MANAGING COMPUTER PROJECTS

François Lustman

Reston Publishing Company, Inc.
A Prentice-Hall Company
Reston, Virginia

Library of Congress Cataloging in Publication Data

Lustman, François.
  Managing computer projects.

  Bibliography: p. 373
  1. Electronic data processing—Management.
I. Title.
QA76.9.M3L87   001.64'068   84-18033
ISBN 0-8359-4186-8

CONTENTS

PREFACE

**PART ONE   THE FUNDAMENTALS OF DATA PROCESSING PROJECT
            MANAGEMENT**   **1**

Chapter 1   Project and Project Management   **3**
    The Project Concept   3
    Computer Project Management   8
    Selected References   13

Chapter 2   The Project Life Cycle   **15**
    Introduction   15
    System Life Cycle   15
    Elementary Planning Definitions   20
    Project Life Cycle   24
    Project Management Life Cycle   30
    Selected References   35

Chapter 3   Methodology for Project Analysis   **37**
    Introduction   37
    Overview of Project Analysis   39
    The Breakdown Process   44
    Integration and Iteration   49
    Estimation Problems   53
    Selected References   58

Chapter 4   Documentation   **60**
    Introduction   60
    Documentation: The Malady of Data Processing   61
    A Document? What For?   64
    The Document Production Process   76
    The Fight Against Inflation: Key Documents   84
    Selected References   89

PART TWO   THE DECISION PHASE   **91**

Chapter 5   Opportunity Study   **92**
    Introduction   92

Overview of the Opportunity Study   94
Problem Assessment   96
Search for Solutions   103
The Opportunity Study Report   108
Selected References   111

PART THREE   PROJECT DESIGN   **115**
Chapter 6   Overview of Project Design   **116**

The Forgotten Stage   116
Analysis of Project Design   118
Selected References   121

Chapter 7   Product Specifications   **123**
Introduction   123
Work Breakdown Structure of Specifications Production   124
System Analysis   130
The Specifications Document   141
The Approval Process   148
Selected References   150

Chapter 8   A Framework for Product Realization   **153**
Introduction   153
Scientific or Technical Decisions   154
Methods and Tools for System Development   156
Standards for System Development   167
Hardware Selection: a Conceptual Approach   173
Selected References   179

Chapter 9   Estimation of Required Resources   **182**
Overview   183
Drawing Up Raw Estimates   187
Factors of Influence   196
Obtaining the Finished Estimates   201
The Project Manager in the Estimating Process   205
Selected References   207

Chapter 10   Planning and Scheduling   **209**
Introduction   209
Overview of Planning and Scheduling   210
Introduction to Formal Planning   213
Planning the Development of a Data Processing System   223
Schedules   227
Selected References   230

Chapter 11   Budgeting   **232**
    Introduction   232
    Why a Project Budget?   234
    Setting Up a Project Budget   237
    Project Management   245
    Selected References   247

PART FOUR   PRODUCT REALIZATION   **249**
Chapter 12   Programming Project: Design, Programming, Testing   **251**
    Introduction   251
    Management Concerns   253
    Design   260
    Programming   275
    Testing   279
    Selected References   286

Chapter 13   Control of a Programming Project   **290**
    Introduction   290
    The Control Function in Project Management   291
    Product Control   294
    Production Control   300
    An Information System for Project Control   307
    Selected References   312

Chapter 14   A Nonprogramming Project: Computer Selection   **314**
    Introduction   314
    System Specifications   316
    The RFP Process   326
    Evaluation   334
    Selection   346
    Selected References   351

PART FIVE   PRODUCT DELIVERY   **353**
Chapter 15   Product Implementation   **355**
    Implementation is More than Delivery   355
    Strategies for System Introduction   361
    Implementation Problems   366
    End of the Project   370
    Selected References   371

BIBLIOGRAPHY   **373**

To the memory of my father,
To my mother,
To my wife Eva, whose patience and encouragement made this
book possible.

PREFACE

This book is the result of several years of teaching at the Department of Computer Sciences, University of Montreal. When asked to take charge of the course on Management of Computer Projects, I looked for textbooks fitting the content as defined in the department curriculum. Some put too much emphasis on computing basics, which my students already possessed, while others were strongly management-oriented and did not put enough focus on the specific aspects of computer projects. It seemed that a balanced presentation of the field would be of interest.

The purpose of the book is to provide senior students in Computer Sciences and Information Systems with the basic elements of project management in data processing. Although no computer science background is required, the reader should be aware of the basic activities in the field: analysis, design, programming.

Project management is often considered to be applicable only to large undertakings in large organizations. This was true in the beginning since the discipline emerged in these surroundings, but it can now be applied with many benefits in small organizations, to small projects. Many remarks and several examples are intended to serve this aim.

In data processing, project management draws from three sources: management, software engineering, and experience. In addition to introducing basic management tools, the book presents many findings of the discipline of software engineering, which tries to deal with the specific aspects of data processing undertakings. Experience both enhances and tempers research findings. Whenever applicable, the results of experience have been used to assess results of theoretical work. In particular, all examples in the book are real projects in which I myself or close colleagues were involved.

The project life cycle was used as a guideline to structure the book. There is, however, an imbalance in the relative importance given to the various topics: the realization part of a project consumes almost all resources, but only three chapters are devoted to it. The reason for this approach is that producing the deliverable in a data processing project involves mostly computing technique. Students usually receive excellent teaching in this field and professionals already possess this knowledge. In addition, a large amount of excellent literature is available. The emphasis was therefore put on the less often covered parts of the field: opportunity study, system analysis, and every thing of concern not so much to the average project participant as to the project manager.

The book is divided into five parts.

Part 1 is an introduction to the basic concepts of a project: system, life cycle, work-breakdown structure, documentation.

Part 2, consisting of Chapter 5 only, deals with the critical stage of the opportunity study, which really brings a project into being.

Part 3, Project Design, is really the project manager's part. It covers all of the preparations required for smooth project realization: estimating, planning, scheduling, budgeting.

Part 4 deals with the realization of two kinds of projects: system development and computer selection. In addition, a chapter is devoted to the control activity, which is the major concern of the project manager during that stage.

Finally, the objective of part 5 is to remind the project manager that producing the deliverable is not enough, it must also be handed over to the user in such a way that he can live with it.

ACKNOWLEDGMENTS

Many thanks go to Professor Nelson Maculan of Federal University of Rio de Janeiro, Brazil; as an invited professor at the University of Montreal, he took the time to review my manuscript and provided me with much valuable advice.

Mister Remi Planche, Partner, Conseillers en Gestion et Informatique, was also of great help in reviewing the material in Chapter 5. His remarks were much appreciated.

I am grateful to the following organizations for providing me with information and allowing its publication:

Lombard Odier Trust Company, especially Mr. Erik Skovsbo, Chairman of the Board.

Notre-Dame Hospital, Montreal, especially Mr. Michel Boisvert, Director of the Data Processing Department.

The Montreal Heart Institute, especially Mr. Paul Lanthier, system analyst.

Raymond, Chabot, Martin, Pare & Ass., especially Mr. Jean-Claude Aube, Partner.

I also owe much to Mister Gregory McCashin for helping me edit the manuscript.

My daughter Laurence overcame her dislike of computers to help me produce the index; many thanks to her.

Finally, I feel deeply indebted to my students who, through their investigative questions, remarks, and criticisms, were of great help in the selection and presentation of many of the topics dealt with in this book.

François Lustman

Part 1

THE FUNDAMENTALS OF DATA PROCESSING PROJECT MANAGEMENT

Much progress has been made since the time when computer systems were developed by a team of analysts and programmers following quick discussion with the user. Despite the technical competence of these data processing specialists, the systems would either be delivered long after the original deadline or not at all. Moreover, they would cost an incredible amount of money and could not do what the users expected them to do. That heroic and disordered time has gradually given way to a more rational, methodical, and efficient era: that of project management.

This specialty—and it is indeed a specialty—is a merging of several disciplines from which it has taken its tools, methods, and modes of thought. From data processing, of course, project management has obtained technical knowledge and, more recently, software engineering. Management has given it an administrative framework, methods of functioning, and especially the basic principles so lacking in data processing.

Finally, from mathematics and more particularly from operational research it has taken scientific management and decision-making tools. Project management then blossomed and became independent, developing and widening its own fields of activity. The life cycle concept, for example (its own study based on numerous experiments), has changed from an empirical definition into a mathematical formulation, with many positive results.

Before exploring project management in detail, it is desirable to define clearly what a project is, who manages it, and what a manager's responsibilities are. This is the object of the first part of this book. With a grasp of basic concepts, the reader should be ready to enter into the project management cycle, the subject of study throughout the remainder of the book.

Chapter 1
PROJECT AND PROJECT MANAGEMENT

THE PROJECT CONCEPT

The "raison d'être" of the Project Concept

The project concept does not owe its origin to data processing. It was introduced at the end of the 1940s in order to carry to successful completion undertakings for which traditional management structures and tools proved to be inefficient. Although very different in nature, such projects had four points in common:

1. Size: Each was large in terms of the scheduling, number of personnel, and money involved.
2. Originality: No prior undertaking was similar enough to be used as a guide.
3. Uniqueness: The resulting product or service was to be supplied only once, not on a repeated basis.
4. Plurality: Elements from various disciplines had to be combined in order to achieve the designated objective.

The structure of an organization, be it public or private, is functional: an administrative unit, no matter what its size, is homogenous and designed to supply a specific product or service. Figure 1.1 illustrates a conventional organization chart of a company's administrative structure. Suppose, for example, that this organization decides to computerize its payroll system. Since all three departments are involved, the following questions may be asked:

1. Who would oversee the project?
2. How would coordination of activities and lines of communication be established among the three departments?
3. Who would hold the decision making power?
4. How would the project be controlled?

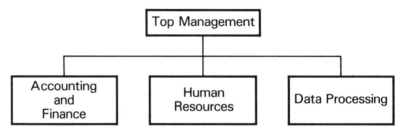

Fig. 1.1. An example of a conventional administrative structure.

The project concept was introduced in order to solve these types of problems. It involves the establishment of a new administrative structure and the introduction of new management tools, leading to the appearance of a new type of administrator known as the project manager. It is the role of the project manager, particularly in data processing projects, which will be examined in this book.

Despite the newly acquired tools and techniques, however, projects did not always remain problem-free. One author after another (Gray, 1981; Lucas, 1981) mentioned the same difficulties: problems in acquiring needed resources in time, straying from schedules, and finished products not meeting specifications. Data processing specialists and users alike are well aware of these problems. The goal of project management, therefore, is to eliminate or at least to minimize them.

Projects in General

Definition

A project is the coordinated putting into operation of a combination of human, technical, administrative, and financial means in order to achieve a specific goal within a fixed time period and by using fixed resources. Diverse examples include construction of a building, establishment of a computerized reservation service for an airline, installation of a new computer system, and writing of a compiler.

Characteristics

SIZE.   A project generally involves several people. There is presently a tendency, however, to attach the project label to smaller and smaller undertakings. The lower limit may be considered to be two people.

LENGTH.   A project is considered to be an undertaking of at least two months duration. All projects have a recognized end point.

ORGANIZATION.   A project does not usually fit into existing administrative structures.
     Additional characteristics include the following:

○ The objective can be clearly defined.
○ The undertaking is unique and nonrecurring.
○ The result is important to the organization.
○ The project involves several disciplines.

Although a project need not have all of these characteristics, the presence of one or two of them will result in the appearance of others.

The Project Concept in Data Processing

Use of the project concept seems to be especially well suited to the data processing field. Yet it has not always received the enthusiastic approval of computer specialists. Rolefson (1978) offered several reasons:

○ The organization was too small.
○ The plan was constantly being changed.
○ Planning was difficult when the system had not yet been designed.
○ Priority-setting by top management was always quite successful.

In a related criticism, Lucas (1982, p379) noted that use of the Critical Path Method (CPM) "requires time to measure and report on progress." Other justifications for not using the project concept in data processing are linked to the stereotypical image of the computer professional as one who is more interested in technical aspects than in management, who dislikes and has little faith in schedules, and who considers systems analysis and programming to be art forms rather than activities subject to quantification.

This image, made popular in the 1960s, has continued to be applied to DP professionals to such an extent that they have adopted it. Yet examination shows the reality of the situation to be entirely different. Frankwicz (1973) published the results of a survey carried out in the St. Louis, Missouri area. This survey found that systems and data processing specialists showed greater understanding and acceptance of the goals set by top management. Furthermore, project managers exhibited a greater degree of motivation and self-discipline than other management employees, and were clearly conscious of their double role as managers and technicians. The extremely rapid growth of computer use in all fields of activity since the 1970s has confirmed this view.

Nevertheless, specific aspects of data processing present problems that are new or more acute than those encountered in other disciplines. First, the uncertainty factor is greater here because it includes the project goal, which is often unclear or undefined. The lack of references for the production of programs (length, time, uniqueness of each program) is another problem, as is the absence of references for making performance predictions, given the rapid rate of change in technologies and methodologies.

Communication between data processing professionals and users is another problem area. Despite its ever-increasing presence, data processing continues to intimidate many managers and users. Adding to communication difficulties are the technological jargon used by computing people and the popular perception that computers are somehow "magical."

Lastly, there is the sheer cost of data processing operations. It is a well-known fact that computerized information systems are expensive, and this constitutes another reason for controlling expenditures connected with such systems.

Different Types of Computer Projects

For most people, a data processing project equals systems development using existing organizational resources. This labeling of terminology originated at the time when internal development of programs constituted the only alternative. The majority of data processing literature and techniques are geared toward systems development to such an extent that confusion in terminology concerning project management and data processing management sometimes exists. Such great advances have been made in data processing, however, that many options are available in almost any given situation. In this book, through the use of both subject topics and examples, every effort will be made to keep the range of problem situations as diverse as possible.

Of the many possible data processing projects, the following represent a typical sample:

System Definition and Development

The principal characteristics of this type of project are the plurality of disciplines involved representing a high degree of involvement of users and management, each playing a critical role; the presence of all the different categories of data processing specialists, ranging from managers to operators; and the availability of numerous techniques and a great store of experience.

System definition and development is the ideal project. A great deal of excellent literature is available on many aspects of such an undertaking, notably the technical ones. The major pitfalls encountered are the failure to meet deadlines and the inability to meet specifications. Chapter 12 deals exclusively with this type of project.

Hardware Selection

Even though hardware selection is as old as data processing itself, it is rarely thought of as a project, save in the form of a collection of recipes. Its principal characteristics are as follows: (a) it is an almost exclusively data processing-oriented project because the users are computing specialists; (b) it demands an extensive knowledge of both the hardware and the market; (c) past experience and/or guidelines tend to be minimal.

Two pitfalls to be avoided include making an incorrect choice and being tempted by technology. This type of project is examined in Chapter 14.

Program Conversion

Although sometimes considered a subproject of hardware selection, program conversion does constitute a project in its own right. It is an undertaking which is exclusively data processing-oriented, since practically no external personnel are involved, and it requires that the technicians have a wide knowledge of both the original and target systems.

The project concept can be very easily applied to program conversion despite the absence of reference material. Possible stumbling blocks are the passing of deadlines and the tendency to want to rework the system instead of converting it. The example studied in Chapter 10 is of this type.

Additional Project Types

Other data processing projects include integrating a group of systems, selecting and installing a software package, and carrying out a requirements study for a noncomputerized organization. (There are still some organizations, not always small ones, which do not possess computer systems.) Despite the variety of tasks and the dimensions of operations undertaken, use of the project concept almost always yields successful results.

COMPUTER PROJECT MANAGEMENT

The Project Team

A project is, by definition, interdisciplinary, crossing functional and hierarchical boundaries. It would be wise, therefore, to define the terms which will be used not only in this section, but also throughout the entire book. The following definitions are either general in nature or are adapted to the specific topic under examination.

Senior manager: an executive having responsibilities of strategic importance to the organization as well as authority over all sectors affected by the project.

Middle manager: an executive having operational responsibilities directly affected by the project.

User: an employee or executive whose work or responsibilities are directly affected by the project.

Project manager: a senior or middle management executive (depending on project size) who is responsible for the realization of the project.

Systems analyst: a professional specializing in the analysis and design of information systems (as defined in Chapter 2).

Data processing analyst: a professional specializing in the design of computerized information systems.

Programmer: a professional specializing in program writing.

The composition of a project team will depend on the type of project to be undertaken. Table 1.1 contains a partial list of the principal team members. Before dealing with the question of how such a team is structured, it is first necessary to establish to whom the team as a whole is responsible. Table 1.1 shows that a team would not include a senior manager as defined at the beginning of this section. His role, in fact, is not to participate in the project but to control it; therefore, he is the person to whom the project manager is administratively responsible. As to the choosing of a specific person to whom the project manager would report, three solutions are possible:

TABLE 1.1
MEMBERS OF A PROJECT TEAM

Team Member	Role	Participates in	
		All Projects	Certain projects
Project Manager	overall project supervision	X	
User	analysis of existing facilities specification of requirements system implementation	X	
Middle Manager	decisions concerning requirements	X	
Systems Analyst	analysis and establishment of requirements		X[a]
Data Processing Analyst	design of the computerized system		X[b]
Programmer	programming, testing, implementing		X[c]
Various Experts	specialized problem solving		X[d]
Support Staff		X	

[a]A systems analyst is not required for some exclusively data processing-oriented projects, such as program conversion and hardware selection.
[b]The data processing analyst, as defined above, is not involved in a hardware selection project.
[c]For projects involving no programming.
[d]Computing professionals in this category specialize in specific subdisciplines such as data bases, optimization, compiler theory, or hardware. Specialists may also come from other disciplines such as financial analysis, accounting, medicine, or electrical engineering.

1. The data processing or information systems department head. For obvious reasons, this is the most frequently adopted solution.

2. The senior manager who is most directly affected by the project. This approach is chosen in organizations where data processing is considered less as a production unit than as a supplier of goods and services for the organization as a whole (the service bureau concept).

3. A steering committee. This solution will be selected whenever the decisions to be made are of critical importance to the various sectors represented on the committee. Two extreme examples are the computerization of an organization totally lacking in data processing systems, and the design of a Management Information System (MIS).

The structure of the team depends on two factors: the type of project and the stage of progress. In contrast to an operational unit, which is stable both in composition and number of personnel, the number of team members will fluctuate depending on project progress. The initial and final phases will require less manpower than the production stages.

Just as the entire project is an ad hoc structure, the organization of the team will be adapted to the work being done. For example, Figure 1.2 depicts

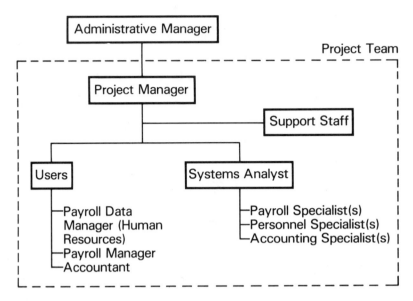

Fig. 1.2. Payroll system project team (requirements study phase).

the structure of the payroll project alluded to at the beginning of this chapter, as it stands at the requirements study stage. It is not necessary to have each task performed by a different person. In the case of small organizations or an uncomplicated system, the same analyst or group of analysts will assume the various functions.

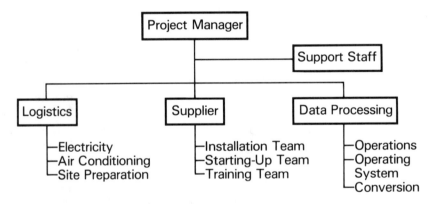

Fig. 1.3. Installation of a new computer system.

Figure 1.3 shows another example: composition of a team for a hardware installation project. As this figure indicates, there are team members from outside the data processing department and even from outside the organization itself. Site preparation work will often, in fact, be carried out by outside firms. Nevertheless, they will be considered part of the team and therefore under the responsibility of the project manager.

Responsibilities of the Project Manager

The project manager supervises a specialized operation which is controlled in terms of time, resources, and specifications of the final product. A variety of techniques intended to promote effective project management have been formulated, published, communicated, and employed with success. Three observations help establish a reasonable perspective in this regard:

> "Project Management is primarily a collection of useful tools and not just a 'cookbook' of procedures and forms" (Rolefson, 1978).

> "It is important to recognize that the various project management packages are 'management aids' and not a substitute for management skills" (Rolefson, 1978).

> "Although PERT and CPM are the project manager's primary tools, use of them does not guarantee success. Project success depends on the competence of management" (Gray, 1981, p. 7).

Technical competence in the use of project supervision tools such as forms, tables, and graphs does not necessarily make for a good project manager. No tool, no matter how sophisticated, can replace administrative competence.

Because the project manager is, first and foremost, an administrator, his role is not so much performing tasks as it is having tasks performed by others. He is not required to do everything himself. One of the secrets of being an effective manager is selecting assistants who can be relied upon. The role of the project manager can be defined in three words: planning, scheduling, and control. Given the entrepreneurial aspect of a project, a fourth responsibility can be added—quite simply, "getting the job done." The responsibilities of a project manager include the following aspects:

1. *Administrative responsibility* to a higher authority for the successful realization of the project. This often-forgotten aspect of the project manager's task does, in fact, demand more than a little of his time.
2. *Communication with the users*, a responsibility of great importance given the very distinct nature of data processing projects, in which objectives-setting is often part of the project itself.
3. *Planning*, a responsibility which includes determining and scheduling all resources and tasks necessary for the realization of the project.
4. *Scheduling* the tasks and resources necessary for successful implementation of the project plan.

5. *Finalizing resource availability* to ensure that needed resources are acquired on a timely basis.

6. *Coordinating project operations,* a typical management task which consists of coordinating the various project components according to the overall plan. Circulating information, directing work groups, and resolving organizational problems which might arise are all part of the coordinating function.

7. *Technical supervision,* requiring the manager to be able to tackle particularly difficult technical problems unresolved by other personnel during the completion of a data processing project.

8. *Controlling,* the responsibility to verify that the project is progressing as planned and to adopt corrective measures if such is not the case. There is often a tendency to restrict this duty to a simple plan-following role. In data processing, conformity of the product to specifications is as important as other considerations, and the risk of "straying" is as great as that of missing deadlines. The problems of documentation and quality control are also of critical importance.

Profile of the Project Manager

Not all first-class administrators make good project managers. The same can be said of brilliant data processing specialists. Two specific aspects of the project concept have a considerable impact on the profile of the manager. First is *originality,* the never-before-attempted aspect of the undertaking. Second is the uncertainty factor always present in data processing projects. Carrying a project to completion involves breaking out of routines, innovating. In short, it involves accepting a challenge. A project manager must be, above all, challenge-oriented, for a project contains more risks and requires greater participation on the part of the manager than does a conventional administrative position.

Besides these characteristics of personality, the project manager must possess skills in the following three areas: technical operations, administration, and human relations.

Technical Profile

The project manager:

o is highly competent in the data processing field with which the project is concerned;

o is highly experienced and particularly knowledgeable of the user's field of activity;

o is not overly technically oriented, i.e., shows technical maturity.

Administrative Profile

The project manager:

- has a sense of organization;
- knows management techniques;
- has a good knowledge of the organization's structures;
- preferably has had previous experience in a management position.

Human Relations Profile

The project manager:

- is able to assume leadership;
- has a sense of responsibility;
- demonstrates ease in handling interpersonal communications,
- is motivated;
- is involved, and not afraid of getting his hands dirty;
- is an entrepreneur.

Contrary to a widely held belief, many experienced computer professionals have these qualifications. The field typically attracts challenge-oriented individuals, and the time of the superprogrammer uninterested in management is no more. The role of project manager is increasingly the testing ground for future data processing executives.

SELECTED REFERENCES

Frankwicz, M. S. 1973. A study of project management techniques. *Journal of Systems Management*, 24, October, 18-22.
 This article reports the results of a survey conducted in the St. Louis (Mo.) area. Many preconceived ideas about data processing are questioned.

Gaydash, A. 1982. *Principles of EDP management.* Reston, Va.: Reston Pub. Co.
 Chapter 4 deals with project management and proposes a profile for project managers. It also warns against too many studies, which is sometimes a part of the data processing specialist's love of perfection.

Gray, C. F. 1981. *Essentials of project management.* Princeton, N.J. Petrocelli Books.
 This technical book deals mainly with the use of network techniques (PERT/CPM) for planning, scheduling, and controlling. The introductory chapter gives

an excellent justification and history of the project concept, as well as good definitions of projects and project management tasks.

Keen, J. S. 1981. *Managing systems development*. New York: John Wiley & Sons.
Appendix 2 gives an extensive description of tasks for project managers.

Kerzner, H. 1981. Project management. *Journal of Systems Management*, 32, October, 26-31.
The author sees project management as being implemented more and more in the future, and project managers as the best-trained people for middle management positions.

Lucas, H. C., Jr. 1981. *The analysis, design and implementation of information systems*. New York: McGraw-Hill.
Chapter 12 deals with computer systems design projects. The author compares computer system projects with research and development projects, and draws attention to the great amount of uncertainty surrounding the definition of user needs.

Lucas, H. C., Jr. 1982. *Information systems concepts for management*. New York: McGraw-Hill.
Chapter 15 deals with project management. In addition to mentioning the high level of uncertainty associated with system analysis and design, the author introduces the concept of user-controlled design for involving users and managers in the management of the project.

Rolefson, J. F. 1978. Project management—Six critical steps. *Journal of Systems Management*, 29, April, 10-17.
The results of a survey mention several reasons for not using project management in data processing. In addition, the author proposes steps to be taken for the success of projects, emphasizes top management involvement, and suggests qualifications for successful projects managers.

Chapter 2
THE PROJECT LIFE CYCLE

INTRODUCTION

The project concept was introduced in order to reposition currently any given problem within its global context, so that the solutions would be analyzed as to how they affect the whole and no longer strictly a specific part. The life cycle principle is an important aspect of the systems concept. Like biological beings, systems are born, grow, mature, age, and die. Because a project has a beginning, a developmental stage, and an end, it fits perfectly into the conceptual framework of the life cycle.

However, contrary to biological systems, which evolve because of their vital energy, a data processing project left to itself can only lose direction and degenerate; it must be guided by some "force" throughout its entire life cycle. One of the characteristics of a project is in fact the high degree of uncertainty surrounding each of its elements. The life cycle must be carefully planned, and its evolution controlled.

SYSTEM LIFE CYCLE

Introduction to Systems

Churchmann (1968) approached the systems concept in an informal but lively manner. Using concrete examples and looking at the problem from, among others, the efficiency point of view, he came to the following conclusion: the procedure which consists in concentrating on the performance of one component can often detract from the performance of the whole. This observation resembles the well-known saying often heard in the operating systems programming area: an algorithm maximizing use of the CPU can consume more resources than it saves. According to Murdick (1980), a system has three characteristics: it is interdisciplinary; its approach is both qualitative and quantitative; and its approach is organized. Note how these characteristics resemble the project concept.

Definition of a System

A system is a set of components and subsystems working together to achieve one or more common objectives. This definition has two fundamental aspects. First, it is a recursive definition: a system is itself composed of other systems. This breakdown will be one of the analyst's crucial tasks. Second, there are common objectives; although having distinct "lives" and objectives, the components must work together toward common goals. This apparent contradiction, mentioned, among others, by Churchmann (1968) and Cleland and King (1968), makes apparent the role of the manager in the framework system: to see that the various components work toward the achievement of the common goal despite their conflicting objectives.

Examples of Systems

- ○ *University*
  Components: administration, faculties, teaching staff, students, classes.
  Common objectives: teaching and research.
- ○ *Automobile manufacturer*
  Components: factories, research and development, network of dealers, marketing, etc.
  Objective: maximizing profit by producing and selling automobiles.
- ○ *Data processing department*
  Components: hardware, software, personnel.
  Objective: satisfying the organization's information processing needs.

There is no one, predetermined method for dividing a system into subsystems. In the case of the data processing department, for example, administration, operation, and development can also be identified as subsystems. The breakdown will therefore depend on the point of view which is adopted.

The components can also belong to several subsystems: in the case of the university, the teaching staff is a system, but professors are also part of the faculties. Even if there are cases in which this grouping is evidence of an incorrect breakdown, sometimes it cannot be avoided; the interrelations are too great. Here again, the point of view which is adopted will have to serve as a guide for the breakdown.

Determining the Limits of a System

Just where does a system stop? An initial answer to this question consisted in attempting to determine the limits of the system's *influence*. Unfortunately, this approach is not always useful, since the influence of the university extends over all of society, the automobile manufacturer influences the market, and so on. The idea of influence was then replaced by the notion of *control*, i.e., the system stops at the point beyond which it no longer exercises control. For example, even though an automobile manufacturer influences the market, it does not control it, except in the case of a monopoly. Even though a university influences and is influenced by society and other universities, it does not control them.

This is a satisfactory definition of the limits of a system because it is thus possible to represent a system by the black box concept (see Figure 2.1). Indeed, the influence of the outside world is accounted for in the form of input data, with output data expressing the effect of the system on its environment.

Fig. 2.1. A system as a black box.

Information Systems

Of all the systems which exist in an organization, those of interest to us here are the *information systems*. Their purpose is to gather, process, manipulate, and supply the information necessary for the betterment of the organization. Throughout the remainder of the book, the term *system* will be used to designate these information systems only.

The Life Cycle Concept

An analogy pertaining to systems which is among the richest in implications is that involving living beings: they are born, grow, mature, then die. In the evolution of a system, similar stages have been identified, leading to the formulation of the life cycle concept.

Table 2.1 displays six definitions, arrived at over a period of 11 years, of the life cycle of a system. The reference list at the end of the chapter gives full information on the works from which these definitions are taken. This comparative table prompts three observations:

○ *Lack of clarity in terminology.* The terms *design* and *analysis* are used with different meanings.

○ *Overall stability of the concept.* The variations from one author to another reflect differing degrees of detail rather than fundamental conceptual differences. During 11 years of evolution, the principal components have remained the same.

○ *Underlying structure.* In spite of variations in terminology and emphasis, four fundamental stages can be identified: birth, development, installation, and operation.

Starting with this experimental concept and focusing on the problem of the consumption of resources necessary for the completion of each phase, Norden (1977) and Putnam (1978) put forward a mathematical life cycle model. Based on the equation

TABLE 2.1
INFORMATION SYSTEM LIFE CYCLE: SIX VIEWS

Rubin 1970	Benjamin 1971	Burch and Strater 1974	Cave and Salisbury 1978	Hall 1980	Lucas 1982
Conception	Feasibility study	System analysis	Project definition	Survey	Inception
Preliminary analysis	System specification		Functional analysis and specification	Analysis	Feasibility study
			Environment analysis and specification		System analysis
					Design
System design	System engineering	System design	System design	Design	Specifications
System programming	Programming and procedure development		Program development		Programming
System documentation			Operational testing		Testing
System installation	Implementation	System implementation	Installation and maintenance	Implementation	Training
System operation	Operations			Review	Conversion and installation
System cessation					Operations

$$y' = 2Kate^{-at^2}$$

in which t = time, $a = 1/(2t_d^2)$, t_d = maximum of y' and K = total effort for the entire cycle: y' represents the percentage of use of manpower at the moment t. The corresponding curve is depicted in Figure 2.2.

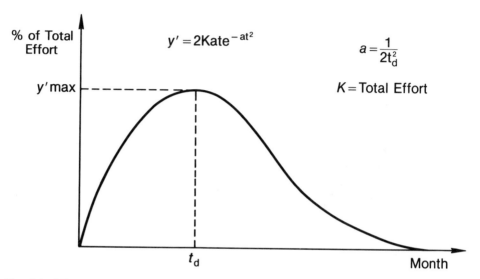

Fig. 2.2. Life cycle: The Norden/Putnam curve.

This model provides a theoretical base for certain facts which are known to systems builders but not always well understood by users or top management. In particular, Putnam shows that:

o The resources necessary for the realization of a system vary considerably from one phase to another; the development phase represents maximum consumption;

o For a given project, production difficulties increase if development time decreases. The relation takes the following form:

$$\text{difficulty} = f\left(\frac{1}{t_d^2}\right)$$

In fact a period of time exists which is known as the feasibility period;

o Decreasing the amount of time allotted for completing a project increases resource consumption.

The life cycle of a system, therefore, cannot be altered at will, and any attempt to shorten the development time will only be to the detriment of the product's quality and the budget. By using this model, Putnam arrives at a development cost which is 40% of the total cost of the system. This figure resembles that given by Benjamin (1971): 40%–50%. Thus, the development of the system is itself a project which will require one-half of the resources consumed during the life cycle. Estimating and controlling the use of these resources are fundamental tasks of the project manager.

ELEMENTARY PLANNING DEFINITIONS

Managing Is Planning

What we have just seen is the "weight" of the development phase in the life cycle of a system and the importance of carefully structuring and controlling it. In data processing, there is something worse than running over budget: not completing the project. There are innumerable quotes from authors on this subject, but we will limit ourselves here to Metzger (1973): the problems encountered in programming projects are caused by:

poor planning

ill-defined contract

poor planning

unstable problem definition

poor planning

etc.

He points out that technical difficulty is not on the list.

The traditional role of the project manager can be defined in three words: planning, scheduling, and controlling. However, correct planning is essential to effective scheduling and controlling. Boehm (1977) outlined seven principles for software engineering, with the first being: "Manage using a sequential life-cycle plan." According to Boehm, the plan must lead to the establishment of the schedule and must incorporate the possibilities and tools for controlling.

The importance of the project manager's fundamental role of planning cannot be stressed enough. There is, in fact, a greater element of uncertainty in data processing projects than in other undertakings. The manager's most important task is to reduce this uncertainty, or at least contain it, through effective planning.

Networks

Any project having several phases can be represented by a network. The undertaking depicted in Figure 2.3 is a computer acquisition project, illustrating the basic principles of a network:

activity: a project element which consumes time (e.g., choosing the computer, waiting for delivery). An activity has a beginning and an end, and is represented by a line segment running from the beginning to the end. Figure 2.3 also shows dotted lines such as the one joining nodes 4 and 50. An activity is, in effect, defined by the numbers of its beginning and end nodes. If, in fact, two activities have the same beginning and end points, they are no longer distinguishable.

dummy activity: an imaginary activity which makes it possible to maintain the interdependence of events.

event: the precise beginning or end of an activity; in other words, a perceivable moment when a perceivable act is accomplished (e.g., computer installed, files converted). An event is represented by a numbered circle and is called a network node. For any activity, the number of the node at the beginning must be lower than that at the end.

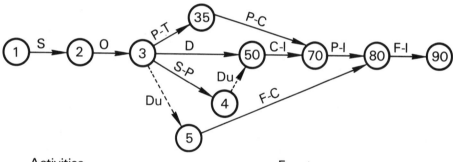

Activities	Events
S: Selection of New Computer	1: Specs of New System Defined
O: Ordering	2: Computer Selected
P-T: Programmers Training	3: Computer Ordered
P-C: Programs Conversion	35: Programmers Trained
D: Delivery Time	4: Site Ready
S-P: Site Preparation	5: Start of File Conversion
F-C: Files Conversion	50: Computer Delivered
C-I: Computer Installation	70: Computer Ready to Run
P-I: Programs Installation	80: Programs Installed
F-I: Files Set Up	90: Everything Ready for
Du: Dummy Activities	Operation

Fig. 2.3. Network of computer acquisition.

critical path: the projected length of the project. Once the network has been structured, time spans are assigned to all of the activities; but then how is the length of the project determined? All of the paths are examined and the time spans of the activities of a path are added together. The path which has the longest time span is called the critical path, and represents the projected length of the undertaking. Any activity located on this path becomes important, since a variation in the time required for its completion similarly affects the project deadline. Figure 2.4 depicts the network shown in 2.3, but this time indicating the time spans, in weeks, of the different activities and paths. The longest path (1, 2, 3, 50, 70, 80, 90) totals 21 weeks. The longest activity on the path is awaiting delivery of the computer.

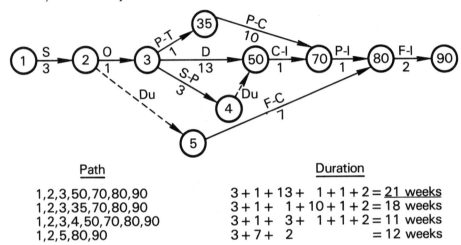

Path	Duration
1,2,3,50,70,80,90	3 + 1 + 13 + 1 + 1 + 2 = <u>21 weeks</u>
1,2,3,35,70,80,90	3 + 1 + 1 + 10 + 1 + 2 = 18 weeks
1,2,3,4,50,70,80,90	3 + 1 + 3 + 1 + 1 + 2 = 11 weeks
1,2,5,80,90	3 + 7 + 2 = 12 weeks

Fig. 2.4. Computer acquisition: Looking for the critical path.

slack: certain paths have a shorter time span than the critical path; this difference, called slack, gives the project manager a certain amount of room to maneuver. He can, for example, delay an activity in order to supply those activities on the critical path with more resources, should the need arise.

Activities Great and Small

Depending on one's point of view, the network in Figure 2.3 is either too detailed or not detailed enough. For the chief programmer, the program conversion activity can in turn be broken down into a complete network. Inversely, management is interested only in the purchase and installation of the computer and the beginning of operations. Therefore, activities and events occur at several levels. The activities of a project can be classed into several categories defined in the following manner:

task: a specific undertaking, carried out by one person, having a beginning and an end.
Example: writing a program

activity: a group of interrelated tasks, under the direct control of one person, the end point of which constitutes an event.
Example: site preparation

stage: a set of activities having a beginning and an end and representing one phase of the project life cycle.
Example: system development

The planning of a project implies the breakdown of the various activities into even smaller elements (see Chapter 3). These definitions will therefore be useful in order to decentralize the breaking down process by the delegating of responsibilities, and to decentralize and spread out the control of the project among those who are most involved in its realization.

Milestones

The event concept as defined in an earlier section is insufficient as a control tool. Some events are more important than others, some more visible than others. In order to distinguish those which play an important role, the milestone concept was introduced.

milestone: a clearly defined and unambiguous event which marks a point of progress in the project.

One of the project manager's major problems is, in effect, choosing the control points, which must meet two criteria:

o Representing an event in a clear, unambiguous manner. Two programming examples will clarify this statement. A program that is 90% ready is not a milestone (for that matter, it is not an event either). When a program has been completely written, it is still not a milestone; it will be corrected, altered, and remodeled during testing time.
o Making it possible to measure the progress of the project. Not all of the events constitute such important information. In the network shown in Figure 2.3, the arrival of the computer is a milestone. On the other hand, the fact that the programmers have finished their training is certainly an event, but undoubtedly not a milestone as far as the project manager is concerned.

In conclusion, it can be said that a milestone is an event which allows the project manager to control progress throughout the project's life cycle.

PROJECT LIFE CYCLE

Project Life Cycle vs Development Life Cycle

The life cycle of a system has already been described as consisting of four phases: birth, development, installation, and operation. Since the operation phase falls under the control of permanent structures, the project itself is made up of the first three stages. Given the fact that the team is dissolved once the system is in the hands of the users, the remaining portion always represents the characteristics of the Norden/Putnam curve.

Even if such a breaking down accurately represents the evolution of a system to be developed, it is not sufficient for the management of the project for two reasons. First is the difficulty of applying this breakdown to projects which do not consist of developing a set of programs (e.g., selection of a computer). The second reason has to do with the running of the project. In effect, even in the case of the development of a system, the entire managerial aspect of the project (technical and administrative planning, resource evaluation and procurement) is not made evident. We will therefore put forward a model which simultaneously takes into account both the product to be delivered and the sequence of tasks necessary for achieving the objective. This project life cycle is depicted in Figure 2.5, and the elements of the model may be described as follows:

Milestone 1–birth of the project through the perception of a problem to be solved.

Opportunity study–stage in which the problem is studied and solutions sought in order to prepare for a decision on a future course of action.

Milestone 2–decision based on the results of the opportunity study. The decision contains two parts: (a) stoppage or continuation, and (b) in the case of continuation, selection of the solution to be put into action.

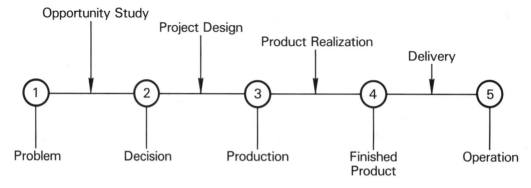

Fig. 2.5. The project life cycle.

Project design–the technical and administrative planning of the remainder of the project, according to the orientation decided on at Milestone 2.

Milestone 3–beginning of product realization.

Product realization–the group of tasks which make it possible to complete the undertaking successfully according to the conditions set out at the project design stage.

Milestone 4–product finished and ready for delivery.

Delivery–transfer of product to the users under conditions which will allow them to use it without help from the project team.

Milestone 5–end of project, with product operating in its normal environment, utilized by its normal users.

This model has numerous advantages. First, it is geared toward reducing the degree of uncertainty linked to data processing projects by concentrating on traditional weaknesses in this field—product definition and organization. Second, the existence of the project design stage is a recognition of the importance of this activity; in the classical life cycle model, it is an overhead to the other stages. Finally, the model is easily adaptable to projects which do not consist in developing a system, since it does not take into account the phases (such as systems analysis, design, and testing) which are specific to this type of undertaking.

Opportunity Study

Table 2.1, which compares different life cycles as proposed by several authors, reveals some discrepancies relative to the birth of a system. Rubin (1970) speaks of conception, Hall (1980) of survey, Lucas (1982) of inception followed by feasibility study. This lack of consistency is evidence of a situation which is specific to data processing projects: their births are surrounded by a certain amount of confusion because the persons involved do not have a very clear idea of what they want, nor of what it entails. Yet, it is on this basis that they propose to launch a lengthy, costly, and major undertaking.

The opportunity study is designed to eliminate these shadowy areas and to bring together all the necessary elements so that a sound decision may be made. Those elements are:

What is the problem?

What is required?

Do solutions exist?

What are the costs and benefits of these solutions?

What suggestions can be made to the decision makers?

This stage is of utmost importance because it makes it possible to give the rest of the project a recognized orientation. The milestone which terminates this stage is, in effect, purely decisional. The total effort will consist in supplying the decision makers (who, in principle, are not part of the project team) with the maximum amount of qualitative and quantitative information necessary in order to help them in their task. The opportunity study, then, will consist of three phases:

1. Examining the problem.
2. Searching for solutions.
3. Compiling the findings in the form of a report.

This stage plays a role of fundamental importance relative to the orientation and quality of the project. Does the consumption of resources required for successful completion of the opportunity study reflect this importance? As can be seen in Figure 2.6, it certainly does not. In this chart, a project life cycle as represented by its stages is superimposed on the Norden/Putnam curve. The consumption of resources between two instances, t_1 and t_2, is the area under the curve between these two abscissas. In the opportunity study, t_1 equals zero, and it can be seen that the area comprises a small part of the entire project.

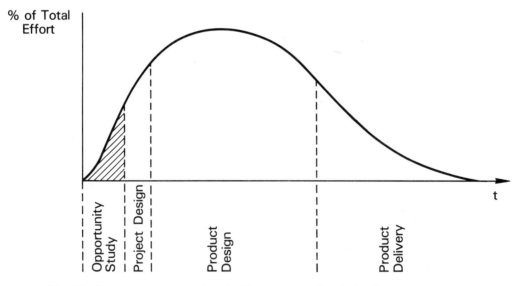

Fig. 2.6. Resource consumption for the opportunity study stage.

It is generally agreed that this stage consumes 10% to 15% of the resources. Although this figure may look excessive when compared to actual practice, it is the best possible investment in the data processing context. It can be compared to what occurs in programming, where the ratio of the analysis costs to actual programming costs has been constantly increasing, evidence of the general tendency to study problems for a long time before beginning to work on the realization of the programs.

Project Design

This stage does not clearly appear in any of the life cycles presented in Table 2.1, with the possible exception of the one put forward by Cave and Salisbury (1978), who speak of environment analysis and specifications. In order to illustrate the role of this stage, development of a personnel system will be used as an example. The result of the opportunity study was the decision to develop a personnel system on the computer of the organization's data processing department. In order that work may begin, answers are needed to the following questions:

1. What are the exact specifications of the system (inputs, outputs, processing)?
2. What development standards will be used?
   —programming language
   —system design method
   —programming standards
   —documentation standards
3. What volume of work (analysis, programming, implementation) will be required?
4. What profile will the personnel who will develop the system be required to have?
5. Who will work on the project? When and for how long?
6. What will be the cost?
7. What equipment is necessary for the operation of the system? What is the cost?
8. What computer resources are required for the development of the system?
9. Will those resources be available?

The project design stage consists in finding answers to all of these questions, and then using them to develop:

a work plan

a schedule

a control plan

Even if the questions to be asked may vary from one project to another, the objective remains the same: to prepare the remainder of the project in such a way that there will be no surprises. This is the ideal stage for the project manager to show his skills. The quality of the final product and the ability to adhere to the schedule as well as the budget depend on the results of this stage.

As can be seen, the activity of system design is not a part of this stage. It is, in fact, part of the product design since it deals with the way in which a system is structured. Moreover, it is an activity which is specific to the development of a system and which has only distant equivalents in other types of projects, such as hardware selection or the conversion of a set of programs.

The resources needed for the project design stage could amount to as much as 10% of the total. The team will be small but very competent, and therefore very costly if one counts in terms of cost-per-man instead of man-hours.

Product Realization

Of all of the stages, this is the best-known and most completely documented. For a conventional system development project, it corresponds to what Burch and Strater (1974) call *system design*, and to what Hall (1980) labels *design*. Cave and Salisbury's cycle (see Table 2.1) lists the activities of this particular type of project as:

system design

program development

operational testing

In the case of hardware selection, for example (see Chapter 14), this stage involves:

obtaining all information on the available systems (e.g., in the form of invitations to tender)

evaluating the different products

selecting the system

negotiating the contract

No matter the type of project involved, this stage is the most data processing-oriented in that it deals more or less exclusively with computing techniques. It is, therefore, the stage which involves the least amount of contact with the users and which consumes the greatest amount of resources (40%–50% of the total). In the case of equipment selection, this figure may seem high; a concrete example will clarify the situation.

EXAMPLE: HARDWARE SELECTION FOR AN EDUCATIONAL SYSTEM

In one of the Canadian provinces, a hardware selection project was set up at the Department of Education. It involved choosing a whole range of equipment for the data processing centers of the elementary and secondary schools and colleges. The computers had to be compatible so that the same information systems could be used in all the centers, which of course have needs of different dimensions. The product realization stage lasted eight months and involved the participation, in various capacities, of 40 people on a part-time basis.

A discussion of the production of a data processing product or service is not complete without speaking of a problem which is specific to the field: *control*. Control usually consists of monitoring the schedule and the consumption of resources. However, care must also be taken that the product does not stray in relation to its specifications. This problem occurs quite easily if safeguards are not employed. For the project manager, responsibility for technical control of the product to be developed will therefore be added to the progress control of the project. According to Boehm (1977), disciplined product control is in fact one of the seven axioms of software engineering.

Product control is of such importance that a new discipline came into being at the end of the 1970s: software quality assurance. This will be dealt with in Chapter 13, especially in the case of systems development, but the same concern will prevail in the hardware selection methodology presented in Chapter 14.

Product Delivery

Data processing specialists like this stage least of all. All of the creative effort has been made and the product is ready—what more could be asked for? Yet, it is only at this stage that the user and the organization finally see results. An implementation which has been badly thought out can ultimately lead to rejection of the product.

No matter what the project, the elements of the product delivery stage are always the same:

1. Preparation of the environment
2. Training of the users
3. Installation of the product into its operational environment
4. Start-up, with the help of the project team
5. Cut-over

Discussion

There is no production of documentation in this stage. It must, in effect, already exist and be part of the production stage. In software quality assurance it is even recommended that documentation precede product realization (see Chapter 4).

The preparation of the environment can take on quite large proportions. In the case of a computer changeover, converting the programs can become the most important activity and undoubtedly the one that consumes the most resources. Start-up, which is assisted by the project team, requires the prior choice of a strategy: complete replacement, parallel operation, or modular replacement. Finally, equipment operators are not the only users to be trained; those users who will work with the output data will also require training.

Project planning traditionally tends to underestimate the length of the product delivery stage and the amount of resources it will consume. It has been estimated that the implantation can require from 20%–40% of the total resources. Benjamin (1971), in fact, goes as high as 50%. Several problems associated with the product delivery stage are responsible for these high estimates:

o The availability of the users, which is often infrequent and irregular.
o The need to rework and make changes. Despite all precautions taken, Murphy's Law will prove correct—if something can go wrong, it will . . . at the worst time. Many changes will have to be made.
o The complexity of the conversion for the users. They must not only be taught how to use the new system, but it is also sometimes necessary to convert manual files, which requires the gathering and verification of a large amount of data. If the system operates on a monthly cycle, the assisted start-up may need to take place over an extended period of time.

The product delivery stage is thankless, frustrating, and invariably underestimated. It is during this stage, however, that the project proves to be a success or a failure. Its importance should never be underestimated.

PROJECT MANAGEMENT LIFE CYCLE

Introduction

Let us suppose that a potential project manager is reading this book and reviewing the topics studied so far. In Chapter 1, following the justification and definition of the project concept, the profile and responsibilities of the project manager were described. In Chapter 2, discussion of the life cycle concept helped the reader gain a clearer understanding of the project. Now, having a general grasp of the task to be accomplished, the manager will naturally pose the following question: "I see quite clearly what has to be done, but what specifically do *I* have to do?" In other words, what are the exact tasks of the project manager in relation to the life cycle?

The traditional view (planning, scheduling, controlling) which places all of the emphasis on management tasks, is, as has been seen, badly adapted to data processing projects. Franckwicz (1973) noted the duality of the data processing project manager's technical and administrative roles. The manager's profile therefore contains a large dose of technical competence. The question then becomes: when must he be a technician and in what proportions?

Part of the answer to the second part of the question lies in the size of the project. Indeed, the smaller the project, the greater the technical role of the manager becomes. Management of small projects is not a full-time job, given the restricted size of the team and the product to be developed. Again because of the restricted size, certain technical tasks are not of a full-time nature, even though they require a high degree of technical competence; this is particularly true in the case of system design.

In order to answer the question in a larger context, however, it is necessary to define clearly the difference between administrative tasks and technical tasks. Tasks considered to be purely administrative are present in non-project and non-data processing environments and are traditional functions of a manager:

communication with superiors

planning

scheduling

controlling

gathering resources

Tasks which correspond to competence in a specific discipline (not necessarily data processing technology) are considered to be technical functions. Examples include the following:

requirements studies for information systems

evaluation of resources

system analysis

data processing analysis

programming

analysis and evaluation of data processing products (equipment, programs, etc.)

Next, the peaks of technical involvement of the project manager will be studied, followed by an examination of the double administrative and technical cycle.

Technical Involvement

Technical competencies may vary from one project to another. Is it possible, then, to establish an overall idea of what is involved? The network in Figure 2.7 represents an opportunity study in which two technical activities appear: (a) examination of the existing system, and (b) evaluation of solutions. Whether it is a case of replacing a computer or putting a new information system into place, these two tasks are present; they do not require the same technical knowledge, but must be carried out. They are of such importance to the rest of the project that the personal involvement of the project manager is indispensable; he will either participate in or supervise the carrying out of the two activities.

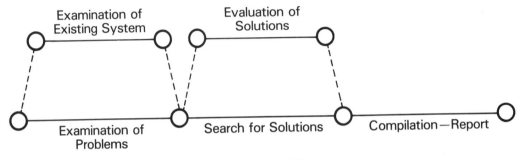

Fig. 2.7. Opportunity study: Technical activities.

Now, let us look at the two networks in Figure 2.8. They represent the product design stage of two projects: Part a describes the development of a system, and Part b the selection of a new computer. Here again it can be seen that even if the disciplines involved are different, the importance of the activities justifies the personal involvement of the project manager in the activity.

On the other hand, for the project design stage, the project manager requires mostly administrative skills since this stage leads to the planning process. It must be remembered, however, that they are data processing management skills. In the same way, the product delivery stage requires a data processing manager's skills.

In conclusion, no matter the nature of the project, the manager must be personally involved at the technical level during the opportunity study and product design stages. The smaller the project, the greater his involvement.

The Project Manager's Life Cycle

The administrative activities of planning, scheduling, and controlling are not equally distributed over the entire project life cycle. Indeed, according to the Norden/Putnam curve, the amount of resources put into play varies to a large

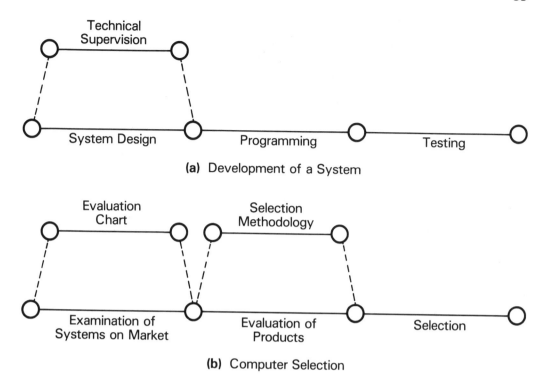

(a) Development of a System

(b) Computer Selection

Fig. 2.8. Product design stage: Project manager's technical activities.

extent from one stage to another, and one must expect these variations in resources to affect the relative importance of the different administrative activities.

In Figure 2.9, the different stages are represented along the horizontal axis. The area above the axis contains the Norden/Putnam resource consumption curve, and the zone below the axis shows the project manager's administrative activity. Three distinct curves of the life cycle are represented in order to show the relative importance of the different stages.

The opportunity study is a project in its own right and must be planned and scheduled. There is therefore a peak in each of these tasks at the beginning of the stage. With the size of the team being restricted, the manager's activity of *control* is moderate in nature.

The team is the smallest during the project design stage. It does, nevertheless, absorb all of the planning and scheduling skills of the project manager since it is during this stage that he must *plan* the remainder of the undertaking. Practically speaking, that is all he does—the activity of control is very restricted, consisting mainly of self-control. During the product design and product delivery stages, control becomes essential because of the quantity of resources involved and the various risks of straying.

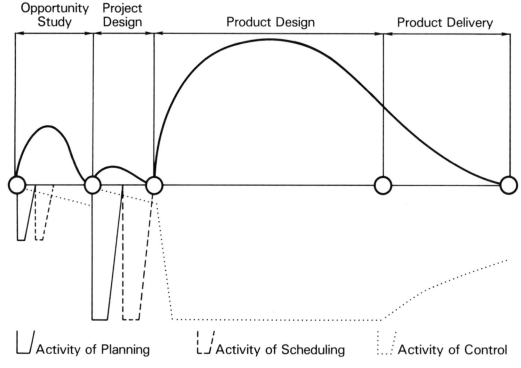

Fig. 2.9. The different administrative activities and the project life cycle.

Planning of the product delivery stage is not shown in Figure 2.9 because, although it is important, it is a task which generally cannot be localized. Depending on the nature of the project, it will take place during the project design stage and will therefore be a part of the overall project planning, or it will be carried out during the product design stage.

The ambivalence of the data processing project manager's role can now be portrayed in Figure 2.10, which depicts the specific peaks of technical and administrative activity. Two major points can be made concerning the division of activities. First, the technical involvement of the project manager is concentrated on the "trouble spots," i.e., those areas where the consequences of an error would seriously affect the entire project. Second, administrative involvement is continuous. It dips slightly towards the end of the opportunity study but immediately becomes extremely important at the beginning of the project design stage, remaining so practically to the end of the project. The only aspect of administrative involvement which changes during the realization of the project is a shift in emphasis from planning to control. The project manager begins as a conceiver and a planner, and finishes as a controller.

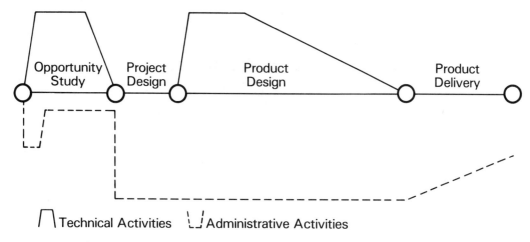

Fig. 2.10. Technical and administrative activities of the project manager.

SELECTED REFERENCES

Benjamin, R. I. 1971. *Control of the information system development cycle*. New York: Wiley Interscience, John Wiley & Sons.
> Despite its age, this condensed book is still of interest today. The system development cycle is presented and justified very well. It also contains an interesting comparison of life cycles formulated by several other authors.

Boehm, B. W. 1977. Seven principles of software engineering. *Infotech State of the Art Report on Software Engineering Techniques*. Infotech International Limited, Nicholson House, Maidenhead, Berkshire, England, 77–113.
> The principles set forth in this article are of fundamental importance and are applicable to all data processing projects. Emphasis is placed in particular on the planning and control of the product to be developed. Here again, the project life cycle is considered to serve as the project manager's basic guideline.

Burch, J. G., Jr, & Strater, F. R., Jr. 1974. *Information systems: Theory and practice*. Santa Barbara, Ca.: Hamilton Publishing Co.
> Directed to quite a wide readership, this book covers all of the topics dealing with information systems. Although the project concept is not explicitly discussed, the system life cycle concept is presented in detail in Chapter 1.

Cave, W. C., & Salisbury, A. B. 1978. Controlling the software life cycle—the project management task. *IEEE Transactions on Software Engineering*, SE-4,4 (July), 326–333.
> This article deals with systems development. The cycle contains seven stages, with the third stage being somewhat similar to the project design stage of this text.

Churchmann, C. W. 1968. *The systems approach*. New York: Dell Publishing Co.
> In an informal and readable presentation, the author introduces and justifies the systems concept and develops it using convincing examples.

Cleland, D. I. & King, W. R. 1968. *Systems analysis and project management*. New York: McGraw-Hill.
> The authors maintain that the project concept is a result of the systems concept. Chapter 8 contains an extensive discussion of organization in a project context as compared to more traditional methods of organization.

Hall, T. P. 1980. Systems life cycle model. *Journal of Systems Management*, 31,4 (April), 29–31.
> The cycle presented in this article contains five stages and is applicable to systems development. Responsibilities, decisions to be made, and results are specified for each stage.

Lucas, H. C., Jr. 1982. *Information systems concepts for management*, 2nd ed. New York: McGraw-Hill.
> A detailed, 10-stage life cycle is presented in Chapter 12. The necessary resources for each stage are described with the help of a bar chart resembling the Norden/Putnam curve.

Metzger, P. W. 1973. *Managing a programming project*. Englewood Cliffs, N.J.: Prentice-Hall.
> This book, which deals exclusively with programming projects, emphasizes the importance of planning, control, and documentation. It is written in a direct and readable style.

Murdick, R. G. 1980. *M.I.S. concepts and design*. Englewood Cliffs, N.J.: Prentice-Hall.
> The book is directed mainly toward managers, and deals with all of the MIS concepts. Chapter 16 discusses the systems concept, while Chapter 7 deals with the project concept and the tasks of the project manager.

Norden, P. V. August 1977. *Project life cycle modeling: Background and application of the life cycle curves*. Airlie, Va.: Software Life Cycle Management Workshop.
> Here the author shows that research and development projects are made up of the planning, design, modeling, release, and product support cycles. Linking the cycles and adding up the required resources leads to the creation of the life cycle curve.

Putnam, L. H. 1978. A general empirical solution to the macro software sizing and estimating problem. *IEEE Trans. on Soft. Eng.*, SE4-4 (July), 345–361.
> The article begins by challenging the bottom-up estimating methods used in software projects. Starting with the Norden curve, the author then goes on to use it to examine several aspects of the life cycle, such as the proportion of resources required for development, the concept of project difficulty, and the influence of the deadline on the total amount of required resources.

Rubin, M. L. 1970. *Introduction to the system life cycle*. Princeton, N.J.: Brandon Systems Press.
> This book is devoted exclusively to systems to be developed and deals with the technical aspects of the undertaking. The life cycle, presented in Chapter 1, is used as the table of contents.

Chapter 3
METHODOLOGY FOR PROJECT ANALYSIS

INTRODUCTION

Let us consider the following system development cycle: analysis, design, programming, testing, implementation. The purpose of the analysis stage is to define the specifications of the system to be developed, that is to say, the inputs, outputs, functions, and constraints. Is it possible to establish a parallel with project management? In order to answer this question, let us return to Figure 2.3 which depicts the activities network for the replacement of a computer. This graph is the starting point of the management activities which have been defined as planning, scheduling, and controlling. There remains only one problem to solve: how was this graph obtained? How does the project manager know that the programs and files must be converted and that the site needs to be prepared? How does he determine the sequence of the activities, their correlation and length? It is the completion of this network, or, more generally speaking, the collecting of the data required for the management activities, that is termed *project analysis*.

Let us return to the system development cycle and the analysis stage. Is it necessary to provide information for each of the subsequent stages of the cycle? It has been seen that the answer to this question is no, and that one need only produce information for the design stage; all of the other information results from it. Is there an activity which plays this same role in the management of the project? The answer is provided by general management principles, one of which is cited by Nelson (1970), as the "Principle of the Primacy of Planning." Among the activities of a manager, that of planning is of the utmost importance and precedes all others. Examination of the definitions of the project manager's various responsibilities (see Chapter 1) shows that, with the exception of technical supervision, all responsibilities are a product of planning, which provides the data.

An in-the-field confirmation of this principle is provided by Thayer, Pyster, and Wood (1981), who reported on the results of a study of the major problems of project management, conducted with the cooperation of several software engineering project managers. The clearest finding of the study was that the planning aspect was the main source of preoccupation of the managers.

Just what then, are these planning problems which are encountered in data processing projects? Kay (1969) mentioned imprecise and changing objectives, as well the fact that the project managers had no basic training in the management of programmers, and that their functions were ill-defined. Sanders (1980) cited, among others, erratic work methods, the lack of estimation data, an oversimplified analysis, and the lack of time for estimation purposes, *this activity being considered to be of marginal importance*. For Pietrasanta (1970), the major estimation problem is that the people involved did not really know what to estimate.

With the exception of imprecise and changing objectives, all of the problems depend on the competency (or lack thereof) of the project manager. Is there a guideline or a primary quality which will allow him to deal with this range of problems? Once again the answer comes from Pietrasanta (1970), for whom an essential prerequisite for estimation is "an intimate understanding of the system development process itself" (p. 90). The relationship to project planning is obvious and leads us to the essential requirement for the planning of the project: a deep understanding of the system development process, or, in other words, the life cycle. Since the objective of the project is to produce a data processing product or service, it includes the production process of this product or service. The conclusion: to plan a data processing project correctly, it is necessary to have a deep knowledge of data processing. After all, an architect plans the construction of a building, an engineer the construction of a road or bridge. Just as they will begin by defining all of the tasks and resources necessary for the achievement of their objective, the data processing project manager will, by means of the project analysis, list everything necessary in order to plan and then organize, coordinate, and control its progress.

After presenting the basis of an analysis method, we will examine the principal problems involved in estimation. Although vaguely felt by practitioners, they are often misunderstood or unseen, particularly by top management.

EXAMPLE A: PATIENT INFORMATION SYSTEM IN A HOSPITAL

Mount Sinai Hospital is a general hospital with 450 beds which receives approximately 15,000 patients per year. Moreover, it has a large outpatient department which handles nearly 500 appointments per day. Having decided to computerize admission-discharge and outpatient appointments, the administration asked several consulting firms to submit proposals for the selection and installation of a turn-key system. The system will have to perform the following functions:

○ Keeping an up-to-date index identifying the patients. Maintained manually at the present time, this index is consulted by the Medical Records, Admissions, Emergency, and Outpatient Departments. The processing of new patients is done exclusively at Admissions.
○ Taking care of admissions and discharges. This activity is also manual at the present time, and involves:
—for a new patient, entry into the index (1 clerk).
—admission: writing up an admission card (3 clerks).
—discharge: compilation of a hospital-stay report, 1 copy to the patient, 1 copy to Accounting for billing purposes (3 clerks).
○ Producing daily, monthly, and yearly statistics.
○ Making appointments for Outpatient Services. There are eight outpatient clinics, each one having its own appointment center. The otorhinolaryngology clinic alone, with two secretaries, handles 200 appointments per day, while the remaining seven clinics have one secretary each.
○ Keeping track of emergency patients. Emergency receives nearly 40 patients a night, and to identify a patient, it is necessary at present to consult the manual index in the Medical Records Department.

The firms submitting proposals must submit: (a) a work plan running up to and including implementation; (b) the list and location of the terminals installed in the different services; and (c) the amount of their fees for the entire study.

OVERVIEW OF PROJECT ANALYSIS

Objectives

In general terms, the goal of project analysis is to provide all of the information necessary for the planning stage. Using this information, it will be possible to define the scheduling and control.

Since the network is the fundamental planning tool, let us examine and analyze the simplest network, composed of a single activity (see Figure 3.1). The

(a) Elementary Project Network

(b) Elementary Project Network: Analysis Objectives

Fig. 3.1. Project analysis objectives.

first component of interest to us is the activity along with its duration. However, an activity is not self-sufficient: it requires human, material, and other resources. Completely defining an activity therefore includes:

—specifying the "work" to be done
—the necessary resources
—the duration of the activity

Since the activity cannot begin until it is defined and the necessary resources are available, it can be seen that the initial event 1 corresponds to the moment these two requirements are met. This will be studied in Chapter 10, dealing with planning.

The second component of the network is event 2. An event represents the instant something identifiable is accomplished. An event will be considered to correspond to something deliverable, be it product or service. A written program is therefore an event, just like a specified report format or a compiled dossier of specifications. Therefore, in order to define an event, it is necessary to specify (a) the deliverable, and (b) the moment of availability.

The network represents the project, and to define it completely, the following elements must be identified:

○ the deliverables
○ the activities to accomplish
○ the necessary resources
○ the time required for realization, which will make it possible to determine the moment of deliverability

Obtaining this information at all levels constitutes the objective of project analysis.

EXAMPLE B: ADMISSION-DISCHARGE SYSTEM

For the consulting firms called upon by the hospital, the project is defined by:

deliverables–work plan, list and installation of terminals, and amount of the fees for the study.

activities–what the firm will have to do in order to supply the hospital with the specified deliverable items.

resources–what the firm will require (manpower, documentation, secretarial services, etc.).

time–the amount of time required by the firm to produce the deliverable items.

A Project Is a System

A system is a set of components and subsystems working together for the attainment of a common goal. This definition applies perfectly to a project. Moreover, given a project's structure, it has little interaction with the outside world, and the black box concept discussed in Chapter 2 also applies.

From the project analysis point of view, input into the box consists of the definition of the product P, with output being the abovementioned parameters:

$$A = \text{activities}$$

$$R = \text{resources}$$

$$D = \text{duration}$$

If the following formulas existed

$$A = f_1(P)$$

$$R = f_2(P)$$

$$D = f_3(P)$$

in which P is the product, we would have an initial answer to the problem, i.e., the global estimates of everything required for project realization. Unfortunately, formulas of this kind do not exist, given the uniqueness of each project. This point will be examined more closely, in the specific case of programming, later in this chapter. The only remaining solution is to analyze the box by breaking it down into subsystems in the hope that, for a given subsystem or component, a formula does exist.

A project, however, is a slightly peculiar system. Let us examine, once again, the automobile manufacturer mentioned in Chapter 2. A breakdown, showing the relation between the different subsystems, is given in Figure 3.2. It can be seen that the output from sales is an input of the production subsystem, that research and development feeds production and marketing, and so forth. The different subsystems interact among themselves in such a way that it is not possible to specify a general rule. The analysis of one subsystem must therefore take into account several others which interact with it.

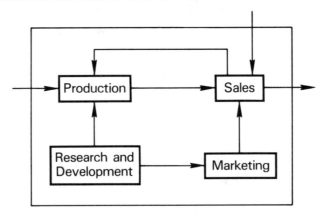

Fig. 3.2. The subsystems of an automobile manufacturer.

Such is not the case, however, in a project. If the life cycle is used as a guideline, a purely sequential breakdown is obtained (see Figure 3.3). Each subsystem receives its input data only from the preceding one (and eventually from the outside world) and transmits its output data to the following subsystem. Analysis thus becomes far easier. If this structure is continued in a repetitive manner, it will be easy to attain a level at which, it is hoped, the parameters being looked for (A,R,D) will become known and the overall information for the project will then be obtainable.

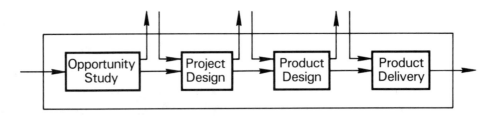

Fig. 3.3. Basic subsystems of a project seen as a system.

The Breakdown-Integration Loop

Project analysis is made up of a series of breakdown-integration phases as shown in Figure 3.4. The breakdown process will be applied to all of the elements, i.e.,

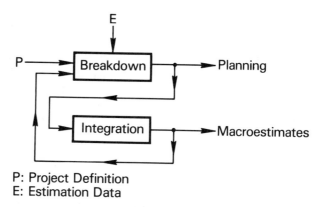

P: Project Definition
E: Estimation Data

Fig. 3.4. The breakdown-integration loop.

the deliverables, activities, resources, and durations, until the components for which the estimation data are available are arrived at.

Definition

A microestimate is an evaluation of deliverables, activities, resources, and durations of elementary components.

HOSPITAL SYSTEM EXAMPLE The number of hours necessary in order to evaluate the equipment of a supplier is a microestimate. The cost of a video display terminal and the type and cost of a printer to be installed in a given department are microestimates.

The results of the breakdown process serve two purposes:

—as data for the integration process
—as the starting point for planning

The integration process consists in gathering together all of the values of a given parameter (A,R,D) in order to arrive at values of significance at the project level.

Definition

A macroestimate is an evaluation of products, activities, resources, or durations of major project components.

HOSPITAL SYSTEM EXAMPLE The cost of all of the equipment is a macroestimate. The time required for implementation and the total number of terminals to be installed are macroestimates.

To start with, the results of the integration process are critically analyzed. Indeed, it will be seen later in this chapter that the microestimate data are frequently inaccurate and subject to question. Once integrated, they may prove to be unrealistic or unworkable. It is at this point that the experience of the project manager and his team comes into play, with the breakdown process being revised either partially or totally, depending on the evaluation of the macro-estimates.

Once the integration results are deemed acceptable, they are used as an overall planning, scheduling, and controlling framework by both the project manager and the higher authority to whom he reports.

Scope of the Macroestimates

For the deliverable elements, the macroestimates cover the identifiable components of the product to be delivered. *Example*: Computer, disks, patient index system, terminals, etc.

For the activities, resources, and durations, the macroestimates will be given for the entire project and the principal milestones. *Example*: Cost of the entire study, duration of the installation stage, number of people needed to make the system selection.

THE BREAKDOWN PROCESS

WBS: Work Breakdown Structure

The work breakdown structure (WBS) method, presented by Tripp and Wah (1980) and Murdick (1980), is the application of the principles of top-down analysis used in program design to the various project elements. It consists of the hierarchical breakdown of the project, level by level, in order to arrive at the level needed for planning and controlling. The project life cycle will be used as a guideline for the initial breakdown.

For each breakdown component, the deliverables, activities, resources, and duration necessary in order to complete the component are specified. In principle, the WBS method is intended to be applied to systems realization projects, with the activity being the element which serves as the breakdown guide. Nothing, however, says that it cannot be applied to something else, in particular to the product itself; if the product is a program, a conventional top-down analysis is involved, but it can also be applied to the equipment, as is shown in the following example.

EXAMPLE C: WBS OF THE HOSPITAL PROJECT

Figure 3.5 depicts part of the breakdown. Examination of the system specifications portion shows that the WBS corresponds to the components of the system;

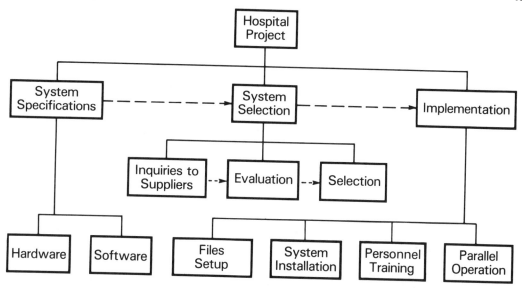

Fig. 3.5. WBS of the hospital project.

if the software element were the particular object of interest, at the next lower level would be found:

patient index

admission-discharge system

outpatient service appointments

This is a classic example of the WBS of a product. Note also in Figure 3.5 that a dotted line links the level 2 elements as well as those at the lower level of system selection; this makes it possible to illustrate the sequences of activities on the breakdown tree.

Lateral Breakdown and Longitudinal Breakdown

There are two distinct types of breakdown. *Lateral breakdown* is the breakdown of an element into components differing in nature, for example:

Software = patient index, admission-discharge, appointments

This makes it possible to enumerate the different elements of a component.
Longitudinal breakdown is the breakdown of an element into components similar in nature, for example:

$$\text{Disk space} = \text{space (index file)}$$
$$\text{space (admission-discharge)}$$
$$\text{space (appointments)}$$

No matter which element is broken down (product, activity, resource, time), the longitudinal fractioning results in components similar in nature, while the lateral fractioning leads to elements differing in nature.

EXAMPLE D: BREAKDOWN OF THE PERSONNEL TRAINING ELEMENT

Lateral breakdown:

Admissions personnel

Personnel handling appointment-making

Emergency personnel

Medical Records personnel

The breakdown is lateral, since the training the various employees are to receive changes from one element to another. The breakdown to determine how many outpatient service personnel will have to be trained is longitudinal, since they will all receive the same training; in this case there are nine people to be instructed in the use of the appointment-making system.

In principle, the four parameters (deliverables, activities, resources, and time) are connected to each box in the breakdown; the purpose of the WBS is to determine them for each component in the tree. It is clear that the values obtained for a given box will depend on and be a result of those of the boxes situated at lower levels.

The Limits of the Process

Until what point, then, should this process be continued? A working limit of the WBS process was defined by Murdick (1980) as the obtaining of workpackages: "A workpackage (WP) establishes the degree of management visibility and control to be exercised on the project" (p. 228). For Murdick, a WP is assigned to one person in particular, with that person being given an account.

This definition, no matter how attractive it may seem, especially from a control point of view, is not very helpful. What happens if the elements (products, activities, resources, and durations) of the WP which are necessary for control purposes cannot be estimated? This illustrates *the fundamental importance of plan-*

ning over other management tasks. In effect, for Tripp and Wah (1980), the goal of planning is to reduce the inherent risks of project realization. According to these authors, if it is admitted that risk is a decreasing function of planning (or analysis), a maximum of planning will result in a minimum of risk. Although the cost of planning itself increases with the amount of effort, there does exist an optimum planning region which takes into account both risk and cost. For Tripp and Wah, the limit therefore becomes the available information, or, in terms of analysis, the availability of estimation data.

These two points of view are in fact complementary and make it possible to arrive at a rule governing the breakdown process:

Stage 1: Continue the breakdown until workpackages are obtained.

Stage 2: If for a WP the elements (products, activities, resources, durations) cannot be estimated, continue the process until elements for which estimation data are available are obtained.

EXAMPLE E: PRODUCT EVALUATION

Let us suppose that we wish to continue the analysis of the evaluation box in Figure 3.5. In order to do this, the characteristic elements must first of all be defined:

product: evaluation of each product under consideration on the market, taking the needs of the hospital into account. An evaluation consists of a mark (rating) accompanied by comments.

activities: all of the tasks and activities necessary in order to carry out the evaluation

resources: number of persons of the various technical profiles required; hours needed per profile

duration: number of days needed to carry out the evaluation

Despite its experience, the consulting firm is unable to provide values for the latter three elements (activities, resources, duration). The breakdown is continued, as illustrated in Figure 3.6. The WPs are second level elements: evaluation of the computer system, of the packages, of the supplier, and consolidation of the results. The firm does have teams which specialize in these activities. Prior experience permits an estimate of 10 work hours to evaluate a computer system. In the same manner, the time required for supplier evaluation is estimated at two hours, and the time required for consolidation of results at three hours per supplier.

On the other hand, it is clear that evaluation of the packages depends on their nature. It was therefore necessary to continue the process until estimable

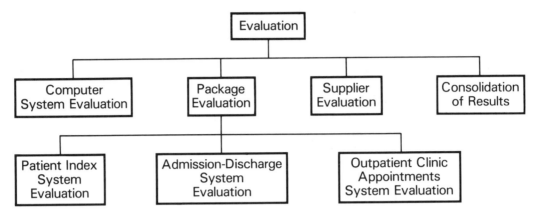

Fig. 3.6. Hospital system: WBS of the evaluation box.

TABLE 3.1.
RESULTS OF THE WBS FOR EVALUATION (PER SYSTEM)

Box	Product	Activities	Resources	Duration
Computer system evaluation	Rating & comments	Evaluation system	Hardware specialists	10 h
Patient index evaluation	Rating & comments	Package evaluation	Hospital systems specialist	3 h
Admission-discharge evaluation	Rating & comments	Package evaluation	Hospital systems specialist	5 h
Appointments evaluation	Rating & comments	Package evaluation	Hospital systems specialist	7 h
Supplier evaluation	Rating & comments	Analysis of supplier reliability	Market specialist	2 h
Consolidation	Rating & comments	Integration of above data	Senior consultant	3 h

products were obtained, i.e., the index, the admission-discharge, and appointments systems. Thanks to specialists in these types of systems, the firm is able to estimate that three hours will be required for evaluation of the index, five hours for the admission-discharge system, and seven hours for the appointments system. In order to obtain uniform evaluations, one principle is always followed: the same person (or team) evaluates a given product component for all suppliers, instead of one person (or team) evaluating all of the components of a single supplier. It is now possible to estimate the elements of all the leaves of the tree in Figure 3.6; the results are contained in Table 3.1.

This example illustrates two important aspects of WBS:

1. The breakdown is not continued to the same level in every branch. Some activities require a greater breakdown than others, regardless of their duration.

2. The estimate data are based on the experience and work methods of the company; this aspect will be discussed more completely in a later section of this chapter.

INTEGRATION AND ITERATION

The Integration Process

The WBS has made it possible to obtain two results:

○ A hierarchical breakdown of the project into ever-smaller, better-defined subsets.

○ Precise definitions, quantitative or not, for the parameters (products, activities, resources, durations) associated with each terminal element of the tree.

The goal of integration is to go back up the tree and assign values to the parameters of the high-level boxes. Let us propose, for example, to determine the number of people required in order to carry out the entire evaluation mentioned in Example D (see also Figure 3.6).

Whereas the breakdown was top-down, the integration is primarily horizontal: for a given parameter, it groups together the elements of one level before moving them up to the next. Before specifying the number of people needed to carry out the evaluation (top of the tree), it will be necessary to determine who will do what at the lower level; the same persons can perform several tasks.

The integration mechanism depends above all on the parameter being studied. Sometimes it is simply a question of additions of microestimates, as will be the case if the object of interest is the number of terminals or the total number of man-hours required to do a certain job. For other parameters, the integration will be a different process: a search for the critical path when the duration is being studied, or complex technical calculations if the amount of memory needed to support 15 simultaneously active terminals is to be determined. The following example illustrates different integration mechanisms.

EXAMPLE F: OBTAINING EVALUATION PARAMETERS

The results obtained in Example E will be integrated under the following hypotheses:

1. Given its knowledge of the market, the firm knows that there are a maximum of eight suppliers that may have a product able to meet the needs of the hospital.
2. In order to avoid making a premature estimate of the durations, it will be assumed that a single person rather than a team will perform each evaluation shown in Figure 3.6; on the other hand, because the different evaluations require different specializations, each one will be carried out by a different person.
3. All of the evaluations will be done by specialists whose rates are \$75/hour. The consolidation shall be done by a senior consultant at the rate of \$90/ hour.

We are now going to integrate three parameters: the time in hours, the cost, and the duration (in days) of the evaluation.

○ Man-hours required for the evaluation
    specialists:

computer system	8 × 10	=	80 hrs
patient index	8 × 3	=	24 hrs
admission-discharge	8 × 5	=	40 hrs
appointments	8 × 7	=	56 hrs
supplier	8 × 2	=	16 hrs
	Total		216 hrs

    senior consultant:

consolidation	8 × 3	=	24 hrs
	Total		240 hrs

○ Cost of the evaluation
    cost = 216 × 75 + 24 × 90 = \$18,360

○ Duration of the evaluation
Taking into account Hypothesis 2, it is now possible to draw the network shown in Figure 3.7. Because of the network's simplicity, it is easy to find the critical path, which is marked by a heavy line and has a duration of 104 hours. Based on an 8-hour workday, the duration is 13 days.

    In summary, for the evaluation, the integration process provides us with:

○ Human resources: at least 5 specialists plus a senior consultant, for a total of 240 hours
○ Cost: \$18,360

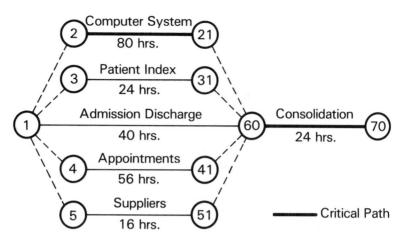

Fig. 3.7. Evaluation activities for system selection.

○ Duration: 13 days

Hypothesis 1 (probable number of suppliers) is necessary; without it, no estimate is possible. Hypothesis 3 is, in reality, simply a fact. The objective of Hypothesis 2, however, is to obtain an unbiased estimate. Indeed, any supposition which results in the assigning of more than one person to an evaluation is based on the resources available. Yet at the time the estimate is done, this factor is unknown, and to assign a value to it amounts to imposing a restriction which will perhaps be impossible to respect during the planning stage. It is important that integration not impose restrictions on subsequent activities.

Results Analysis and Iteration

The macroestimates obtained by integration must not be considered final; they must be open to the critical judgment of their authors and the people responsible for them. Indeed, breakdown and integration have neither the rigor nor the uniqueness of a mathematical algorithm which, when applied to the same object, always yields the same results. The macroestimates, therefore, can be questioned for three reasons: microestimate errors, unacceptable situations provoked by the process, and inadequate breakdown.

The problem of microestimation accuracy will be discussed more completely in the following section; in Example F, the duration of the evaluation of a computer system could very well be 7 hours instead of 10.

An unacceptable situation is the creation *by the integration process itself* of an unnecessary restriction on a project parameter, as would be the case, for example, if a specialist were required to have two parallel activities or if a cost surpassed fixed constraints. It would then be necessary to retrace the integration process in reverse, and perhaps the breakdown as well, in order to find the source of the problem and attempt to resolve it.

EXAMPLE G: DURATION OF THE EVALUATION

Let us suppose that the project manager decides that a duration of 13 days for the evaluation would make the final deadline unacceptable to the client. Going back through the integration, he discovers that the evaluation of the computer system alone requires 80 hours, if carried out by a single specialist. He may then decide that he will have no choice but to assign two people to this activity, thereby reducing its duration to 50 hours. (It will be seen later that doubling the personnel does not cut the time in half.) The critical path then passes through the appointments activity, which lasts 56 hours (see Figure 3.7), with the total duration of the evaluation now becoming 56 + 24 = 80 hours or 10 days.

An inadequate breakdown is the result of an error or incorrect approach in the process. Although not all errors can be detected at the macroestimate level, it can nonetheless happen, as is illustrated by the following example.

EXAMPLE H: REWORKING THE WBS

Let us suppose that the project manager considers the total cost of the evaluation ($18,360) to be too high. The most extensive component is the computer system evaluation. Having consulted a hospital systems specialist, the manager then discovers that certain products correspond to a service bureau: terminals are to be installed in the hospital connected to the supplier's computer. For these products, the computer system evaluation element no longer exists, and the only evaluations necessary are those for the packages and the suppliers. We are now faced with two breakdowns which are a function of the product: one with a computer, the other without. The integration performed in Example F must be revised in the following manner:

○ Man-hours required for the evaluation
   specialist:

computer system	5 × 10	=	50 hrs
all other evaluations remain the same		=	136 hrs
	Total		186 hrs
senior consultant:			24 hrs
	Total		210 hrs

- Cost of the evaluation

$$cost = 186 \times 75 + 24 \times 90 = \$16,110$$

- Duration of the evaluation

As in Example F, the critical path now passes through the appointments activity, with the duration of the evaluation becoming

$$56 + 24 = 80 \text{ hrs} = 10 \text{ days.}$$

While the microestimates and their eventual calling into question involve only the breakdown phase and demand only the knowledge of the elements concerned, revision of the macroestimates includes the entire analysis process and requires a deep understanding of the project management process, product realization, and the environment in which the project is being carried out. As Pietrasanta (1970) indicated, "an intimate understanding of the development process itself" is required.

ESTIMATION PROBLEMS

Microestimation

The breakdown into a WBS can be compared to the construction of the skeleton of the project. The microestimates constitute the flesh which is added to the skeleton, with the macroestimates being the characteristics of the major components. While the breakdown process has been demonstrated and is based on a well-established discipline, top-down structured analysis, what can be said about the estimation of the components? To try to answer this question, the sources of the microestimates will first be examined, followed by the related problems, and finally an attempt will be made to find ideas which will help the project manager in his task.

We have already established that there currently exists no magic formula of the type $e = f(P)$, where e is the estimation of a parameter and P the description of the product to be developed; thus the necessity of the WBS. In fact, the problem has simply been shifted: for a given object which is to be estimated, is such a formula available? Except in the case where the object to be estimated is already on the market, the answer is no, and the people in charge can rely only on their experience.

Use of past data can be employed in three progressively more sophisticated ways.

Individual Experience

The data are drawn from personal experience and are in the minds of the estimators. A good programmer, for example, knows how to estimate the work required to produce a certain type of program. The disadvantages of this method are obvious: relying too heavily on individual experience and opinions, the lack of references, no guarantee of repetition.

Company Database

The results obtained during previous undertakings were entered into a manual or computerized data base and can therefore be studied. The advantages of this method over the previous one are: (a) data are nonindividualized; (b) data are based on results; and (c) values are based on a large number of data.

In example D, the estimates in Table 3.1 come from just such a source. The disadvantage of this method is a lack of quality and homogeneity in the data contained in the base. Moreover, very often the data base does not exist, no data having been gathered or documented.

Mathematical Models

A model is built using a base like the one just described, usually by employing simple or multiple regression techniques. The advantage of this method is that in principle the famous "magic formula" can now be employed. An excellent example of this can be seen in the presentation made by Nelson (1970), in which he uses multiple regression techniques to estimate programming and computer times. Unfortunately, there are several problems which, although general in nature in all three methods, are more visible here, the major ones being the quality of the data and the choice of variables.

The use of previously collected data poses a certain number of problems that are well known to researchers: the conditions under which they were obtained, measuring instruments, and context. Putnam (1978) clearly puts forward the case of the "man-day." Is it an 8-hour day (working day), or 8 hours of actual work? Moreover, there is the problem of paid holidays, times of sickness, and so on. However, a solution does exist: collecting data on a prospective basis. If the data from previous projects are gathered with the idea of using them at some future time as estimation sources, many of the problems cited will be alleviated to a great extent.

The problem of choosing variables is clearly illustrated by estimating the effort required to produce one or several programs. The conventional approach is to find a way to formulate the equation

$$MH = f(S)$$

in which *MH* is the programming duration (in hours, for example) and *S* the number of source statements. How can *S* be estimated by using the product description as the starting point? There are no more methods for this than there are for MH: the problem has simply been shifted. Is *S* a valid reference? The answer to this question is no, as shown by the following example, well known to programmers.

Program to Calculate the Prime Numbers between 1 and N

This exercise has been done by every student of data processing. The author participated in or was witness to the following solutions:

o A single-statement APL program, produced and tested in 10 minutes.
o An 80-instruction Assembly-language program, produced and tested in six hours.
o A Fortran program of roughly 20 lines, produced and tested in one hour.

The effort required to produce a program depends on:

the programming language chosen,

the nature and complexity of the problem to be programmed, and

the experience of the programmer in programming and in the particular type of problem.

These points have been illustrated by several authors (Burton, 1975; Pietrasanta, 1970; Putnam, 1978).

In summary, the analytical methods (i.e., those used to find a model of the type $e = f(P1, P2, \ldots PN)$) still face the problems of the choice and expression of the variables P1, P2, ... PN.

What conclusions, therefore, can be drawn from this rather disappointing examination of the microestimation sources? They are set out by Pietrasanta (1970) and Tripp (1980), and can be summarized as follows:

o Incorrect estimates are almost always underestimates.
o Underestimates result from estimate omissions.
o A bad estimate is better than none at all.
o If doubts arise regarding the estimation of an element, the breakdown must be continued.

In summary, the quality of the WBS is more important for the estimate than the quality of the microestimates themselves.

Some Characteristics of Macroestimates

Macroestimates are a result of the integration process; if the WBS has been well done they should be accurate, provided the same can be said of the microestimates. However, as has been illustrated by Brooks' (1975) model in "The Mythical Man-Month," this is not entirely true. If n persons are working on a project, in addition to their regular tasks, there is an intercommunications factor proportional to:

$$x = \frac{n(n-1)}{2}$$

The resources consumed by intercommunications vary as the square of the number of persons involved. Even though, as Gaydash (1982) pointed out, intercommunications account for only a small portion of the total (10%), an increase in available resources does not result in a proportional decrease in the amount of the time required. In example 3.7, when the number of team members responsible for the computer system evaluation was doubled, the time required to carry it out went from 80 hours to 50, and not to 40 as might have been expected. It is a question here of the classic cost-time tradeoff problem, which can be formulated as follows: people and time are not interchangeable.

Besides Brooks' intercommunications parameter, there is also that of the degree of difficulty. It is intuitively known that the more difficult a problem is, the more expensive it will be to solve. Moreover, the degree of difficulty is itself increased if the time allotted is reduced. For Putnam (1978), the difficulty of a project is expressed by

$$D = K/t_d^2$$

where K is the total cost and t_d the development time of the system. It is obvious that if K is constant, D increases if t_d decreases. Unfortunately, it has been seen that the cost increases as a function of the degree of difficulty. Result: if the allotted time of the project decreases, the cost increases. Pietrasanta (1970) intuitively illustrated this as shown in Figure 3.8.

Figure 3.8 depicts the development portion of the Putnam life cycle under three development time assumptions, $t_1>t_2>t_3$. y' represents the effort required at time t, with the total cost being given by

$$K = \int_0^{t_i} y'dt \qquad \text{for } t_i = t_1, t_2, t_3$$

The hypothesis which states that K is a constant depending only on the nature of the product to be delivered is false; the fact is that

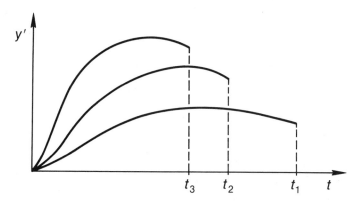

Fig. 3.8. Development cycle under three-time assumptions.

$$K_1 < K_2 < K_3$$

What happens if K and t are decreased at the same time? For Putnam, the project can no longer be completed because the increased difficulty puts it out of reach of the project team, the size of which is determined by K. For Pietrasanta, the conclusion is clear: if t and K are decreased simultaneously, the product to be delivered will also be reduced, be it in quality or in scope.

An attempt can be made to summarize these different aspects in the following manner. Let P be the product to be delivered, K the cost, and T the completion time. P, K, and T are linked by a formula of the type

(1) $\qquad\qquad f(P,K,T) = c \qquad c = \text{constant}$

If P is given a value of P_o, for example, the formula then becomes

(2) $\qquad\qquad f(P_o,K,T) = c$ which can be changed into

(3) $\qquad\qquad K = g_{P_o}(T)$

g_{P_o} decreases as a function of T: if the allotted time decreases, the cost of the project increases. Inversely, if the allotted cost decreases, the time required to complete the project increases. On the other hand, according to equation (3), it is impossible to decrease K and T simultaneously.

Let us now look at equations (4) and (5) below:

(4) $\qquad\qquad\qquad P = g_{K_o}(T)$

(5) $\qquad\qquad\qquad P = g_{T_o}(K)$

In contrast to g_{P_o}, g_{K_o} and g_{T_o} increase as a function of T and K respectively: for a total fixed cost K_o, decreasing the completion time results in a deterioration of the delivered product; the same thing happens if the cost is reduced while the time is maintained as a constant. In the specific case of program development, Putnam arrives at

$$(K^{1/3} \, T^{4/3}) \, / \, P \, = \, C$$

where P is defined as the number of instructions to be delivered.

In conclusion, the classic time-cost tradeoff changes into a time-cost-product tradeoff:

o It is possible to reduce the time (within certain limits) and obtain the product decided upon at the outset, provided that an increase in cost is acceptable.
o It is possible to reduce the cost and still obtain the same product, as long as pushing back the deadlines is acceptable.
o It is impossible to reduce the cost and the deadlines simultaneously without adversely affecting the final product.

Generally speaking, these reductions never come from the project manager; they are imposed on him by the administration, who are rarely aware of the time-cost-product triangle. The project manager should be aware of this problem in order to avoid finding himself in impossible situations resulting from his ill-considered submission to pressures whose consequences are all too predictable.

SELECTED REFERENCES

Brooks, F. P. 1975. *The mythical man-month.* Reading, Mass.: Addison-Wesley.
        The author attacks the belief that it is possible to save a past-deadline project simply through the introduction of additional personnel. In particular, he presents a model of the intercommunication between N people, which has since become a classic.

Burton, B. J. 1975. Manpower estimating for systems projects. *Journal of Systems Management*, January, 29–33.
        This article proposes a method for estimating the number of man-days needed to produce a given system. The author insists on the necessity of the most complete breakdown possible, and presents estimating formulas which take into account the complexity of the problem and the experience of the analyst or programmer.

Gaydash, A., Jr. 1982. *Principles of EDP management.* Reston, Va.: Reston Publishing Co.
        In Chapter 4, dealing with project management, the author discusses the applicability of Brooks' formula. He presents the partitionable project concept, in which the necessity of intercommunication almost totally disappears.

Kay, R. J. 1969. The management and organization of large scale software development projects. *Proceedings Spring Joint Computer Conferences*, 34, 425–433.

A summary of a series of presentations, this publication gives an excellent state-of-the-art report. It includes attention to the problem of imprecise and changing objectives and the absence of management training in project managers.

Murdick, R. G. 1980. *MIS concepts and design.* Englewood Cliffs, N.J.: Prentice-Hall, Inc.

In Chapter 7 the author presents the work breakdown structure (WBS) method and the concept of the workpackage as the breakdown process limit; the discussion is control-oriented.

Nelson, E. A. 1970. Some recent contributions to computer programming management. In Weinwurm, G. F. (ed.), *On the management of computer programming.* Princeton, N.J.: Auerbach Publishers, Inc.

This presentation reaffirms the famous principle of the primacy of planning in management activities. It also contains formulas for resource estimation obtained through multiple regression techniques using a database of 169 projects.

Pietrasanta, A. M. 1970. Resource analysis of computer program system development. Functional estimating of computer program system development. In Weinwurm, G. F. (ed). *On the management of computer programming.* Auerbach Publishers, Inc.

These two presentations are essential reading for anyone interested in project management and more particularly in estimating and planning problems. Discussion topics include: the overhead concept introduced by logistics and the problems in communication; the necessity of carefully specifying and listing the products to be delivered; and a brilliant exposé of the time-cost trade-off problem and product quality. The author also insists that each supposition made during the estimating stage be documented.

Sanders, J. 1980. Barriers to estimating DP projects effectively. *Infosystems*, December, 64–70.

This is an excellent description of the principal estimating problems: the absence of reference data; unrealistic restrictions on time and money; and the lack of time allotted for the actual estimating process.

Thayer, R. H., Pyster, A. B., Wood, R. C. 1981. Major issues in software engineering project management. *IEEE Transactions on Software Engineering*, SE-7, 4, July, 333–342.

This article presents the results of a survey conducted among software engineering project managers. The objective was to determine the main problems encountered and to define their causes. Although several results are nonconclusive, there is a consensus on three subjects: planning problems are the most important, project managers are promoted to this position without prior training and very few universities provide a course in software engineering project management.

Tripp, L. L., & Wah, P. N. 1980. How much planning in systems development? *Journal of Systems Management*, October, 6–15.

This excellent article presents the work breakdown structure (WBS) method. The authors introduce the cost of the planning process and that of the risk incurred due to lack of planning. They discuss the factors which influence the level at which the process must stop: cost, experience, complexity, duration, and so on.

Chapter 4
DOCUMENTATION

INTRODUCTION

Documentation is the Achilles' heel of data processing. Lack of documentation has been the object of countless complaints, analyses of causes, and proposed solutions (Lucas, 1982; Menkus, 1970; Weinberg, 1971). For the project manager, lack of documentation contributes to loss of control over deadlines, costs, and even the final product itself.

The process used in documentation is analogous to that employed in medicine. First, the symptoms are identified. They may be manifested in changing and unclear specifications as well as in systems which users are incapable of using and programmers unable to correct or modify.

Next, a diagnosis is made to determine the causes which produced the symptoms, such as programmers' reluctance to document, ineffective management approaches, or absence of standards. Finally, as in medical science, ways to cure the sickness are proposed. In most organizations, therapy consists of approaches such as the use of norms, methods, checklists, formats, and persuasive advice.

EXAMPLE A: PORTFOLIO MANAGEMENT SYSTEM

Savings Management Trust (SMT) specializes in stock portfolio management for individual and institutional clients. A new subsidiary of a larger business organization, the company carries out its operations manually. The parent company's data processing department is given the task of automating SMT's operations, either by packages acquisition or inhouse development.

The system selected will have to perform the following short-term functions: issue a monthly statement of each client's cash account; issue a monthly statement of each client's stock account; issue reports for control of custodian banks (where the securities are actually deposited); and estimate client portfolios. On a long-term basis, the system must allow online access to client accounts and perform portfolio management.

The organization does not have a strong background in documentation. Existing systems have little documentation and no standards exist. As for systems development, there are no references, the approach having always been to create a system whenever the need arose, without estimation or control of costs and schedules.

Three favorable circumstances led Andrew Crawford, head of data processing, to use this project as a development and documentation experiment: (a) the deadlines for this system are not rigid; (b) the absence of documentation and control is beginning to worry management; and (c) a new analyst trained in modern development and documentation techniques was hired six months ago.

The project will be managed by the analyst, Michael Bernstein, under Crawford's supervision. Because it is a first-time experiment, Crawford will exercise stricter control over the project manager than is typical of most projects. Among other requests he asks Bernstein to propose documentation requirements for the project.

DOCUMENTATION: THE MALADY OF DATA PROCESSING

Diagnosis, Treatment, and Outcome

The risks associated with undocumented systems have been recognized for years, and documentation is thus primarily seen as an insurance policy (Keen, 1981; Rubin, 1970). As a precaution, it is a package policy to protect against all risks: including programming errors, personnel turnover, and lack of understanding on the part of the users. For Lucas (1982), documentation is "almost anything written about the information system." Areas typically covered include system documentation, program documentation, implementation documentation, user documentation, and operations documentation, with each of these being subdivided into subchapters, sections, etc.

While the intentions are good (let us not forget that the documentation must help to avoid any incidents), the pill seems to be hard to swallow, and if it is taken according to the prescription, the increase in paper results. However, the patient refuses the medication without even knowing the consequences. Why?

Weinberg (1971, p. 262) noted that "documentation is the castor oil of programmers—managers think it is good for programmers and programmers hate it." Some programmers consider documentation to be a task which is beneath them (Menkus, 1970), while others fail to see any advantage in it and consider it an imposition on their already heavy workload (Keen, 1981; Lucas, 1982). In addition, pressure by management to produce results quickly may persuade project personnel that documentation is of low priority. Once again, according to Weinberg, "It's a wonderful thing to have good documentation, but not if it has to be paid for" (p. 264).

What, then, are the proposed solutions? There are three avenues of approach:

○ *Management commitment*: Management must see documentation as an important project element.
○ *Psychological approach*: This involves use of noncoercive, tactful persuasion to convince project personnel that documentation is both good and necessary.
○ *Standards*: For many people, standards will facilitate the production of coherent, useful documentation and will provide a task framework for the programmer.

EXAMPLE B: PROGRAMS DOCUMENTATION PROPOSAL

Eager to do a good job, Michael Bernstein, head of the portfolio management project at SMT, extensively studies the literature on documentation. He then presents his superior with a proposal, part of which is shown in Table 4.1. Extremely impressed and even a little ashamed, Andrew Crawford goes into his office to study the document. Indeed, he does not know what a structured walkthrough is. Somewhat reassured after researching the definition, he examines the manual, then calls Bernstein and asks him a few questions.

Andrew: Doesn't the compiler make it possible to obtain a variable cross-reference list?

Michael: Yes.

Andrew: So why make it a separate item? Don't programming standards stipulate that all of the variables must be described at the beginning of the program?

Michael: Yes.

Andrew: So why make it a separate item? Are the inputs and outputs described again in the user documentation section?

Michael: No, that's useless repetition.

TABLE 4.1

A PORTION OF THE SYSTEM SMT.PM DOCUMENTATION MANUAL

Section	Subsection
1 Documentation standards	
2 General description	
3 System design	
4 Programs	4.1 List of programs
	4.2 For each program: History Narrative description Flowchart Decision tables Listing Structured walk-throughs reports Variables list Variables cross-reference list Inputs description Outputs description Error messages Test data Test procedures Test results
5 Files description	5.1 Files list
	5.2 For each file: Name Medium, device Organization Access methods Record format Record length Key
	For each data item: Name Function Position Type Length
6 Programs-files cross-reference list	6.1 Per file: list of programs accessing the file Per program: type of access (I,O,U)
	6.2 Per program: list of files accessed by the program Per file: type of access (I,O,U)
7 Operations	
8 User	

Andrew: So if a user doesn't understand a report, he has to sift through the program documentation section to find the explanation.

Michael: Apparently.

Andrew: Is there an error messages list in the user documentation?

Michael: Yes, of course. The reason I put it in the programs documentation as well was to help the programmers.

Andrew: Do you mean that a complete list of all the error messages is not provided at the end of the program?

Michael: No, I don't believe so.

Andrew: Don't you think the programming would be a lot neater and wouldn't require a document?

Michael: Yes, of course.

A Second Opinion

Let us investigate the reasons for not having good documentation: the author involved sees no use in it; he finds it heavy, tedious, below him; management finds documentation expensive. According to Benjamin (1971), documentation is an integral part of the design process; each phase has outputs (documents) which are used as inputs for the succeeding phase. The HIPO method (Katzan, 1976) is as typical example of a document which *is* the design of a data processing system. Even user documentation can be made to be of use to the developer: in quality assurance it is recommended that documentation be produced before design begins in order to eliminate any possible misunderstandings between the user and the design team. The project manager uses a Gantt chart to monitor the progress of the work. Ingrassia's (1978) Unit Development Folder (UDF) makes it possible, in the case of programming, to monitor the work and control its quality at the same time.

Documenting can also be unnecessarily expensive if the programmer, despite his credentials and training, does not know how to document correctly. Perhaps he was told what to do (see Example A) but not how to do it. Not surprising that he finds it heavy, tedious, and tiresome! Neither computer science curricula nor information systems programs have any courses in documentation (see DPMA, 1981; Nunamaker, Couger, & Davis, 1982).

A DOCUMENT? WHAT FOR?

What Is a Document?

Once a document is in use, it can be considered to be the *input* to a given process (Figure 4.1); thus, it has a function (as input to the process). Because it is deliv-

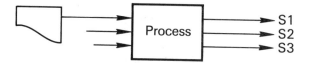

Fig. 4.1. A document as input to a process.

erable (as defined in Chapter 3), a document is also itself an *output* of a certain production process.

EXAMPLE C: DESIGN OF THE SMT.PM SYSTEM

The manual presented in Table 4.1 contains a document entitled System Design. For which process is it used as input? To answer this question, let us use the work breakdown structure (WBS) of the development stage presented in Figure 4.2. The general design process corresponds to the definition of the data processing system's general architecture: organization of the programs and data. The objective of the detailed design process is to define architecture of the individual components: programs, files. The system design document then falls naturally into place—it is the product of general design and serves as input to the detailed design, as illustrated in Figure 4.3. Are there cases in which a document serves as input to two different processes? If so, how is it defined?

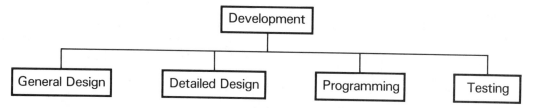

Fig. 4.2. WBS of the development phase of a system.

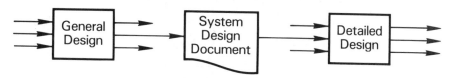

Fig. 4.3. The system design document as input to a process.

EXAMPLE D: OPPORTUNITY STUDY REPORT

The upper portion of the diagram shown in Figure 4.4 contains the SMT.PM project network, while the lower contains a partial WBS. The opportunity study report (OSR) serves as input to the process of deciding between purchase of a package or inhouse development. Figure 4.4 is based on the assumption that inhouse development was chosen.

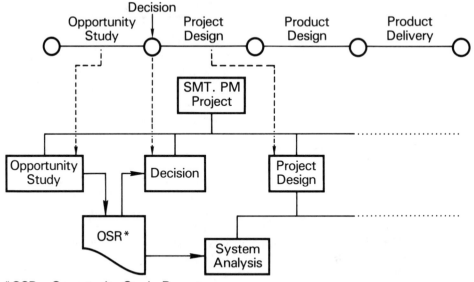

*OSR = Opportunity Study Report

Fig. 4.4. A document as input to several processes.

The system analysis process consists of a detailed study of the existing system and what is required in order to build the future system. The OSR is obviously an input to this process. But in relation to which process is the OSR defined? Weinberg (1971) answers this question by suggesting that a document must fulfill *one specific objective*. If others are met, it is an added benefit. The following rule can therefore be stated:

> If a document can serve as an input to several processes, it is defined in relation to the process for which it is the most important. The document function thus defined will be called the primary function.

It is clear that the decision making function is the primary one in this example. Let us now consider the following example.

EXAMPLE E: PLAN OF THE SMT.PM PROJECT

As indicated in Chapter 3, project analysis provides the elements required for planning, management, and control. Figure 4.5 illustrates a partial WBS of this portion of the project, where it is shown that the project plan is an input to the scheduling activity. Scheduling, defined more precisely in Chapter 10, involves

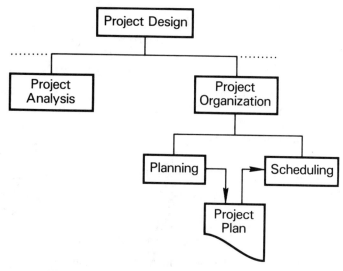

Fig. 4.5. The project plan as input to scheduling.

establishing a schedule containing the ordered list of activities, each of which is accompanied by a description of

o the nature of the activity,
o the person(s) carrying it out,
o starting date, and
o ending date.

The project start date and all available human resources constitute other inputs into the scheduling activity. The project plan must contain: the activities, the events, their sequencing, and the duration of each. The contents of a document are therefore determined by the process to which it serves as input.

A data processing project is carried out by human beings. The data contained in a document must be adapted to the people using it. The person(s) executing the primary process to which a document serves as input will be called the *target(s)*.

EXAMPLE F: USER DOCUMENTATION OF THE SMT.PM SYSTEM

Figure 4.6 depicts a page of the user documentation dealing with stock entry. The upper portion represents the screen, the lower the definitions of the authorized codes and formats. Note that the items SYMBOL and CUSIP have been described by their COBOL formats. It is obvious that the document was produced by a programmer who did not realize that the user had no idea of the meaning

```
┌─────────────────────────────────────────────────────────────────┐
│                         SYSTEM: SMT.PM                            │
│                         STOCK-ENTRY                               │
│                                                                   │
│     1–CURRENCY:              2–SYMBOL:              3–CUSIP:       │
│     4–DESCRIPTION:                                                │
│                                                                   │
│                                                                   │
│     5–COUNTRY:                                                    │
│                                                    6–COM/PREF:    │
│     7–DATE QUOTATION:                              8–QUOTATION:   │
│              9–OTHER ACTION:              10–END                  │
│                                                                   │
└─────────────────────────────────────────────────────────────────┘

                         Formats and codes

     CURRENCY:   Three digits. Most common are:
                    404: US DOLLAR
                    385: JAPANESE YEN
                    101: CANADIAN DOLLAR
                    For others see section 3.2

     SYMBOL: PIC X (8) Consult stock codes, section 4.1
     CUSIP PIC X (9) Consult stock codes, section 4.1
```

Fig. 4.6. A page of the SMT.PM system's user manual.

of PIC X(8). CURRENCY, on the other hand, is described in prose: "three digits," a language the user understands.

In summary, a document is a *product* which serves as input to a process which defines its characteristics: function, contents, and target.

Documents as Part of the Work Process

A document has been defined by the role it plays once it has been completed. The creation of a document may play a role in the principal activity of its author. The two case studies that follow illustrate the use of documents in the creative process, either as a starting point or in a support role.

Case 1: Producing the Document = Performing the Activity

The HIPO method (see p. 64) makes it possible to design and document a system simultaneously. The method itself utilizes the hierarchical breakdown of the functions. The document is composed of:

o A visual table of contents, an initial breakdown of the system

o Overview diagrams which specify the breakdown, inputs, functions, and outputs of each process

o Detailed diagrams which show the logic of the functions and provide the technical details of the inputs and outputs.

In the following example the method is applied to the SMT.PM system.

EXAMPLE G: SMT.PM SYSTEM DESIGN

Figure 4.7 contains the initial table of contents drawn up by Mike Bernstein. Figure 4.8 illustrates the overview diagrams of boxes 3.0 and 4.0. Study of the overview diagrams reveals that there is something wrong:

1. Each transaction is analyzed twice: once for the cash accounts, once for the stock accounts.

2. A portfolio estimate can be performed only for the updated stock and cash values.

Bernstein therefore revises the visual table of contents (see Figure 4.9). The new overview diagrams shown in Figure 4.10 tell him that this time the operations will occur in a more coherent, more uniform manner.

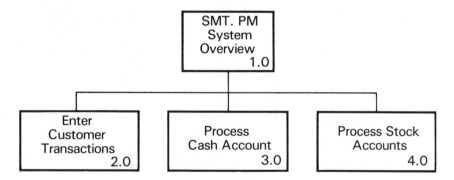

Fig. 4.7. Portion of visual table of contents of SMT.PM system.

Case 2: The Document Makes Completion of the Activity Possible

In the preceding case the document was produced as design progressed. Here, on the other hand, two documents are available, and it is through their utilization that the activity can be completed.

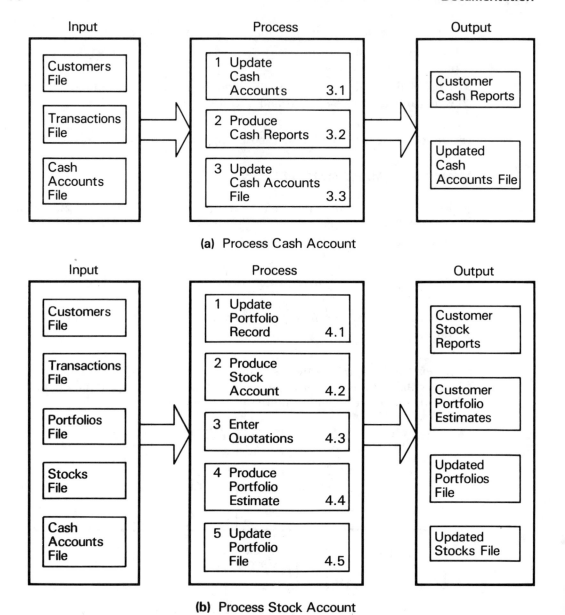

Input | Process | Output

Customers File

Transactions File

Cash Accounts File

1 Update Cash Accounts   3.1

2 Produce Cash Reports   3.2

3 Update Cash Accounts File   3.3

Customer Cash Reports

Updated Cash Accounts File

(a) Process Cash Account

Input | Process | Output

Customers File

Transactions File

Portfolios File

Stocks File

Cash Accounts File

1 Update Portfolio Record   4.1

2 Produce Stock Account   4.2

3 Enter Quotations   4.3

4 Produce Portfolio Estimate   4.4

5 Update Portfolio File   4.5

Customer Stock Reports

Customer Portfolio Estimates

Updated Portfolios File

Updated Stocks File

(b) Process Stock Account

Fig. 4.8. SMT.PM system: Two overview diagrams.

EXAMPLE H: PLANNING OF PROGRAMMING

To develop the system, Mike Bernstein has three programmers as members of his team: Susan Pratt, senior programmer; Marvin Phister, medium program-

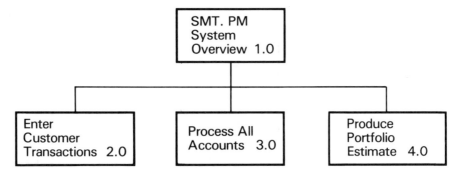

Fig. 4.9. SMT.PM: Revised visual table of contents.

mer; and John Paintree, junior programmer. Having decided to have the trans-actions entry programs written first (box 2.0 in Figure 4.7), and having little planning experience, Bernstein proceeds in the following manner. He draws up a list of the modules to be developed and assigns them according to their com-plexity and the experience levels of his programmers [see Figure 4.11(a)]. At the same time, he draws a network for this phase in relation to possible parallel activities. Finally, he writes the names of the programmers on the network [see Fig. 4.11(b)].

One glance at the result tells him that it is not satisfactory; Susan Pratt has too much work, while John Paintree has practically nothing to do. He therefore changes the assignments; together, Marvin Phister and John Paintree can easily do the dividends and interest entry program in 15 days. A much more satisfactory network is depicted in Figure 4.11(c).

Different Roles of Documents

The various documents of a project have five major functions:

reference,

production tool,

decision tool,

contract, and,

baseline.

Figure 4.12 shows each type of document in relation to the process in which it is used as a work tool.

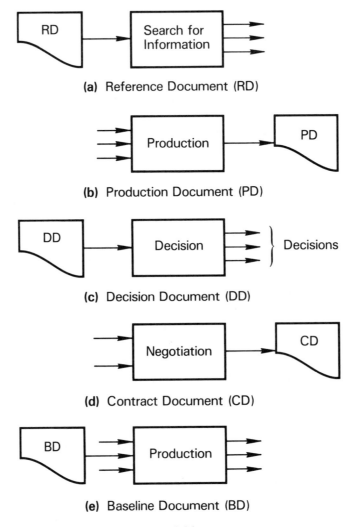

(a) Reference Document (RD)

(b) Production Document (PD)

(c) Decision Document (DD)

(d) Contract Document (CD)

(e) Baseline Document (BD)

Fig. 4.12. Relation of documents and activities.

references, repetitions) to enable the reader to locate the information he is looking for rapidly.

Production Tool (Figure 4.12b)

This is the principal, if not the sole, result of an activity. The system design document is the classic example. It is the result of the iterative exercise which involves defining the architecture of the data processing system to be developed.

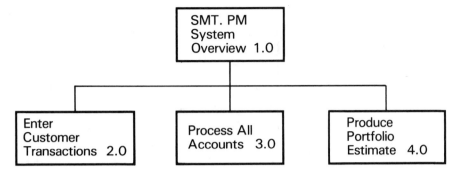

Fig. 4.9. SMT.PM: Revised visual table of contents.

mer; and John Paintree, junior programmer. Having decided to have the transactions entry programs written first (box 2.0 in Figure 4.7), and having little
planning experience, Bernstein proceeds in the following manner. He draws up
a list of the modules to be developed and assigns them according to their complexity and the experience levels of his programmers [see Figure 4.11(a)]. At
the same time, he draws a network for this phase in relation to possible parallel
activities. Finally, he writes the names of the programmers on the network [see
Fig. 4.11(b)].

One glance at the result tells him that it is not satisfactory; Susan Pratt has
too much work, while John Paintree has practically nothing to do. He therefore
changes the assignments; together, Marvin Phister and John Paintree can easily
do the dividends and interest entry program in 15 days. A much more satisfactory
network is depicted in Figure 4.11(c).

Different Roles of Documents

The various documents of a project have five major functions:

reference,

production tool,

decision tool,

contract, and,

baseline.

Figure 4.12 shows each type of document in relation to the process in which it
is used as a work tool.

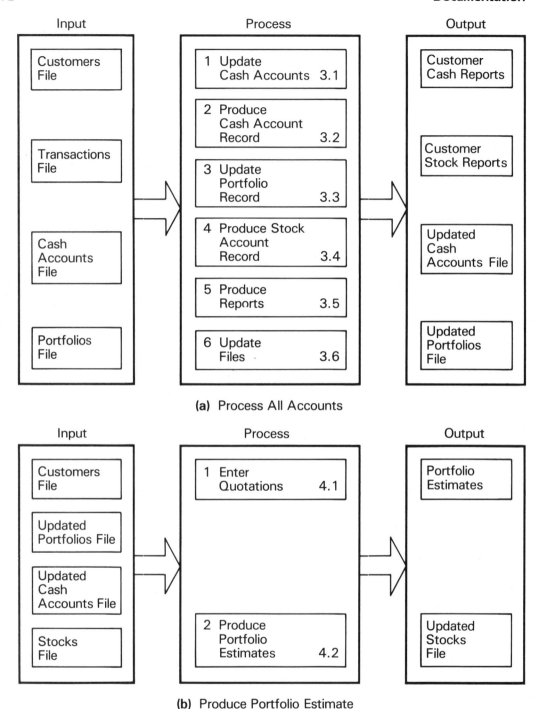

(a) Process All Accounts

(b) Produce Portfolio Estimate

Fig. 4.10. Revised overview diagrams.

Module	Duration (days)	Complexity	Programmer
Customer profile	5	easy	JP
Daily transactions	30	very difficult	SP
Stocks description	10	easy	MP
Dividends and interest	20	difficult	MP or SP

(a) Assignment of Modules to Programmers

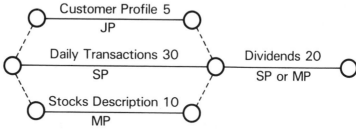

(b) Network of Data Entry Programming

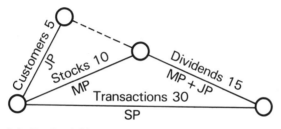

(c) Revised Network of Data Entry Programming

Fig. 4.11. Documents as inputs to the planning process.

Reference Document (Figure 4.12a)

The primary function of a reference document is as a source of information. A system's users manual is the classic example:

- Function: provides all information concerning the operation of the system.
- Content: general description of the system; description of the sessions and screen formats; description of the entry forms; description of the reports; message errors list; codes list, etc.
- Target: the various users of the system.

Any reference document must be written in the target's language. It must be complete, clear, and include a large amount of redundancy (lists, index, cross-

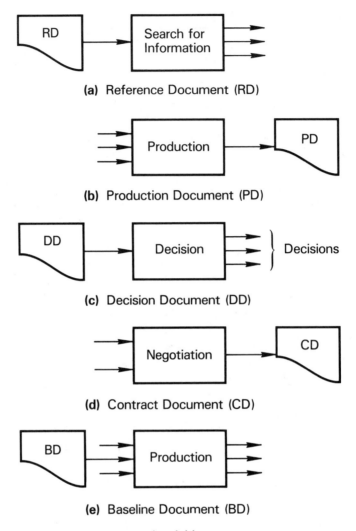

Fig. 4.12. Relation of documents and activities.

references, repetitions) to enable the reader to locate the information he is looking for rapidly.

Production Tool (Figure 4.12b)

This is the principal, if not the sole, result of an activity. The system design document is the classic example. It is the result of the iterative exercise which involves defining the architecture of the data processing system to be developed.

o Function: describe the architecture of the system.
o Content: general architecture of the system; each module's relation with the other modules, functions, inputs, and outputs; general architecture of the data; description of the inputs; description of the outputs.
o Target: designers (detailed design).

Decision Tool (Figure 4.12c)

This is the only input to a decision process. The typical example is the Opportunity Study Report (OSR):

o Function: determine the orientation of the remainder of the project.
o Content: analysis of existing system, requirements, solutions, recommendations.
o Target: decision makers.

As with the user manual, this document is structured in its entirety according to its target and function. It contains *only* the data required for the decision making process and uses the forms and language of the target.

Contract (Figure 4.12d)

This document describes a product on which two parties have agreed, and which the supplier must deliver to his client. The specifications of the system to be developed are an excellent example of a contract document.

o Function: describe the capabilities of the system, as understood by the user.
o Content: general description, functions to be developed, inputs, outputs, procedures.
o Target: user (supervisors and operators).

   Why is such a document a contract?

1. It defines for the developer the product to be delivered. (The document can therefore be expected to serve as input to a production activity.)
2. It defines for the user the product he can expect to receive.
3. It can only be modified following agreement between the two parties.

Baseline Document (Figure 4.12e)

A baseline document is the description of a result to be obtained. A schedule is a good example of a baseline document.

○ Function: specify the dates on which the various activities will be completed.
○ Content: list of activities, each accompanied by a description of the nature of the activity, starting date, and ending date.
○ Target: performers of the different activities.

The baseline document differs from reference and contract documents as follows:

1. The reference document does not define a result to be obtained. (It is not a production activity input.)
2. The baseline document does not require agreement between two parties. A document may, however, be both baseline and contractual, as in the system specifications example previously described.

Example D indicated that the opportunity study report and the specifications each had two functions. The chart in Table 4.2 indicates that this is more often the rule than the exception.

THE DOCUMENT PRODUCTION PROCESS

A Document Is a Product

We have seen that a document can be defined by its three characteristics: function, content, target. Like any product, once it has been defined it can be de-

TABLE 4.2
DIFFERENT FUNCTIONS OF PROJECT DOCUMENTS

Documents	Reference	Production tool	Decision tool	Contract	Baseline
Opportunity study report			⊗		
System specifications				⊗[a]	x
General design document	x	⊗			x
User manual	⊗			x	
Schedule	x				⊗
Budget	x	x[b]	⊗		x
Program listing	⊗[c]	x			

⊗: primary function of the document.
[a]The system specifications document is also baseline since it is used by data processing analysts as a description. Its contract function, however, must be given priority (see Chapters 1 and 2, dealing with the problems of changing objectives and uncertainty surrounding the product).
[b]The budget is a production tool since it is the result of the budgeting activity. Its primary function, however, is decisional: approval and control of expenditures.
[c]The program listing is primarily a reference document; this is why it must be as self-sufficient as possible if a program is to be understood.

veloped through a simple or complex process. The black box concept can be used to represent the process and to determine its inputs and some of its activities.

EXAMPLE I: SMT.PM SYSTEM USER MANUAL

Figure 4.13 depicts the inputs required for the production of a user manual. Just as for a tertiary product (service), the following elements are needed: knowledge (description), specialized personnel, and administrative support. It is assumed that if these elements are available, development of the product can be defined and organized.

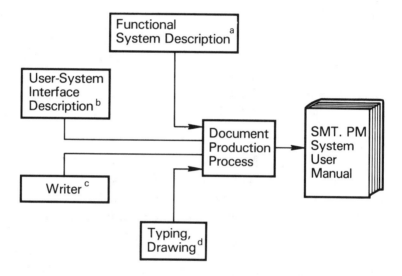

[a]The user is not interested in how the system works but in what it can accomplish.
[b]The manual must help the user put the system into operation and therefore must describe the interface.
[c]Obviously, the manual must be authored.
[d]Once written, it must be typed, copied, and bound.

Fig. 4.13. User manual production process.

The Document Development Cycle

While the production of a document is a complex task, it is not at all mysterious. One of the objectives of modern software engineering and project management methods is to structure systems production. Similarly, the goal of the document production approach presented here is to make this operation logical and constructive.

Table 4.3 illustrates the close parallel between the development of a software system and that of a data processing document. The analogy is even found

TABLE 4.3
SYSTEM AND DOCUMENT DEVELOPMENT LIFE CYCLES

System Development Life Cycle	*Document Development Cycle*
Systems specifications	Function, content, target
General design	Table of contents
Detailed design	Design of each section
Programming	Section writing
Unit testing	Review of written section
Integration tests	Review of the whole document
Implementation	Typing, editing

in the testing loops of the activities. The reading of one section may result in corrections or even redefinition of content. Similarly, the reading of the entire document may lead to text corrections, revisions to the content of a section or, if worse comes to worst, modification of the table of contents.

As noted earlier, planning the development of a document thus consists of defining and listing the activities, estimating the resources required for each activity, estimating the duration of the activities, and scheduling the activities. The problems encountered here are the same as those occurring in system development:

o Necessity of a general design (in this case, a table of contents) in order to provide a list of the activities.

o Difficulty in obtaining microestimates.

o Communication problems resulting from the involvement of several parties.

Just as in a project, sound management can only be obtained by extensive knowledge of the production process. To achieve this level of knowledge it is necessary to analyze the various activities involved in document production.

The Activities

Using the SMT.PM system user manual as an example, we shall review the activities defined in the preceding section.

Function, Content, Target

This activity consists of defining the role of the document as precisely as possible by carrying out the following tasks: (a) list all topics the document must cover, (b) assemble all necessary data.

EXAMPLE J: USER MANUAL

The SMT.PM user manual document will have to cover the following topics: all input screens, all reports produced, input documents, error messages, procedures, and codes used. Necessary data to be gathered includes description of screens with associated codes, description of reports, comprehensive code lists, and procedures.

Production of the Table of Contents

Drawing up a table of contents involves more than simply listing the contents of a document. Its content, target, and function are in reality defined by the titles chosen and their order of presentation. The table of contents must therefore be established before the document itself, thereby making it genuinely possible to speak of "design."

EXAMPLE K: TABLE OF CONTENTS

Let us once again point out three characteristics of this document:

o Function: reference
o Content: SMT.PM system functions and user interface
o Target: Screen operators and those to whom reports are directed

One possible table of contents for this document is as follows:

1. System Overview
   1.1 Functions of the system
   1.2 Daily and monthly operations
2. Input Procedures
   2.1 Enter, update, consult customer data
      2.1.1 Procedure description
      2.1.2 Input document
      2.1.3 Display terminal operation
   2.2 Enter, update a stock
      2.2.1 Procedure description
      2.2.2 Display terminal operation
   2.3 Enter a dividend or interest
      2.3.1 Procedure description
      2.3.2 Dividend or interest data entry
      2.3.3 Update of the interim report
      2.3.4 Customer earnings input

2.4 Enter a customer transaction
    2.4.1 Procedure description
    2.4.2 Shares data entry
    2.4.3 Bonds data entry
    2.4.4 Treasury bills data entry
    2.4.5 Options data entry

3. Reports Description
  3.1 Daily reports
    3.1.1 Transaction notice
    3.1.2 Transactions daily journal
  3.2 Monthly reports
    3.2.1 Trial balance
    3.2.2 Customer cash report
    3.2.3 Customer stock report
    3.2.4 Customer bank report
    3.2.5 Portfolio estimate

4. Help Lists
  4.1 Data input codes
  4.2 Reports codes
  4.3 Error messages

Note that no mention is made of the system's construction. The document contains a large amount of redundancy; the codes and error messages appear twice (once in the description of the corresponding procedure, once in the help lists). The document can, in effect, be used for learning (procedures) and for troubleshooting (help list). The order of presentation corresponds to the natural order of user operations.

Design of Each Section

Contrary to a literary work, a data processing document is not the product of inspiration. Before a section is written, it must be organized and its content specified, just as a program is designed before it is written. The tasks are:

listing what will be said,

organizing the content, and

choosing the modes of expression (text, diagrams, tables).

EXAMPLE L: CUSTOMER CASH REPORT

This report is similar to a bank account statement. The user is the employee in charge of verifying the report and having it sent to the client.

The list of topics to be covered is: (a) definition of the report; (b) Detailed description of the report; (c) frequency; (d) use; (e) what to do in case of problems. Content is organized as follows, with modes of expression in parentheses:

1. Definition of the report (text)
2. Description (annotated copy of the report and explanation table)
3. Use (text)
4. Problems (text)

Section Writing

This is actually the production of the document. Here again, by way of analogy with programming, the nature of the work involved is similar to coding, given the level of detail and organization in Example L.

EXAMPLE M: CUSTOMER CASH REPORT: EXTRACT FROM USER MANUAL

DEFINITION.   Monthly statement of a client's cash account, produced in triplicate around the 3rd of the following month. There is one report per client per currency; if a client has one account in U.S. dollars and another in Canadian dollars, he receives two reports.

DESCRIPTION.   The SMT account statement as of March 31, 1983, is shown in Figure 4.14. Zone numbers and their explanations are:

1	Account number
2	Name and address of account holder
3	Currency used in statement
4	End-date of period covered by statement
5	Pagination (verify that all pages of statement are present)
6,7	Balance forward (must equal the final balance of the preceding month's statement)
8	Description of transaction (corresponds to text written on corresponding transaction notice)
9	Number of corresponding transaction notice (enables its location for verification purposes)
10	Date transaction occurred
11	Date transaction took effect (Example: purchase of shares, 2/15; date effective, 2/20)
12	Nature of transaction; corresponds to the square checked off on the input slip (D = deposit; T = transfer; P = purchase; S = sale; W = withdrawal)
13	Amount of transaction (in the currency indicated in Zone 3); verification is provided by the input slip; if followed by a minus ($-$), it is a debit
14,15	Final balance

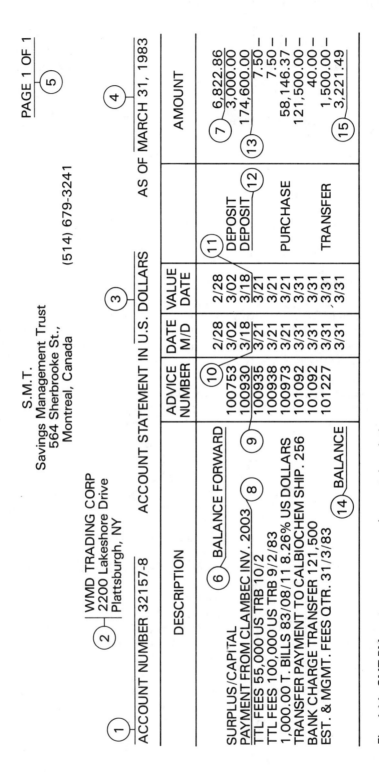

Fig. 4.14. SMT.PM system user manual report description.

USE.   Verify that it is complete and accurate. Have it approved by the account manager, then sent to client.

PROBLEMS.   For incorrect balance forward, see accounting department; for an incorrect amount, see data processing; for a transaction omission, see the account manager; for a page missing, see data processing (operations).

Review of Written Section

The document must be read at the component level in order to verify that the section is complete, accurate, clear, and meets its objective. Although this examination can be done by the author, ideally it is carried out by someone else if a qualified person who is familiar with the material is available to act as controller.

EXAMPLE N: CUSTOMER CASH REPORT: REVIEW OF TEXT

Careful reading of the document (Example M) reveals an oversight. Under the heading *Definition*, a report done in triplicate is mentioned; yet under the heading *Use*, only the copy to be sent to the client is mentioned. To make it complete, the *Use* section should read as follows:

Copy 1: sent to account manager for approval and then to client

Copy 2: sent to account manager for his files

Copy 3: sent to accounting department

Review of the Entire Document

A document written by a single author should be reread completely by that author. In all cases, however, a document should also be reviewed by someone other than its author (ideally by its target), the objective being to verify that the document does in fact perform as expected.

Typing, Editing

The importance of this final activity must not be underestimated. Because secretarial services often have a heavy workload, advance planning and allotment of sufficient time for typing and editing is important. Proofreading is also a necessary task, long and tedious but critical to the accuracy of the final version of the document.

Documentation Problems

Updating

While it is not easy to have a document produced, it is even more difficult to keep it up to date. There are, in effect, two problems: updating, and mention of the update. The first can only be solved if someone is explicitly put in charge of the updating. To solve the second problem, standards are required.

Standards

The conventional approach to documentation standards has been to unify their presentation. Unfortunately, this approach can transform document production into a heavy, boring task. A more reasonable approach, which will be outlined in Chapter 7, is to give the standards the objective of defining everything the documentation must contain.

Accessibility

The documentation must be accessible to all interested parties. Multiple copies present an updating problem; a single-copy document is, of course, inaccessible. Ideally, all of the documentation is contained in the computer, thus providing a solution for both the updating problem and the lack of accessibility. Word processing systems capable of producing texts, graphics, and charts are also helpful.

Documentation Management

Each project document must be produced, organized, stored, controlled, and distributed. Documentation management is just as much a project function as program, personnel, and budget management. If the project is large enough, documentation management will be one person's full-time responsibility. For a small project, the project manager will have to assign it as a part-time task or even assume it himself.

THE FIGHT AGAINST INFLATION: KEY DOCUMENTS

Overly zealous efforts to compensate for the past failures to provide documentation run the risk of promoting an invasion of paper, exorbitant costs, and computer specialists who produce documentation instead of systems. The presumption that documentation time is equal to programming time is also questionable. Although everyone agrees on the necessity of documentation, its proliferation can perhaps be challenged. But where does one begin to trim the excess? The risk management approach, already used in business and security, will help us begin to answer this question.

The Risk Management Concept

The term risk *refers to the cost resulting from an accident in which security measures were absent.*

Given the possible occurrence of a major or minor catastrophe, and given the means to prevent it or to limit its consequences, risk management consists in quantifying the various elements involved in order to make a rational decision concerning the advisability of installing preventive measures.

Let us consider one possible catastrophe: the organization's computer is completely destroyed by fire, and no security measures have been taken to prevent it. The cost (C_T) includes the replacement of the installation, the eventual loss of revenue following the accident, and so forth.

Let p be the probability of the accident happening. Let k be the cost resulting from the installation of preventive measures. If C_T, p, and k are calculated on an annual basis, risk management involves comparing $p \times C_T$ and k:

$p \times C_T \gg k$: The cost of prevention is low given the risk;

steps will be taken to obtain it.

$p \times C_T \simeq k$: The two costs are comparable;

the value of prevention is now debatable.

$p \times C_T < k$: Prevention becomes a waste of money.

Some accidents have irreparable consequences. Loss of the master files of a business system, for example, can make it impossible for the organization to operate, pushing it into bankruptcy. Such a case can be easily dealt with by assigning to C_T a value equal to the assets of the company.

Application to Documentation

Let D be a certain document having a production cost of k, determined on a 12-month basis. To complete our risk analysis it is necessary (a) to determine what occurs when the document is needed and to assess the additional costs (C_T)

resulting from its absence; and (b) to determine the probability (p) of the document being needed.

EXAMPLE O: USER MANUAL

The 12-month probability of the manual being needed is 1. All evidence shows that the user often requires explanations concerning the utilization of the system.

Let us calculate the production cost: we estimate 150 hours of work by the authors at $10/hour, 30 hours of typing at $7/hour, and $40 for the printing of several copies:

$$150 \times 10 + 30 \times 7 + 40 = \$1750$$

If the system is to be in operation 5 years, the annual cost is

$$k = 1750/5 = \$350$$

Now, what happens if the manual does not exist, but the authors of the system are available? We assume that approximately 100 questions are asked per year, each requiring 10 minutes of one author's time (at $10/hour) and 10 minutes of one user's time (at $10/hour).

$$C_T = (10 \times \frac{1}{6} + 10 \times \frac{1}{6}) \ 100 = \$333$$

We see that $p \times C_T < k$, thereby making user documentation of questionable interest.

On the other hand, if the manual does not exist and the authors are not available to answer questions, the system cannot be used. In this case, C_T is given the value ∞ (infinity), and user documentation becomes absolutely necessary.

The second hypothesis has the greatest chance of being true over the long term, thereby making the user document indispensable.

Key Product Documents

Without going so far as to calculate actual costs, prior experience makes it possible to classify documents into three categories according to the risk involved. Category 1 is key documents; if these are absent, the resulting product $p \times C_T$ is an unacceptable amount. Category 2 is useful documents, where the product $p \times C_T$ is higher than the cost of production but could eventually be acceptable. Category 3 is debatable documents; where $p \times C_T$ is equivalent or lower than the cost of producing the document.

Table 4.4 contains a categorized list of documents for a software system development project. It can be seen that there are six key documents whose

TABLE 4.4
SYSTEM DOCUMENTATION: KEY DOCUMENTS

Document	Category Related to Risk
System specifications	1
General design	1
Detailed design	2
File description	1
Program listing	1
Additional program documentation (unstructured programming)	2
Additional program documentation (structured programming)	3
Tests documentation	2
User manual	1
Operations documentation	1

Legend: 1 = unacceptable; 2 = costly but manageable; 3 = debatable.

existence is easy to justify. System specifications, general design, and file description are baseline documents without which the problem to be solved cannot be defined. The other three—program listing, user manual, and operation documents—are reference documents; they are, in fact, the only ones which enable interested parties to interact with the system.

The detailed design refines the results of the general design up to the programming level. Nonetheless, with a general design and listings which are even slightly documented, detailed design documents could be reconstructed. While test documentation is indeed useful, the cost of its absence is certainly acceptable. The most interesting case is that of the additional programming documentation. Following are a few observations which, although open to discussion, are the fruit of experience:

1. If other documents (specifications, general design, file description) are available, no program is indecipherable. The simple fact is that programmers detest this type of work.
2. Unstructured program documentation is as difficult to understand as the programs themselves.
3. Modern compilers are equipped with a number of documentation tools, such as a list of variables, external procedures, and cross-references.
4. A program written according to structured programming principles and containing a minimum of information in the form of comments (explanation of the variables, file records, major operations) has a self-sufficient listing.

Key Project Documents

A document has been defined as a *key* document if its nonexistence results in an unacceptable risk. To analyze these risks, let us once again look at the role of the project manager, whose activities have been summarized as planning, scheduling, and controlling.

Can the manager plan without documents? The answer is, of course, no. Even if the project were reduced to a single person, that individual would need to record what is to be done and in what order—in short, a plan is needed. The most widely used tool for planning is the network, and this subject will be developed in Chapter 10.

Since a project involves more than one individual, their individual schedules of project-related activities must be updated in a coordinated manner. Scheduling therefore requires its own documentation in the form of the project "appointment book," which will also be discussed in Chapter 10.

Traditionally, the purpose of control is to ensure steady and timely progress as the project proceeds. Control documents, examined in Chapter 10, are used for the purpose of controlling and monitoring project activities, milestones, and changes. However, in data processing the product itself must also be controlled. Given the length of a project, the number of internal and external personnel (developers and users), it is unrealistic to think that the product can be controlled without documents. This activity is known as product or configuration management and requires documentation that will be described in greater detail in Chapter 13.

The project manager must maintain regular communication with his supervisors and users as the work progresses. The documents which have been described so far have either been too technical or too static. Others are required. These are the *opportunity study report*, which makes it possible to define the project, and *progress reports*, which are used to keep management informed at regular intervals along the way. Table 4.5 lists the responsibilities of the project manager, with the addition (in italics) of these two documentary work tools. Another new document has also been added to the planning: the *budget*. The ultimate design of a project depends on the resources which are available for its development.

TABLE 4.5
PROJECT KEY DOCUMENTS

Project Manager's Responsibilities	Documents
Administrative responsibility	*opportunity study report, progress reports*
Communication with the users	*opportunity study report, progress reports*
Planning	plan, *budget*
Scheduling	plan, schedule
Finalizing resource availability	*budget,* plan, schedule
Coordinating project operations	plan, schedule
Technical supervision	product documents
Control	project control documents product control documents *budget*

A budget is, in essence, a list of the necessary resources converted into a common standard: money. The budget document will make it possible to assemble the resources and control their consumption.

In summary, the key project documents are:

opportunity study report

progress reports

plan

budget

schedule

key product documents

project control documents

product control documents

A well designed document is a work tool both for its author and for his closest colleagues. Document production is therefore a task which is very closely linked to the principal project activity.

SELECTED REFERENCES

Benjamin, R. I. 1971. *Control of the information system development cycle.* New York: Wiley Interscience, John Wiley & Sons.
>The notion of a document serving as an input datum to a project phase is presented as being part of the project management methodology.

DPMA model curriculum for undergraduate computer information systems education. 1981. Park Ridge, Ill.: DPMA.
>This is one of the very few data processing management curriculums which examines how to produce documents.

Ingrassia, F. S. 1978. Combating the 90%-complete syndrome. *Datamation,* January, 171–176.
>This article defines the Unit Development Folder (UDF), a complete programming file containing the design and testing elements and the milestones on the program development progress.

Katzan, H., Jr. 1976. *Systems design and documentation: An introduction to the HIPO method.* New York: Van Nostrand Reinhold.
>The HIPO documentation and system design method is presented, and it is the perfect example of a document work tool. The breakdown method is based on the black box concept and uses the hierarchical decomposition approach.

Keen, J. S. 1981. *Managing systems development.* New York: John Wiley & Sons.
In Chapter 8, documentation is justified by the minimizing of risk. A major problem discussed is the fact that the people in charge of producing the documentation see very little use in it.

Lucas, H. C., Jr. 1982. *Information systems concepts for management.* New York: McGraw-Hill.
Chapter 14 examines the reasons why computer specialists do not like documentation work.

Menkus, B. 1970. Defining systems documentation. *Journal of Systems Management,* December, 16–21.
In this article, documentation is considered to be both a process and a product. Five documentation functions are presented.

Nunamaker, J. F., Jr., Couger, J. D., & Davis, G. B. 1982. Information systems curriculum recommendations for the 80s: Undergraduate and graduate programs. A report of the ACM Curriculum Committee on Information Systems. *Comm. ACM,* 25, 11, 781–805.
This second ACM curriculum in information systems (the first was in 1973) is complete, up-to-date, and contains excellent bibliographic references. However, documentation is not dealt with, either as a product or as a process.

Rubin, M. L. 1970. *Introduction to the system life cycle.* Princeton, N.J.: Brandon Systems Press.
Documentation is first of all treated as an insurance policy (Chapter 5). Interestingly, poor quality documentation is attributed to the manager's attitude.

Weinberg, G. M. 1971. *The psychology of computer programming.* New York: Van Nostrand Reinhold.
Even though documentation is a secondary topic in this well-known work, it does provide the most thorough analysis of the causes of poor documentation and the solutions to be adopted. It is essential reading.

Part 2
THE DECISION PHASE

Suppose a young woman just finishing high school must decide whether to enter the work force or go on to higher studies. After weighing a variety of career options in light of her personal interest as well as her financial resources, she finally decides to enter the field of data processing. Her future now has direction; a course of action has been set. However, she has not yet chosen the school, let alone the specific courses she will take. In short, she has not yet defined her program.

This student's situation is analogous to the opportunity study stage. The project itself does not yet exist—only a problem or a desire for change. It will be necessary to analyze the situation, specify the problems, list and evaluate the alternatives, and finally to make a choice. It will then be clearly known in what direction to funnel the resources, although the specific details of the project remain undetermined.

The opportunity study makes it possible to give direction to the project, whose rigorous definition can only be arrived at once this basic orientation has been established. The opportunity study does not provide either the detailed specifications of the system or a budget, let alone a detailed plan. It must, however, provide a maximum amount of data so that a well informed decision may be made.

Chapter 5
OPPORTUNITY STUDY

INTRODUCTION

The conventional approach to this important stage is comprised of two phases: the preliminary survey and the feasibility study (Gaydash, 1982; Lucas, 1981). The objective of the former is to understand the problems and to decide if any action should be taken (i.e., the implementation of a system). The preliminary survey is usually brief (according to Gaydash, a maximum of one week of work by one person) and the resources allocated for it are modest. A brief report is issued and, if warranted, the feasibility study takes place; this time the problems are more deeply examined, alternatives sought, and solutions proposed. Unfortunately, nearly all of the work of the preliminary survey has to be repeated in the feasibility study. It might as well be done right from the beginning.

In order to understand clearly the role of the opportunity study, it is essential to remember that it results in a decision. The conventional model of the decision making mechanism can be summarized as follows:

defining the problem,

searching for and evaluating alternatives, and

making a choice.

The objective of defining the problem is to assess the current situation and identify the causes of the problems, and determine what would have to be done to correct the situation. This is Lundeberg's (1979) change analysis. Unfortunately, seeking and evaluating solutions are too often of no concern to hardcore computer specialists, for whom only one solution exists: developing the system they had unconsciously constructed during the preliminary study. In most situations, however, there are several possible solutions, the trick is being able to evaluate them as logically as possible. It is not up to the project manager to make the final choice, but he is responsible for summarizing all of the necessary data and presenting his views in a report. The major outcome of this stage, therefore, is a set of documents, and a section of the present chapter will be devoted to its format and content.

Finally, it is during the opportunity study stage that the contact between the user and the project team will be the closest. User involvement and participation is critical at this stage (Canning, 1977; Lundeberg, 1979). The project manager's skill in human relations and his understanding of the area being studied are particularly important.

EXAMPLE A: INVENTORY CONTROL

The Great River Transit Commission provides public transportation for the city of Great River and its suburbs, serving a population of half a million people with a fleet of 300 buses. Maintenance and repairs are done in two garages, G1 and G2, each having its own parts warehouse. Five thousand different parts are available. The value of the inventory is estimated to be $800,000, with annual expenditures close to $1 million. Figure 5.1 shows the organization of the supplies department. When a repairman needs parts he fills out a work order, one copy of which is sent to inventory control.

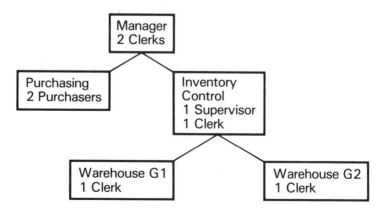

Fig. 5.1. The structure of the supplies department.

No effective inventory control is taking place; no standard numbering system exists in the warehouses; and parts are often in short supply, thereby leading to rush purchasing at higher cost. The data processing department of the company was set up one year ago, and after dealing with payroll and general accounting, is now ready to enter the field of inventory control.

OVERVIEW OF THE OPPORTUNITY STUDY

Figure 5.2 breaks down the three successive steps of the opportunity study (analyzing problems, searching for solutions, and producing a report) into finer detail. As shown in the figure, problem analysis is comprised of two successive groups of activities. The first (branches 1 and 2) allows the team to specify the problem and its environment. During the second activity (branches 3 and 4), project managers and computer specialists should bear in mind that users know their own fields and have ideas which they should be encouraged to express (Willoughby, 1975).

Solutions can then be sought in specific directions and evaluated according to user-suggested guidelines. Finally, the project manager must commit himself to a specific position by making written recommendations.

Participating Personnel

The active involvement of the users has been stressed again and again as a key factor in the success of this phase (Canning, 1977). A good opportunity study

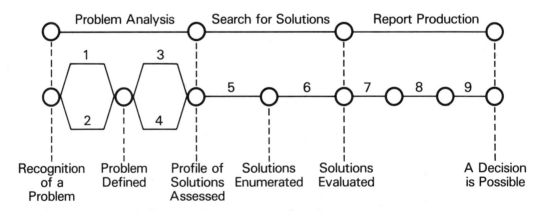

Legend: 1 = Study of the Existing System; 2 = Problems; 3 = Objectives; 4 = Requirements; 5 = Solutions Inventory; 6 = Solutions Evaluation; 7, 8, 9 = Report Writing.

Fig. 5.2. Detailed graph of an opportunity study.

is carried out by a team consisting of users and analysts. The project manager usually comes from outside the departments involved, not only because the ensuing steps of the study require knowledge of the computer field, but also because an outsider has a more objective view of the department and its problems.

The size of the team, at this stage is usually small compared with those involved in any subsequent project stages which might occur. Figure 5.3 illustrates one example of a team working on the opportunity study of a medium- to large-scale project. The project manager's duties include:

1. Planning of the study.
2. Coordination and control of the team.
3. Continuous contact with the users.
4. Orientation of the study.
5. Making final recommendations.

A user representative from the middle management level should co-head the team or assist the project manager. He is, in fact, the project manager's main collaborator. The user representative will:

1. Introduce the project team to his staff and smooth over any psychological barriers which might arise.
2. Present the problems in an integrated manner.
3. Propose ideas and suggestions.
4. Assist the project manager in setting criteria to evaluate solutions.

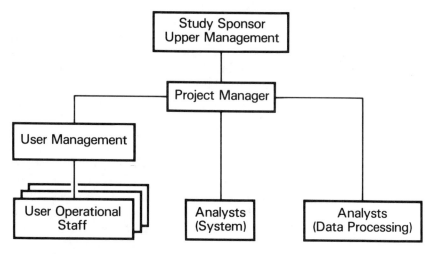

Fig. 5.3. Example of a team for an opportunity study.

The user operational staff representatives are to work closely with the analysts.

EXAMPLE B: OPPORTUNITY STUDY TEAM

Following several requests from the supplies department manager, the data processing department is asked to undertake an opportunity study concerning computerized inventory control. Bill Mason (head of data processing) and one of his analysts once set up an inventory control system for a wholesale hardware company. If it is assumed that Mason will act as project manager, what will be the composition of the remainder of the team? The supplies department manager will be the sponsor; the supervisor of inventory control will be the team's user representative; and, because Mason is unable to work fulltime on the study, his analyst will be involved as well. The project team will therefore consist of:

the project manager (head of data processing),

the supervisor of inventory control (user), and

one analyst.

PROBLEM ASSESSMENT

Analysis of the Existing Situation

The objective of the analysis is for the project team to become familiar with the current situation and the problems which gave rise to the study. It is an information gathering activity during which investigators should concentrate as much as possible on listening and observing; they should not be concerned with formulating any ideas of their own. Although the final objective is to gain knowledge of the information system, the focus should not be restricted to that area. A department or organization does not exist for the purpose of running an information system. It has production work to do, and the team should become familiar with that work. Davis (1982) called this "synthesis from characteristics of the utilizing system."

If the project team simply takes a random approach—observing the system, asking questions, and taking notes—it will obtain random results. Fortunately, however, more sophisticated methods and tools are available. The first is the work breakdown structure (WBS), already described in connection with the analysis of project tasks (see Chapter 3). It can also be used for system analysis. WBS applied to a system is nothing more than top-down analysis (see Figure 5.4). The objective, however, is to investigate the system. The method is therefore

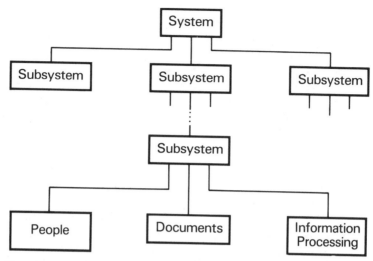

Fig. 5.4. First-level breakdown of an administrative system.

used not so much for representing the system as it is for enumerating all of the topics of interest. These can be grouped into three major components as shown in the figure: people, documents, and information processing. Each component can be further subdivided as follows. The *people* component may be divided into the categories of administrative structure and job descriptions. The component labeled *documents* contains the six categories of format, content, volumes, origin, destination, and location (if stored). Finally, the category of *information processing* may be subdivided into information processed, place of processing, time of processing, nature of processing, and rules (procedures, controls).

EXAMPLE C: BREAKDOWN OF THE INVENTORY SYSTEM

The system described in Example A can be broken down as follows. The inventory system consists of the incoming parts subsystem, the outgoing parts subsystem, and the inventory control subsystem. All three are present in garages G1 and G2.

Let us proceed with the inventory control for each garage:

○ People: supervisor and clerks managing the inventories,
○ Documents: Parts catalogue (the suppliers' catalogues are used); inventory status (one kardex card per part, insufficiently updated); delivery slips; work orders; activity reports.
○ Information processing: Delivery slips and work orders are checked by the inventory control staff and used to update the kardex cards. They are also supposed to be compiled each week to produce weekly and monthly activity reports.

Each incoming parts subsystem is composed of:

o People: warehouse clerk.
o Documents: purchase orders, delivery slips.
o Information processing: Delivery slips are checked against purchase orders. The parts are put on the shelves and the slips, once signed, are sent with corresponding purchase orders to the inventory control group.

Each outgoing parts subsystem consists of:

o People: warehouse clerk.
o Documents: work orders.
o Information processing: work orders are checked for authorization and parts are then provided to the repairman, with one copy of the order being kept by the clerk. At the end of the working day, the entire batch of work orders is sent to inventory control. If a part is in short supply, the clerk calls inventory control and a rush order is issued to a supplier.

Tools Available for Analysis

Interviews

There are two types of interviews. *Unstructured* interviews are used for a first contact, to exchange general ideas, gauge the user's feelings, and so forth. Although they serve as a good starting point, they do not yield any precise data. During *structured interviews* the investigator looks for specific data or information. He usually asks the questions and records the user's answers on a prepared questionnaire. The investigator runs the risk of missing some important point during a structured (i.e., prepared) interview. Thus, it is used only when the analyst knows exactly what he is looking for.

Visits to the Workplace

The objective of a visit to the actual workplace is to gain a real knowledge of the particular context in which the system operates and perhaps discover new facts or insights in the process.

Questionnaires

Questionaires can be handed out to the users, who are to complete them to the best of their knowledge. Although the objective here is to collect easily quantifiable data, the reliability of the information received may be questionable. We will return to this point shortly.

Study of the System Documents

All documents pertaining to the system should be assembled and studied, e.g., forms, cards, slips, and so on. These documents describe the information carried by the system, and, taken as a whole, comprise the database scheme of the system.

All of these tools must be utilized in the opportunity study for at least two reasons. First, each one has a specific field of application; none meets all needs. The second reason is related to efforts to obtain reliable data, which is often an extremely serious problem in opportunity studies. If we look at the scope of the various tools that have been described, we find a certain amount of redundancy. No effort should be made to eliminate it. On the contrary, a large amount of redundancy is useful in checking findings.

In effect, a major problem in opportunity studies is related to the uncertainty regarding the findings. For example, the same data coming from two different sources may have quite different values. A major source of these uncertainties lies in the individual characteristics of those users and analysts who participate in the process. An interesting analysis of this situation (Davis, 1982) can be summarized as follows:

o Users are aware of and report only parts of problems.

o Users have a tendency to focus on the closest and most recent events.

o People (both users and analysts) form opinions based on impressions and tend to make generalizations from single isolated facts.

o Analysts may not always select the approach which is best suited to a specific user.

Redundancy and overlap, although unable to ensure reliability, can at least help eliminate some of these problems. It is therefore not unwanted in an opportunity study; it is a useful part of the process.

EXAMPLE D: SETUP OF THE STUDY

Which tools should be used in the investigation? Let us use the results of the WBS performed in Example C. Four unstructured interviews and five structured interviews are recommended, all to be conducted in the workplace of the people involved. (Except for very simple cases, two interviews are usually required.) These interviews may be broken down as follows:

sponsor of the study: 2 unstructured meetings

supervisor and clerk together: 1 unstructured meeting

clerk alone: 1 structured interview

supervisor alone: 1 unstructured meeting

warehouse clerks (2): 2 structured interviews each

Since all of the people working on the system will be interviewed, there is no need for questionnaires. Seven documents must be studied: parts catalogue, kardex cards, purchase orders, delivery slips, work orders, weekly statistics, monthly statistics. This is a small study which could be conducted over a period of two to three weeks, depending on the availability of the user personnel.

Problems

As mentioned by Lundeberg (1979), great uncertainty surrounds the problems to be dealt with. The problems initially identified tend to be distorted by distance and administrative fog, or else they prove to be only the tip of the iceberg. The reality of the situation will progressively emerge during the investigation. All problems must then be listed, with a specific activity devoted to their analysis.

Problems can be put into two categories (Figure 5.5). Some are purely administrative in nature, such as outdated working procedures or lack of controls. They cannot be solved by technical means, but only by the user. Their solution is usually a prerequisite to the use of technical help (see Example G at the end of this chapter).

The second type of problem can be solved or greatly ameliorated with the use of computers. Those most frequently identified include problems with workload, costs, and deadlines, arising when all or part of document handling and information processing is performed manually; problems with poor quality information (a result of manual processing, loose controls, and/or poor input data); and lack of information. Integrated and elaborate data which is of particular

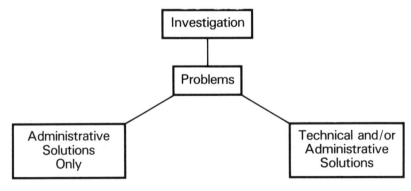

Fig. 5.5. The two kinds of problems uncovered during an opportunity study.

interest to management (e.g., sales statistics, budget controls, etc.) cannot be obtained manually, or are worthless if the quality of input data is not perfect.

EXAMPLE E: INVENTORY SYSTEM'S PROBLEMS

Returning to our example, the visible problems initially identified by the manager of the supplies department are as follows:

1. Too often, needed parts are in short supply.
2. The real status of the inventory is almost unknown.
3. Consumption data is lacking or late.
4. Staff are overloaded with paperwork because they must update all of the documents manually.
5. In spite of point 1, the inventory seems to be too large; parts are being ordered in too large quantities.

The investigation provided some insight into the causes of these problems by showing that:

○ No uniform numbering system exists for use in both warehouses.
○ The main supplier's part numbers are used, but the inventory also contains parts from other suppliers.
○ If a part is in short supply in one warehouse, no attempt is made to find it in the other.
○ Communications are slow. For example, work orders are sent to the inventory control group within 24 hours, but may take up to a week to be processed.

Objectives and Requirements

We are now entering a new stage of the study: the emphasis is no longer on how things are, but on how they should be. At the beginning there is much confusion—objectives are taken for requirements, requirements are stated as objectives. This confusion is present not only in the minds of many users but also in the approach taken by many analysts who hunt for outputs and procedures in order to define the system precisely. In top-down analysis, generality precedes detail; the same should apply to user needs. Objectives come first; requirements are the tools needed to achieve them.

The objective(s) of a system is (are) the business goal(s) to be achieved through the use of the system.

Canning (1979) gives an example of an interactive order-shipping-billing system nicely defined by all it inputs, outputs, and procedures. Discussions that take place as the preliminary plans are presented to the managers reveal that no real business objective was assigned to the system, and that, if taken into account, the managers' opinions would profoundly change the planned system.

Table 5.1 offers examples of systems with stated objectives. The example of portfolio management is interesting because it shows how different objectives can lead to different systems. A computerized portfolio management system for a broker or financial trust company is basically a filing and reporting system containing all data on clients, their securities, profits, losses, and earnings. As a reporting system, it will be without memory; in other words, it will contain the current but not the past status of a client's portfolio. However, if the objective is investment policy analysis, the system will need past data on clients, securities, and earnings. This requirement necessitates storing a large amount of historical data. Every computer professional knows that the second system is larger and more complex than the first.

A requirement is a specific function to be performed by the system.

Examples of requirements are monthly statements for customers in banking or credit card systems, admissions and discharges for hospital systems, or weekly status of parts in an inventory system. Requirements do *not* constitute the specifications of the system (see Ross, 1977). Although requirements state what the system should be able to do, they are not precise enough to be called specifications. As will be seen in Chapter 7, specifications should describe in every detail what the system is to do. Requirements do not; they merely indicate in general terms the various functions to be accomplished.

Let us now suppose that we have identified requirements that are compatible with the system's objectives. They must still be screened and then classified into three groups.

1. "Artificial" requirements are unreasonable requests which are usually costly and do not help to solve any problems. A good example is the executive's

TABLE 5.1
EXAMPLES OF SYSTEMS AND THEIR OBJECTIVES

System	Objectives
University department results system	Documented history of the teaching activity of the department
Hospital patient information system	Patient's cumulative record
Inventory control	Decrease fixed assets or eliminate back orders
Portfolio management	Customer information and/or investment policy analysis

request for a display terminal in his office in order to have the company budget at his fingertips. Few executives have the time or the interest to learn how to operate a CRT. Moreover, the painstaking task of examining a budget is actually more easily done if the figures are on paper. Another example is the payroll system request to have the entire yearly payfile on line in order to answer quickly employee inquiries concerning pay status. The probability of an employee being unable to wait a few hours or days to receive such information on paper is so small that the request is unreasonable.

2. Requirements stemming from the current state of affairs. Although these are genuine requirements, they will automatically be taken care of when the new system is put in place. For example, if the future system provides up-to-date status reports on parts, the problem of short supplies should disappear.

3. Requirements that the new system must indeed meet. Examples include basic information (e.g., status of a part); basic results (e.g., weekly consumption); consolidated results (e.g., monthly and yearly consumption, dollar value of the inventory); and deadlines (e.g., established time for reordering before supplies run short).

SEARCH FOR SOLUTIONS

Solutions Survey

At this stage, the team knows all it needs to know about the current situation and what the user wants. The word *system*, used throughout this chapter, represents, in fact, a mixture of administrative and technical elements. A good example of this is a manual payroll system in which the paychecks are drawn up using an old accounting machine (there are still some left!). Any solution will have to be a mixture of (a) administrative and/or manual elements, and (b) automated elements. The solution should, of course, increase the proportion of (b) and decrease that of (a). Care should be taken, however, not to try to decrease the administrative elements too drastically, especially in the controversial area of decision making. There is good reason for this. First, the human mind is still much better than a computer. Second, loss of decision making power directly threatens the human ego and, in an incidental way, employee jobs (or so they think).

First, possible solutions must be defined and identified (see Table 5.2). Maintaining the status quo should not be ruled out, since it is possible that some solutions could, in fact, do more harm than good. Procedure modification occasionally works well and costs little, although it may be painful to implement. In today's burgeoning market, computer-based solutions exist by the dozen. Let us mention just a few:

TABLE 5.2
SAMPLE SOLUTIONS

Without New Technologies	With New Technologies
Status quo Procedure modifications	Computer-based (many possibilities) Word processing Microfiche Photocopies

in-house computer, design of programs,

in-house computer, purchase or leasing of packages,

outside computer, design of programs,

etc.

Although the solutions listed in Table 5.2 are discrete, any mixture of them can be easily imagined. The survey is now beginning to appear more and more complex, and the following questions could be asked: Where does one start? Where does one look for solutions? Until the 1970s, there was only one answer: design a system. Now, however, people and organizations are more careful, and this path is usually taken only if nothing else really meets the need.

In the search for solutions, there are four sources of information: the project manager's background and experience; user suggestions; situations or places similar to the one examined; and a market survey. All four sources are equally good, but may not all be present in a given situation.

EXAMPLE F: SOLUTIONS FOR THE INVENTORY SYSTEM

Let us examine all four sources of information.

PROJECT MANAGER'S BACKGROUND AND EXPERIENCE. During his previous assignment, he designed and implemented an inventory system; at the same time, he conducted a market survey but found no package to solve his problem; however, this was three years earlier, in a different industry and for a different computer.

USER SUGGESTIONS. The supervisor has seen an advertisement for a standalone turnkey system on a small minicomputer. He prefers this solution, since he would remain in complete control of the situation. Unfortunately, the system is designed for a single warehouse.

SIMILAR SITUATIONS. The transit commission in a nearby city of approximately the same size has designed its own system and is willing to share it. Moreover, it runs on the same computer model.

MARKET SURVEY.   Three products are of particular interest:

1. The computer manufacturer's package. The company already uses the general accounting and payroll systems and all are compatible. Unfortunately, the inventory system is primarily designed for wholesalers and contains many customer and sales analysis features which are almost useless to the transit company.
2. An inventory control package designed by a large and reliable software company. The system is available for the transit commission's computer but is not compatible with the accounting packages.
3. A specialized package designed for bus and truck repair shops. It is part of an overall maintenance system and runs on a minicomputer.

Evaluation of Solutions

In this segment of the process, the project manager really shows his skills; consequently, results are strongly related to abilities. The results of the opportunity study will be presented to people who are neither narrow-minded nor ignorant. They will highly appreciate a job done in a professional manner. A well-prepared case is hard to reject and difficult to attack. Since any case is open to debate, the better it is prepared, the more profitable the discusson will be.

Evaluating solutions is a difficult process, and biases are easily introduced. Following is a methodology which can be used in many similar situations (see Figure 5.6). This three-step process is composed of two selections and one evaluation. The first selection step is based on the following criteria:

1. Does the solution meet the objectives?
2. Does it meet the requirements?
3. Does it meet the constraints?

Any solution which does not satisfy these criteria should be rejected. If any solutions remain after the first selection step, we can proceed to step 2. If no solutions are left, the solutions survey may have been incomplete. If, however, it was exhaustive, the requirements and/or constraints must be revised by the user (not by the project manager, who can only be an advisor in this situation). Step 2 consists of examining the feasibility constraints, the most common being costs, deadlines, technical practicality, and organizational constraints. Here, too, a solution which fails to meet any one of these criteria should be rejected. If no solutions remain, the process described for step 1 should be repeated.

After completing those two steps, we are left with a solution (or solutions) that fits the user's needs and wishes, and that is acceptable on a practical basis. From this point on, nothing else will be eliminated. In step 3, the remaining

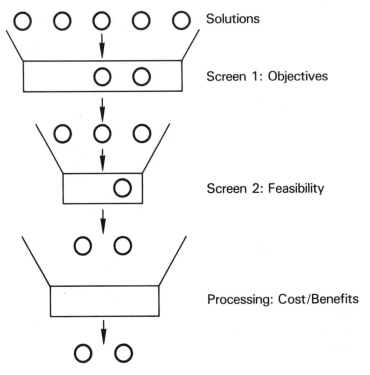

Fig. 5.6. Methodology for project evaluation.

solutions could be distinguished according to subjective or objective criteria. An interesting example of this is Land's (1976) system goals weighting method. The principle is a top-down decomposition of the system's goals as defined by the various users. Weights are then given to the nodes of the tree, and the contribution of each solution to a given leaf-goal is valued according to a specific scale. Results are then compiled upwards, finally producing an overall mark for a given solution. A similar method will be used in Chapter 14 to compare different solutions for hardware acquisition.

Cost/Benefits Analysis

Of all criteria used to compare solutions, money is the least subjective, and a cost/benefits analysis should always be performed. We agree with Knutson and Nolan (1974) that costs and benefits should be evaluated separately instead of trying to present an integrated cost/benefit figure. At this stage of the project, knowledge of costs is grossly inaccurate. In addition, many benefits are not financial, or more precisely, it is nearly impossible to assess the financial value of such benefits as budget control.

There are two reasons for performing a cost/benefits analysis. First, it will provide managers, if not with precise figures, at least with an idea of the amount they will have to invest and the returns they can expect. Second, it is used primarily to compare different solutions. Even if the amounts are inaccurate, the same inexactness is linked to all of the solutions, and the analysis has served its purpose.

Table 5.3 outlines the fixed and operational costs involved in a system. Fixed costs apply only once, while operational costs occur continuously once the system is in service. For budgeting reasons, a one-year period is usually used as a basis for the cost/benefits analysis. In some cases, however, a 3- to 5-year time frame gives a fairer comparison, especially when comparing solutions involving leases or licenses against purchases and/or inhouse development.

TABLE 5.3
PROJECT COSTS

Fixed Costs	Operational Costs
Hardware and software (if purchased) Wages, fees (project set-up) Supplies, travel Installation Computer time (for project programming, if applicable)	Hardware (if rented or leased) Software (if rented or licensed or royalties paid) Telecommunications Maintenance (hardware, software if applicable) Computer time (if applicable) Personnel (if needed) Supplies

As illustrated in Table 5.4, not all benefits are financially measurable. Direct financial benefits are obvious, but occur less and less frequently. Indirect benefits are of greater value, but their assessment and reliability are difficult to pinpoint. In our inventory system, for example, a 2% decrease in reordering would represent a saving of $20,000. If this amount seems small, it must be remembered that it does not apply to development costs but to operational costs, which occur year after year. The difficulty here is to assess the reliability of the 2% decrease in ordering.

An interesting example of unmeasurable benefits in portfolio management is the elapsed time between a dividend being declared and the stockholder (or his broker) being advised of it. Even if the problem is inconsequential on a small

TABLE 5.4
FINANCIAL BENEFITS BROUGHT ABOUT BY A PROJECT

Measurable		Unmeasurable
Direct	Indirect	
Decrease in staff Elimination of certain costs	Decrease in system-related expenses Increase in system-related returns	Shortening of deadlines Increase in the quality of information Better controls Data impossible to obtain otherwise

scale, it takes on another dimension when hundreds or thousands of shares of stock are involved. A computerized system may advise in advance when dividends (or interest) will be paid, thereby enabling the holder to make timely investment decisions.

THE OPPORTUNITY STUDY REPORT

Objectives, Target Readers

In Chapter 4 we saw that a document is defined by its function, its target, and its content. The opportunity study report serves as the decisional tool for setting the orientation of the project (function); its target is the decision makers (upper management); and its content includes all that is required to make a rational decision.

Because managers, as the target of the report, are often not technical people, an opportunity study report is therefore not a technical document. If technical data are necessary, they can be placed in appendices. Proposed solutions should be presented in functional rather than technical terms. For example, "4 disk drives with 130 megabytes each" should be specified in the appendix; in the main body of the report, the phrase "on-line storage for 300,000 patient records" would be more meaningful to the reader.

The opportunity study, and therefore the report it generates, follows the basic steps involved in the decision making process: stating the problem, finding solutions, weighing the alternatives, and making a decision (see Table 5.5). The executive summary and the recommendations are the two key chapters in the document, and sometimes they are the only ones read by busy executives. Thus they warrant special attention.

TABLE 5.5
THE OPPORTUNITY STUDY REPORT

Report Outline	Corresponding Step in the Decision Making Process
Executive summary	All steps
Introduction	State problem
Scope	State problem
Current situation	State problem
Objectives and requirements	State problem
Solutions	Find solutions
Recommendations	Weigh alternatives
Conclusions	Make a decision

The Executive Summary

Let us begin by stating what it is not.

- It is not a summary. Its content has neither the same weight nor is it in the same order as the rest of the report.
- It is not a propaganda document. Presenting merely the author's preferred recommendation and its many justifications is not appropriate.

The executive summary is a reader-adapted document presenting the main points of the report along with the importance *the reader attaches to them*. Thus, the purpose and scope of the study should be stated briefly (since the manager is usually aware of them), and there is no need to describe the current situation except to *identify the problems*. The most interesting solutions should be mentioned, and the recommendations should be presented along with their justifications. The executive summary should, in principle, comprise 5% to 15% of the report itself; ideally, it should never exceed 10 pages in length.

EXAMPLE G: EXECUTIVE SUMMARY OF THE INVENTORY SYSTEM OPPORTUNITY STUDY

This study was undertaken to determine whether the use of data processing could be of some help in the management of the inventory system. The team, composed of members from inventory control and data processing, investigated the system during a four-week period and came to the following conclusions.

Several problems hinder the efficient operation of the system:

1. Part numbering. There is no uniform coding for parts in both warehouses.
2. Short supply. Inventory status is always behind schedule.
3. Lack of communication. Each warehouse is operated independently of the other.
4. Poor reporting. Reporting is done manually when time is available.

This state of affairs has the following consequences.

1. Parts are ordered for one warehouse without inquiring if they are available in the other.
2. Purchasing on a rush basis means paying higher prices and sometimes leads to oversupply.
3. Consumption data is lacking, reports being late or nonexistent.
4. The real status of the inventory is unknown.

It is obvious that computerization would help to solve these problems. However, any solution would require a change in the present system: all parts in both warehouses should be numbered with the same coding system. Given this change, the following solutions are possible:

1. Renting the inventory control system (ICS) package from our computer manufacturer. It would require one display terminal at each warehouse, one at inventory control, and a small printer. Investment would be around $15,000 and operating costs would run approximately $4,500 per year. The major advantage is that it could later be integrated with our accounting system. Moreover, the supplier is reliable and well-known. Less convenient is the fact that the system was designed primarily for wholesalers, meaning that some functions are useless and some reports are not exactly as the user would want them.

2. Entering into an agreement with the Borden City Transit Authority, which designed a system almost identical to the one we need and which runs on the same type of computer we have. Investment would be about the same amount, i.e., $15,000 (the same equipment is required), with operating costs being slightly lower ($4,000). The main advantage is that the system is perfectly suited to our needs. The inconvenience is in the area of support, which might be less reliable than our manufacturer's. In addition, we would have to program the integration with our accounting system.

3. Designing our own system. We have the experience and staff to do it. The result would suit our needs exactly and could be adapted to new requirements. The cost in equipment would be the same. The main disadvantage is the time required to set up the system (approximately six months longer than implementation of the other two solutions).

We recommend solution 1, i.e., leasing the ICS package from our computer manufacturer. It is more expensive than the others but can be implemented faster, allows integration with other systems, and has a secure support environment.

From Scope to Evaluation

These sections of the report will be read either by management or by assistants and/or professionals, and should be more detailed. The section identified as *scope* is used to situate the study and define quickly how, when, and by whom it has been carried out. In the following section, the *current situation* (existing system) is described, as well as the main information flows and activities. Volumes and frequencies should be mentioned if they are related to the problems or used to describe the size of the system. A special section should be devoted to a description of identified problems and their consequences.

The *objectives* of each remedy are presented and classified as general objectives and specific objectives. The main *requirements* of each solution should also be listed, and every *solution* examined should be presented, even those which are later rejected. The *evaluation* part of this section includes a presentation of the methodology, the evaluation process, and the results. The *cost/benefit analysis* part should be presented in a way that permits easy comparison of the solutions. All hypotheses such as time frame, salaries, etc., should be mentioned, as well as the sources of all data.

Recommendations

Up to this point, the project manager has never had to take a stand. All information has been objectively presented, and only his technical skills have been at work. Now, however, he is asked to advise the reader on what solutions are preferable. In other words, pure objectivity stops here and he has to argue. Making recommendations consists in making statements which cannot always be scientifically or numerically justified. It is assuming a responsibility, and this is exactly what the project manager must do. No one but he has mastered not only the extent and depth of the problem, but also the content of the report itself, and his readers should be able to benefit from this knowledge.

There is no obligation to make only one recommendation. Several solutions may be proposed, with all of equal value or else listed in order of preference. Every recommendation should be justified.

If a project manager's recommendations are followed, we may conclude that he did his job well. However, recommendations may not be followed for reasons that are unrelated to the study or the problem. Thus, the fact that they may not be followed is not necessarily an indictment of the quality of the study or of the report.

SELECTED REFERENCES

Canning, R. G. 1977. Getting the requirements right. *EDP Analyzer*, 15, 7 (July), 1–14.
In this article on requirements and specifications, the author emphasizes the importance of user participation and the necessity of dealing with the real problems. He suggests using a progressive approach based on a divide-and-conquer strategy and top-down analysis.

Canning, R. G. 1979. The analysis of user needs. *EDP Analyzer*, 17, 1 (January), 1–13.

> After presenting two systems analysis methods (SADT and IA), the author examines the general problems surrounding the analysis of user requirements. The change analysis stage of the IA method in particular is strongly recommended, despite the fact it is often neglected by analysts and users. A lively example is given providing excellent justification for its use.

Davis, G. B. 1982. Strategies for information requirements determination. *IBM System Journal*, 21, 1, 4–30.

> This article is essential reading for any analyst who must perform a requirements study. Of special interest is the analysis of the problems caused by the behavior and characteristics of the humans involved in the process. The principal strategies for requirements determination and the associated methods are defined and analyzed, while the context of their use is specified. Finally, a method is presented for selecting a strategy to reduce the uncertainty related to the requirements determination process.

Gaydash, A. 1982. *Principles of EDP management.* Reston, Va.: Reston Publishing Co.

> Chapter 6 deals with the opportunity study by way of the conventional preliminary investigation—feasibility study approach. For the author, the survey must not last longer than a week and must be carried out by only one person. The feasibility study, on the other hand, goes much further than in some conventional models since it includes a description of the proposed system and a development plan.

Knutson, K. E., Nolan, R. L. 1974. Assessing computer costs and benefits. *Journal of Systems Management*, February, 28–33.

> The article begins by attacking, with the use of an example, the financial justification of a system based on the conventional direct benefits (or return-on-investment) approach. The justification results from the uncertainty surrounding the costs and benefits at this stage of the project. The article proposes carrying out separate evaluations and differentiating between quantitative and qualitative benefits.

Land, F. F. 1976. Evaluation of system goals in determining a design strategy for a computer-based information system. *The Computer Journal*, 19,4, 290–294.

> The article describes a method for evaluating alternative solutions. An interesting aspect is being able to compare the different alternatives either on an overall basis or relative to a specific objective.

Lucas, H. C., Jr. 1981. *The analysis, design and implementation of information systems.* New York: McGraw-Hill.

> Chapter 8 approaches the opportunity study in the conventional manner, i.e., the preliminary survey followed by the feasibility study. However, besides the fact that there are two separate reports, there is no clearly distinguishable difference between the two phases of the study. The activities are exactly the same as those in the opportunity study presented in this text.

Lundeberg, M. 1979. An approach for involving the users in the specification of information systems. In *Formal models and practical tools for information systems design*, edited by M. J. Schneider. North-Holland, Amsterdam, The Netherlands.

The article describes Lundeberg and Langfors' ISAC method, of which IA is the systems analysis portion. Emphasis is placed on the involvement of users, particularly in the change analysis phase, which corresponds to the objectives and requirements determination stage of an opportunity study. Emphasis is also placed on the uncertainty surrounding the problems to be solved.

Ross, D. T. 1977. Reflections on requirements. Guest Editorial. *IEEE Tans. on Soft. Eng.*, SE-3, 1, January, 2–5.

These reflections are in fact a remarkable analysis of the reasons why systems do not perform as expected. By means of an analogy with geometrical optics, Ross demonstrates the fact that even if a system is imperfect, it can be corrected provided it is possible to determine its imperfections. The proposed procedure makes, in particular, a clear distinction between requirements and specifications.

Willoughby, T. C. 1975. Origins of systems projects. *Journal of Systems Management*, October, 18–26.

This article analyzes how projects are selected and where they are born. Much attention is devoted to the user department, as well as the data processing department, upper management, and outside services.

Part 3
PROJECT DESIGN

Chapter 6
OVERVIEW OF PROJECT DESIGN

THE FORGOTTEN STAGE

Taking Stock of the Situation

The opportunity study has been finished and the decision to proceed has been made. But where exactly are we in the system development cycle? As depicted in Figure 6.1, our position is fixed at a turning point. We know what must be produced (one of the alternatives has been selected), and we have a general knowledge of the resources that will be required (from the cost/benefits portion

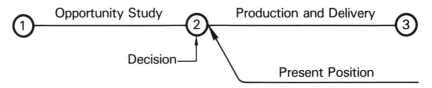

Fig. 6.1. Where we stand in the project life cycle.

116

of the opportunity study). Many information systems have been developed with less data than that, so why not start?

Programming without Design

Project design is to a project what design is to programs: preparation for the coherent development of a quality product. Brown (1974) described two programmers: Mr. Blunder and Mr. Look. Mr. Blunder is obviously a hard worker. The description of the program to be developed has only just been given to him, and already he is at the terminal. In fact, he is there night and day, constantly programming, testing, perfecting. Mr. Look, on the other hand, seems to spend a good deal of time reading, thinking, and writing. He is not seen all that often working with the equipment. He analyzes, structures, documents. Like the hare and the tortoise, not only will Mr. Look finish first, but he will have spent less time on his program and it will be better than Mr. Blunder's (if, indeed, Mr. Blunder ever gets his program to work).

There is no mistaking the parallel with product development in a project: he who starts "manufacturing" as soon as the problem has been defined will take an inordinate amount of time, an unacceptable amount of money, and will end up with an inadequate product. Computer specialists understood this problem, and the discipline of software engineering was born. Given the disastrous consequences of hurried and disordered programming, they perfected an entire arsenal of principles, tools, and techniques which make the development of quality products possible. During the remainder of this book, elements will be borrowed from the field of software engineering and applied to system development projects.

However, having good tools, good methods, and good personnel is not enough; they must be well-organized. Let us remember that poor planning was cited as the prime culprit in unsuccessful projects (see Chapter 2). On the same subject, Zmud (1980) noted that large application systems development projects (as opposed to pure software systems) suffer from managerial rather than technical problems.

The Main Stage of Project Management

A general leading his best troops does not go into battle without a plan of attack; neither does a coach count on his best players' ability to improvise to win a game. For Daly (1977), planning is the first phase of development. Knutson and Scotto (1978) stated that work can only begin once the planning and scheduling has been done. Miller (1978) echoed the caution that planning must precede working.

Why draw up the plan at this point? Until the opportunity study was completed, a decision had not been made on what was to be done. Furthermore, a quick glance at the Norden/Putnam curve (see Figure 2.6 in Chapter 2) shows that the production stage will consume the most resources in a project life cycle; it therefore deserves the most attention.

Project design is the most crucial stage for the project manager; the ultimate success or failure of the project depends on its outcome. During this stage, the project manager must make maximum use of the administrative skills of planning, scheduling, and resource gathering.

The structure of this stage is the same, regardless of the type of data processing project involved. No transposition or adaptation is necessary. The objectives remain the same, and the activities and tools do not change.

ANALYSIS OF PROJECT DESIGN

The Work Breakdown Structure (WBS) of Project Design

To analyze this stage, let us use once again the WBS method presented in Chapter 3. Our goal for the project design stage is to obtain the following four parameters: deliverables, activities, resources, and duration.

Deliverables

The objective of the project design stage is to make possible the coordinated development of the subsequent stages. It must therefore establish the exact definition of the product to be developed, since the opportunity study provided only very general data. The design must also specify operating processes, the financial and human resources necessary for operation, and the planning and scheduling of production.

Knowing what the project design stage must produce, it is now possible to draw up the WBS presented in Figure 6.2.

Activities

The project design stage contains six activities:

1. **Definition of specifications.** Analysis of the system and drawing up the specifications document are crucial here (see Chapter 7).
2. **Operating processes.** Production norms must be defined, and some very general technical decisions must be made concerning the tools to be used (see Chapter 8).

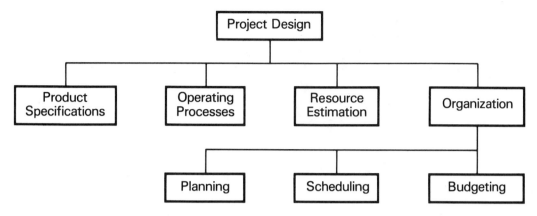

Fig. 6.2. WBS of project design.

   3. Resource estimation. Chapter 9 will explore the sensitive area of estimating the programming times for a system that is as yet undesigned.

4-5. Planning and scheduling. Because of the high degree of interaction between these two activities, they are grouped together for purposes of discussion (see Chapter 10).

   6. Budgeting. This "schedule" of the consumption of monetary resources will be discussed in Chapter 11.

Resources

Human resources will vary from one activity to another, but will always involve experienced, high-level specialists: analysts for the specifications, chief programmers or similar individuals for estimation purposes, and personnel with planning experience for the other activities. Other important resources are the tools that make the accomplishment of these activities possible, namely, analytical methods, estimation data, and budget planning methods. All will be described in detail in later chapters.

The personal involvement of the project manager will be inversely proportional to the size of the project. For large undertakings, he will have access to specialists in the various disciplines. For small projects (or small organizations), he himself will perform the activities in the project design stage either in whole or in part.

Duration

Despite the restricted size of the team, this stage will be long, for three reasons.

First is the *intrinsic duration* of certain activities. Defining the specifications will take time; it is a sizable and difficult task, its quality directly affecting that of the product and other project design results.

The second reason is the *high degree of interaction* among the different activities. Is it possible to find parallel activities in project design? Figure 6.3 provides a theoretical response to this question. Although the specifications are not yet available, it is possible to start work immediately on the operating processes. On one hand, the data processing environment in which the product will be developed imposes or prompts the use of certain tools and methods. On the other hand, the opportunity study provides enough data to make it possible to determine where the technical problems will arise.

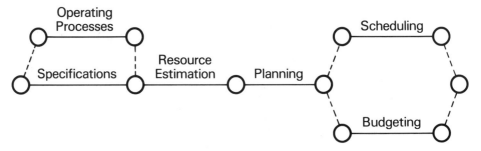

Fig. 6.3. Network of project design.

Resource estimation, however, requires specifications and technical decisions. Planning cannot be done without a list of the activities and the duration of each. The results of the planning stage are used for the scheduling and budgeting phases.

The sequencing is unfortunately both theoretical and optimistic. In effect, if the specifications and technical choices must precede the other activities, the real situation with regard to these remaining activities is more likely to resemble the diagram shown in Figure 6.4. The plan can be called into question because of the budgeting or scheduling; high and low points in activities or expenditures

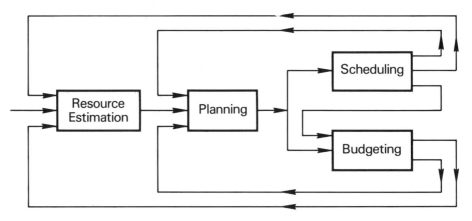

Fig. 6.4. Interaction among the activities of project design.

caused by poor distribution, utilization of the same resource at the same time for two different activities, and so forth. In the same way, estimates known to be inaccurate (see Chapter 3) may have to be revised depending on the budgeting and scheduling results.

The *repetitive aspect* of the activities is the third reason for the long duration of the project design stage. The completion of each activity requires a good deal of backtracking. This is true for defining the specifications as well as for estimating and planning purposes. For each of these activities there exists no single solution for a given problem. A choice can only be evaluated in relation to its effect on the remainder of the activity. This repetitive aspect will always be present, since the current state of affairs in data processing rarely makes it possible to determine the consequences of a particular decision immediately. A judgment can be made only after the effects have been analyzed, thereby resulting in much backtracking.

The project design stage will therefore last a long time—from a few weeks (even for small projects) to several months (for large undertakings). Let us not forget, however, that Mr. Look ultimately won the race. Also to be remembered is the comment made by Tripp and Pietrasanta (see p. 000) concerning estimates: a bad estimate is better than no estimate at all. To paraphrase them: "bad planning is better than no planning," and "when in doubt, plan in greater detail!"

SELECTED REFERENCES

Brown, P. J. 1974. Programming and documenting software projects. *ACM Computing Survey*, 6, 4 (December), 214–220.

> The article deals with the need to control, structure, and document the programming and testing activities. This is illustrated by two fictitious programmers: Mr. Blunder, who is above all a coder, and Mr. Look, who thinks out his programs before writing them. The author emphasizes the difference between local code optimization, which is machine-oriented, and overall long-term program performance.

Daly, E. B. 1977. Management of software development. *IEEE Trans. on Soft. Eng.*, SE-3, 3, May, 229–242.

> The author begins by analyzing the different types of programs, the rates of output of programmers, and the resource consumption of the different life cycle stages. He then presents a development cycle whose first stage is planning, and discusses the problem of configuration management.

Knutson, J., & Scotto, M. 1978. Development of a project plan. *Journal of Systems Management*, October, 36–41.

> The three phases of project management are identified as planning, scheduling, and controlling. The authors maintain that production cannot begin until the

planning has been finished. An analytical method similar to WBS, as well as a variety of unconventional planning and scheduling tools, are also presented.

Miller, W. B. 1978. Fundamentals of project management. *Journal of Systems Management*, November, 22–29.

This article should be read or reread by all project managers. Written in a direct and concise manner, it describes the principles and problems of planning, scheduling, controlling, and documenting. It is a record which is complete, clear, and exact. Here again, planning must precede production and anticipate the measures to be taken in case of straying.

Zmud, R. D. 1980. Management of large software development efforts. *MIS Quarterly*, June, 45–55.

For the author, the fundamental problem in this type of project is the basic uncertainty of its nature. To reduce this uncertainty, a repetitive development is proposed, involving increasingly more precise versions. The author strongly emphasizes the importance of controlling and planning for changes.

Chapter 7
PRODUCT SPECIFICATIONS

INTRODUCTION

Why are specifications needed? Freeman (1980) provided an implicit answer to this question by making a distinction between the traditional approach, in which analysis and design comprise a single activity, and the new one in which they are regarded as two distinct activities. Anyone who has worked long enough in the area of applications is aware of the weight of maintenance problems and the frustrations of users and programmers whenever a system has been developed without enough time being taken beforehand to define it. Boehm (1977) stressed two points:

1. Most of the errors in a system are introduced before programming (i.e., at the specifications and design stages).
2. The later an error is detected, the more expensive it is to correct.

An error in the specifications of a system is exactly the same as an error in an examination question; when the users (the students taking the exam) encounter the error, the test is usually cancelled! The necessity of specifications is not even a matter of debate in data processing project management.

What exactly, then, are specifications? Their primary objective is to serve as a *contract* between the user and the project team—one that specifies the product to be delivered. Primary emphasis will therefore be placed on this aspect, and the readability of the contract will be stressed. For software engineering specialists, specifications constitute above all a *baseline document* which enables the project personnel to know exactly what they are to produce; this, however, is only a secondary objective (see Chapter 4).

Once approved, the specifications will inform the user of exactly what he is receiving, allow the project manager to plan and organize the remainder of the project, and provide the project team members with a description—a "specs manual"—of the product to be developed.

EXAMPLE A: ADMISSION-DISCHARGE IN A LARGE HOSPITAL

Good Samaritan Hospital is a Canadian hospital which has 800 beds. The institution also has its own data processing department. Admission-discharge was one of the first applications developed, using the means available at that time—i.e., the batch method. Later, a few online capabilities were added, but the system was clumsy, unadapted to the new regulations, and almost completely inefficient. The central computer was recently replaced with a new, truly interactive system having database management capabilities. An opportunity study on updating the admission system was conducted, and it was decided that the system must be revamped.

All of the work will be done by the hospital's data processing department. The team which developed the initial system is no longer in existence, but a certain number of analysts worked on its maintenance and are familiar with the problem. Michael Greenwood, head of the data processing department, has named an experienced colleague, Donald White, as project manager. White's task will be to form an analysis team, draw up the specifications, and get them approved within 4 months.

WORK BREAKDOWN STRUCTURE OF SPECIFICATIONS PRODUCTION

In order to analyze a group of activities ending in a milestone, it is necessary to define four parameters (see Chapter 3):

the deliverables,

the activities required to produce them,

the resources needed to ensure the successful outcome of these activities, and the duration of the process.

The Deliverables

The specifications of a product are the detailed description of the tasks that the product will have to perform for the user.

Note that the specifications are *not* a description of a system's files and programs, a description of a machine's CPU cycle, the size of its storage, etc., nor are they the budget and development schedule of a system.

EXAMPLE B: ADMISSION-DISCHARGE SYSTEM

A proposed summary of the specifications reads as follows: "To automate the admission, transfer, and discharge procedures of patients at Good Samaritan Hospital." This summary is unsatisfactory because: (a) it is not detailed; (b) it does not define what is meant by the term *automate*; (c) it is not clear whether or not the production of the plastic card is included (making it possible to identify all of the documents concerning a particular patient); and (d) it is not clear whether or not the statistics are included.

The summary specifications obviously need clarification of the nature outlined in Figure 7.1. Acceptable specifications are:

1. Complete—they must describe all aspects of the product to be delivered.
2. Consistent—there must be no contradictions between different elements (e.g., entering a patient's age and wanting to specify his date of birth in a report).
3. Unambiguous—ambiguity constitutes a nightmare for analysts and programmers.

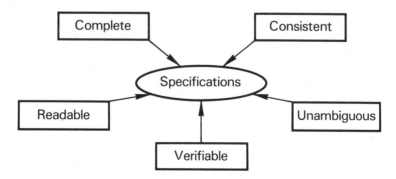

Fig. 7.1. Qualities of specifications.

4. Verifiable—this characteristic, while desirable, is difficult to achieve without a specialized program.
5. Readable—in order to be of any value to the user.

The Activities

If the specifications are considered to be a contract, the activities required for the "signing" can be defined very simply (see Figure 7.2). *Information gathering* is systems analysis. In order to develop a product having the characteristics described above, we will need a method. *Contract writing* is the actual drawing up of the specifications. This step is included in certain analysis methods. *Negotiation and approval* is the final activity, without which no contract can exist.

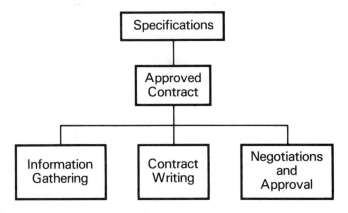

Fig. 7.2. Activities of specifications production.

Although analysis, writing, and approval are ideally sequential (Figure 7.3a), systems analysis in reality requires a high degree of interaction between users and analysts. As a result of problems in communication and comprehension, the process more closely resembles Figure 7.3b. It is, in fact, repetitive and composed of loops, nested or not. A change in the specifications makes rewriting necessary and can even result in a revision of the analysis. The process may be either iterative or sequential, so long as it converges in a finite period of time. Analysis methods and management procedures are both necessary here.

The process depicted in Figure 7.3b holds true regardless of the type of product to be delivered. While it is true that some systems analysis methods do produce the specifications document, this does not apply to all methods.

Resources and Duration

Four types of resources are necessary for determining specifications:

1. *Manpower* in the form of analysts with a great deal of experience in systems analysis coupled with a good knowledge of the milieu in which the product to be described is situated.

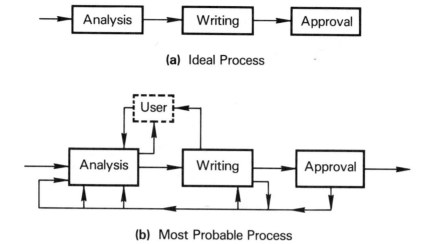

(a) Ideal Process

(b) Most Probable Process

Fig. 7.3. The specifications production and approval process.

2. *Data* come from two sources: (a) the opportunity study (for major guidelines, direction, and quantitative data); and (b) the users, who will help the analysts deepen their knowledge of the product desired.

3. *Technology* of software engineering, which will donate its principles, major guidelines, and, if possible, its methods.

4. *Users*, who (in addition to their role during analysis) will form one of the two components of the specifications negotiation and approval process.

The duration of the overall activity must not be underestimated. The complexity of some systems, the repetitive nature of the process, and the problems surrounding user availability must all be taken into account. Indeed, it is important to remember that while specifications production is the analyst's job, the user's participation in this activity constitutes an addition to his regular workload.

Specifications production may take time. The overall benefit for the project will, however, be substantial as can be seen in Figure 7.4, where the later stages are shorter, and there is no more costly backtracking at the beginning.

In summary, producing the specifications "contract" requires expertise, time, data, and user availability.

EXAMPLE C: ADMISSION SYSTEM: SPECIFICATIONS DEVELOPMENT TEAM

Donald White knows the system very well, since he directed the opportunity study. One year ago, he and Jean Coolidge, an analyst, attended a seminar on system analysis methods and they liked the ISAC method (see p. 138). White decides to use it, and then forms his team:

Jean Coolidge: 9 years experience, 2 on the old admission system.

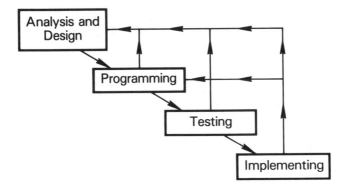

(a) Development Without Specifications

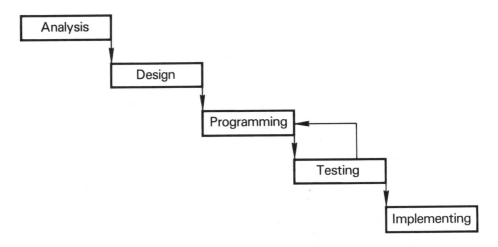

(b) Development with Specifications

Fig. 7.4. The development process.

Charles Blain: 7 years experience, 6 months on the old system.

Ronald Norton: ex-programmer just promoted to analyst, previously in charge
of maintenance of the system.

Besides managing the project, White decides to assume responsibility for
that portion of the analysis covering the requirements of management. Coolidge
will deal with the admissions, discharges, and the patient index, while Blain and
Norton will be responsible for the transfers and statistics of operation. Because

the personnel and management are quite readily available, the specifications should be approved in three months.

Project Management Problems

The formation of a competent team is the primary concern of the project manager. Once it has been formed, the planning and scheduling activities related to this phase are relatively minor. Control, on the other hand, becomes very important given the crucial role that the specifications play in the remainder of the project. Moreover, it is once again necessary to differentiate between product and project control.

With regard to *product control*, there are two concerns which the project manager must keep in mind. First, the specifications must describe *what* the final product will do, and not *how* it will be done: *specifications* are expected, not a *design*. Second, the specifications must be complete, consistent, unambiguous, and readable. In order to monitor specifications quality more effectively, the project manager should be well aware of the most common types of errors. (Canning, 1977). Bell and Thayer (1976) recorded a very large number of errors in specifications (sometimes more than one per page). They found that 30% were incorrect specifications, 25% incomplete, and 9% to 30% ambiguous, depending on the particular project. According to Black (1976), most cases of missed deadlines are not attributable to incorrect estimates of planned tasks, but rather to the omission of tasks the system is to perform—i.e., to incomplete specifications.

With regard to *project control*, it has been established that the process is not purely sequential, but repetitive, and it is essential to ensure that all of the elements converge. There are three necessary conditions:

1. Having an analysis method. Several are available for analyzing a system to be developed or for producing a computer's specifications. If none of these can be used, a method must be developed, since even an imperfect method is better than none at all.

2. Monitoring the results. It must be possible to assess the progress of the process, thus requiring a method of analysis which ensures that the *results* are visible and, for negotiations, a procedure which ensures that the *progress* is visible.

3. Leading the negotiations process. Because the user is less available than the project team, it is the responsibility of the project manager to supervise the implementation, progress, and conclusion of the process.

During the life of the project, the project manager will have ample opportunity to display his technical knowledge (system analysis), his administrative abilities (organization and control), and his skills in human relations as he leads the negotiations process.

SYSTEM ANALYSIS

Objectives and Principles

The goal of system analysis is to construct a model of the product desired. But what kind of model? Is it, for example, an exact replica? Absolutely not. It is a description written in a specialized language. Moreover, priority will be given to a static rather than an operational view of the system. There are two reasons for this. First, it is difficult to "see" the system, to grasp it. Second, a dynamic model might require as great an effort to build as the system itself. It is a regrettable situation, but fortunately some methods do make it possible to build an operational model of part of the system.

What, then, are the model building methods that we can use? Freeman (1980) proposed a classification which has since been adopted and is composed of three sets of elements:

1. Tools—such as programs, languages, and symbols.
2. Methods—ways of performing a specific task.
3. Methodologies—well organized collections of methods and tools which include management and human elements.

These elements, although they may previously have been used by analysts in a disorganized way, are products of the software engineering field.

Software engineering has established seven principles of system analysis which have been examined by, among others, Canning (1977, 1979) and Wasserman (1980). They are presented in Figure 7.5 and discussed in the sections that follow.

Top-down

This approach involves analyzing the components of a system by starting with the whole and working progressively toward the parts, in contrast to the method which starts with the parts and works toward the whole (bottom-up).

Modularization

This application of the divide-and-conquer principle involves the breaking down of a complex problem into less complicated ones, continuing until an easily

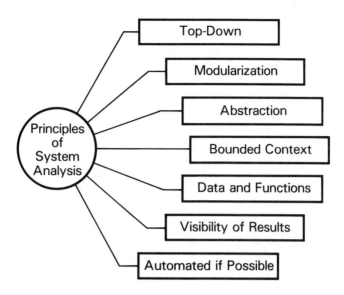

Fig. 7.5. Principles of system analysis.

solvable problem is arrived at. An application of this principle has already been
seen for the WBS method in Chapter 3.

Abstraction

This principle has two applications. A given problem must be studied in abstract
terms, independent of its concrete characteristics; for example, the patient-
admission function is studied independently of the admission data input. This
principle can also be applied to those data whose abstract concept (e.g., admission
data) will be defined long before the data items themselves are listed. When this
principle is combined with the top-down approach, it leads to the concept of
levels of abstraction which make it possible to determine at any moment the level
of detail which must be addressed. For the patient-admission function, for example, the admission data will not be listed one by one, but will be grouped into
their component parts in relation to the corresponding function (see Figure 7.6).

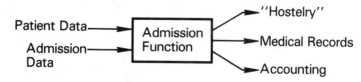

Fig. 7.6. Same level of abstraction for functions and data.

Bounded Context

Whenever an object (datum, function, subsystem) is studied, it is necessary to determine its boundaries; everything inside the boundaries must be analyzed, everything outside is to be left alone. It is the application of this principle which makes modularization effective.

Data and Functions

In system analysis, the data must receive as much attention as the functions.

Visibility of Results

What applies to programming also applies to systems analysis: an analysis that is 90% complete is worthless. It must be possible to "see" the model at every moment of the process.

Automated if Possible

This would be a desirable aspect of many methods. The concept is, in effect, that an analysis method should make it possible to verify that the model meets the required specifications characteristics (i.e., that it is complete, consistent, and unambiguous). At the very least, it should be possible to conduct a formal verification.

These software engineering principles of course apply to systems (programs) to be developed. However, their scope of application is in fact much more extensive, and it will be seen (particularly in Chapter 14) that they are very useful for computer system selection.

Overview of System Analysis Methods

Many analysis methods have been developed since the beginning of the 1970s. In addition to those described in the sections that follow, they include Belford, Bond, Henderson, and Selers (1980), Mendes (1980), and Warnier (1981). DeMarco (1981) has also developed a version of Structured Systems Analysis (SSA).

Structured Analysis and Design Technique (SADT)

Developed by Ross and his colleagues (1977), this top-down analysis method involves the progressively more precise definition of the system functions. It uses graphic language with two types of diagrams: functions and data flows.

There are documentation, validation, and control procedures. Extremely complete, this method is heavily based on processes and requires extensive training in its use.

Information Analysis Approach

This method was designed by King and Cleland (1975) to analyze the requirements of Management Information Systems (MIS). In contrast to the others, which must construct a model of a concrete operating process, this method is designed to illustrate the decision making mechanisms and the necessary data. Therefore, it does not involve a graphic language, but rather a rigorous procedure which calls for extensive user participation. Applicable to decision support systems, it could be valuable in determining the objectives and requirements of new operating systems (not for replacing an existing system).

Software Requirements Engineering Methodology (SREM)

Developed at TRW (Bell, Bixler & Dyer, 1977), this method is very well adapted to real-time systems analysis. A PASCAL-like language called Requirements Statement Language (RSL) makes it possible to describe the objects (processes), the data, and their interrelations. Using this completely automated method, it is possible to validate specifications, conduct a static analysis of the system, and carry out simulations. An interesting characteristic is the possibility of adding specifications analysis functions. Geared in fact toward software specifications, the method requires extensive training on the part of the user and analyst.

Systematic Activity Modeling Method (SAMM)

Developed at Boeing (Stephens & Tripp, 1978), this method is composed of three tools for system description: (a) a tree used to describe the hierarchy of the activities; (b) activity diagrams to define the relationships between activities and data flows; and (c) condition charts to define the input/output and conditions of an activity. SAMM also has a computer system making it possible to enter and modify a description and to conduct analyses (consistency, connectivity). The method is very much based on top-down analysis, levels of abstraction, and bounded context. Its limits are those of hierarchical systems.

Problem Statement Language (PSL/PSA)

Developed by Teichroew and Hershey (1977), PSL/PSA must be considered separately from the other methods. While it is extremely useful for documenting and validating specifications, it cannot be considered an analysis method since it does not contain a procedure for investigating the system under study. It is, rather, a data processing system which makes it possible to use a language (PSL) to describe a system, to document it, and to analyze the specifications (PSA).

Structured Systems Analysis (SSA): A Method Based on Data Flows

Developed by Gane and Sarson (1979), the method is comprised of four elements:

o Logical flow diagrams.
o The use of a data dictionary.
o Tools for describing the logic of the process.
o Methods for determining the contents of the data stores.

Logical flow diagrams are designed to describe the flow of data and operations. Figure 7.7 shows the general diagram of the admission-discharge-transfer (ADT) system and the definitions of the various symbols. Starting with a general diagram, the method consists in "exploding" each process into one or several more detailed data flow diagrams (DFDs). In Figure 7.8, this was performed for the single process shown in Figure 7.7a. The explosion could be continued, with the admission process being a possible target, for example.

Before going on to discuss the data dictionary, a few comments concerning data flow diagrams must be made. It is impossible to do the DFD without carrying out an extensive system analysis; thus, the DFD is, in fact, an effective working document (as it is for all methods of this type). Drawing the DFD poses planar topology problems for the analyst which have nothing to do with understanding the system itself. The levels-of-abstraction concept is not part of the method, as it is for ISAC or SADT; it is up to the analyst to incorporate this himself.

The method plans explosions only for the processes, not for the data or external entities (at least in regard to the DFD). There is therefore a certain imbalance between the abstraction level of the processes and that of the other entities.

There is no way of indicating the triggering event of a process; in other words, the "control" can only be expressed on the DFD if it consists of data, although such is not always the case. In Figure 7.8, for example, the search waiting-list operation is activated every morning because it is the first task of a certain employee; in the same way, the produce-statistics operation is activated on the first of every month.

The *data dictionary* is an essential element, whether automated or manual. It makes it possible to list and describe the objects of the system, namely, data flow, data stores, processes, and external entities. Table 7.1 summarizes the data

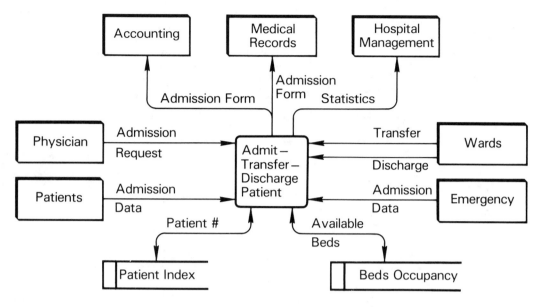

(a) Overall Data Flow Diagram for ADT

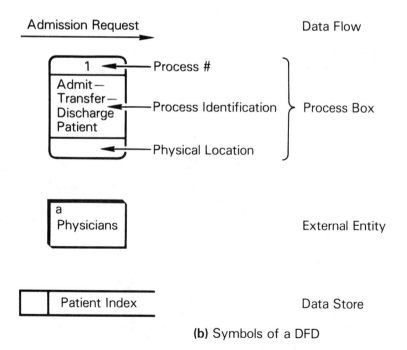

(b) Symbols of a DFD

Fig. 7.7. SSA method: DFD diagram and symbols.

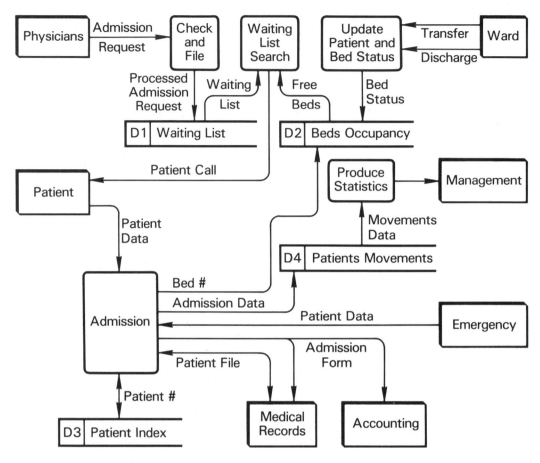

Fig. 7.8. SSA method: Exploded ADT data flow diagram.

the dictionary should contain. The data dictionary also describes all of the objects defined by the DFD, along with their interrelations.

We now see all of the power of such a system, first because the DFD is the tool which makes it possible to analyze and understand the system under study, and second, because the dictionary contains in prose the description of the entire system. Reorganized according to the guidelines given later in this chapter (see p. 000), it becomes the specifications of the system. If automated and equipped with analysis programs, it is capable not only of producing but also verifying the specifications of a system.

It is a well-known fact that prose is an inadequate mode of expression to describe a logical process. Gane and Sarson therefore propose three alternative *tools for describing the logic of the process*: decision trees, decision tables, and structured English. As an example, Figure 7.9 illustrates the decision tree for the admission process.

TABLE 7.1
SSA METHOD: CONTENT OF A DATA DICTIONARY

Object	Content of Object Description
Data element	Name, aliases Related data elements Range of values Length of element External coding Other editing information
Data structure	Elements list Optional data elements Alternative data elements
Data flow	List of data structures Source Destination Volume of each structure Actual physical implementation
Data stores	Data elements and structures Incoming data flows Outgoing data flows
Processes	Name Short description Summary of logic
External entities	Name Incoming or outgoing data flows

Determining the contents of the data stores involves entering and validating the contents, as well as analyzing and structuring them through use of the relational model and the theory of normalization. This analysis is carried out at the logic level and not at the implementation level.

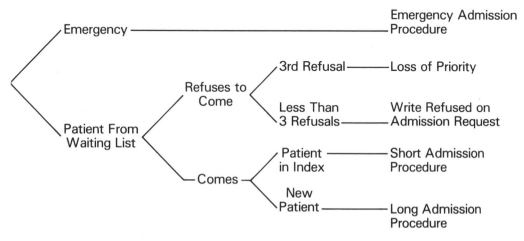

Fig. 7.9. SSA method: decision tree for admission process.

Discussion of the SSA Method

There is too great a tendency to associate this method with the production of the DFDs alone. When coupled with an automatic dictionary, it is a powerful and effective system analysis and specifications production method. It is simple, uses few symbols, and yields excellent results. However, it is remarkably well adapted to systems in which the complexity of the data flows is greater than that of the functions. Its use is especially effective for existing systems (manual or computerized) that are to be replaced or upgraded. It could prove to be less valuable for systems which do not exist at the time of analysis, even at the manual stage.

At the theoretical level, the method does not incorporate the application of some of the principles set out in Figure 7.5—in particular, modularization, abstraction, and bounded context. It is up to the analyst to include them. SSA also does not allow a clearcut division to be made between system analysis and design. The analyst will be tempted, either consciously or subconsciously, to consider the DFD to be a development model and the data stores to be a logic structure to be implemented.

The ISAC Method: Principles Enforcement

This data processing systems analysis and design method was developed at the University of Stockholm, Sweden, by a team led by M. Lundeberg (1979). The systems analysis portion of the method will be summarized here. It is particularly interesting in that it requires the application of nearly all of the systems analysis principles described in Figure 7.5.

There are three stages to the ISAC methodology: (a) *change analysis*, which corresponds more or less exactly to the opportunity study in Chapter 5; (b) *activity analysis*, which is a top-down breakdown of the activities and related data; and (c) *information analysis*, which is the study and breakdown of the data linked to all of the activities.

The user is deeply involved in the process, so much so that it is sometimes his task to draw the activity diagrams. The five tools, listed in the order in which they are used, are as follows:

1. A-graphs: activity diagrams
2. I-graphs: data relation diagrams
3. C-graphs: data components
4. process lists
5. process tables that describe each process

It is interesting to note that the description of a process comes at the end, a remarkable application of the abstraction principle (Canning, 1979).

The different tools will be presented by analyzing the ADT system. The first A-graph of the system can be seen in Figure 7.10. In this figure, a system, subsystem, or activity is described within a large square. All of the input data *and products* are drawn above in lozenges; all output data are drawn below in lozenges. The square illustrates the principle of bounded context.

Within the square (Figure 7.10), the breakdown into activities or subactivities is done using a point for a component activity. Only a title makes identification possible. Lines are drawn from the inputs toward the activities and from the activities toward the outputs. The data, products, and/or people moving from one activity to another are indicated by lozenges. The lines always identify a data flow from the top toward the bottom; if the complexity requires that an ascending line be drawn, that line must be indicated by an arrow. However, there can only be from four to six activities in a square (bounded rationality principle).

If necessary, the breakdown is then continued, activity by activity. Figure 7.11, for example, illustrates the breakdown of the admission activity. Note that the bed-reservation and bed-allocation data, which are interior for the ADT activity (Figure 7.10), are exterior in this breakdown.

When the breakdown has reached an adequate level, the information analysis stage follows. The necessary data are established for every activity, along with the transformations each will undergo and the sequence in which they will occur. Figure 7.12 shows the I-graph of the admission-form-filling activity in Figure 7.11. Once again, the starting point is a square, with the input data above and the data to be produced below. What takes place next is a stage-by-stage analysis of the information required to produce these data. Hence, for the example being considered, the diagnosis and referring physician are required. Since these data appear on the admission request, a change will be made to Figures 7.10 and 7.11; the admission request must be available during the admission activity.

The following stage involves breaking down each set of data by using C-graphs, which identify the subsets and then each datum. The activities list is obtained through a numbering system, with the processes description being done with the help of decision tables.

Discussion of the ISAC Method

The change analysis stage of the method contains what we call the opportunity study, including the cost/benefits analysis. More specifically, the system to be developed is represented by an A-graph. In some other methods, this emphasis on the preliminary analysis of problems and the search for overall solutions is either lacking or else it is part of the analysis stage.

Breaking down activities with the use of A-graphs imposes nearly all of the principles of analysis, including the simultaneous analysis of the activities and data. The information analysis stage, which is applied to the activities, links the

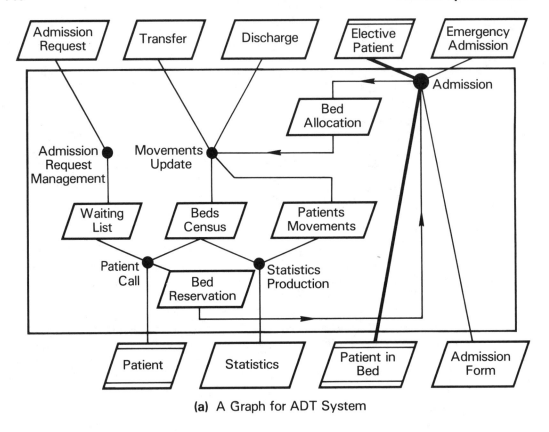

(a) A Graph for ADT System

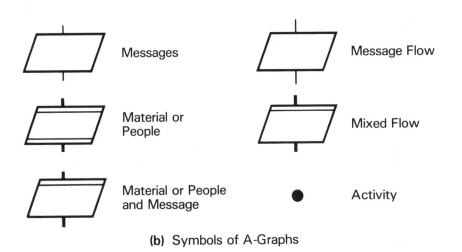

(b) Symbols of A-Graphs

Fig. 7.10. The ISAC method: A-graphs.

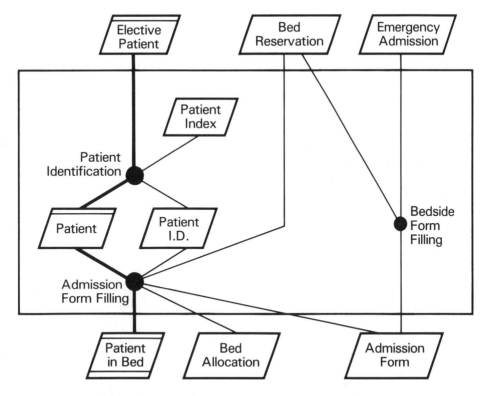

Fig. 7.11. ISAC method: A-graph for admission activity.

two components of any information system even more closely. Control, i.e. the ordering of the activities, is also imposed by the use of the tools.

There are, however, a few missing elements. First, the triggering event concept is missing (in contrast to SADT or SREM), although many management systems contain triggering events which are not data (end-of-the-day or end-of-the-month operations, for example). Second, although very much geared toward automation, the ISAC method does not appear to have been computerized.

THE SPECIFICATIONS DOCUMENT

Overview

Most system analysis methods have been designed by software engineering specialists. Their goal is to provide designers and developers with a formula which will enable them to work without any unwanted surprises: the baseline document.

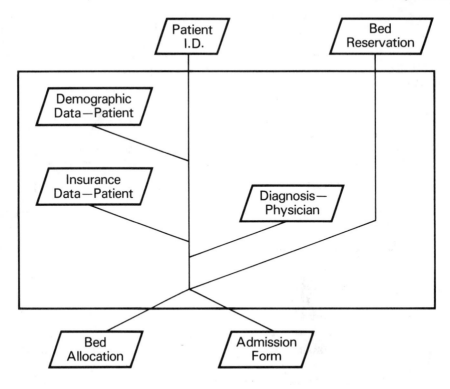

Fig. 7.12. ISAC method: I-graph for admission form completion.

However, for the project manager, the primary role of the specifications is to act as a contract with the user. The user must be able to read and understand the document submitted to him, or be willing to take the time to learn the method. Conventional users are certainly capable of interpreting narrative prose, lists and tables, provided the material is clearly presented (see Hershauer, 1978).

However, the precision and rigor obtained in the specifications must not be lost during the transformation of the results into a more conventionally presented document. Ideally, the method would be automated and capable of producing a final document which any user could read. Since most methods are not automated, it is up to the analyst to perform this task, and he will have to be careful to maintain the complete, consistent, and unambiguous quality of the original document specifications.

To illustrate, we will use the results of the analysis in order to establish the structure of the document. Figure 7.13 depicts the organization of a table of contents for a specifications document. Shown at the left is the breakdown tree of a system into subsystems, sub-subsystems, etc. At what point do we stop? The answer depends on the target, i.e., the user. A section will be devoted to a subsystem *if there is user interaction with that subsystem*. The functions of each

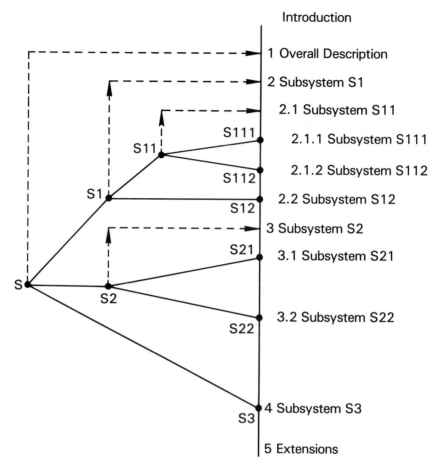

Introduction

1 Overall Description

2 Subsystem S1

2.1 Subsystem S11

2.1.1 Subsystem S111

2.1.2 Subsystem S112

2.2 Subsystem S12

3 Subsystem S2

3.1 Subsystem S21

3.2 Subsystem S22

4 Subsystem S3

5 Extensions

Fig. 7.13. Construction of a table of contents for a specifications document.

subsystem will be described, as well as its interface with the user. A final section of the document will mention the planned extensions in relation to the current specifications.

Following is the ADT system table of contents obtained from the analysis done with the ISAC method. Although admission was the only activity described in detail in the section on the ISAC method, the table of contents contains a detailed breakdown of all the subsystems mentioned in Figure 7.10.

EXAMPLE D: TABLE OF CONTENTS FOR ADT SYSTEM SPECIFICATIONS

1. Overall description
2. Admission request management

3. Patient movements update
   3.1 Admission
   3.2 Discharge
   3.3 Transfer
4. Patient admission
   4.1 Elective patient admission
       4.1.1 Patient identification
       4.1.2 Admission form filling
   4.2 Emergency admission
5. Patient call for admission
   5.1 Patient selection
   5.2 Patient call
6. Statistics production
   6.1 Daily statistics
   6.2 Monthly statistics
7. Extensions

The Interface Description

The interface of a system or subsystem is the portion which is in direct contact with the user. It consists of (a) the type of interface; (b) the users involved; (c) the procedures for interacting with the system; and (d) the input or output data.

There are four types of interface: input forms, printed reports, input screens, and output screens.

With regard to the users involved, it is necessary to specify explicitly who is interacting with the interface in question, i.e., the position and department involved.

Interaction procedures for the input forms should specify the circumstances under which they are to be completed, the data which are used to complete them, and their ultimate disposition. For reports, only the circumstances under which they are produced are required. The screens constitute a slightly more complex situation. It is not only necessary to specify the conditions under which the interaction takes place, but sometimes the sequence of commands necessary for data input or output as well.

Data must be described according to the nature and format of each one, in particular, the code list for coded data (e.g., sex, M or F). In addition to the individual format, is it necessary to define exactly the overall format of the report or screen? There is no clearcut answer to this controversial question; some users demand it, others do not. However, it is a decision which can be put off without any problems. Once the content and medium have been determined, the general presentation format can be defined at a later point without affecting what the user expects of the system, and without changing the design.

In what order must the different interfaces be presented? Every system (or activity) corresponds to a logical sequence of operations, and for the user, to a sequence of inputs and outputs. The order which will be adopted is the one determined by this sequence. The following examples contain the interface specifications for the admission-form-filling activity (see Example D).

EXAMPLE E: ADT SYSTEM SPECIFICATIONS FOR ADMISSION DATA ENTRY

4.1.2 Admission form filling
    4.1.2.1 Data entry

Type: display screen

Entered by: admission clerk, admissions office

Procedure: For elective patients, patient already has a patient ID. Enter "A-D form filling" on the terminal, then fill in the blanks.

Content: type of admission, *E* (elective)
last name (maximum 30 characters)
first name (maximum 15 characters)
initial (if none, push RETURN key)
sex (M or F)
date of birth (YYMMDD)
insurance company (maximum 30 characters; if none, push RETURN key)
policy number (maximum 15 characters; if none, push RETURN key)
physician (code from admission request form)
diagnosis (code from admission request form)

EXAMPLE F: ADT SYSTEM SPECIFICATIONS FOR ADMISSION FORM

4.1.2 Admission form filling
    4.1.2.2 Admission form

Type: report (form AH101, 4 copies)

Produced at: admission office

Procedure: Copy 1 to medical records; Copy 2 to accounting; Copy 3 to daily admissions, admission office; Copy 4 to ward (patient file).

Content: patient ID, admission number
date, type of admission
patient name: last, first, initial
patient sex
date of birth

address, telephone number
insurance (name of company, policy number)
physician (code)
diagnosis (code)

Note that Example F contains data not entered by the admissions employee in Example E, namely, the patient's ID number, admission number, and date of admission. These are, in effect, provided by the system. Any existing pre-printed form on which reports will be produced must be included with the description.

Functions and Control

Most analysis methods concentrate on the ordered listing of the activities and on their inputs and outputs. However, when it comes to specifying the details of an activity—the algorithm—the tools are less refined: decision tables, structured English, and so forth. Defining a system correctly (the activities, their input/output, and their sequencing) is of paramount importance. If an error occurs in this portion, the system will not perform as expected and repair will be costly. On the other hand, if an error occurs in a calculation formula, repair will be easy.

The method used to express the *details* of a function is therefore less important than it seems. If the user accepts decision tables and diagrams, so much the better; if not, prose will simply be used. What is important, however, is knowing what to talk about.

The description of a function includes the following elements: (a) a general description; (b) the conditions for activation of the function; and (c) the detailed description. The *general description*, in one or two sentences, defines the function in an unambiguous manner acceptable to the user. *Conditions for activation* involve the element of control: when or why does the function activate itself? There are two activation modes, one programmed in relation to time (e.g., daily or monthly execution), the other in relation to one of three triggering events:

1. End of execution of another function (e.g., the admission-form-filling function is executed when patient identification has ended).
2. Internal condition (e.g., the patient-call function is activated only if there are beds available).
3. Outside request by the user (e.g., the emergency-admission function is activated only when a patient is admitted from emergency).

The *detailed description* outlines in complete detail the operations to be performed, in the order of execution and with reference to the inputs and outputs involved.

Example G contains the detailed description of the patient-identification function.

EXAMPLE G: ADT SYSTEM PATIENT IDENTIFICATION FUNCTION

4.1.1 Patient identification
      4.1.1.1 Identification data
      4.1.1.2 Patient ID card
      4.1.1.3 Identification function

Generic description: To identify a patient without ambiguity and to associate him with an ID number; to produce a patient ID card for a new patient.

Conditions: Elective admission; patient present at the admissions office.

Detailed description:
(a) Patient has an ID card.
    Enter ID number; the system displays identification data which must be checked with the patient. If wrong patient, go to (b). In case of discrepancies, enter new data which replaces the existing data.
(b) Patient does not have an ID card.
    Enter identification data as required by the screen (see 4.1.1.1). An ID number is provided by the system and an ID card is printed (see 4.1.1.2).

Extensions

An information system is an open and evolving entity. Believing that the specifications define an eternal limit is an illusion. Not only will there be internal modifications to the system, but sooner or later other functions and other systems will be added. It is important to indicate these possible extensions in the specifications.

Remember, the document is directed at two individuals—the user and the developer. For the user, mentioning the extensions places the present system in a wider perspective. The system defined by the specifications is often a compromise between the requirements of the user and the means of the organization. Indicating possible extensions beyond the specifications allows the user to envision that all of his needs may eventually be met.

For example, the admission system in the hospital is concerned only with the input/output of the patient. Yet during the time he is hospitalized, other departments such as nursing care, radiology, and labs would like to have access to portions of his medical data. One extension of interest to them would be the "medical summary," containing a few key data such as name, bed, treating physician, diagnosis, and current treatment. All of the departments involved should have access to this summary.

The extensions are even more important for the developer. Specifying the extensions often determines important aspects of the design of the current system. In the admission system, for example, the medical summary extension tells the designer that some of the admission data, although not kept in the present system, will at some future time have to be contained in the database and be directly accessible. This is valuable information for the designer.

In contrast to the specifications of the current system, the extensions need only be described in very general terms. Identifying them, rather than giving a detailed description, is the important thing, for example:

Admission summary, directly accessible.

Appointment system for outpatient clinics.

Medical data file in coded form for research purposes.

THE APPROVAL PROCESS

Objectives

It is important to differentiate clearly between verifying and approving specifications. The objective of verification is to control specifications quality, i.e., to make certain that they are complete, consistent, unambiguous, and readable. If this is done by the user during analysis, step 2 described below has already occurred. Unfortunately, the process is often carried out by the analyst in an isolated environment, and must therefore be repeated by and with the user.

The negotiation stage has four objectives:

1. To verify that the system is indeed the one requested by the user. Figure 7.14 describes the all-too-frequent case in which the specifications meet all of the criteria perfectly but describe a system different from the one desired.
2. To have the user verify the quality of the specifications. If he takes the specifications seriously (since they represent his contract), it is certain that he will detect a certain number of ambiguities, errors, and inconsistencies. This stage is particularly important because the singular term "user" is misleading. All personnel who will interact with the system should study the specifications either in part or in whole.
3. To lead to the signing of the "contract" as formal recognition of the primary role of the document.

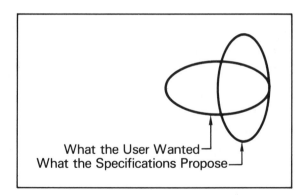

Fig. 7.14. User needs and analyst's specifications.

4. To produce a baseline document for the developers. More than simply a description of the product to be created, the baseline document will serve as the basis for the configuration-management activity, which involves controlling eventual changes that may be made to the system during development (see Chapter 13).

Process and Outcome

The three-step specifications approval process is illustrated in Figure 7.15. The *general review* consists in obtaining an agreement regarding the major functions of the system or, in other words, getting the chapter headings in the table of contents approved. This initial review should reduce the differences between user needs and analyst's specifications, as illustrated in Figure 7.14, to irregularities between two superimposed drawings.

Fig. 7.15. The specifications approval process.

During the *detailed review*, on the other hand, each element of the proposed system will be analyzed. Much of the process will take place outside the formal meetings. As a practical matter, it is impossible for all of the users to take part in these meetings, but they must nevertheless study the section of the specifications which concerns them. Any comments are relayed by spokespersons.

The *signature* corresponds to a formal approval of the version of the specifications on which there was overall agreement. Two elements are required: a revised version of the specifications, and managerial approval. The latter may be in the form of a letter which refers to the document and which designates it as the contract. In principle the document is signed by the user in charge of the entire system.

The approval committee is composed of:

the project manager,

the analyst in charge of the study,

the user manager, and

the user's colleagues most directly affected by the system.

The primary role of the project manager will be to guarantee the continuity of the process, i.e., that the meetings take place and that progress is made in the study of the document. The analyst, in addition to being the person who maintains the closest communication with the users, must also act as secretary; it will be his responsibility to record all of the modifications adopted during one meeting and to review them at the beginning of the next. Once the document has been reviewed, he will have to write the final version. A final meeting should then be held to make certain of the overall consensus and to settle the administrative aspects of the signing. Once the document has been signed, the project can officially begin.

SELECTED REFERENCES

Belford, P. C., Bond, A. F., Henderson, D. G., Sellers, L. S. 1976. Specifications: A key to effective software development. *Proc. 2nd Int. Conf. on Soft. Eng.*, Oct. 13–15, San Francisco, 71–79.
> This specifications verification method is geared toward defense systems. The approach consists of an I-P-O (input-process-output) type of breakdown into smaller elements. The method presents verification graphs and analysis and simulation tools.

Bell, T. E., Bixler, D. C., Dyer, M. E. 1977. An extendable approach to computer-aided software requirements engineering. *IEEE Trans. on Soft. Eng.*, SE-3,1, January, 49–60.
> This article describes the SREM method.

Bell, T. E., & Thayer, T. A. 1976. Software requirements: Are they really a problem? *Proc. 2nd Int. Conf. on Soft. Eng.*, Oct. 13–15, San Francisco, 61–68.
> Through the analysis of several experiments, the article gives an affirmative answer to the question posed in the title. In particular, interesting statistics are given regarding the number of errors per page in specifications and the distribution of errors according to type.

Black, W. W. 1976. The role of software engineering in successful computer applications. *Proc. 2nd Int. Conf. on Soft. Eng.*, Oct. 13–15, San Francisco, 201–205.

This is an excellent summary of the procedure which should be followed in the development of a computer application. Included is the concept that missed deadlines are not caused by errors but by oversights in the specifications.

Canning, R. G. 1977. Getting the requirements right. *EDP Analyzer*, 15,7 (July), 1–14.
This excellent article states clearly all of the problems linked to specifications: form, quality, process. It raises the problem of errors and proposes a certain number of guidelines to follow when dealing with the different problems.

Canning, R. G. 1979. The analysis of user needs. *EDP Analyzer*, 17,1, January, 1–13.
Following a brief look at the HIPO method, the article presents and discusses two systems analysis methods: SADT and ISAC. In a third section, the author proposes the characteristics that a good analysis method should have.

DeMarco, T. 1978. Structured analysis and system specification. New York: Yourdon, Inc.
This book presents a structured analysis method similar to that of Gane and Sarson. Included are data flow diagrams structured according to the levels concept, a data dictionary, and process specification done with the help of structured English and decision tables. The modeling concept and a construction procedure are presented in the two final sections.

Freeman, P. 1980. A perspective on requirements analysis techniques: Tutorial on software design techniques, 3rd ed., edited by P. Freeman & A. I. Wasserman. IEEE Computer Society.
In this overview of systems analysis problems, the author classifies the approaches into implicit design/explicit design, and into outside-in/inside-out. He then defines the principles of software development technology.

Gane C., & Sarson, T. 1979. *Structured systems analysis*. Englewood Cliffs, N.J.: Prentice-Hall.
The book presents the structured analysis method, and is essential reading for anyone interested in systems analysis.

Hershauer, J. C. 1978. What's wrong with system design methods? It's our assumptions. *Journal of Systems Management*, April 25–28.
This article, slightly iconoclastic toward computer specialists, is refreshing. It openly challenges a number of assertions which are the product of the conventional approaches to data processing: dominance of technology, superiority of machine over man, and ignorance on the part of the user, who must be trained. After putting forward his own principles, the author states that a system must be defined, above all, according to its outputs.

King, W. R., & Cleland, D. I. 1975. The design of management information systems: An information analysis approach. *Management Science*, 22, 3 (November), 286–297.
Designed specifically for MIS, this eight-stage method attempts to obtain a user consensus on a model for decision making. This extremely interesting approach is applicable to all cases involving specifications definition for systems which do not exist in manual or other form.

Lundeberg, M. 1979. An approach for involving the users in the specification of information systems. In *Formal models and practical tools for information systems design*, edited by M. J. Schneider. North Holland Pub. Co.
This article presents the ISAC method.

Mendes, K. M. 1980. Structured system analysis: A technique to define business requirements. *Sloan Management Review*, 21, 4, 51–63.
> Based on the works of Jackson and of Yourdon-Constantine, this method, perfected by Exxon, uses an approach based on the operation of the existing system. It uses five diagrams (global model, function matrix, data flow, activities breakdown, data structure) and contains a rigorous analysis and verification procedure.

Ross, D. T. 1977. Structured Analysis (SA): A language for communicating ideas. *IEEE Trans. on Soft Eng.*, SE-3,1, January, 16–34.
> This article presents the SADT method developed by the author and his colleagues—a milestone in systems analysis.

Stephens, S. A., & Tripp, L. L. 1978. Requirements expression and verification aid. *Proc. 3rd Int. Conf. on Soft. Eng.*, May 10–12, Atlanta, 101–108.
> This article presents the SAMM method.

Teichroew, D., & Hershey, E. A. 1977. PSL/PSA: A computer-aided technique for structured documentation and analysis of information processing systems. *IEEE Trans on Soft. Eng.*, SE-3, January, 41–48.
> This article presents the widely known PSL/PSA system.

Warnier, J. D. 1981. *Logical construction of systems*. New York: Van Nostrand Reinhold.
> This method begins with a study of the unit in which a system is to be implemented. The system is first of all defined by its outputs; the approach is hierarchical and structured. Using the output, systems specialists then define the system's database, followed by the operations and finishing with the input.

Wasserman, A. I. 1980. Information system design methodology. *Journal of the American Society for Information Science*, 31, 1, January, 5–24.
> This excellent article begins by mentioning the life cycle concept as the development framework of a system. It then presents the characteristics of information systems and the concepts on which all analysis methods must be based. The rest of the article is devoted to a study of various systems analysis and design methods. An excellent bibliography is appended.

Chapter 8
A FRAMEWORK FOR PRODUCT REALIZATION

INTRODUCTION

The objective of the project design stage is to define the elements making the manufacture of the product or service possible. The specifications clarify *what* is to be produced, and through planning and scheduling, it is determined *who* will perform each task, and *when*. It is now necessary to know *how* to perform each task, and which tools and operating procedures to use. The objectives of the activities covered in this chapter are:

- To choose the production tools.
- To choose (or define) the operating methods.
- To make certain that personnel are able to work together in a coordinated fashion.
- To ensure the visibility of the work being done.
- To ensure high work and product quality.
- To ensure the best possible productivity.

The 1970s witnessed the development of several techniques for improving quality control over the products delivered, improving productivity, and even facilitating cooperation among those individualists known as computer specialists. These techniques will, of course, vary from one project to another. A project is always a unique undertaking, and some may pose special difficulties. No operating procedure may be known, or choosing one may in itself pose a problem, whether the project is business-oriented or whether it is of the traditional research and development or software systems type.

EXAMPLE A: DEVELOPING A PORTFOLIO MANAGEMENT SYSTEM

The SMT.PM system described in Chapter 4 may be defined according to its inputs and outputs. *Inputs* include clients (entering a new client or modifying an existing one), stocks (entering new stocks), quotations, and transactions. *Outputs* include clients list (on demand), stocks list (on demand), transaction statement for each client (monthly), statement of stock holdings for each client (monthly), and estimate of the value of the stocks of each client (monthly).

Inputs are entered on a daily basis, and transactions must be completely processed immediately following entry. At a later stage, in fact, direct access to up-to-date client accounts should be possible.

SCIENTIFIC OR TECHNICAL DECISIONS

There is one stage in research and development projects with which we have not yet dealt: choosing the scientific or technical methods to be used in order to develop the product desired. The development of a compiler will serve as a good example.

A compiler is a program which translates a user program written in a high-level programming language such as COBOL into a set of equivalent machine-language instructions. One of the major problems encountered is selecting the process (called the algorithm) which will allow the compiler to recognize an instruction in high-level language and therefore proceed to translate it. This process is called syntactic analysis, and several such analysis methods are currently available. There are even systems known as compiler generators which can be fed the description of the source language as input (COBOL, for example), and which will produce a syntactic analyzer as output. How must the COBOL compiler development team proceed? Does it have a compiler generator at hand? If not, which algorithm should it select? Is there a specialist on the team who can solve these problems and define the implementation of the algorithm selected?

During the development of the Multics operating system, these same problems cropped up right from the outset (Corbato & Clingen, 1980):

- The computer for which the system was designed (General Electric GE635) was itself being developed, and some parts had to be redefined so that the Multics specifications could be implemented.
- All of the existing assemblers or compilers were then outdated and an assembler had to be developed so the system could be programmed.
- The language to be implemented was PL/I, and the complexity of the problems posed by the development of the compiler were such that this became a project in itself.

Because both of these examples are software development projects, we might be tempted to conclude that an information system development project in a business enterprise will not experience problems of this type. However, the following cases demonstrate that such is not the case:

- *Banking system:* In any handling of client files, the account number (or the patient number in hospital systems) must contain a check-code making it possible to detect, and if possible correct, an error in the file number. The selection or specification of such a code is usually a problem that is resolved before design begins.
- *Data encryption:* More and more, the problem of protecting data against unauthorized access is solved through the use of this technique, which employs an extremely sophisticated mathematic arsenal familiar only to specialists.
- *Routing:* Optimizing a merchandise supplier's distribution routes or a school bus operator's pickup routes involves the use of operational research techniques which require specialized knowledge and necessitate making choices or decisions before the information system itself is designed.

It would appear, perhaps, that some of these problems could be dealt with during the definition of the specifications, others during design. They are dealt with as a separate activity at the product design stage because, by nature (even in management systems), they are research and development problems with the following characteristics:

1. The outcome is unforeseeable; there is no guarantee that they will be solved, nor how.
2. Their solution requires intervention by scientific or technical specialists who are not normally available within the organization.
3. The time required to identify a problem and the cost of implementing its solution are totally unpredictable.

If the estimating, planning, and scheduling activities are to take these problems into account, they must be solved beforehand. If they remain unsolved, as pointed out by Corbato and Clingen, 1980, missed deadlines and cost overruns will result.

METHODS AND TOOLS FOR SYSTEM DEVELOPMENT

Producing an object or service requires work tools and methods. Once the production process reaches a certain dimension because of the size or complexity of the product, the people involved must organize it and establish an environment that promotes easier, more effective task performance. The following sections describe the principal tools, methods, and concepts which can be used to enhance overall productivity of the development team.

Production Tools

These are the fundamental tools of the system developer. If a mechanic is used as an analogy, the complexity of the instruments involved ranges from the screwdriver to machine tools.

Computer Selection

The project team rarely has the option of computer selection, since the system is usually developed on the organization's existing computer. If, however, it is part of the product to be delivered, it becomes not only a tool but also one of the project deliverables, and its selection must be one of the stages of development (see Chapter 14).

Programming Language

The long-lived arguing over high-level and assembler languages appears to be over. Assembler languages have lost the war in the field of application programs, and even in most software areas. There is really only one question to ask: which high-level language to choose.

The classic answer is the language best adapted to the particular application, such as COBOL for management applications and FORTRAN for scientific problems. However, the question is no longer that simple. First of all, there is sometimes more than one language for a given application (e.g., PL/I for management (or scientists), Pascal, BASIC . . .; the possibilities are almost endless). Second, the system life cycle concept (i.e., realizing that a system has a long life and must be maintained and updated) tips the scales in favor of "clean" languages which make possible the production of clear, readable, easily changeable programs. The life cycle concept also introduces a third consideration: the fact that the applications outlive their authors and exist within the organization for a longer time than the machines on which they were developed. The programming language must therefore be one which is widely used so that it is certain to be found on almost any computer and so that programmers familiar with it will be readily available.

In summary, the long-term considerations are gradually given priority over the short-term ones, leading us to select a language according to the following criteria:

1. Adaptation to the problem
2. Quality (resulting in "clean" programming)
3. Availability on the various computers currently on the market
4. Familiarity to the data processing community

Text-editors

These systems allow programmers to enter, correct, and manage their programs interactively. Nearly all of the operating systems currently available are equipped with such tools, but the punched-card work philosophy has left a deeper impression than believed. A text-editor is an essential tool of modern application development projects, and the project manager has every right to make its use by the programming team compulsory. Moreover, as noted in a later section, editors are often coupled with systems that make possible the development of program support libraries.

Report Generators

Management applications require the production of many reports, and next to documenting, writing a report program is undoubtedly the task programmers find most boring. There do exist a certain number of systems which are autonomous or are linked to a programming language (usually COBOL) and which make it possible to produce reports much more easily than in a standard programming language. Some, such as Easytrieve or Mark IV, make it possible to define at the same time, through the use of quite complex selection criteria, the data which will be examined in the report.

The advantage of such a system is seen in increased productivity and ease in modifying existing reports. There is, of course, a price to pay—the cost of the product (in money, memory space, and operating performance) and the fact that the personnel must be trained in its use, occasionally a lengthy process.

The use of such systems will therefore depend on their availability (they may already be in place and in use), and on the size of the application with regard to the number of reports required or anticipated at the present time.

Data Base Management Systems (DBMS)

In the traditional approach, all of the data of an application are contained in files. A file is typically made up of entries, all (or almost all) in the same format, that represent an element of the problem in question: for example, a clientele or bills file. The database concept consists in building a more complex data organization model that permits grouping various objects that have a logical relationship; for example, all of the bills sent to a client, or all clients having a certain stock in their portfolios. In the files approach, the application program must know how the file fits into the system, how the entry-making process is organized, and how each variable fits into the entry-making process.

In a database, the application program need only know the logical organization of the data (the scheme) and the names of the different variables. The results are as follows:

1. Elimination of redundancy. Reproducing the same datum in several files, creating the risk of inconsistency, is no longer necessary.
2. Better integrated data. Thanks to the scheme, elements of different origin can be grouped together.
3. Independent programs, i.e., programs which are not linked to database structure. This is controlled by the DBMS. For more about DBMS, see Date, 1977; Martin, 1977; and Ullman, 1980.

As with report generators, there is a price to pay for these advantages: the cost, size, and performance of the DBMS compared with those of conventional files; the necessity of specialists to put it into operation; and the need for an administrator to manage the sets of data thus established. Therefore, a DBMS will be used in a project if: (a) the size of the project (amount and complexity of data) warrants it; (b) the organization already utilizes a DBMS; or (c) the project, although modest in size, is to be followed by many others which will utilize data interrelated with those of the current project.

Debugging Tools

This author's experience with debugging tools has not been very rewarding. Although they did not enable him to find his errors, he did obtain large piles of paper or endless lists of meaningless messages on the screen. There was the strange feeling that the errors would have been found if only the trace indicators could have been set at the right location, i.e., at the location of the error! Fortunately for the author's ego, he is not the only one of this opinion. Mills (1980) remarked:

> A good number of debugging tools have been devised to take the place of good programming—they can't. Programs should be written correctly to begin with.

Debugging poorly designed and coded software is veterinary medicine for dinosaurs. The real solution is to get rid of the dinosaurs, even though they pose interesting questions indeed for veterinarians. The best debugging tool, given a properly specified and implemented programming language, is the human mind. (p. 101)

The problem of a clean language was noted earlier and in Chapter 12 we will see what is meant by a well-written program. In our opinion, no more need be said about debugging tools.

EXAMPLE B: CHOOSING THE PROGRAMMING TOOLS FOR THE SMT.PM SYSTEM

Bernstein, the SMT.PM project manager (see Chapter 4), analyzes the various requirements of the project and submits his conclusions to Andrew Crawford, his superior. These are summarized in Table 8.1.

Crawford smiles at the reason given for not using any debugging tools, but agrees. He also approves the decision not to acquire a DBMS, since he is worried about the project deadlines. He is happy to see that his project manager wishes to use a report generator, since he has been looking for an opportunity to introduce one into the department for a long time. He concludes that his project manager is becoming increasingly realistic and competent.

Work Methods

System and Program Design Methods

Whereas the objective of programming is to manufacture the data processing system, the design activity consists of defining its architecture. Generally, a dif-

TABLE 8.1
USE OF PRODUCTION TOOLS IN THE SMT.PM PROJECT

Tool	Use	Justification
Programming language	Cobol	Cobol, Fortran, and Best (manufacturer's language) are the only languages available on the company's computer.
Text editor	Yes	There is no other way to enter programs in the computer.
Report generator	Yes	Forecasted reports will undergo many changes during development. In addition, new reports will be requested during the system's life cycle.
DBMS	No	The system is small and simple. In addition, acquiring a DBMS and becoming familiar with it would take too much time.
Debugging aids	No	Bernstein and the programming staff hate them.

ferentiation is made between general and detailed design, the latter dealing more particularly with the architecture of the individual programs.

The major methods are based on certain principles of which the following are most common:

○ Top-down design. We have encountered this principle twice already, once during project analysis and once during system analysis. It will be used systematically during design, and involves beginning at the top and descending toward increasingly simpler elements.
○ System breakdown based on the architecture of the data. It must be remembered that a system transforms data and that the best guideline in this area is undoubtedly the structure of the data and the sequence in which they are transformed.
○ Definition of a single component (the program) model or of a (uniform) breakdown rule.

The difference in the various methods will be the breakdown rule and the choice of the single component model. Stevens, Myers, and Constantine's (1974) structured design technique, for example, is based on the following principles:

○ Breakdown by adopting input-process-output structures.
○ Breakdown according to the flow of transformations undergone by the data.
○ One module performs one function.

A variation of the technique as applied to the SMT.PM system will be presented in Chapter 12.

Nearly all design methods make use of these principles in one way or another (see also Jackson, 1975, and Warnier, 1981).

Data Modeling Methods

Data modeling consists in using a model to describe all of the data which will be inputted, outputted, or stored in the data processing system, as well as their interrelations. It differs from describing the files or drawing the schema of a database, where an implementation is being described—physical implementation if files are involved, and logical implementation in the case of DBMS. Modeling is concerned neither with files nor databases; it is interested only in the universe of information as perceived by the user. The use of Chen's (1976) entity relationship model as applied to the data of the SMT.PM system will be discussed in Chapter 12.

Programming Methods

At the present time there is only one really accepted programming method, structured programming. However, it goes hand in hand with the stepwise refinement method, which will be presented first. It involves applying to programming the top-down decomposition principle, which consists in subdividing the problem into increasingly simpler elements. Here again we are guided by the problem functions to be developed, without worrying about statement groupings or corresponding machine functions. Let us consider, for example, a program for estimating each stock in a portfolio: if its structure is defined by stepwise refinement, the diagram shown in Figure 8.1 will be obtained. This diagram is not a flow chart since it defines the hierarchy of the operations to be performed rather than the flow of control. One of the reasons why there is no need to worry about statement groupings is that languages well suited to structured programming offer a set of statements perfectly adapted to this type of breakdown.

Structured programming is based on the fact that any program can be written by using only the following three forms of control flow:

1. statement sequence
2. WHILE expression DO statement—which makes it possible to repeat the execution of one or several statements as long as the expression is true
3. IF expression THEN statement ELSE statement—which makes it possible to illustrate the two branches of an alternative. For example, in structured programming, the function "calculate stock value according to stock nature" (see Figure 8.1) will appear as:

```
if NATSTOCK = 'share' then
    STOCKVALUE : = STOCKQUOTATION * STOCKQTY
else STOCKVALUE : = (STOCKAMOUNT/1000) * BONDQUOTATION;
```

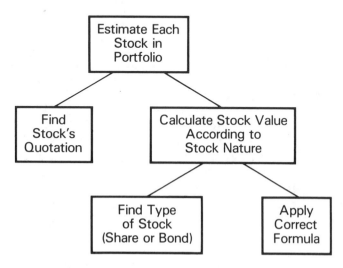

Fig. 8.1. Stepwise refinement: Estimate of stock in portfolio.

Of interest is that there are no GOTO statements, thereby making the sequence more readable. It must be remembered that a GOTO is, in fact, a machine instruction telling the computer where to go in the memory to find the next instruction; it is not a "problem" statement. A more complete look at structured programming can be found in Dijkstra (1976).

Structured design and data structuring methods are now well known; as for structured programming, it is a part of all data processing curricula. The project manager, who has the responsibility of choosing which work methods his team will use, must make his selection before the project begins. Here again, what is important is not really the method chosen, but rather the fact that a choice is indeed made. Having *any* method is better than having no method at all.

Development Process

Figure 8.2 depicts the conventional system development cycle, a purely sequential graph in which the activities follow in succession. Anyone who has participated in a system development project knows that this ideal representation does not correspond to what happens in real situations, where many iterations occur. But is this design-programming-testing sequence in fact ideal? It means that the system must be designed in its entirety before programming begins, and must be completely programmed before testing can be started. This is neither reasonable nor, more importantly, is it efficient since programming will result in corrections in design, and so on. Another more realistic and more efficient approach gradually made its way to the forefront.

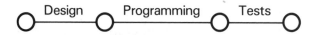

Fig. 8.2. Classical cycle of system development.

Top-down Implementation

Presented by McGowan (1980), top-down implementation can be quickly summarized: code a little, test a little. In other words, testing can begin before all of the programming has been completed. Given that design begins at the top, programming follows the same order. As soon as an element has been designed and programmed, it can be tested, with the elements not yet programmed (sometimes not even designed) being replaced by "stubs," i.e., simulators. The definition then becomes: design a little, code a little, test a little (see Figure 8.3).

The advantages of this type of organization are:

○ An increase in productivity. For program development, juxtaposing the three activities results in maximum performance.

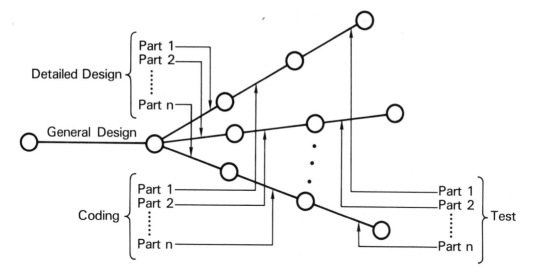

Fig. 8.3. Development network: Applying the design-code-test-a-little principle.

○ A shortening of deadlines as a result of the possibility of parallel development.
○ Visibility of results. Numerous significant milestones are easy to define.

Bootstrap Implementation

This approach was presented by Corbato and Clingen (1980) in regard to the Multics system, and can be summarized as "Use the system to develop the system." It is not too difficult to imagine its implementation in a software project in which, for example, the assembler will be developed first, thereby facilitating the production of the compiler. But what about its use in a management system? The answer is simple.

> Let A1, A2, . . . An be the elements to be developed as defined by the top-down implementation approach. Let A1, A2, . . . Ak be the elements necessary for developing and testing Ak + 1. A1, A2 . . . Ak will therefore have to be produced before (Ak + 1).

The advantages of this approach are immediately visible: elimination (reduction) of the need to create an artificial testing environment; increased productivity; increased visibility of results; and shorter deadlines.

The importance of linking good general design with top-down and bootstrap implementation in the organization of the system realization stage cannot be stressed enough. It results in efficient, faster, and more easily controlled development, and also serves as a valuable guide for the project manager during planning.

EXAMPLE C: BOOTSTRAP IMPLEMENTATION OF THE SMT.PM SYSTEM

Figure 8.4 depicts a possible SMT.PM system breakdown. In what order will the elements be produced? An initial proposal is indicated by the circled numbers. The production order closely respects the principles of top-down implementation. However, to test "update portfolios" (⑧), it is necessary either:

to create a shares test file, or

to test "update stocks" (⑨) first.

With the second solution there is no need to create a shares test file (it will be created by testing "update stocks"), thereby resulting in the numbering sequence shown in squares (Figure 8.4).

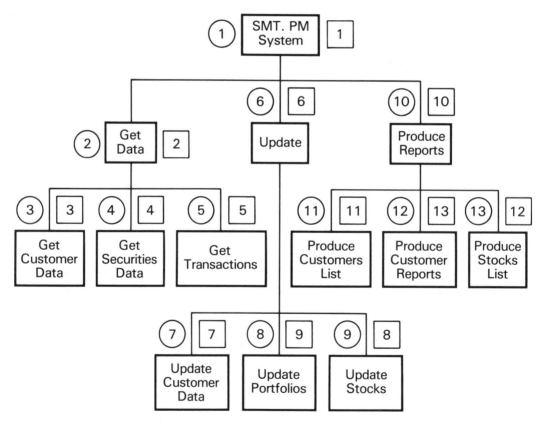

Fig. 8.4. Bootstrap implementation of SMT.PM system.

Support Tools

Having seen the tools and methods that can help increase productivity at the level of the individual team member, we will now examine collective production services which make it possible to create a productive work environment. These are the concepts of the program support library and the software warehouse.

Program Support Library (PSL)

Introduced by Baker (1972) as one element of the chief programmer team concept, this method consists in setting up a computerized library of all documents relating to the programs being developed (programs themselves, documents, test data and results, etc.) and in designating a "librarian" whose main responsibility will be the management of this library. It is known that the individual and overall management of programs and their different versions is a problem encountered in projects of any size which involve several people. Figure 8.5 illustrates an example of PSL.

The librarian is responsible for managing the baseline libraries, which contain those system elements considered to be completed. Each programmer has his own development library which he himself manages and keeps up to date by using a text-editor. When a programmer wishes to test a module or set of modules, he can use the object modules contained in the baseline library; the librarian, alone in having access to the baseline library, will make them available

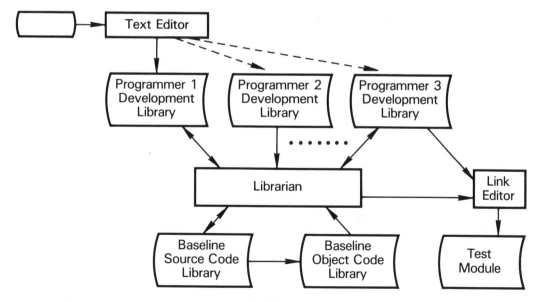

Fig. 8.5. Program support library (PSL).

to the programmer by combining them with those he wishes to test. When a module has finally been certified, the librarian will copy it from the programmer's library into the baseline library. Should a programmer be forced to modify a program already contained in the baseline library (e.g., change in specifications), it is once again the librarian who will retrieve and copy it into the programmer's library.

With a program support library, the programmer has a tool for managing his own production and the project manager has a tool for controlling and managing overall production. Some believe that the latter is of paramount value, whereas the former must be considered marginal. Our own experience does not reflect this line of thought. In order to expect the programmer to accept the apparent restrictions created by the introduction of an intermediary (the librarian), he must see some advantage in it. Indeed, the librarian can be viewed as a support person managing the programmer's personal affairs (certified programs) for him and providing him with the resources he needs to do his work (i.e., programs developed by his colleagues which he needs in order to develop and test his own).

The librarian plays a critical role. In large projects it is a full-time responsibility. In smaller projects a programmer or programmer-analyst may assume this function, but must remain clearly conscious of the fact that his primary role is that of librarian rather than programmer or programmer-analyst.

Software Warehouse

The concept of the software warehouse involves the much-debated notion of reusable software; in other words, the possibility of using existing programs to develop a new system. This usually ends in failure because the programs have been developed for another environment. Their adaptation usually takes as much effort as would be required to rewrite them, and results in poor quality products that are almost impossible to maintain.

However, the analogy with a parts warehouse is more appropriate, since the objects (programs) stored in the software warehouse are elements (like parts) which, right from the outset, have been designed to be used in the manufacture of many different systems. Following are a few examples of programs which many software warehouses would do well to have:

○ Error handling programs
○ An unending calendar making it possible to shift from a duration to a date and vice-versa
○ Screen formatting program, if not supplied by the system
○ Character string processing programs for software projects
○ Standard files access modules dealing with verification problems regarding their status and positioning

○ A report-heading production program dealing with pagination (in the absence of a report generator)

It is difficult to design a priori the contents of a software warehouse. The programs are therefore created during the course of an organization's successive projects. The process involves the following steps:

1. It is recognized that a function to be developed is general in nature and may reappear in other projects or project elements.
2. The module's specifications are defined based on its warehouse role. (The general aspect of the function is retained, while those aspects specific to the problem which led to the module's creation are discarded.)
3. The module is designed through application of the black box concept.
4. Production is assigned to a highly qualified programmer.

A software warehouse has many advantages. Productivity is increased at both the programming and design levels. The system is more easily understood, since it is comprised of many familiar elements. A greater standardization effort concerning systems production is gained. Finally, in the case of a changeover to a different system, applications are more easily converted. The list of examples cited earlier involve almost exclusively service tasks. This is quite understandable, since these are the tasks which are common to all systems. Experience has shown that they represent nearly 80% of the total programming effort, which implementing the functions of the problem always requires a lesser amount of work. The software warehouse therefore attacks the largest portion of the work involved in systems production. It also represents the unseen part of the iceberg; there is always a tendency to forget the "housekeeping" part of a set of programs.

According to this author's experience, the program support library and software warehouse were the two most effective and most easily implemented support tools of the 1970s. Many developments have since taken place and are gradually being integrated in the work environment of computer specialists. An excellent presentation of these developments can be found in an article by Newmann (1982). The integration of all of the development, support, and project management tools was envisaged by Bratman and Court (1975) under the very apt name "Software Factory." Any project manager planning to work in an organized, efficient, and up-to-date manner should read these two articles.

STANDARDS FOR SYSTEM DEVELOPMENT

Design Standards

Is it possible to impose standards on an activity as creative as design? Is creativity not hampered by the imposition of standards? Composers, painters, and poets must work within the guidelines of an extremely elaborate system of rules, conventions, and norms which are as numerous and varied as those which the field of data processing is attempting to impose on computer specialists in general and analysts in particular. Artistic revolutions do not represent the abandonment of standards, but rather, the replacement of one set of standards by another. Being at least as disciplined as artists, we therefore admit the need for design standards. Design standards have three objectives:

1. To facilitate communication among the persons involved.
2. To facilitate communication and compatibility among the objects involved (programs and data).
3. To increase productivity.

We will therefore have standards concerning the work methods and the resulting product.

The design activity involves data and programs. It can be summarized as follows:

○ data: modelization, implementation
○ programs: general architecture, detailed architecture

Who is going to define the design standards? It is the project manager's responsibility to see that standards exist. In large projects, one analyst will be in charge of design; it will be his responsibility to define the design standards and to make certain they are enforced. If the team involved is small (i.e., one designer), the project manager will ask the analyst to define the standards and will then have to see that they are respected. In exceptional cases, the project manager will be the analyst in question.

Programming Standards

Programming standards are only accepted by those programmers who have had to maintain programs written by others. The objectives of the standards are, in effect, to produce programs which are easier to read and understand. Every programmer understands very well what he himself has just written. However, if a long enough period of time elapses, even the parent has a difficult time understanding its offspring. This fact is what has kept programming standards alive and well. There are four types of programming standards: object name standards, presentation standards, structural conventions, and processing conventions.

Name Standards

All of the objects contained in a system will have to follow the rules concerning names: programs, variables, labels, files, reports, screens. The most conventional approach consists in using a two-step method to define names: a *prefix* characterizing the category of the object (program, file, report), and a *suffix*, usually a number, making it possible to differentiate among the different objects in a given category. For example, PR413 specifies a program, F103 a file. The procedure can be further refined by adopting a structured prefix.

This method is widely practiced and quite effective, but does have one disadvantage: the name PR413 is hardly instructive, and makes it difficult to determine the function of the program. This is perhaps only a minor inconvenience, since a program name is seldom used. On the other hand, applying such conventions to internal objects—variables and statement labels—would mean that a program could not even be read by its own author! The standardization rule, which is simply a principle of sound programming, will be:

The name of an object must reflect the function that object performs in relation to the problem, and not in relation to the program.

A device which counts the number of transactions read during input, for example, will not be called COUNTER, but perhaps NBER-TRANS.

Presentation Standards

PROGRAM HEADING.   Every program must begin by a comment of predefined content that specifies, for example, the object of the program, the author's name, date of writing, dates of any modifications, and so forth.

SPACES.   Like any printed text, a well-written program must be well spaced both vertically and horizontally. Although with some languages such as PASCAL it is possible to write several statements per line, there is no need to fill the page completely.

FRAMES.   The framing of certain parts of a program (procedure header, perform start) with the use of symbols (* or +) is of considerable help in understanding a program's structure.

INDENTATION.   This is the horizontal spacing of statements in order to show those sets of statements involved in executing the same tasks, as well as to illustrate the hierarchy of the tasks. Once again, there is an attempt to make the program as readable as possible by illustrating the "problem" functions rather than the statement flow which constitutes their implementation.

Structural Conventions

The structure of a program must reflect that of the problem to be solved. In other words, if the principles of structured programming are followed, the problem is solved. Of course, this depends on the availability of a programming language that can be used in the particular context—a language such as PASCAL, for example. If not, a certain number of conventions make it possible to "simulate" the structures contained in structured programming. An example is the IF-THEN-ELSE PASCAL statement (see p. 000), rewritten here in FORTRAN:

```
C       COMPUTATION OF THE VALUE OF THE STOCK IN PORTFOLIO
        IF (NATSTOCK.NE.SHARE) GO TO 100
C----------------STOCK IS A SHARE
        STOCK = STOCKQUOT*STOCKQTY
        GOTO 200
C----------------STOCK IS A BOND
100     STOCKVAL = (STOCKAMT/1000)*BONDQUOT
C-CONTINUATION OF THE PROGRAM
200     OTHER STATEMENTS
```

The sequences following the IF statement are in the same order as in the IF . . . THEN . . . ELSE statements in PASCAL.

Processing Conventions

Involved here are conventions regarding the way in which certain functions are performed. Yet, for conventions to be possible, these must be operations which are not unique and which are likely to be encountered in many programs. For example, if a buffer must be repeatedly used, one convention is to decide if it will be initialized by blanks or zeros before or following its use. This problem has been the cause of countless programming errors, and as far as possible, one convention should be adopted for all levels of the project.

Autocontrol is another useful convention. A program manipulates two types of objects: (a) those of the problem (i.e., the user's data), which may be inaccurate and whose values are monitored, and (b) objects (such as indexes and parameters) which are created by the programmer to *solve* the problem and which are assumed to be correct. (Unfortunately, this assertion holds true only if the program is exact, which is not the case during development.) The verification of objects, even internal ones, is a powerful testing tool. Moreover, it defines the conditions under which the program is supposed to perform well; these conditions are, in a manner of speaking, its technical specifications.

As in the case of design standards, the question arises as to who must define the programming standards and monitor their application. It is up to the head of the programming team to perform this task, and the responsibility of the project manager to see that he does it.

Documentation Standards

Documentation is the area in which there are the greatest number of standards; this is probably the reason that documentation is so boring to produce. Let us attempt, therefore, to adopt a more realistic point of view. If we had to define documentation, how would we proceed? We would successively specify

1. which documents are wanted,
2. their contents, and
3. their presentation.

Documentation standards are too often confused with presentation, yet this element is in fact the least important. The importance of the standards decreases as we pass from point 1 to point 3. (Remember the risk analysis method used in Chapter 4: What would happen in the absence of . . .?)

Documents

A list of the documents involved in the development stage is contained in Table 8.2. Note that programming seems to generate few documents; it must not be forgotten that the listing of a well designed program is self-documented. The mention of flowcharts is, in fact, a concession made to tradition. Note also that the interfaces with the outside world (reports, screens, etc.) are mentioned twice; they may be differentiated according to content.

TABLE 8.2
DOCUMENTS OF THE DEVELOPMENT PHASE

Activity	Documents
General design	Data description System architecture Reports Screens Other inputs
Detailed design	Files description or Data base scheme Program descriptions Report layouts Screen layouts Other inputs layouts
Programming	Program listings Flowcharts
Tests	Test data Test results

Contents

The contents can be obtained quite easily if the principle of stepwise refinement is used to define them. From the general design stage through to programming, the problem is examined in increasingly greater detail, and the corresponding documents reflect this trend.

The general design documents will only contain general data, namely:

o Data description: description of the data, their nature, and their interrelations (through use of a model).
o System architecture: general organization of the system into subsystems and modules; a brief description of the function performed and the inputs are given for each one.
o Screens, reports, other inputs: a simple list.

The detailed design documents, those which make programming possible, will contain all information required for this activity. This information includes:

o File descriptions: name, organization, format and contents of the records (including name, type, position, length, and explanation for each field); if a DBMS is used, the scheme produced by the system takes the place of the document.
o Programs: name, detailed description of the function to be developed, accessed files, inputs (screens or other), outputs (reports or screens).
o Screens, reports, other input layouts: a detailed description of the contents and exact format of each of the system's interfaces with the outside world.

In principle, the program documentation is summarized in the listing, provided the listing is well commented and organized. In particular, the data given in the detailed design should be restated in a heading.

The test documentation must contain (a) a full description of the test data; and (b) test results in the form of listings of the test runs, reporting the results achieved and the follow-up performed.

Presentation

Although presentation was cited as perhaps the least important aspect of documentation standards, this is not to say that it should be completely ignored. Fortunately, a large portion of the presentation work is already done.

Some documents correspond to an activity performed with a given method (data modelization, design, programming), and in this case, the method dictates a presentation format of the results which is in itself a readymade standard (structured design, entity relationship model, etc.). Some documents, such as screens and report layouts, are standards of the data processing profession. Imagining formats for the few remaining documents does not pose much of a problem. Figure 8.6 gives one example of a file description form.

FILE DESCRIPTION				DATE:
PROJECT: SMT.PM		NAME: F-CUST		
ORGANIZATION: Indented sequential RECORD-TYPE: fixed RECORD-LENGTH: 128		KEY:START: 1 LENGTH: 8		
ITEM	START	LENGTH	FORMAT	DESCRIPTION
CUST-NUMBER	1	8	9(8)	custom number
CUST-NAME	9	20	X(20)	customer name
CUST-ADDR1	29	30	X(30)	1st line of address
CUST-ADDR2	59	30	X(30)	2nd line of address
CUST-TEL	89	12	9(12)	area code—number
FILLER	101	28	X(28)	filler
TOTAL		128		

Fig. 8.6. File description.

HARDWARE SELECTION: A CONCEPTUAL APPROACH

From Short-term to Long-term Performance

The traditional concern when choosing a computer system is to make sure the equipment can handle the workload. What does the term "workload" mean? Traditionally speaking, it refers to the processing power of the CPU; indeed, for several decades this was considered the computer's major characteristic as well as its bottleneck. However, much has happened since the mid-1970s and this is no longer the case.

CPU power dramatically increased while cost decreased. Moreover, in the field of business in particular, applications are only slightly CPU-bound. (An application is CPU-bound if it consists essentially of CPU operations.) In addition, computers gradually evolved from simple calculators into archives (storage and information retrieval) and telecommunications centers (interactive and remote use).

As a result, the parameters by which computer performance was defined evolved, and other elements were considered along with CPU power; or sometimes even replaced it. These elements included storage and rapid information retrieval capabilities, and communication capabilities with the outside world.

What we have just examined is the evolution of computer performance and, more specifically, the development of instant performance. Yet, computers were the object of the same phenomenon that occurred in programming: concern with instant performance gave way to interest in long-term performance. It must not be forgotten that the computer represents the largest capital investment in data processing and, as with all investments, there is a desire that it be profitable for as long a time as possible.

Three of the parameters for determining the long-term performance of a computer are as follows:

1. *"Upgradability"* denotes the possibility of enhancing the capabilities of some components when needs increase in order to avoid the necessity of changing the entire system too quickly. When the original computer can "grow" no larger, the term refers to the possibility of obtaining a more powerful system from the same line of hardware.

2. *Compatibility* refers to the fact that the computer must not be a "rare specimen" because: (a) it must be capable of handling products (hardware or software) coming from other sources; (b) it must constitute a standard work environment in order to make data or product exchanges with other centers possible; and (c) the organization must be able to find personnel who either know the machine or can easily learn to use it.

3. *Maintenance* requires that the design and technology of the computer are recent enough so that it will not be obsolete before the end of its profitability cycle. Technical support (hardware or software) must be readily available, of good quality, and projected to be still on the market three or four years down the line.

This new way of viewing computer performance is going to influence the choice of the system, the form of the selection process, and the assessment parameters.

Basic Concepts

Timmereck (1973) believes that hardware selection can be undertaken in two ways: the objective and subjective approaches. We will add a third, which is the pragmatic approach.

The *objective approach* is based on the principle that the computers under consideration can be evaluated and compared in a rational and even quantitative manner. It presupposes that a set of requirements has been established beforehand.

The *pragmatic approach* differs from the objective approach in that it is not based on an a priori study of requirements but rather, given the various proposals, seeks to determine the most advantageous.

The *subjective approach* maintains that the final choice of a computer is often based on totally unsupported (if not to say unprofessional) factors, and that what we call objectivity is sometimes no more than a preference dressed up with numbers in order to give it an air of respectability. As a result, the involved procedure required by the objective and pragmatic approaches is seen as a waste of time and money. One need only quickly examine the proposals or put the entire matter in the hands of the organization's usual or preferred supplier.

Table 8.3 compares the advantages and disadvantages of the three approaches. The experience of this author leads to his unequivocal preference for the objective approach. Arguments in its favor can be found in Timmereck (1973). The only serious disadvantage of the objective approach is that it can be biased. Any selection methodology utilizing this approach will have to make sure all risks of bias or veiled subjectivity are eliminated. While it is impossible to guarantee total objectivity, we will see in Chapter 14 that nearly every risk can be dealt with.

Technical versus Functional Specifications

For any particular problem, the variety of possible solutions is such that comparing the technical capabilities of two computer systems becomes meaningless. For example, how can one machine equipped with real memory be compared to another computer using virtual memory? How is it possible to compare a system incorporating a single CPU with another containing several specialized processors? As Timmereck (1973) says: "Machines should be compared according to what they do, not what they are" (p. 201).

TABLE 8.3
THE THREE APPROACHES TO COMPUTER SYSTEM SELECTION

Approach	Advantages	Disadvantages
Objective	Best possible choice related to requirements	Expensive Time-consuming Objectivity debatable
Subjective	Fast Inexpensive	Result may be completely outside requirements
Pragmatic	Realistic Objective	Some requirements may be missed

What we want the machine to do for us constitutes the functional speci-fications. The key word here is *functional*, as compared to technical. In an in-formation system, the specifications are a description of what the system will do for the user. And who are the users of a computer? They are the application programmers, the operators, and the endline users (through interaction). The requirements must therefore be determined according to their needs. For ex-ample, disk space will be defined by the quantity of information to be stored and not by the nominal capacity of the disk. All data processing specialists know that 1,000 bytes of physical space can only store a smaller number of characters of information. As a second example, there is no reason to say we require a 512 kilobyte memory; from a functional standpoint, it would be better to say that the system must be able to run 8 terminals simultaneously, each of which is communicating with a program of roughly 60 kilobytes.

Minimal Set of Requirements

The objective approach is based on this concept. Termed the "wanted items category" by Joslin (1974) and the "minimal set of requirements" by Lustman et al. (1978), it consists in specifying in advance the elements considered indis-pensable in an acceptable system. This makes it possible to avoid the risk (pointed out in Table 8.3 with respect to the subjective or pragmatic approaches) of selecting a system which does not meet basic needs.

Invitation-to-tender Procedure

Hardware selection is no different from design or analysis with respect to the truism that any method is better than none at all. Yet, there is one administrative procedure related to the purchasing of goods or services which is compulsory in all public and parapublic institutions: the invitation to tender. It was estab-lished to eliminate any problems relating to subjectivity or the influence of a given supplier, and is therefore particularly well suited to hardware acquisition. Moreover, the specifications manual assures that all requirements have been defined beforehand. The procedure will therefore be used as a model even though it is not imposed by administrative regulations. A detailed definition will be given in Chapter 14.

The Hardware Selection Life Cycle

Whether or not there is a formal invitation-to-tender procedure, the selection cycle of the objective approach remains the same. It is depicted in Figure 8.7 and is comprised of four stages.

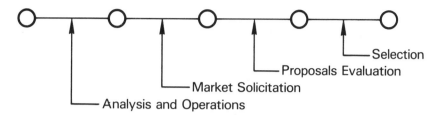

Fig. 8.7. The hardware selection life cycle.

Analysis and Specifications

This stage is identical in its intent and objectives to the system analysis stage described in Chapter 7. In principle, the result is a "specifications manual" containing, among others, functional specifications.

Market Solicitation

The goal of this study is to obtain proposals from potential suppliers. It is during this stage that the procedure will change depending on whether or not a formal invitation to tender has been issued. If tenders have been called for, extremely strict procedural constraints will have been imposed on the suppliers, but some of these may not be needed to guarantee a successful outcome of the procedure within a private business enterprise.

Proposal Evaluation

Termed *validation* by Joslin (1974), this stage consists of two closely related activities:

1. Verifying the truth and exactitude of the contents of the proposals. Because it is a question of functional specifications, this is not an easy task, and it requires extensive knowledge of the computers and operating systems involved.
2. Producing one or more quantitative assessments of each proposal.

Selection

The objective approach has been criticized for attempting to quantify the unmeasurable and compare the uncomparable. It is because of the latter problem that it is preferable to obtain several assessments (or rather, to obtain independent assessments of factors of a dissimilar nature). As for the attempt to quantify the unmeasurable, it is in itself the justification of the selection stage. The assessment, in effect, quantified everything possible, but the elements were not all grouped together and assigned a specific value. Selection will therefore consist of two activities:

1. Choosing the factors (based on comparative values) which are to be evaluated. (Each individual factor has been assigned a specific value.)
2. If the need arises, leave room for subjective factors which will complement the objective assessment data.

Methods and Tools

Just as for systems analysis, hardware selection will require a methodology, techniques, and tools. The process is based on the objective approach, and in this context the methodology to be utilized is the invitation to tender. Given this framework, the principal methods and tools are defined below.

Methods

In order to maintain consistency of point of view in the assessment, it is important that the same portion of the system be evaluated by the same team or person for each of the proposals. Another approach consists of distributing the different systems among the various teams, which of course opens the door to every bias possible, either conscious or subconscious. Moreover, even if complete objectivity on the part of the teams can be assumed, there is a risk that the assessments will not be conducted with the same rigor (or open-mindedness) from one team to another.

The most widely used assessment method is the *scoring method*, a variation of which was presented by Lustman and colleagues (1978). Using a previously established marking scale, a mark is assigned to each of the elements in the system to be evaluated. A system of weights makes it possible to assign greater or lesser values according to the requirements being considered. The major criticism of this method is that the calculations require such a large amount of work that one loses sight of the basic objectives of the procedure. It will be seen in Chapter 14 that this criticism is valid only if the assessment is limited to the technical aspects of the proposals.

One method which is enjoying considerable success was developed by Joslin (1977). Known as the *requirements cost evaluation technique*, it reduces everything to a financial assessment. First of all, each system which does not meet the mandatory requirements is eliminated, regardless of price. The Lustman (1978) variation of the scoring technique works exactly the same way (see Chapter 14). Second, added to the amount of each proposal is a financial estimate of each desirable feature which is *not* supplied. This amount is calculated a priori by the evaluation team. (The idea is the same as that discussed in Chapter 4, on documentation: How much would it cost to purchase the element in question somewhere else?) The proposal with the lowest total is the one chosen. Paradoxically, this technique seems to be the object of the same criticism made of the scoring method, i.e., the length and complexity of the procedure.

Insofar as both techniques examine more than just the purely technical aspects, we believe they are equivalent.

Tools

The two presented here are of fundamental importance to the procedure. The *specifications manual* is similar to the specifications document described in Chapter 7. It must specify which data are to be included in the proposal and contain the functional specifications. Present-day specifications manuals go so far as to contain a series of answer sheets on which the bidder must make his proposal. Examples of such forms are given in Chapter 14. Whether the scoring technique or the requirements cost evaluation technique is used, *evaluation forms* on which the results of the different evaluations can be recorded must be designated beforehand.

SELECTED REFERENCES

Baker, F. T. 1972. Chief programmer team management of production programming. *IBM Systems Journal*, 11, 1, 66–73.
> In this well-known article, the author presents a large data processing project as it was carried through to completion at the New York Times. The principal concepts presented are: structured programming; the makeup of the chief programmer team, centered around a chief and a back-up programmer; the role of the librarian, who has the responsibility of managing all project documentation; and the program support library, which enables the librarian to perform his duties in cooperation with the programmers. The article is a milestone in data processing project management.

Bratman, H., & Court, T. 1975. The software factory. *Computer*, 8, 5, May, 28–37.
> The starting point of the article is a series of problems which afflict development projects. Despite the creation of many tools (structured programming, top-down analysis, program support library, etc.), the entire process is still not effective since the tools are neither integrated nor available on a regular basis. The authors therefore introduce the software factory concept, composed of a database, support library, test case generator, documentation tool, and finally a project management module, which is the heart of the system and which obtains its data from a development database.

Chen, P. P. 1976. The entity-relationship model—Towards a unified view of data. *ACM Trans. on Database Syst.* 1, 1, March, 9–35.
> The power of this model in the field of data analysis has gradually made it into a systems analysis tool which can be utilized for all systems.

Corbato, F. J., & Clingen, C. J. 1980. A managerial view of the Multics system development. In *Research directions in software technology*, edited by P. Wegner. The MIT Press, 138–158, Cambridge, Mass.
> This article is interesting for two reasons. First of all, it examines some problems which are specific to large projects, such as personnel turnover, training, and participant communication. Second, since there is quite an extensive research and development side to the project, the authors look at the influence that highly specialized scientific or technical problems could have on project management.

Joslin, E. O. 1974. *Analysis, design and selection of computer systems.* Arlington, Va.: College Readings.
> This book reviews all of the problems related to hardware selection. The first section deals with requirements analysis, while the second examines the actual selection process. Chapter 18 contains an exposé of the "requirements cost evaluation" technique.

Lustman, F., Lanthier, P., Charbonneau, D., DaLadurantaye, P., & Gagnon, P. 1978. A systematic approach to choosing a computer. *Canadian Data Systems*, April, 24–32.
> This article presents a case in which the scoring method for computer evaluation is used. It also introduces the minimal set of requirements concept and an assessment procedure resulting in several different evaluations for each system.

McGowan, C. L. 1980. Software management. In *Research directions in software technology*, edited by P. Wegner. The MIT Press, 207–253.
> This article examines the current state of affairs regarding systems development problems. It looks at the principal technical milestones such as structured programming, systems analysis, and design methods. It also presents a number of organizational instruments such as top-down implementation, the chief programmer team concept, and the program support library.

Mills, H. D. 1980. Software development. In *Research directions in software technology*, edited by P. Wegner. The MIT Press, 87–105.
> The author reviews 25 years of data processing project evolution and highlights the exceptionally high cost of maintenance. Moving on next to the various technical and methodological instruments, he presents the software design and development methodologies and emphasizes the fact that nearly 80% of code is devoted to "housekeeping."

Newmann, P. S. 1982. Towards an integrated development environment. *IBM Systems Journal.* 21, 1, 81–107.
> This article examines the current state of systems development support tools. It reviews the following topics in particular: documentation systems; interconnection languages making it possible to integrate elements of diverse origin; extensions to high level languages; and very high level languages which enable programmers to describe an application almost at the specifications level.

Stevens, W. P., Myers, G. J., & Constantine, L. L. 1974. Structured design. *IBM Systems Journal*, 13, 2, 114–139.

> This article is one of the first presentations of the structured design method. It also contains an outstanding analysis of the characteristics which make up a good program.

Timmereck, E. E. 1973. Computer selection methodology. *ACM Computer Surveys*, 5,4 (December), 199–222.

> The article reviews the various problems related to computer selection, and presents the different approaches (objective and subjective), the futility of comparing technical aspects, and the problem of divergent buyer and seller objectives. The author then presents the different phases of the selection process and the various evaluation methods along with their advantages and disadvantages. Finally, he examines the different acquisition alternatives.

Chapter 9
ESTIMATION OF REQUIRED RESOURCES

The institute is a 150-bed hospital engaged in heart research and affiliated with the university. Its data processing department deals with medical and administrative applications and with clinical research projects. Until 1977 the department had been linked by terminals to the university's computer, a Control Data 6600. Because of rising costs, however, the Institute decides to purchase its own computer, scheduled to be installed in September 1977. The applications will be converted in two stages, the first being the object of this example. Each of the programs to be converted is described in Table 9.1.

All of the programs were developed by the data processing department in FORTRAN. At the technical level, three problems must be solved:

1. File format differences between the two computer systems.
2. Differences in the machine-word formats. (The source computer uses words composed of ten 6-bit characters, while the target machine uses words composed of four 8-bit characters.)
3. Differences between the two FORTRANs.

TABLE 9.1
SYSTEMS TO CONVERT AT THE INSTITUTE OF CARDIOLOGY

System Number	System Description	Number of Programs or Routines	Number of Lines of Code
1	UTILITIES (software warehouse)	20	790
2	MEDIC: database management system	41	5680
3	MUPDATE: update of patient data files	24	2280
4	INQUIRY: inquiry system on patient data files	23	2960
5	DISC: application: discharge and hospital statistics	8	1300
6	DIET: application: dietary habits	15	1500
7	PMC: application: pacemakers clinic	40	6900
8	HEMO: application: hemodynamics reports	50	5000
	TOTAL	221	26410

Conversion work will begin in March 1977, with each application (systems 5 to 8) being put into operation as conversion is completed.

Available personnel consists of four programmer-analysts who have extensive knowledge of the applications, either because they are the authors or because they are involved at the maintenance level. Due to the amount of work required for the maintenance of the existing systems, this personnel is available only 70% of the time. Nonetheless, the supplier offers the Institute five programmer-analyst man-months on a contractual basis and access to a computer. In February 1977, the manager of data processing assigns the conversion project to Diana Charters and asks her to submit estimates to him at the end of the month.

OVERVIEW

Definition and Goals

In Figure 6.3 (see Chapter 6), the estimation activity is situated between the established specifications and technical framework on one side and the planning, scheduling, and budgeting activities on the other. If the network depicted in Figure 6.3 is correct, the results of the preceding activities will necessarily serve as input to the estimation step, which will, in turn, feed the subsequent activities. What, therefore, is required for planning, scheduling, and budgeting?

1. A detailed list of the activities.

2. A detailed list of the types of resources needed to complete the activities successfully.

3. For each type of resource, the quantity required to complete the activities successfully.

The tools we have to work with include *specifications*, which enable us to give a detailed description of the product to be delivered, and *operating procedures*, which make it possible to define the activities necessary for the production of each product component. We will therefore be able to supply the lists that are required. To estimate quantity, on the other hand, we need something else: the formula described in Chapter 3, which here takes the following form:

$$q_r = f_r (p,m)$$

in which q_r is the amount of resource (r) needed to produce the product or component (p) by using the tool or method (m). Obtaining or approximating formula f will be the most delicate part of the estimation activity, which can be summarized by the black box depicted in Figure 9.1.

The estimating process is that which makes it possible to establish the qualitative and quantitative description of all of the resources needed to develop the product.

The qualitative description of a resource is its precise definition. The quantitative description will be provided both on an overall scale (macroestimates) and on a detailed activities-breakdown scale (microestimates). This description at the detailed breakdown level is required in order to make planning possible.

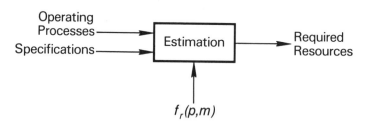

Fig. 9.1. Inputs and outputs of the estimating process.

The Estimation Process

The process is usually composed of the four activities shown in Figure 9.2. While activities (1) and (2) are quite easily completed once the specifications and op-

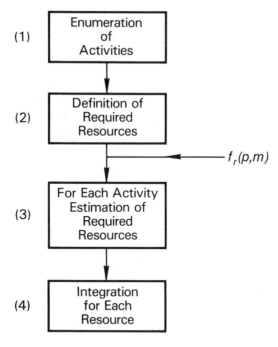

Fig. 9.2. Overall description of the estimating process.

erating methods have been established, such is not the case for the subsequent ones.

Indeed, with respect to a program, what does p represent in the formula $q_r = f_r(p,m)$? If p represents the program specifications, a formula such as this does not currently exist except in isolated cases and at a relatively elementary level. It is therefore necessary to attempt to break the program down into a set of smaller programs. If, on the other hand, p stands for the finished product (i.e. a set of specific statements), it is p itself which is unknown and which must then be estimated by using the specifications as a starting point. It is first necessary in each case to establish an approximate value for p before implementing our formula.

Given the current state of the art, the function $f_r(p,m)$ itself is relatively imprecise. It is therefore no surprise that after two approximations the result will have to be readjusted to a large extent. This brings us to a more complex process, outlined in Figure 9.3 and discussed in subsequent sections of this chapter. In order to be able to make the required adjustments, we will first examine the factors affecting productivity and estimates; later, we will deal with the production of revised estimates. Why "revised" instead of "final" estimates? Here, as in many other data processing and project management activities, nothing is ever final; everything must be redone, often more than once.

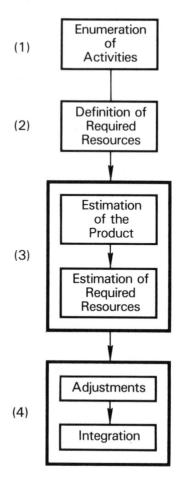

Fig. 9.3. Detailed estimating process.

Estimating Is an Iterative Activity

Given the approximate nature of the estimates defined above, it is possible that the real situation will differ from the predictions despite the adjustments made. Unfortunately, the progress and outcome of a data processing project is not as rigorous as assembly line production. The estimates will therefore have to be revised as the project progresses. There are three types of revisions.

Revisions Resulting from a Better Knowledge of the Product

It was seen that the first estimate dealt with the product itself. The first stage of the project, no matter what the product, consists in defining its components.

In the case of systems development, it means general and then detailed design. In the case of conversion, it involves specifying program by program the elements to be converted. This better understanding of the final product makes it possible to verify or recalculate any estimates. The resource estimation and adjustment formulas are applied in their original form to the new product estimates. This type of revision may take place one or several times, depending on the size of the project and the number of design milestones.

Revisions Resulting from a Better Knowledge of Productivity

Here, development is actually underway, and this type of revision is one of the control activities. All of the elements in the estimating process can therefore be revised: the estimates of the products yet to be developed, based on those already produced; the productivity estimates, based on the productivity so far registered; and the adjustments made, based on current progress. These revisions will be described in greater detail in Chapter 13.

Revisions Resulting from Unforeseen Events

Examples of unforeseen events that might disrupt the project or affect the estimates include:

○ A change in the specifications, resulting in a reevaluation of the product estimate.
○ The replacement of an experienced programmer by a less productive one.
○ Discovery of an error resulting in the need for additional work.

There is no fixed rule regarding what portion of the estimate must be revised. In each case, the effects of the incident must be analyzed and the process reworked beginning with the earliest point at which the incident had an effect on the project.

DRAWING UP RAW ESTIMATES

Inventory

Using the WBS method (see Chapter 3), the process consists in decomposing the production stage and determining the deliverables, the activities, the resources, and the duration for each component. For example, let us apply this breakdown to the Institute's project.

EXAMPLE B: CONVERSION PROJECT WBS

Diana Charters believes the method to be somewhat childish and quickly draws the WBS contained in Figure 9.4a. She proudly shows it to her supervisor, who is sure to be pleased—she has even thought of the operations documentation.

The head of data processing gives his approval. Two days later, he receives a call from Dr. Dawson, chief physician at the Institute: "When will I be able to consult my file on 'our computer'?" He then realizes that the conversion of the existing files is not part of the WBS! Moreover, these files contain enough information for 40 million bytes. He calls Charters and informs her of the omission. It was serious, since all of the files are of a single format (MEDIC), except those of the HEMO application, which was designed before the DBMS and never converted. Not overly upset (after all, the boss had forgotten as well), she analyzes everything and returns with the WBS depicted in Figure 9.4b. This example serves to illustrate the crucial problem of any breakdown: not forgetting anything.

Once the WBS has been established, the deliverables and resources required for each activity can be defined. Clear definitions are critical. For example, the activity which involves producing a program is usually called programming, but what does that mean?

Does it involve only the coding activity?

Is the detailed design included?

Are the individual tests included?

Is the documentation included?

It is obvious that the programming estimates will vary, depending on whether or not some or all of these tasks are included.

Let us consider the programmer-analyst resource in the same manner. Is the individual an applications specialist or a systems specialist? Here again the definition will have to be as precise as possible, as much for estimation requirements as for planning needs.

EXAMPLE C: RESOURCES NECESSARY FOR PROGRAMS CONVERSION

Converting the programs will first of all require programmer-analysts who are familiar with FORTRAN. Closer examination of the systems to be converted leads Charters to the following assessment:

System 1 (UTILITIES): systems programmer-analysts

System 2 (MEDIC): analysts familiar with databases

System 3 (MUPDATE): experienced programmer-analyst

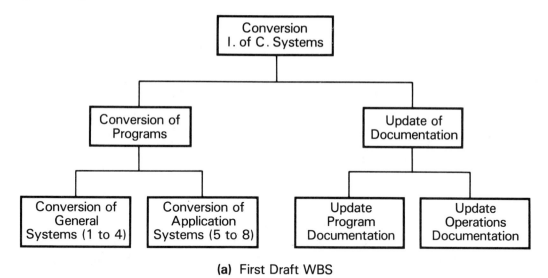

(a) First Draft WBS

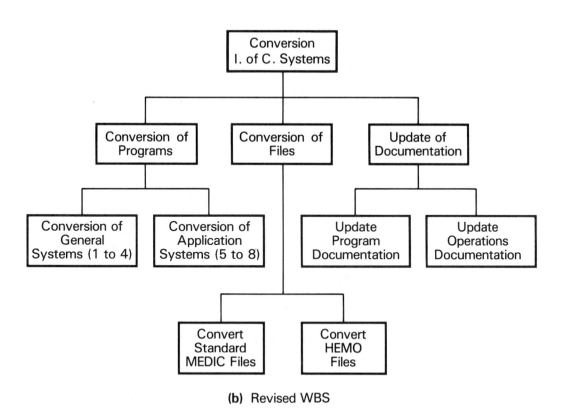

(b) Revised WBS

Fig. 9.4. WBS of the conversion project.

System 4 (INQUIRY): compilers specialist

Systems 5 to 8 (applications): programmer-analysts who are experienced or who are familiar with the applications.

Studying this list, she sees that if any systems must be assigned to outside personnel (employees of the supplier), these will first of all be systems 1, 2, or 4.

The conversion must begin in March, but the machine will only arrive in September. Access to a similar computer and a disk on which to store the work are therefore required.

Moreover, because a new system is involved, with which no one in the department is very familiar, the following resources are also needed:

○ Documentation (operating system, files management, FORTRAN).
○ Training courses: introductory courses for all of the conversion personnel and a systems course for the person in charge of the operating system.

Documentation and training courses are in fact included in the contract, but Charters is concerned that they may not be sufficient.

Estimating the Product or the Activities

At this point, either the final product or the activities necessary to develop it must be estimated, and the only way of accomplishing this is by breaking down the product or the activities. But breaking down the product is the same as designing it. Designing the product when the objective is to estimate the design activity is quite a paradox! (see Metzger, 1973, in Chapter 3). Its justification was discussed earlier in this chapter (p. 000).

The goal, of course, is not to design the product completely, but to come up with an outline that will make estimation possible. Consider, for example, the SMT.PM system in Chapter 4; by using the results of the HIPO approach (p. 000), we were quickly able to achieve a good understanding of the system's modules and files. While it is not certain this will be the chosen design, it is an acceptable one because it has been done according to a sound method and is therefore a good basis for estimation work. In cases where the final product is better known, the activities can be immediately analyzed.

EXAMPLE D: PROGRAMS CONVERSION ACTIVITIES

It was seen in Example A that conversion involved three problems: differences between the FORTRANs; differences in the machine-word formats; and differences in the file formats. Close study of the systems to be converted reveals the following specific activities:

System 1 (UTILITIES): adapt to the new machine word format
   adapt to the new FORTRAN

System 2 (MEDIC): define a new MEDIC file format
   adapt to the new FORTRAN

Systems 3 to 7: adapt to the new FORTRAN

System 8: adapt to the new file format
   adapt to the new FORTRAN

Units of Measurement

A problem arises whenever the product is expressed—that of the unit involved. What unit of measurement will be used to estimate one or a set of programs? The most widely used unit for programs is the *number of lines*. Here again, it must be specified whether or not the measurement includes the comments and declarations (Data Division in COBOL). There are several schools of thought concerning this problem, but in this author's opinion, everything should be counted.

Another unit of measurement is the *work unit*, i.e., a set of statements of a certain length. In a highly structured work environment, the programs or modules have an average length which is roughly constant. Let us examine, for example, the Institute of Cardiology's system. Except for system 1 (utilities), which has an average program length of 40 instructions, all of the others have programs with lengths varying between 100 and 160 statements (an average of 130). And, as will be noted in a later section, many computer specialists detest the idea of basing an estimate of programming time on a given number of statements. On the other hand, in a less structured environment, they are willing to say that a program requires X hours (or days or months) of work.

The choice of which unit to use depends on the work and estimating practices of the organization. Our preference is for the work unit. If it is a program or set of programs, a work unit corresponds to a set of tasks which is the same from one unit to another: detailed design, coding, individual tests. Moreover, all integration efforts are based directly on the number of work units.

No matter the unit selected, the result of this activity consists in stating that development of the product involves producing X number of type Y units. It can easily be said in the case of the conversion project that it is necessary

to convert 26,410 lines of FORTRAN

or

to convert 221 FORTRAN programs each containing roughly 130 lines.

Estimating the Required Resources

Whenever the resources needed to perform an activity are to be estimated, two types of resources must be identified: (a) those which can be deduced from the activity (e.g.), programming time; and (b) those which can be deduced from another resource (e.g., number of copies of the documentation, which depends on the number of programmers).

Of course, in order to estimate the latter, it is necessary to know the former. For example, how can the number of man-hours (or days or months) needed to develop a set of programs be estimated? *Experience is the best guide* (see Abdel-Hamid & Madnick, 1983). Indeed, the productivity of a group of people working in a particular environment is more or less constant. This productivity is available either through statistics or through the people involved.

In Table 9.2, for example, productivity values are given in numbers of lines of code (LOC) per day. These values are taken from data processing literature or are a product of this author's experience. In every case the activities involved cover the totality of the project stages, i.e., general and detailed design, coding, tests, documentation. Although it does not appear possible to draw any conclusions from such dissimilar data, we will soon see that an extensive knowledge of the environment of each situation makes it possible to draw instructive conclusions.

A number of authors have used all of the accumulated experience in order to attempt to discover the "magic formula" given on p. 000. Here, it takes the form

$$E = f(L)$$

in which E = effort (usually in man-months)
L = thousands of lines of code produced

TABLE 9.2
SOME DATA ON LINES OF CODE PER DAY
AS A MEASURE OF DEVELOPMENT PRODUCTIVITY

Reference	Type of Projects	Languages	Productivity (LOC/day)
Johnson (1977)	Business applications (from small to large)	COBOL, PL/I	8–100
Walston & Felix (1977)	All kinds, all sizes	28 high level languages	12.5 (average)
Corbato (reported by Brooks, 1975)	Operating system	PL/I	5.5
Lustman (unpublished)	Compilers, database management systems	FORTRAN	15–25
Lustman (unpublished)	Business applications	FORTRAN, COBOL	25–80

Benbasat and Vessey (1980) give an interesting review of the different work done in this area. Let us look at a few examples.

Based on a database containing 60 projects varying in size from 10,000 to 59,000 lines of code, Walston and Felix (1977) proposed the following formula:

$$E = 5.2 \times L^{0.91}$$

For these authors, L represents the number of statements, not including declarations, comments, etc.

Bailey and Basili (1981) proposed a two-stage formula based on the data obtained from 19 projects. The first stage produces a background equation.

$$E = 0.73 \times L^{1.16} + 3.5$$

Here, L represents *all* of the lines of the program. Notice the constant 3.5, indicating that there is a certain amount of effort independent of all programming. The Bailey-Basili formula takes into account the software-warehouse concept; if the decision is made to reuse an existing program without modification, then the amount of work needed to integrate it is assumed to be 20% of the number of lines it contains.

In his book, "The Mythical Man-month," Brooks (1975) first of all reviews a large number of results and then states that any formula to be used should take the form

$$E = kL^{1.5}$$

Although all of these formulas are mathematically expressed in the same manner, i.e. $E = kL^a$, the value of the exponent a deserves further study. Let P be the productivity in thousands of lines per month:

$$P = {}^L/_E = {}^L/_{kL}{}^a = k_1 L^{1-a}$$

in which $k_1 = {}^1/_k$.

Let us take the first derivative of P, P′:

$$P' = k_1 (1-a)L^{-a}$$

If $a = 1, P' = 0$ productivity is constant.

If $a < 1, P' > 0$ productivity increases with the size of the system.

If $a > 1, P' < 0$ productivity *decreases* with the size of the system.

We will see in a later section that most of the evidence tends to support the final hypothesis ($a > 1$).

Getting back to our estimation work, why not immediately apply such a formula instead of consulting other people, something that can be a little embarrassing? Following is an example of what can happen.

EXAMPLE E: CASE IN POINT: THE SMT.PM PROJECT

The SMT.PM project used as an example in Chapters 4 and 8 was a real project. It involved a system containing 22,000 lines of COBOL, including 10,000 statements in the Procedure Division, with the Data Division and comments excluded (see Lustman, 1983). Table 9.3 shows the results of the application of the Walston-Felix and Bailey-Basili formulas compared with what actually happened. The activities involved range from design through implementation.

What is the problem? Are the formulas totally incorrect? Absolutely not. Was the project completed much more quickly than anticipated? Not at all, since actual resource consumption exceeded estimates by about 10%. The problem is that these formulas are based on a specific experiment (no matter the number of projects involved, in each case they were all from the same work environment), and are valid under the conditions surrounding that experiment. Before using these formulas, it would be advisable to determine whether or not the conditions are the same.

Another problem with these formulas is their generality; they provide total productivity but no details. If estimation work is to be useful for planning purposes, it would be a good idea to have a few more microestimates. Work units provide this breakdown. The size of a system is estimated in number of programs involved, and the time required to produce a program is approximately constant. This method also makes it possible to adjust estimates according to program type. Following, for example, is how the method was used for estimating the work involved in the SMT.PM system.

Estimating by Program Type

A conventional management system contains three types of modules:

1. Input or interaction programs

TABLE 9.3
APPLICATION OF SOME FORMULAS TO THE REAL SMT.PM PROJECT

Formula Used	Lines of Code Considered	Effort in Man-months
Walston & Felix (1977) (procedure division only, no comments)	10,000	42.3
Bailey & Basili (1981) (all lines of the programs)	22,000	29.8
Actual results	not considered	18.5

2. Report production programs

3. Processing programs

The programs in categories 1 and 2 are common enough that, when given the number of data to be handled and the description of the report, a programmer can estimate quite accurately the amount of work needed to produce them. Moreover, the number of screens, the number of data, and the number and complexity of the reports are known because of the specifications. What remains is to estimate the processing programs (category 3). Here we can only rely on programmer experience, which is less reliable since processes are not as similar as inputs or outputs. However, all is not lost. In effect, in a management system, the processing portions only represent from 20% to 30% of the total programming effort. An error in one of these programs therefore has little effect on the overall estimate. In the SMT.PM system one processing program was incorrectly estimated; in reality, the estimate should have been double, but the effect of the error on overall result was only about 5%.

This method (estimating by program type), although more involved and longer than the global estimation method, yields excellent results and is very easily used, as can be seen in the following example.

EXAMPLE F: ESTIMATING THE WORK NEEDED FOR CONVERSION

Having met with her colleagues to discuss the differences between the machine-words, the physical formats of the files, and the two FORTRANs, Charters comes to the following conclusions:

1. All programs which carry out character manipulation or which, more generally, are not independent of machine-word format will have to be rewritten. Their detailed design, on the other hand, can be retained. Involved here are the S1 system (UTILITIES) programs, and two days of work can be estimated per program, since these are relatively short.

2. Programs directly manipulating files will also have to be rewritten. The design can be retained here as well.

3. For those programs involving only the difference between the two FORTRANs, conversion will require two days of work per program.

She then proceeds to draw up the following assessment:

```
System S1: 20 programs at 2 days per program                    =  40 days
System S2: 5 programs to be rewritten (6 days per program
           5 × 6                                                 =  30 days
           36 programs to be corrected
           36 × 2                                                =  72 days
Systems S3 to S7: 110 programs at 2 days per program            = 220 days
System S8: 10 programs to be rewritten (6 days per program)
           10 × 6                                                =  60 days
           40 programs to be corrected
           40 × 2                                                =  80 days
                                                         Total = 502 days
                        1 month = 22 working days: 22.8 months
```

What resources are available? Four persons are available 70% of the time from March 15 to September 1, meaning:

$$5.5 \times 4 \times .7 = 15.4 \text{ months}$$

The evidence seems to indicate that unless outside help is obtained, all of the conversion work will not be completed when the computer arrives. In fact, we will see that the actual situation is worse than that.

FACTORS OF INFLUENCE

Introduction: The Forest Is Hidden by the Trees

At first glance the estimating methods presented in the preceding section are scarcely encouraging. Given such great uncertainty and such debatable references, is there not a risk of making a mistake in estimating the workload? Although the answer is yes, estimating errors are perhaps not really as serious as might be believed. In a study of data processing projects, Gildersleeve (1973) enumerated 17 types of errors resulting in missed deadlines, all of them much more serious than estimating errors. Such errors include nearly all of the classic management errors made in a data processing project.

In an article on the study of project dynamics, Abdel-Hamid and Madnick (1983) reported the following experiment. Having constructed a system making it possible to simulate the evolution of a project by taking into account various factors which could affect its development, they defined a hypothetical project and carried out four successive tests:

Test 1: A perfect project is progressing without incident.

Test 2: An error discovered at an advanced stage of the project has required a rework.

Test 3: In addition to the problem cited in Test 2, there is a certain amount of employee turnover.

Test 4: Added to everything else is an estimating error of roughly 20%.

The results are compiled in Table 9.4, with the variations in relation to the initial estimates given in percentages. While it is not possible to draw any definite conclusions from this experiment (since it is a simulation), it is clear that the effect of a rework and personnel turnover *nearly neutralize the effects of an estimating error* (minimal difference between tests 3 and 4). This is the "safeguard" of estimates; their effects are much less serious than those of the other factors.

TABLE 9.4
INFLUENCE OF VARIOUS FACTORS ON PROJECT OUTCOME[a]

Test #	Type of Perturbation	Variation in Cost (%)	Variation in Duration (%)
1	none	0	0
2	rework	18	10
3	2 + personnel turnover	30	27
4	3 + estimation error (20%)	31	27

[a]Simulation by Abdel-Hamid & Madnick (1983)

However, it should be noted that the principal (and by far the most serious) type of estimating error is the *omission* of an element from an estimate. Pietrasanta was arguing in this vein as early as 1970 (see Chapter 3).

EXAMPLE G: CONVERSION PROJECT

It is clear that the estimate done in Example F is incomplete, even if we are only interested in the programmer time. Two elements are missing: (a) the time needed to update the documentation, and (b) the resources necessary to convert the existing files.

With regard to program documentation, only the documents on the rewritten programs have to be updated. The documentation of the 20 programs in system 1 is short and can be updated in four days. The documentation of the other rewritten programs (systems S2 and S8) must be redone entirely and should require 15 days of work for the former and 20 for the latter.

The operation documentation must be completely redone. There are 32 different procedures corresponding to the various operations (daily, monthly, annual, on request), and each one will require about one day of work to be designed, implemented, and tested.

Therefore, to summarize the time requirements for updating the documentation:

```
System S1                    =  4 days
Other systems: 20 + 15       = 35 days
Operation documentation      = 32 days
                             ─────────
                        Total: 71 days
```

With regard to conversion of existing files, there are two file formats: those of the HEMO system, and all of the others. In each case, a program could be produced in 15 days once the new format has been defined (this being done during conversion of the programs).

Therefore, in review:

Documentation	= 71 days
Files conversion	= 30 days
Programs conversion	= 502 days

Total: 603 days or 27.4 months

Given the manpower available, the September 1 deadline is increasingly unrealistic.

Productivity: A Function of Many Variables

Earlier, it was stated that the omission of needed elements was the primary factor of influence on estimates. The second factor is productivity, which is affected by an extremely large number of variables. Metzger (1973), for example, deals with up to 45 factors that may inflate estimates; nearly all of them affect productivity. Walston and Felix (1977) found 29 factors affecting productivity, with another 30 being added by Bailey and Basili (1981). Their findings may be summarized in four major factors which influence the productivity of system developers: the system, the developers themselves, the users, and the work environment.

Influence of the System

The size and complexity of a system have an adverse effect on productivity. Brooks (1975) and Johnson (1977) recorded variations in productivity ranging from 1 to 9. The effect produced by complexity needs no explanation. Size affects productivity indirectly, since increasing the size of the team requires a greater amount of interaction. Reexamination of the formulas presented on page 000 reveals that those in which the exponent is greater than 1 reflect the effect of project size better than the others.

Influence of the Developers

In this case, intuition is confirmed by experience: more experienced personnel have a higher productivity. The effect of this factor can be to double or triple productivity. But what is meant by experience? It can, in fact, take extremely different forms, such as:

general professional experience,

knowledge of the type of problem involved, or

experience with work tools and methods (machines, languages, design methods, programming methods, and so on).

In this author's opinion, productivity is much more seriously affected by the first two factors than by the third.

Influence of the User

There is a general consensus that (a) a user who knows what he wants has a positive effect on productivity, and (b) user involvement in specifications production also increases productivity. Indeed, the user's crucial role in this activity has already been stressed (see Chapter 7). It is impossible to assign a value to the effect of users on productivity. Our experience shows that a user who does not know clearly what he wants decreases productivity, and pushes back deadlines. Related results include poorer product quality and an increase in the amount of maintenance work required. Minimal user involvement in specifications production has the same effect.

Influence of the Work Environment

Involved here are the issues discussed in Chapter 8, as well as project management methodology itself. Limited tests have shown, for example, that structured programming increases productivity by at least 20%. Even though quantitative results showing the effects of modern work methods are not yet available, the computer community and the organizations involved are categorical: systems are developed more quickly with modern work tools and methods than without. However, the most outstanding advantage of this arsenal is the quality and durability of the final product.

The factors which influence productivity, as well as their effects, are summarized in Table 9.5. Even though the numbers proposed are not always based on scientific data, they are nonetheless the results of a large number of experiments.

An estimator must take into account these factors of influence by following a relatively simple three-step procedure:

1. Determine the factors of influence which apply to the project.

TABLE 9.5
FACTORS INFLUENCING PRODUCTIVITY

Factor of Influence	Productivity Variation
Project size and complexity	1 to 9
Team experience	1 to 3
User	increases with user involvement
Work environment (methods and tools)	20% to 50%

2. Determine those factors which the estimates done thus far have not accounted for.

3. Make the necessary adjustments to productivity or to the microestimates involved.

EXAMPLE H: SYSTEMS CONVERSION

Charters systematically evaluates each of the possible factors of influence. Project size and complexity presents no problem since the project is typical of those generally handled by the department. The developers are very experienced in all areas except one: they are not familiar with the computer system. The users are the developers themselves, plus the operations group, and all are involved in the project. The work environment is the same as in previous projects.

Assessment is straightforward: the new machine is the only element which may affect productivity. The project team is composed of highly experienced individuals; the task is converting from one version of a language to another.

During the first two months of work, productivity should be running at about 50%, after which everyone should be working at normal speed. What is required, therefore, is to increase the total estimate by:

$$4 \times .7 \times 2 \times .5 = 2.8 \text{ months}$$

This brings the estimate of the total amount of work required to:

$$E = 27.4 + 2.8 = 30.2 \text{ man-months}$$

The project manager is fortunate because the estimates are affected by very few factors, and the adjustments are minor (10% of the total).

Factors Affecting the Macroestimates

These factors do not directly influence productivity, but do affect the value of the estimates. They are contingencies which must be taken into account since their probability of occurrence is 1.

The Necessity to Rework

Any plan or estimate is based on the assumption that events will unfold as forecast; for example, that all of the errors in a module will be found during its testing stage. Anyone who has worked on more than one project knows that such will never be the case. There will *always* be an error discovered later than projected which will require unplanned-for resources to correct. If no historical data are available, increasing the estimates by 10% is a good idea.

Personnel Turnover

This is a risk which must be dealt with once a project goes beyond a certain duration or number of participants. In this case, well-documented data can be found within the personnel department, and will appear in one of two forms:

average length of service in organization = X months (or years)

rate of personnel turnover = Y%/year

with one, moreover, being the inverse of the other. Armed with this information, and knowing the duration of the project and the size of the team, it is not very difficult to anticipate a certain number of new personnel, with all that that implies in the way of hiring, training, and integration. In the experiment carried out by Abdel-Hamid and Madnick (1983), the cost increased by more than 10% in comparison to that involving a rework (see Table 9.4).

Absence from Work

While there are roughly 22 working days in a month and 264 in a year, it would be folly to believe that these are all actual workdays. Statutory holidays, earned vacation time, illness, and personal leave all represent days that will not be worked. Once again, based on its records, the personnel department can tell the estimator how many actual days of work there are likely to be in a year or month, and the necessary adjustment can easily be made.

Lost work time assessed in terms of days also pertains to hours. Does a workday of n hours really correspond to n hours of work on the project? Coffee breaks, conversations, personal phone calls, and so on have already been allowed for in the productivity estimate. We want to determine the proportion of actual worktime which will be devoted to the project rather than to other tasks such as the maintenance of other systems and attendance at regular meetings. These statistics should be available from the data processing department and, once again, adjustments will have to be made. It was seen in the conversion project that this was planned for right at the outset.

OBTAINING THE FINISHED ESTIMATES

Expected Results

So far we have estimated the resources necessary for product realization. Some, however, depend on the number of personnel, and for the moment we have no idea how many participants will be involved. Moreover, some adjustments, such as those resulting from personnel turnover, depend on the duration of the project. For the estimate to be complete, three variables must be known: the necessary resources, the team size and make-up, and the duration of the project. Most of the time the estimator does not have three degrees of freedom, since management or the particular project conditions dictate the value of at least one of the three variables.

In the case of a fixed-deadline project, it is frequently necessary to evaluate:

1. The possibility of completion, using the equation

$$f(K, T, P) = \text{constant}$$

(see Chapter 3), in which

$$K = \text{resources}, \ T = \text{time}, \ P = \text{product}$$

Assuming that P is invariable, if T becomes invariable as well, then it could be impossible to develop the product, no matter what K may be.

2. The size and make-up of the project team
3. The other necessary resources.

Projects which use personnel already available within the organization frequently have a *fixed number of personnel*. The assessment in this case must include the necessary resources and the duration of the project.

The project which has *fixed total resources* represents the classic case of the "contract." It is necessary:

1. To assess the possibility of completion, since the values of the variables P and K in the equation

$$f(K, T, P) = \text{constant}$$

are imposed

2. To determine the makeup of the team
3. To determine the duration of the project.

The last two variables are related, and the estimation of one results in the estimation of the other.

EXAMPLE I: CONVERSION PROJECT ESTIMATE

This is a case of a fixed number of personnel: four programmer-analysts from the data processing department and one from the supplier. The assessment of the resources required has been estimated at 30.2 man-months of work. Charters can subtract 5 man-months from this estimate (namely, the supplier's programmer-analyst), leaving 25.2 man-months. Given that each department member can devote 70% of his time to the project, one calendar month equals 2.8 man-months. The minimum duration of the project is therefore

$$T_{min} = 25.2/2.8 = 9 \text{ months}$$

If work begins around March 15, the conversion will be finished at the end of the year at the earliest.

Charters takes this report to her superior, who considers it for a few moments and then asks: "Of course you allowed for vacation time?" Somewhat embarrassed, she admits that this was overlooked. They quickly do some calculations, ignoring absences due to sickness or personal reasons, since the employees of the department are rarely absent. Given that the 3-week vacation time is paid, this cost is part of the project budget, therefore resulting in

$$4 \times .75 \times .7 = 2.1$$

more months in resources and .75 more months in time. The assessment is:

total resources: $30.2 + 2.1 = 32.3$ man-months

minimum duration: $9 + .75 = 9.75$ months

Integration

So far we have estimated variables that are directly linked to production, and in fact nearly all of these have been the human resources directly involved. Yet, there are others which must also be estimated. The major ones include:

○ Computer resources, usually assessed in dollars. However, when the company does not apply any chargeback, it is estimated in hours. This is a difficult estimate to make under any circumstances, and experience is about the only guideline available. It seems that the most accurate hypothesis is to consider computer cost (or time) proportional to effort. In terms of dollars, the experience of this author would tend to favor a formula of the type

CC = 15% CHR

CC = computer costs

CHR = total cost of human resources involved in development

o Training costs, which depend on the size of the team and the rate of personnel turnover. The costs are calculated both in dollars (to pay for the courses) and in nonproductive days for the individuals involved.

o Administrative resources, which include the managers involved in the project, whose number increases with project size. Clerical personnel are also included. A rule based on experience says that one secretary can handle the work submitted by 5 to 7 members of a development team.

o Supplies, including office supplies as well as data processing supplies. The amounts involved should never exceed more than 5% of the total cost.

o Transportation, which can become an expensive element in the case of a multisite project or when the supplier and user are not at the same location.

Integrating the estimates therefore involves:

1. Adding the estimates of resources of similar type.
2. Using the major resources as an estimating base for the auxiliary resources.
3. Drawing up a complete detailed version of the estimate.

EXAMPLE J: CONVERSION PROJECT REVISED ESTIMATES

Having estimated the duration and necessary human resources, Charters can calculate the auxiliary resources involved in her project. The supplier is offering 40 hours of computer time free of charge, the rest at $80/hr. The average cost of an analyst is roughly $2500/month.

$$\text{Total cost: } 2500 \times 32.3 = \$80,750$$

Applying the 15% formula, Diana obtains the following result:

$$\text{Computer cost} = 80,750 \times .15 = \$12,112.50$$

$$\text{or } 12,112.50/80 = 151.4 \text{ hours.}$$

Since there are 40 free hours, it is necessary to plan for 112 hours at $80/hr, resulting in a cost of $8,900.

The training costs are not applicable, since they are included in the purchase contract. The data processing department will provide the administrative resources and there will be no transportation costs. Only the documentation remains: two complete sets are provided for in the contract; yet, at least two more will be required at a cost of $240 each to the project. The assessment can now be drawn up, and it is depicted in Table 9.6.

TABLE 9.6
INTEGRATED ESTIMATION RESULTS FOR CONVERSION PROJECT

Resource	Total Amount Required	Provided by Supplier	To Be Provided by the Institute
Analyst-programmer	32.3 man-month	5 man-month	27.3 man-month
Computer time	151.4 hrs	40 hrs	111.4 hrs
Documentation	4 sets	2 sets	2 sets
Duration	9.75 months	NA	NA
Staff	5	1 (5 months)	4

THE PROJECT MANAGER IN THE ESTIMATING PROCESS

The Institute of Cardiology project was quite small, at least in terms of number of personnel involved, and we saw that the project manager did all the work. Such will not always be the case, and in larger projects the work will be distributed among all of the individuals concerned. It is therefore once again necessary to distinguish between the two roles of the project manager: manager and technician.

Managing the Estimating Function

It has been said that managing is planning, scheduling, and controlling. How does this apply to the estimating activity? Planning tasks which relate to the estimating process are as follows:

1. Performing the first-level WBS, which involves defining the principal areas to be estimated.
2. Defining or choosing the estimation methods; which is an important decision. As will be seen shortly, the actual estimating activity will be distributed among several groups or individuals. For the results to be compatible, it is necessary that everyone use the same method.
3. Defining the expected results; which involves the variables for which we wish to obtain estimates.
4. Assignment of estimating tasks. In principle, the estimate of a certain element is done by the person in charge who is closest to those performing the activity; this person knows the capabilities of the employees better than anyone else.

Since the scheduling activity is very limited, nothing in particular stands out.

The controlling activity will, of course, be concerned with meeting deadlines, but especially with product quality (i.e. with the estimates). More precisely, it will be necessary

to verify the proposed estimates,

to verify the consistency of the various results,

to analyze the adjustments made or to be made, and

to revise the estimates or have them revised.

Participating in the Estimating Function

As always, any intervention by the project manager in a production process should only happen at the overall project level. In the case of the estimating activity, this means that he must perform the following tasks:

1. Adjustments. We have seen that these directly affect either productivity or the macroestimates. The project manager will either have to make the adjustments himself (in medium-sized projects) or exercise strict control over them (in large projects).

2. Integration. This is also the responsibility of the project manager, since the compilation of all the results is involved. Indeed, very often there will be an iterative loop between the different tasks, as depicted in Figure 9.5.

3. Estimate and results database input. Time and time again, we have noted that experience is the best estimating guide and that data based on experience are difficult to apply to other projects. If the organization in which the project is being performed has an estimate and results database, the project manager must see that the pertinent data are fed into it. If no such database exists, he should set one up. In this way, he will have available over the long term his own estimating formulas, adapted to his own environment and therefore reliable.

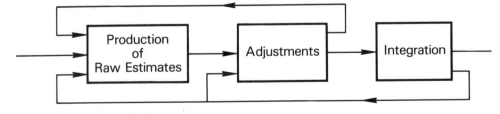

Fig. 9.5. Iteration of the production of estimates.

SELECTED REFERENCES

Abdel-Hamid, T. K., & Madnick, S. E. 1983. The dynamics of software project scheduling. *Com. of the ACM*, 26, 5 (May), 340–346.
> In this article the authors use a dynamic simulation model to study the behavior of project parameters while the project is in progress. One experiment, dealing with the effects caused by various problems, is presented in this chapter of this book. The other demonstrates the effects which the estimates themselves can have on the evolution of the project.

Bailey, J. W., Basili, V. R. 1981. A meta model for software development resource estimating. *Proc., 5th Int. Conf. on Soft. Eng.*, March 9–12, San Diego, 107–116.
> The starting point is the fact that estimating formulas are usually specific to the environment in which they have been conceived. Their goal being to create an adaptable tool, the authors developed a two-component formula: the basic formula as well as another component taking into account specific environmental factors. This latter component can be adapted to each particular environment.

Benbasat, I., & Vessey, I. 1980. Programmer and analyst time/cost estimating. *MIS Quarterly*, June, 31–43.
> This article presents an excellent review of the major estimating methods. It begins by studying programming estimates and then moves on to the overall project estimates.

Brooks, F. P. 1975. *The mythical man-month*. Reading, Mass.: Addison-Wesley.
> This book contains an interesting review of the estimating experiences of various authors. The problems relating to estimate adjustments are examined, as are the causes which result in unrespected schedules.

Gildersleeve, T. R. 1973. The time-estimating myth. *Datamation*, 19, 1 (January), 47–48.
> The author challenges the obsession for accurate estimates that managers have; in fact, he considers it to be an excuse for bad management. He also attacks project management systems which, because of the way they are used, distort the time data normally used as estimating bases.

Johnson, J. R. 1977. A working measure of productivity. *Datamation*, February, 106–112.
> This article analyzes the problems related to the units used for estimating the product, productivity, and the factors affecting productivity. The results, based on a bank of 19 projects, are compared with those obtained by Brooks.

Kustanowicz, A. L. 1977. System Life Cycle Estimation (SLICE): A new approach to estimating resources for application program development. *Proc. IEEE Comp. Soft. and Appl. Conference*, Chicago, 226–232.
> The estimating method presented here has the advantage of being workable and usable by many organizations. Its starting point is an estimation of the sizes of the different project life cycle stages. Using the number of instructions per day to determine the product estimate, the author uses this to determine the programming estimate and then carries it progressively further to cover the entire life cycle.

Walston, C. E., & Felix, C. P. 1977. A method of programming measurement and estimation. *IBM Systems Journal*, 16,1, 54–73.

> This article contains one of the most exhaustive studies done on estimation problems. Using a database of 60 projects, the authors analyze the distribution of work over the entire life cycle, propose a formula for estimating the amount of work required for production, determine 29 factors which may influence productivity, and propose a formula making it possible to take their effects in account. They also set out formulas for computer costs, project team size, and duration of project. This article is must reading for anyone interested in the estimation of data processing systems development projects.

Chapter 10
PLANNING AND SCHEDULING

INTRODUCTION

In a book on advanced project management techniques, Harrison (1981) stated: "Planning is a philosophy, not so much in the literal sense of the word, but as an attitude, or way of life" (p. 35). Our experience can only confirm that statement. Planning is much more than a technique; it is a state of mind. We have known at least two managers who were completely against any kind of planning—one because he considered it a substitute for action, the other because he saw it as a waste of time. Nevertheless, both were extremely brilliant and had successful careers.

The most concise definition of planning is "thinking before acting." Increasingly sophisticated and more widely applied formal techniques have resulted from over 40 years of study of this area. (See Ansof's (1977) article on the evolution of these techniques.) Unfortunately they enjoyed a period of intensive use and then were gradually discarded by disenchanted users, especially in data processing. As is always the case, excess creates problems. Excessive polarization on formal planning systems (see Harrison, 1981), eventually let to rejection—also excessive—of the methods themselves.

A balanced dose best guarantees success. Formal planning techniques must be considered the basis or framework within which we will work. To these will be added those factors that are difficult to incorporate into a highly structured system, the specificity of data processing projects in particular.

EXAMPLE A: PROGRAMS CONVERSION

It was seen at the end of Chapter 9 that Diana Charters had produced estimates for the conversion of the first set of programs. She presented them to her superior who, after considering them with a sigh (nothing will be ready on September 1), says: "Very good. Now, could you draw me up a plan and a schedule?"

This time Diana is really perplexed. "What do you mean by a plan? Aren't the estimates enough?" Her superior explains: "What I'd like is a calendar and also a general idea of who is doing what, and when." Diana leaves, but instead of rushing back to her office, she heads for the university library.

OVERVIEW OF PLANNING AND SCHEDULING

Definitions

The widest and most concise definition will be taken from Gray, (1981).

Planning is the process of deciding a future course of action.

More specifically, it consists in answering the following three questions: *what* to do, *when* to do it, and *how* to do it. Since this definition has an extremely wide field of application, we will attempt to narrow it somewhat:

Strategic planning applies to the organization itself and covers a 3- to 5-year period.

Tactical planning (within the framework defined by the strategic planning) applies to a sector of the organization over a period of 1 to 3 years.

Let us attempt to apply these concepts to a project (see Figure 10.1). It can be seen in this figure that the project, its objective, and its work methods are in fact a product of strategic planning. Within this framework, tactical planning consists in determining in detail which activities will be carried out, when, and with what resources in order to produce the desired result.

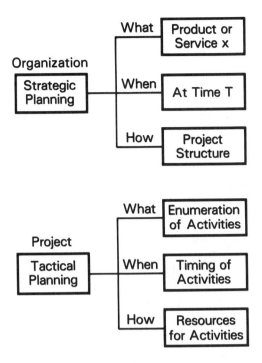

Fig. 10.1. Strategic planning, tactical planning, and the project.

Scheduling an activity involves deciding when and how it will be executed.

Project scheduling consists in drawing up a calendar showing the dates of execution of all activities required for project completion. Because the gross results of the planning phase are not always compatible with the time and financial restrictions imposed, the scheduling phase will have to supply a pragmatic calendar taking these restrictions into account.

But what exactly is planned; what is scheduled? The answer is *activities*. However, any activity to be performed requires resources which must be available when needed. It is important to keep in mind that planning and scheduling involve *both* activities and resources. In many cases, resource planning dictates activities planning.

EXAMPLE B: DESIRED RESULTS

Charters has just read the definitions of planning and scheduling. "So," she says, "that's what he wants: who does what, and when." Being a practical person, she draws a form (see Figure 10.2) and thinks, "Once this form has been filled in, I'll take it to him and that will be the end of it." We will see, however, that a

System	Person Responsible	Starting Date	Ending Date
UTILITIES			
MEDIC Database			
MUPDATE			
INQUIRY			
DISC			
DIET			
PMC			
HEMO			

Fig. 10.2. Result of planning-scheduling as seen by the project manager.

good number of stages will have to be gone through before "the end of it" arrives.

Planning the Process

As with all of the other activities, planning and scheduling must also be planned. The diagram of this process is illustrated in Figure 10.3. In the first stage, the interrelations among activities are analyzed through the use of a network, for

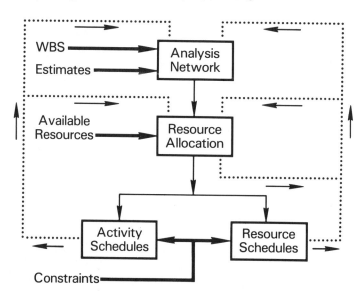

Fig. 10.3. Planning-scheduling process.

example; the data are provided by the WBS of the activities and the estimates. Once the network has been established, the available resources must be allocated to the various activities. It is then possible to draw up the activity and resource schedules.

Once again, this sequence of events is idealistic. The reality of the situation may be entirely different. The resources that are available may make it necessary to revise the initial network (see Figure 10.3). In the same way, other restrictions involving the calendars may make it necessary to rework resource allocation and even the network. There may be a large amount of iteration, and even the estimates themselves might have to be revised. Figure 10.3 shows that planning and scheduling are, in fact, extensively intertwined. Throughout the remainder of this chapter we will restrict the term *scheduling* to the quasi-mechanical production of calendars once the problems caused by the various constraints have been settled.

INTRODUCTION TO FORMAL PLANNING

Review of Basic Network Concepts

An excellent presentation of networks can be found in Gray (1981) and Harrison (1981). Here, we will simply review a few basic definitions introduced in Chapter 2 and completed in Chapter 3.

activity: a project element occurring over a period of time. With respect to planning, an activity can be considered defined once the following have been specified: (a) its nature, (b) the resources necessary for its execution, and (c) its duration.

event: The beginning or end of an activity. With respect to the network, an event is considered completely defined when (a) the deliverable, and (b) the moment of delivery are both known.

critical path: the path running from the initial to the final event and having the longest duration.

slack: difference between the time duration of a path and that of the critical path. It constitutes "free" time which can be used for a number of purposes: shifting activities within the time framework in order to take external constraints into account; or delaying certain activities in order to shift resources (toward the critical path, for example) if the need arises.

EXAMPLE C: PARTIAL CONVERSION NETWORK

The network in Figure 10.4 represents the conversion of three systems—MUP-DATE, DIET, and INQUIRY. The activities are defined each time as the system

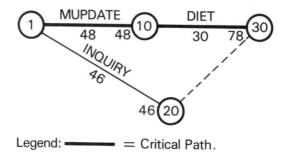

Legend: ━━━━━ = Critical Path.

Legend. ━━ = critical path.

Fig. 10.4. Partial network of conversion project.

conversion, tests, and production of the corresponding documentation. Each event therefore corresponds to a system operational on the new computer. Duration is expressed in days, and it can be seen that the critical path (indicated by the heavy line) is formed by activities 1-10 and 10-30 and has a duration of 78 days. There are 32 days (78 minus 46) of slack time for activity 1-20. How this slack is used will be seen in the remainder of this chapter.

It has been mentioned that each activity consists of program conversion, tests and documentation. Why was this level of detail not used for the network? Diana Charters, our project manager, could answer this question by saying that this network is for her boss and that he is only interested in knowing when each system will be ready, not the details. It is, in fact, possible to construct a network depicting the detailed breakdown of every project activity and task. In our conversion project, for example, there are 221 programs, resulting in a network of 221 activities. If these are then subdivided into programming, tests, and documentation, this number is tripled. The network then becomes unreadable and therefore useless. The level of detail of a network must correspond to what the network is to be used for. The manager of a project involving 3,000 activities and 60 people does not require the same network as a chief programmer supervising 5 programmers assigned to produce 40 programs.

Level of Detail of a Network

It must not be forgotten that, among other things, the plan will have to be used for control purposes. The level of detail of a network can therefore be defined very simply as the level at which the network's user participates in and controls the project. Since we usually differentiate among three levels of responsibility, there will be three levels of networks:

1. *General network.* Intended for the highest level of management (the project manager), its events will be the principal milestones, and its activities those which result in these milestones.

2. *Intermediate network.* Intended for an intermediate level superior, it is the detailed breakdown of the general network activity of which he is in charge. Its level of detail corresponds to the milestones enabling him to control the teams under his supervision.

3. *Detailed network.* Intended for front-line supervisors, this network usually takes the form of a workpackage. It provides detailed task breakdown and also makes it possible to monitor work progress.

Figure 10.5 depicts the three network levels of the INQUIRY system. The first level is for the use of the project manager. The second is a breakdown of the system into three independent modules which can be assigned to three separate individuals or teams. The third level corresponds to the main programs of the compiler module; each represents one conversion task.

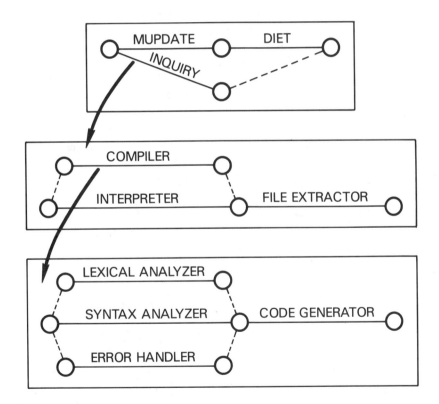

Fig. 10.5. Three levels of networks.

Setup of the Initial Network

Setting up the network is the first step in the planning process (see Figure 10.3). It is the most human part of the process in that it is not automated. Brooks

(1975) and others believe it is the most interesting part, since it calls for an indepth analysis of the entire undertaking. The base data are provided by the WBS and estimates, and by the list of activities and the duration of each.

Setting up a network consists in defining the sequence of the activities and determining any possible parallel activities. But where does one start? At the beginning or at the end? Most prefer to start at the end (i.e., the final event) and work back toward the beginning (see Gray, 1981, & Miller, 1978). It is relatively easy to take one activity and determine those which precede it, since they are the ones that make that activity possible. Thus, the parallelisms naturally occur. But at what level do we place ourselves? Which milestones do we use? We will always begin with the most important milestones and then go into greater detail.

EXAMPLE D: SETUP OF THE CONVERSION NETWORK

Diana Charters applies the principles of top-down and bootstrap implementation; thus each system is to be converted, tested, and documented before considered completed, and the systems are developed in reciprocal order of use: if A uses B, B will be converted before A.

First of all, she draws up a list of the activities and the duration of each one (see Table 10.1). Then, starting at the end, she goes back towards the beginning:

o For everything to be operational, the operating procedures are needed: this requires activity K (see Figure 10.6a).

o All of the operating systems correspond in reality to operating applications (i.e., activities, E, F, G, H, I (in Figure 10.6b).

o The DIET and PMC systems used the UPDATE system. Moreover, for the HEMO system to be operational, programs conversion is not the only element

TABLE 10.1
ACTIVITIES OF THE CONVERSION PROJECT

Activity	Description	Duration (in days)
A	Convert utilities	44
B	Convert MEDIC system	117
C	Transport MEDIC files	15
D	Convert MUPDATE system	48
E	Convert INQUIRY system	46
F	Convert DISC system	16
G	Convert DIET system	30
H	Convert PMC system	80
I	Convert HEMO system	160
J	Transport HEMO files	15
K	Write operations documentation	32

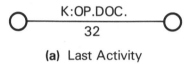

(a) Last Activity

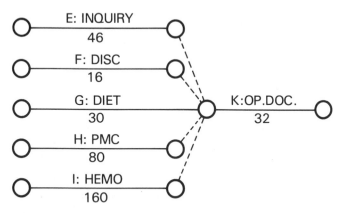

(b) Working Backward to the Start

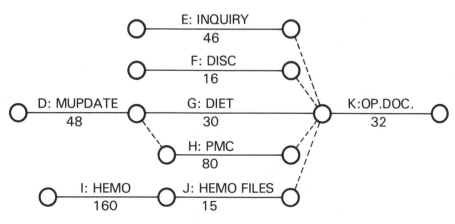

(c) Working Backward : Next Step

Fig. 10.6. Developing the conversion network.

involved; once the programs have been converted, it is also necessary to move the files, meaning that activity J comes after activity I. This new stage in construction of the network is depicted in Figure 10.6c.

o Finally, all of the systems except HEMO use MEDIC, and absolutely all, MEDIC included, require UTILITIES. Similar to HEMO, the MEDIC files will be converted after the MEDIC programs. The finished network is depicted in Figure 10.7.

Once the network has been defined, it becomes possible to perform every imaginable type of calculation and in particular, to determine the critical path. To do this, one starts at the beginning and traces every path to the end while following these rules:

The ending date of an activity is the starting date plus its duration.

The starting date of an activity is that of the longest path ending at the starting event of this activity.

Thus, for conversion, the critical path passes through events 1-5-10-20-45-50-60-100-110 and lasts 336 days. In Figure 10.7, the nearest possible starting date of each activity is indicated in a square adjacent to the activity, with the critical path being illustrated by a heavy line.

Although there is no slack for producing the operations documentation, the following time slacks are available:

    82   days   for   INQUIRY
   112   days   for   DISC
    50   days   for   DIET
    85   days   for   HEMO

Use of CPM or PERT

Originally two distinct methods, CPM (critical path method) concentrates on the critical path concept and the use of slack time, whereas PERT (program evaluation and review technique) enables the users to take into account the uncertainty surrounding estimates, and is strongly geared toward control. The packages available today are sophisticated enough that we generally speak of CPM/PERT methods.

We saw that the use of these techniques in data processing has been the subject of much debate. Certainly a small project can be planned without using a computer, and feeding a program a stack of data would only complicate the situation. Large projects, even in the field of data processing, can make good use of these packages provided they are given input. The criticism that they require too many update data, even though it is occasionally justified, may in fact serve to hide a reluctance to control project members too strictly.

Hypothesis Concerning Resources

The procedure followed to develop the network is based on the assumption that there are unlimited resources. Indeed, whenever the parallelism of several ac-

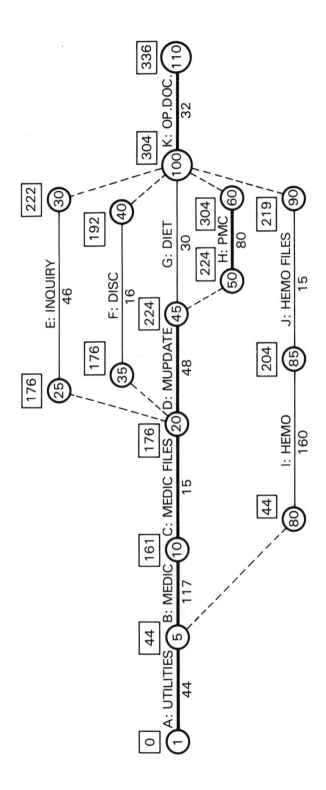

Fig. 10.7. General network of conversion.

tivities is defined, knowing if enough resources will be available to allow the activities to be executed simultaneously is not important. Similarly, nothing allows us to state that the necessary resources will be available long enough to make it possible to execute theoretically sequential activities one after the other. For example, there is a point in the network in Figure 10.7 at which it is assumed that five programmers will be working on parallel activities. Yet, the data processing department has only assigned four, and there is no proof that the fifth, to be provided by the supplier, will be available at that time. Therefore, the network that has just been established is actually a starting point and may later be modified, depending on available resources.

Resource Allocation

This activity, often termed resource scheduling, consists in allocating a portion of the available resources to each activity in the network. To do this, however, it is necessary to have the list of available resources. This brings us to the resource library concept presented by Koenig (1978). The *resource library* is a list indicating the different types of resources available for the project, the quantity of each and, if warranted, the period of availability. This "inventory" will be helpful in determining whether the resources required for a given activity are available or whether they have already been exhausted. Allocation of resources to activities is done using the resource library as a basis and attempting to ensure that no resources are overtaxed. As is evidenced by the conversion project, this is not always an easy task.

EXAMPLE E: RESOURCES FOR THE CONVERSION

Table 10.2 contains Diana Charter's list of available resources. Note that the four programmer-analysts from the data processing department are considered separate resources; this is, in effect, the only way of determining afterwards if the workload has been correctly distributed.

EXAMPLE F: ALLOCATION OF THE CONVERSION PROJECT RESOURCES

It is clear that if there is a distribution of one person per system, half of the team will be idle until event 20 (see Figure 10.7). Moreover, whenever one of the department's programmer-analysts works on a project, he is there only 70% of the time, resulting in longer deadlines. The supplier's programmer-analyst should therefore be used on the critical path and prior to activity 10. Diana decides to assign him the MEDIC system; she will do UTILITIES herself and gives Paul Loews the responsibility of converting the HEMO system programs and files. Unfortunately, no matter what she tries, the final portion of the net-

TABLE 10.2
CONVERSION PROJECT'S RESOURCE LIBRARY

Type of Resource	Resource	Amount Available	Time When Available
Analyst-programmer	Diana Charters	15.4 days/month	project duration
	Paul Loews	15.4 days/month	project duration
	Peter Deladdy	15.4 days/month	project duration
	Michael Green	15.4 days/month	project duration
	provided by supplier	110 days (5 months, full-time)	starting April 1st
Computer time	supplier's computer	40 hrs	to be negotiated
	own computer	unlimited	after Sept. 1st

work cannot be completed unless she assigns two parallel activities to one person, something she will do only as a last resort. Indeed, there are five parallel activities (see Figure 10.7), and since the five months of time assigned to the supplier's analyst were allotted to converting MEDIC, there are now only four people available.

Different Project Types

With respect to planning and scheduling, there are two types of projects. In time-bounded projects, if the resources required for the parallel activities are not available through the usual channels, they will have to be procured. Although these resources may be "purchased," such expenses will be kept as low as possible by "reclaiming" resources available due to the slack in various activities.

In the case of *resource-bounded projects*, the pool of available resources is limited. If there are not enough to cover the parallel activities in the network, unplanned sequences must be introduced, possibly resulting in a delayed completion date. Here again the available slack will be used to minimize delays.

EXAMPLE G: USE OF SLACK IN A RESOURCE-BOUNDED PROJECT

A glance at Figure 10.7 reveals that it is possible to complete the INQUIRY and DISC systems one after the other without affecting the date of event 100. This leads us to the network in Figure 10.8 illustrating task assignment. There is no guarantee that this distribution results in the most balanced workload.

The four programmer-analysts from the data processing department have the following workloads:

Diana Charters: 89 days
Michael Green: 128 days
Peter Deladdy: 94 days
Paul Loews: 175 days

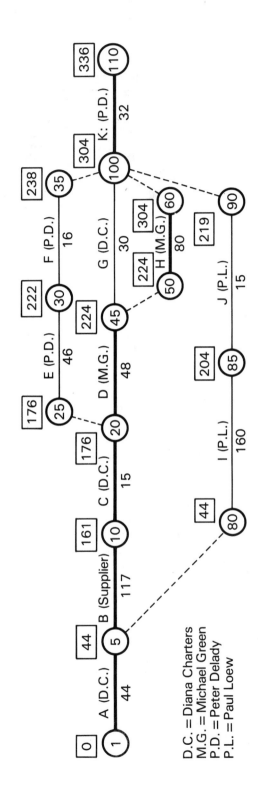

Fig. 10.8. Revised conversion network.

D.C. = Diana Charters
M.G. = Michael Green
P.D. = Peter Delady
P.L. = Paul Loew

Paul is really overloaded, and given the slack time, Diana or Peter could easily take charge of activity J. However, it was not by chance that Diana assigned Paul tasks I and J; he designed the HEMO system, and the time estimates for these two tasks are valid only for him, not for the others.

This gradually brings us to the limits of formal planning and scheduling techniques, and in particular to the limits imposed on them by the strange and somewhat unpredictable nature of data processing.

PLANNING THE DEVELOPMENT OF A DATA PROCESSING SYSTEM

A Cookbook May Help

As we have already seen, data processing and research and development (R&D) projects have some common characteristics. There is much uncertainty surrounding estimates and work procedures; unforeseen events may occur at any time, and so on. It is clear that the direct and inflexible application of formal planning techniques can only lead to undesirable results. This rigidity must be tempered by factors specific to the area of activity involved.

It was stated in the preface that this book would not be a collection of recipes, and so far the author has done his best to avoid such a situation. However, in order to present the fruit of his own experience and that of others, he sees no other way than to put it in the form of a series of recipes. After all, to a gourmet, cookbooks are quite respectable.

Networking the System's Development

Recipe 1: A Milestone Is a Flagpole.

As noted in Chapter 3, an event can be considered defined if the activity which it terminates produces a deliverable. In other words, the events in the network must produce something visible. The case of the 90%-complete program is only too well known. If, for example, the detailed design consists of a document, it is a milestone. Otherwise, it is not (as is frequently the case whenever the detailed design is done by the programmer). A completed subprogram is a milestone provided it can be demonstrated as operational.

Recipe 2: Try Piecemeal Delivery.

Unfortunately, resource-bounded projects are all too often time-bounded projects in disguise. One of the most effective ways of calming user impatience is to deliver the product component by component. This makes a longer deadline possible while at the same time providing usable results more quickly. Business systems lend themselves well to this type of breakdown.

Recipe 3: Use Top-down Implementation.

This approach, which consists of programming as design progresses, makes it possible to sequence the work more logically, make results more visible, and, especially, to take advantage of recipe 2. At the highest level, the top-down decomposition corresponds to the subsystems of a given system.

Recipe 4: Use Bootstrap Implementation.

The advantages of using the system to build the system were described in Chapter 8. When coupled with top-down implementation, this approach probably constitutes the most dependable guide for planning the development of a data processing system. It has, among others, two advantages: a progressive speedup in production as development advances; and the reduction and occasionally even the elimination of the reworks.

Activities and Resources

Recipe 5: In Data Processing Development, the Progress of an Activity Is Measured in the Binary System.

In conventional activities such as construction, there is no problem in referring to an activity as being X% complete. Such is not the case in data processing development. When 80% of the allocated time has been used up, there is no guarantee that 80% of the activity has been completed. In fact, nothing is known for certain, and wisdom dictates that 0% and 100% be the only values used for measuring the state of progress of a given activity. Using such an approach naturally means that a large portion of the activity may be uncontrolled. The solution to this problem does not consist in trying to pinpoint inevitably unrealistic percentages. (How does one know when 90% of the tests have been completed?) Rather, it consists in defining activities small enough to be controlled.

Recipe 6: A Data Processing Activity Is Not Interrupted Once It Has Begun.

This procedure is often used to speed up activities which are behind schedule. A bulldozer can be shifted from job A to job B and then back to job A without causing any real problems. However, having a programmer stop in the middle of program A in order to do program B and then return to program A is not particularly productive.

Recipe 7: A Human Being Is a Very Inefficient Time-sharing Machine.

Consequently, assigning several parallel activities to the same person is not recommended in data processing development.

Recipe 8: The Most Critical Tasks Are Assigned to the Most Reliable People.

Because of the uncertainty surrounding estimates and personnel performance, it is preferable to assign a task to a slower but reliable person than to a periodically dispirited genius (see Gildersleeve, 1974).

Recipe 9: A Good Project Manager Sees to It That No One Becomes Irreplaceable.

All of the activities carried out by an "irreplaceable" individual constitute a second critical path.

Critical Paths

Recipe 10: The Critical Path Must Not Be a Private Path.

If all or nearly all of the activities along the critical path are assigned to the same person or team, the path becomes doubly critical since it is practically impossible to make up any lost time. Unfortunately, this type of task assignment is quite probable in small projects and/or with small teams.

Recipe 11: The Critical Path Is Not the Only Critical Element.

An activity located on the critical path is important because any delay in completing it results in a delay at the overall project level. There are other activities which require at least as much attention as those situated on the critical path, and whose completion can be blocked by such problems as technical difficulties.

Recipe 12: In the Field of Data Processing, the Critical Path Is Very Unstable.

Once the development of the system is under way, the actual durations of the activities may result in an extensive shift of the critical path. Moreover, it will shift not just once, but continuously as the project progresses. In the field of data processing, those activities which are critical because of their very nature require the attention of the project manager more than the critical path itself.

Does Slack Exist in System Development?

Recipe 13: Murphy's Law: If Something Must Go Wrong, It Will—at the Worst Time.

This law is considered dogma by good data processing specialists. It leads them to regard with skepticism the varying amounts of slack appearing in the initial network. They know that the slack will often be negated because of estimating errors or unforeseen difficulties.

Recipe 14: A Project with No Slack Will Run behind Schedule.

This truism follows logically from the preceding recipe.

Recipe 15: A Good Project Manager, Like a Squirrel, Stores away Slack for More Difficult Times.

If possible, whenever the project manager has control over the final deadline date (as is the case in resource-bounded projects), he leaves some room to maneuver when selecting the date he will submit to his superiors. Moreover, when assigning activities, he will reserve half of the slack contained in any activity for himself and give the other half to the development team.

Recipe 16: Be Able to Recognize Genuine Slack.

In a data processing project, slack time contained in any activity can be considered to provide real room for maneuvering only if it meets the following two conditions:

1. The estimate of the activity is sound.
2. The resources allocated for the activity are interchangeable.

The first condition is justified by recipe 12; the second can be justified by applying recipes 2 and 13 to the activity, preceding the one in question and making use of the same resource.

SCHEDULES

Objectives

Once the network and resource allocation have been revised in accordance with the various constraints (including those listed on p. 000), the results of the planning activity—in other words, the schedules—have to be produced. To put them into proper perspective, let us examine the two objectives of this operation: organizing and controlling the work.

Organizing the work means specifying what to do, when, and with what resources. We will therefore need activity and resource schedules. *Controlling development* involves (a) assessing (determining how much progress has been made); and (b) measuring performance (i.e., comparing the actual situation to forecasts). Here again, schedules will control activities and resources.

A schedule can therefore be defined by two characteristics:

the item concerned: activity or resource, and

the function: organization or control.

Because a classification system must be adopted, the schedules will be grouped as follows: those involving activities will be presented first, and those involving resources second. Although this classification is arbitrary, it is preferable to a simple listing.

Activity Schedules

Gantt Charts

The oldest, most widely used, and apparently most effective tool is the Gantt Chart or bar chart. Invented in the early 1900s by H. L. Gantt, it contains one line per activity, with the horizontal axis starting at the beginning of the project and defining the time.

EXAMPLE H: GANTT CHART OF THE CONVERSION PROJECT

Using the network in Figure 10.8, Diana Charters draws the chart depicted in Figure 10.9. To do this she must convert man-days into calendar weeks. Yet the Institute's employees can only give 70% of their time; for them, one calendar week = 5 × .7 days = 3.5 workdays. For the supplier's analyst, on the other hand, one week of work represents 5 days. This is why the 117 days of the MEDIC system lasts only 23.4 weeks, compared with the 22.9 weeks of the PMC system which requires only 80 days of work.

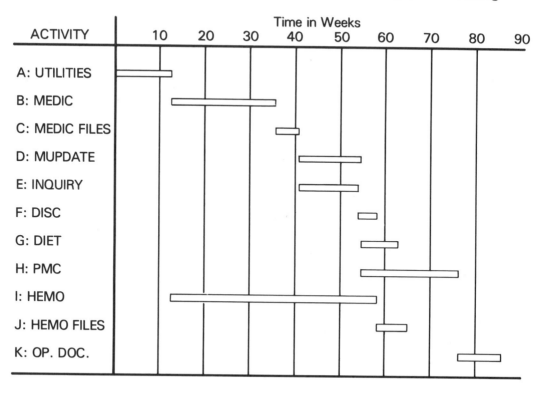

Fig. 10.9. Gantt Chart of conversion project.

The advantages of a Gantt Chart are that it is easy to draw up, easy to read, and can be used as a tool for controlling the progress of a project by shading in the portions of the activities which have already been completed. The disadvantages are that a Gantt Chart does not illustrate the interrelations between activities; it cannot be used once the number of activities reaches a certain limit; and it poses updating problems. These arguments are constantly offered to justify the use of networks instead of Gantt Charts (see Brandon & Gray, 1970; Gray, 1981). However, we believe that the Gantt Chart does not replace but in fact complements a network, and is very effective in small and medium-sized projects. Moreover, modern data processing systems involving networks invariably contain a report which is practically a Gantt Chart in itself.

Milestone Charts

For the people in charge, who are more interested in results than in the detailed task breakdown, a milestone chart constitutes a very effective control tool. Table 10.3 illustrates the simplest form of a milestone chart.

The only elements of information contained are the milestones and the forecasted and actual dates of completion. The table can be refined by adding

TABLE 10.3
MILESTONE CHART AS OF JUNE 1, 1978

Milestone	Forecast	Achieved
DISC	4/15/78	4/30/78
DIET	5/20/78	5/20/78
PMC	9/1/78	
HEMO	4/15/78	5/10/78

columns for the revised forecasts, the state of progress at the time of the revisions, and so on. Experience does not lead us to favor these refinements, since their significance in data processing is questionable, and their use also implies the expectation that the milestone chart can play a role of which it is incapable: that of being a complete control tool. It is, above all, a tool that allows one to determine how fast the project has progressed. If more extensive information is needed, Gantt Charts and the other control tools (see Chapter 13) are more useful.

Resource Schedules

Resource load charts are graphs depicting the consumption-time relation for each resource (see Figure 10.10). These charts have two advantages. First, their use makes it possible to determine if the load is evenly distributed over the entire project. Second, they permit comparison of forecasted and actual consumption of a given resource. In data processing projects, in which human resources represent the greatest portion of the resources used, these graphs will be very useful as control tools whenever real budgeting control (in dollars) is lacking. They are, in effect, the only way of learning the amount of resources consumed and when.

An *individual schedule* is a kind of personalized and condensed Gantt Chart. It may resemble Figure 10.11, for example, and will indicate the activities to be completed by a particular person or team. The forecasted and actual starting

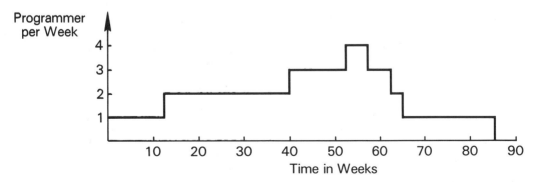

Fig. 10.10. Example of resource workload.

Individual Schedule Name: Diana Charters				
Activity	Forecasted		Actual	
	Start	End	Start	End
Utilities Medic Files Diet	3/1/77 11/15/77 3/15/78	6/1/77 12/20/77 5/20/78	3/5/77 11/20/77 3/15/78	6/11/77 12/20/77 5/20/78

Fig. 10.11. Example of individual schedule.

and ending dates are indicated for each activity. This type of schedule is especially useful to team leaders such as chief programmers, since a simple glance affords them an overall view of the situation.

The various scheduling tools must not be regarded as a collection of alternative methods but, rather, as complementary techniques. Each is adapted to a specific project management function. However, at no time can they be considered substitutes for planning and its basic tool, the network.

SELECTED REFERENCES

Brandon, D. H., Gray, M. 1970. *Project control standards.* Auerbach Publishers.
    Despite its title, the book covers much more than just the actual controls, since it examines development processes, project selection, and estimates. Devoted exclusively to systems development projects, the book strongly emphasizes the need for control documents.

Gildersleeve, T. R. 1974. *Data processing project management.* New York: Van Nostrand Reinhold.
    Dealing exclusively with development projects, this book is obviously the fruit of extensive experience. The introduction takes the form of a series of documents within an organization (memos, department messages, etc.) describing a failure. In this way the real problems faced by a project manager are illustrated. One interesting aspect of the book (for computer specialists) is that it contains no "data processing lessons"; it deals only with project management and provides much practical advice.

Gray, C. F. 1981. *Essentials of project management.* New York: Petrocelli Books.
    This work constitutes an excellent introduction to networks and their use in planning. Using a simple and clear approach, the book enables the reader to absorb the basic knowledge needed to manage small or medium-sized projects.

In particular, the methods used in dealing with both time- and resource-bounded projects are examined.

Harrison, F. L. 1981. *Advanced project management.* Aldershot, England: Gower Pub. Co.
Contrary to Gray's work, Harrison assumes that the reader has already mastered the basic network concepts and therefore introduces modern project planning and control techniques. It is very enriching reading for those interested in well-structured management of large projects.

Koenig, M. H. 1978. Management guide to resource scheduling. *Journal of Systems Management,* January, 24-29.
The article gives a detailed analysis of the scheduling process and the reports or outputs that programs of this type can provide. For the author, the starting point is the resource library indicating which resources are limited in quantity.

Miller, W. B. 1978. Fundamentals of project management. *Journal of Systems Management,* November, 22-29.
Devoted to planning and control, the article presents the basic characteristics of these two activities. Special emphasis is placed on the fact that the planning documentation forms the basis of the control activity.

Chapter 11
BUDGETING

INTRODUCTION

In past years, data processing professionals usually had little background in accounting and finance. The computer science curricula in most universities left little room for these disciplines, and even where they did, students were not interested. They would graduate and jump into what they liked doing most: programming, analyzing, and designing—in other words, building systems. Those who were eventually promoted to higher management levels through technical supervising positions managed to learn the problems involved in planning, organizing, and directing people. They even learned to write reports. But budget? Because the present breed of computer science students seems no different, it is still useful to review accounting and budgeting concepts on a very basic level.

EXAMPLE A: ADMISSION-DISCHARGE-TRANSFER SYSTEM BUDGET

Good Samaritan Hospital has approved the specifications of the admission-discharge-transfer (ADT) system (see examples in Chapter 7). Donald White, the project manager, has completed the entire planning and estimating process. Tables 11.1 and 11.2, respectively, contain a summary of his development estimates and of the hardware requirements of the new system. In Table 11.1,

TABLE 11.1
ADT SYSTEM DEVELOPMENT ESTIMATES

Activity	Number of People	Duration (in weeks)	Total Requirements	
			Analysts	Programmers
A: General design	2 analysts	20	40	
B: Identification	2 programmers	25		50
C: Waiting list	1 programmer	15		15
D: Admission	2 programmers	20		40
E: Discharge	1 programmer	15		15
F: Transfer	1 programmer	10		10
G: Patient movements	2 programmers	10		20
H: Reports	2 programmers	10		20
		Total	40	170

TABLE 11.2
ADT SYSTEM HARDWARE REQUIREMENTS

Hardware	Location	Time Required
5 display terminals	Admission	admissions ready
2 printers	Admission	admissions ready
1 card printing machine	Admission	admissions ready
2 display terminals	Medical Records	identification ready
1 printer	Medical Records	identification ready
2 display terminals	Emergency	admissions ready

Activity A is the general design of the system. Activities B to H are summaries of more detailed estimates; each represents the detailed design, programming, testing, and implementation of the corresponding system. The related network is shown in Figure 11.1, and the milestone schedule is presented in Table 11.3. On each activity segment (Figure 11.1), the first number is the duration, with the second, in parentheses, representing the number of people involved. White's next step is to present a budget for final project approval.

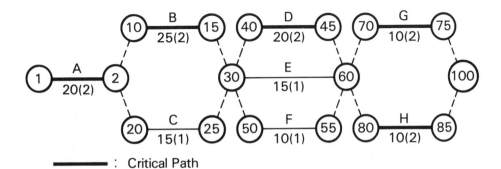

——— : Critical Path

Fig. 11.1. Network of ADT system development.

TABLE 11.3
MILESTONE SCHEDULE OF ADT SYSTEM DEVELOPMENT

Milestone	Date
Start of the project	February 15, 1978
General design ready (A)	July 15, 1978
Identification ready (B)	January 10, 1979
Waiting list ready (C)	October 10, 1978
Admission-Discharge-Transfer ready (D, E, F)	June 10, 1979
Patient movements ready (G)	August 31, 1979
Reports ready (H)	August 31, 1979

WHY A PROJECT BUDGET?

Different Budget Functions

Of the three functions of the budget document—decision tool, baseline, and reference, the first is the most important because it represents the last time the project can be cancelled before production begins and large amounts of money have been committed to it. This will be discussed later in greater detail.

You will recall that a baseline document defines a result to be achieved (see Chapter 4). Table 11.4 illustrates the fact that the budget is the overall *resources* baseline document, just as the specifications constitute the *product* baseline document, and the plan and schedule the *time* baselines. While the specifications define only the final product, the budget, like the schedule, specifies not only the final results but also intermediate goals, which will be helpful for financial planning and control.

The budget is also a reference document. It can be used as a source of information when the project manager wants to know how much money was spent, how well it was spent, and whether there are any resources left—in other words, when he wants to control overall resource consumption. This function will be dealt with later, and we will see that it will deeply affect the structure of the budget itself.

TABLE 11.4
THE BUDGET AS ONE OF THE THREE PROJECT BASELINE DOCUMENTS

Project Constraints	Baseline Document
Specific product	Specifications
Fixed time frame	Schedule
Fixed amount of resources	Budget

Conventional Accounting and Its Problems

The accounting of any organization records incoming and outgoing flows of money. Let us suppose, for example, that the monthly report of the computing department is as presented in Table 11.5. Note that expenses (or income) are recorded in terms of three dimensions:

1. Location within the organization (in this case, the computing department).
2. Time (in this case, March 31).
3. Type of expense or income.

While this may be sufficient in a stable environment where the flow of activities is constant, it creates several problems in the project context.

- o Time: An expense (or any income) is recorded when it occurs. In a project, however, an expense is related to a resource, and the point of interest is not when it is paid for, but when it was used.
- o Location: With the conventional system, there is no way of consolidating expenses occurring in different departments. The entire dimension is inadequate.
- o Activities: As can be seen in Table 11.5, there is nothing relating an expense to the use of the corresponding resource; there is no way of knowing which activities have been performed.

These problems have been mentioned again and again (e.g., Block, 1971; Harrison, 1981; Maciariello, 1974), and a budget must provide the solutions if it is to be of some help to the project manager.

The Project Budget

A conventional budget can be considered a projection of an organization's income and expenses. It is always organized along the time and category dimen-

TABLE 11.5
MONTHLY INCOME-EXPENSE STATEMENT

Department: Computing   Period ending: March 31, 1978

Code	Item	Period income	Period expenses	To Date income	To Date expenses
31003	Salaries		$78,483.77		$236,943.28
31004	Benefits		5,348.51		15,732.28
57005	Computing equipment (rental)		41,382.45		134,147.35
57006	Computing equipment (purchase)		2,325.00		8,640.00
81413	Supplies		3,540.21		7,413.32
	Total Computing		$131,079.94		$402,876.23

sions, and sometimes along the department or "activity centers" dimensions, if the organization is large enough.

We know that the time dimension in a project is of critical importance. The category dimension is also important, as long as it can be related to an activity. The activities in a project will therefore play the same role as the activity centers in an organization. A project will be organized along the following three dimensions:

time,

type of expense, and

activity for which the expense is incurred.

Given these characteristics, a project budget is nothing more than the projection of the project's plan and schedule on the money dimension.

EXAMPLE B: SUMMARY BUDGET OF THE ADT PROJECT

If, for purposes of summary, the ADT project is divided into two parts—design and programming-testing, one possible budget is presented in Table 11.6. Here, the unit of time used is the year. This unit is much too large for control purposes—the month or week would be better. However, budgets are like plans; they can be presented on several levels, depending on what they are to be used for. The type of summary budget shown in Table 11.6 will be useful for overall evaluation and financial planning. For control purposes, a more detailed presentation will be required.

A conventional budget does not usually make it possible to relate amounts to activities. It only shows categories of expenses (or income) such as salaries,

TABLE 11.6
ADT SYSTEM DEVELOPMENT SUMMARY BUDGET

Item	1978	1979	Total
Design			
Salaries (including fringe benefits)	13,500	13,500	
Total Design	13,500		13,500
Programming-Testing			
Salaries (including fringe benefits)	29,865	53,295	83,160
Equipment (rental)	425	9,300	9,725
Computer time	6,000	12,000	18,000
Others	3,000	3,000	6,000
Total Programming	39,290	77,595	116,885
Total Project	52,790	77,595	130,385

computer time, and so forth. However, as will be seen in a later section, the main control problem is to relate progress (activities completed) to expenses (resources spent). An organization's normal accounting system does not provide for this link. If the project manager does not insert it into his budget, he will later experience much difficulty trying to find it using two separate control systems.

Some environments, however, provide this kind of accounting framework, namely, those organizations whose products are projects or contracts: consulting and engineering firms, software companies, and so on. Usually, a reporting system enables the project managers and team leaders to monitor resource consumption as related to activity type. Later we will examine some of the tools which are available for this purpose.

SETTING UP A PROJECT BUDGET

The Process

Preparing any kind of budget is a long and tedious task which may require many iterations. (We should now be accustomed to starting things over and over again.) The basic cycle is illustrated in Figure 11.2.

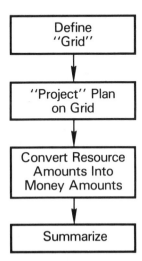

Fig. 11.2. Process of project budgeting.

Define Grid

This step consists in specifying the units or items in the three dimensions.

TIME.   The month is usually the unit of time chosen; for long projects, however, it could be the quarter or even the year.

CATEGORIES.   In principle, it should be possible to differentiate among the categories of resources used; for example, human resources could be broken down into analysts and programmers instead of being grouped together as in Example B.

ACTIVITIES.   The objective here is to make it possible to link expenses to specific project work. The level of detail used in the detailed budget usually corresponds to that used in the detailed plan, while the budget summary corresponds to the highest-level plan and schedule.

EXAMPLE C: THE BUDGET GRID FOR THE ADT SYSTEM

The unit of time used for the detailed budget will be the month, since the hospital accounting system provides for monthly budget control and expenses reports.

The hospital accounting and reporting system provides for different categories of salaries, making it possible to include the following categories in the detailed budget:

salaries, analysts

salaries, programmers

computer equipment (rental)

computer time (charged by the computer department back to the project)

other expenses

Activities will be grouped into the following subsystems (see Table 11.1):

general design

identification

waiting list

admission, discharge, transfer

patient movements and reports

In principle, this will lead to a grid having 25 lines (5 activities, 5 categories of expenses) and 19 columns (19 months, from February 1978, to August 1979). All 475 cells will have to be completed with the relevant data.

Project the Plan onto the Grid

This step involves taking a given activity from the plan and putting it into the time columns corresponding to its schedule and duration, as well as placing it into the activity group to which it belongs. The amounts of the various resources needed to perform the activities will then be written down according to the categories available in the budget. This will be done for all activities belonging to the same activity group and time frame. The results will be added up for each cell.

EXAMPLE D: ADMISSION-DISCHARGE-TRANSFER BUDGET WORKSHEET

The time period involved is the months from January to June 1979. There are three systems to be programmed, debugged, and implemented: admission, discharge, and transfer.

- Human resources: (see Figure 11.1 and Table 11.2). Admission: 40 weeks or 10 months of programming spread equally over the 5 months. Discharge: 15 weeks or 3.75 months starting January 10. Transfer: 10 weeks or 2.5 months starting January 10.
- Computer equipment: There are already two display terminals and one printer in the medical records department. With respect to the admissions and emergency departments, the equipment for testing the programs will be installed in May 1979.
- Computer time: Admission: 7 hours/month starting April 1979. Discharge: 3 hours/month (March and April). Transfer: 3 hours in March.

A worksheet like the one depicted in Table 11.7 will be drawn up. As noted in Example C, the only lines of interest with respect to the budget are the "total" lines of each resource category. The other lines are present because it is the only way of obtaining the results.

Convert Resource Amounts into Money Amounts

This is an easy step, provided the data needed to perform it are available. Some data sources will be discussed shortly.

EXAMPLE E: DETAILED BUDGET

Let us suppose that the rates of the various resources involved are as follows:

- Programmers: $1980/month

TABLE 11.7
DETAILED BUDGET WORKSHEET
ADMISSION-DISCHARGE-TRANSFER SUBSYSTEM

	Jan. 1979	Feb. 1979	Mar. 1979	Apr. 1979	May 1979	June 1979	Total
Programmers (man-months)							
activity D	1.33	2	2	2	2	.67	10
activity E	.67	1	1	1	.08		3.75
activity F	.67	1	.83				2.50
total programmers	2.67	4	3.83	3	2.08	.67	16.25
Equipment (T = terminal; P = printer; C = card printer)							
admissions dept.					5T,2P,C	5T,2P,C	
medical records dept.	2T,P	2T,P	2T,P	2T,P	2T,P	2T,P	
emergency dept.					2T	2T	
total equipment	2T,P	2T,P	2T,P	2T,P	9T,3P,C	9T,3P,C	
Computer time							
activity D				7	7	7	21
activity E			3	3			6
activity F			3				3
total computer time	0	0	6	10	7	7	30

○ Equipment: display terminal, $125/month; printer, $175/month; card printer, $250/month

○ Computer time: $300/hour

Once these rates have been established, the budget in Table 11.8 is easy to draw up.

Summarize

Summaries from the detailed budget are usually obtained by compressing or even eliminating one of the three dimensions.

TABLE 11.8
PARTIAL DETAILED BUDGET, ADT SUBSYSTEM

	Jan. 79	Feb. 79	Mar. 79	Apr. 79	May 79	June 79	Total
Admission-Discharge-Transfer Subsystem							
Salaries, programmers	5,286.60	7,920	7,583.40	5,940	4,118.40	1,326.60	32,175
Equipment	425	425	425	425	1,900	1,900	5,500
Computer time			1,800	3,000	2,100	2,100	9,000
Total	5,711.60	8,345	9,808.40	9,365	8,118.40	5,326.60	46,675

Data Sources

When trying to draw up his first budget, the project manager sometimes has no idea of the rates to apply when converting resource amounts into money amounts. This is especially true for human resources, since salaries are always surrounded by a certain amount of secrecy. There are, however, several available sources of data:

○ In-house salaries: The personnel department has a record of both individual and average salaries by category, and a project manager has access to these data.

○ Market salaries: If the project manager has to hire people and figure out what it could cost to do so, several sources of data are available, such as the local Board of Trade, professional journals, etc.

○ Consultant rates: A rule of thumb for estimating consultant fees is to budget 4 times the hourly rate of the same in-house specialist.

Budgeting chargeable computer time is another problem facing the project manager. Although there are no effective rules for doing this, the formulas projecting 15% of the total cost of human resources were mentioned in Chapter 9. This sum is then spread over the programming and testing periods in increasing amounts.

Finally, several potentially useful guidelines regarding the proportions of the various budget components can be offered. In most computer projects and especially in system development, human resources make up the largest part of the budget, ranging from 70% in projects involving equipment and/or computer time to 95% in projects with no goods to acquire over the course of the undertaking (e.g., a computer selection project).

What are the cost proportions of the various activities in system development projects? Many results have been published, some of which are summarized in Figure 11.3. Their comparison makes it obvious that harmony among results does not seem to be a quality present in resource consumption data. However, such divergent findings, which are due to the wide variety of projects and environments from which the data are drawn, should in fact make the project manager feel more at ease should his own results differ from any of those he has studied. As long as they are consistent with inhouse experience, he need not be too concerned.

To summarize the topics of data sources and cost proportions, the following rules of thumb should always be kept in mind:

○ Manpower costs constitute the main account in a data processing project, using up more than 70% of the total budget.

○ Hardware-related costs are the second largest expense. Together with salaries, they represent over 95% of the cost of a project.

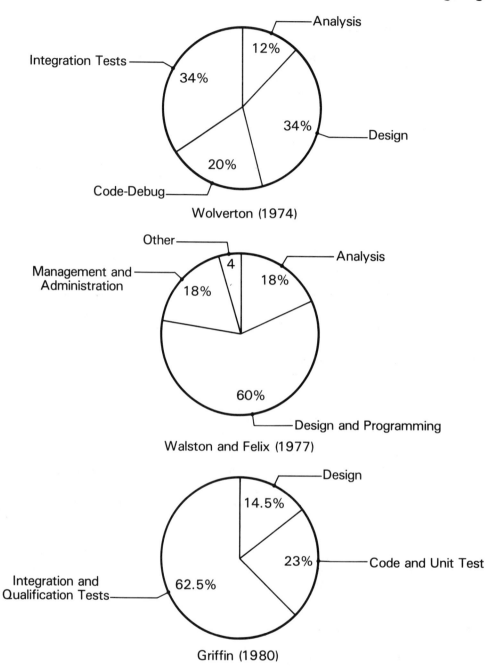

Fig. 11.3. Some proportions of life-cycle resource consumption.

Hidden Expenses

In this section we are interested in those expenses which are usually not predicted. For this reason they would perhaps more appropriately be called forgotten expenses.

A hidden expense is not a direct result of the estimating-planning-scheduling activities.

Following are the most important ones.

Salary-related Expenses

Salary-related expenses are the largest, since they relate to the main entry in the budget. These hidden expenses may include:

FRINGE BENEFITS. These constitute the employer's contribution to his employee's paid vacation, pension plans, medical insurance plans, life insurance plans, and so on. Varying from one sector of the economy to another, they can represent from 6% to 15% of the gross salaries.

INFLATION. If a project is to be spread over several years, inflation will increase salaries by 3% to 10%, depending on economic conditions.

SALARY INCREASES. Apart from the expected effects of inflation, salaries are usually expected to increase from one year to the next, depending on employee performance, organization-established criteria, or market conditions.

OVERTIME. Although in principle, professionals are not paid for overtime, programmers may receive overtime pay in some instances. Support staff are always being paid for overtime work. The cost of overtime may be 150% of the normal rate, and a project manager would be well advised to take this hidden expense into consideration if he has a tight schedule.

Hardware-related Expenses

The nice thing about equipment rental is that the cost includes almost everything. However, this is not always true when an equipment purchase is made, and some additional costs should be budgeted for.

INSTALLATION COSTS. Some are specified in the supplier's proposal; if not, the buyer should ask about them. In addition, site preparation costs are at the customer's expense and should be forecasted. Such costs can involve large amounts of money. For example, one of the departments in a large university purchased a minicomputer for approximately $30,000. At the time of installation, it was discovered that the substation supplying power to the department was saturated. A new substation had to be added to the electrical network and, with all of the related requirements, installation costs came to roughly $70,000.

MAINTENANCE COSTS.   Often forgotten or ignored in the budgeting exercise, yearly maintenance costs run from 6% to 12% of the purchase of a piece of equipment.

OVERHEAD.   This includes costs such as office rental, power, and telephone. In some organizations it does not have to be budgeted into the project; in others it does. Except in very special situations, it never constitutes a large proportion of the project budget.

TRAVEL EXPENSES.   It is always a good idea to budget for some travel costs, even if no trips are planned, since the allotted money can always be used as a buffer to compensate for overruns. However, it is typically a very small budget entry except in cases where the project is to be carried out at a location other than the staff's usual workplace, or when multi-location projects are involved.

Reserve Fund

This is the time to use some of the slack set aside in the planning process (see recipe 11 in Chapter 10). One method advocated by Maciariello (1974) involves withholding a certain amount of money from each authorized workpackage. Another is to budget for some portions of slack which fall into the "dubious" category (see recipes 8 and 9 in Chapter 10). Although this practice could be considered debatable, it has nonetheless been used several times and always with success; the slack "set aside" was in fact consumed by the activity it was related to. Although the most straightforward approach would be to put a "reserve-for-unexpected-problems" item in the project budget, such an item has, in our experience, *always* been withdrawn by finance or upper management personnel.

The Final Product

In its final form, a project budget is composed of four documents, a detailed budget like the one presented in Table 11.8, and three summaries along the three dimensions of time, activities, and categories of expenses. The role of the *detailed budget* is:

1. To act as a basis for the preparation of the summaries.
2. To be a working tool for the allocation of resources to workpackages.

3. To act as a control tool for the consumption of these resources.

To an accountant, the *expense categories summary* looks more like a regular budget than a summary. The costs of the different activities have been added together, leaving a conventional budget with the time and expense categories dimensions. The financial arm of the organization will use this tool to procure the means necessary for carrying out the project.

The *time summary* is a summary of great interest to management. Like the one shown in Table 11.6, it shows yearly budgets for long projects or quarterly summaries for other types. It is useful for evaluation and approval, as well as for long-term financial planning.

In the *activities summary*, the category expenses dimension has disappeared, leaving only activity costs related to time. This summary is intended for internal use by project management for high-level activity-related cost control.

PROJECT MANAGEMENT

Project Evaluation

The last time there was an evaluation of any kind in the life cycle of the project was at the end of the opportunity study. Going back to Chapter 5, we find that all of the financial data were approximate. (Specifications precisely defining a product constitute a contract on what is to be done, not an authorization to proceed.) The budget stage will therefore be the first time that more precise cost and schedule data are available, and the least which can be done is to compare these with the estimates. There are three possible outcomes.

1. *Budget is roughly equal with opportunity-study estimates.* When this wonderful situation happens, it means that the project manager is exceptionally skillful and the users extremely reasonable. Usually, the project can be continued in this perfect organization.
2. *Budget is under opportunity-study estimates.* Before heralding his findings, the project manager should verify that the product for which he prepared the production budget is the same product which was considered in the opportunity study. In other words, was a part of the originally planned system dropped or forgotten during system analysis? If this did in fact occur as a deliberate act, it should be so stated; if it occurred by chance, the entire exercise should be repeated, beginning with system analysis.
3. *Budget is over opportunity-study estimates.* This time we find ourselves in familiar surroundings. The most common reasons for this overrun are: (a) additions to the initially forecasted system, whereby during system analysis the user

asked for and obtained additions to the product which were not provided for in the opportunity study, (b) resource underestimates during the cost-benefit analysis, especially in the area of human resources, (c) omission of hidden costs, which is typical of opportunity study cost estimates, but does not usually represent very large amounts.

When a budget runs over the initial estimates, there is no solution other than to present the data along with the appropriate explanations. It is then up to upper management to decide on the future of the project.

Financial Planning

Typically, the project manager is not a financial expert. He sees to the planning and scheduling of activities and resources, and relies on the organization to provide the means of acquiring the resources. No organization has unlimited amounts of money at its disposal; like other resources, money must be planned and scheduled.

The basic information sheet used for this purpose is the budget-time summary which shows the money schedule of the project. The organization will use it to schedule the funds needed to acquire the resources, or even to produce those funds. This is particularly true in very large projects, where the development organization does not have funds available for the required investments. Unavailability of funds occurs more often when project-required expenses have not been forecast in the currrent financial year. This can affect the project schedule or plan if the project manager is required to delay some expenses until the following financial year, as often happens in the case of hardware acquisition, a large capital expense.

Control

What kind of control can be achieved by monitoring the money flow in a project? Clearly neither product control nor activity progress—the budget does not convey enough information for that. What will be controlled is the cost of performing the various project activities. Merely knowing how much money was spent as of a given date does not provide the project manager with enough information about activities progress. He needs to know which activities held to cost, which ones incurred overruns, and which ones yielded savings in money (usually along with savings in time).

In order to control the costs of activities, the project manager needs tools. The three most widely used are cost accounts, computer accounts, and time sheets. *Cost accounts* are segments of the project defined in order to monitor progress on a more manageable scale. They are subdivisions which contain all of the planning, scheduling, and budget characteristics of a complete project (see Harrison, 1981).

Going back to Example C, we see that the subsystems used to make up the detailed budget (general design, identification, waiting list, admission-discharge-transfer, and patient movements and reports) could well be defined as cost accounts. The important point is that if a cost account is to be useful, the budget should provide the data for its baseline.

Computer accounts are well-known tools which are underutilized for project control. Every mainframe and even some minicomputers have accounting systems that permit sophisticated cost reporting. To monitor computer-time expenses, a project entry is needed, as well as entries for the various cost accounts. Some systems offer a two-level entries system, while others are limited according to project and user. It is then up to the project management team to adapt a given tool to its needs.

Time sheets are used by project participants to record time spent on a given project. Human resources are the project's most expensive resources, and monitoring them represents the major function of resource control. The information recorded on time sheets is fed into a reporting system which indicates resource consumption on both a time and money basis. For a time sheet to be useful at the cost account level, each cost account must be assigned a code in addition to the project code. Time sheets will be discussed in greater detail in Chapter 13.

SELECTED REFERENCES

Block, E. B. 1971. Accomplishment/cost: Better project control. *Harvard Business Review,* May–June, 110-124.

> The paper presents a method called ACP (Accomplishment/Cost Procedure) designed for better project control. The basic problem to be solved is the difficulty in relating costs to schedule accomplishments. In ACP, costs are related to "units" of work performed. An interesting aspect is that for one-time (i.e., nonrepetitive) activities, the accounting value is zero as long as the unit of work is not finished.

Griffin, E. L. 1980. Real time estimating. *Datamation,* June 188-197.

> Real time is interpreted to mean that the estimate is required almost immediately upon request. Conventional methods cannot be applied, since carrying them out requires too much time and data. The approach is to identify factors influencing each activity of the development life cycle and to find equivalencies for the various aspects of the planned project. One of the frames of reference is the life cycle resource consumption.

Harrison, F. L. 1981. *Advanced project management.* Aldershot, England: Gower Pub. Co.
> Chapter 7 of this book deals exclusively with project budgeting and control. It discusses in depth the problem of whether or not to change a budget to reflect new situations such as inflation or the cost of a given resource. The cost account is defined and extensively discussed, especially with respect to very large projects.

Maciariello, J. A. 1974. Making program management work, part 2. *Journal of Systems Management,* July, 20-27.
> Once more, the problems surrounding conventional expense reporting systems are discussed. After defining the project budget, the author shows how it can be produced by using the project's work breakdown structure. He also mentions the necessity of creating a reserve fund for unforeseen problems by retaining a small portion of each workpackage authorization.

Wolverton, R. W. 1974. The cost of developing large-scale software. *IEEE Trans. on Comp.*, C-23, 6 (June), 615-636.
> The article is devoted to cost estimates of very large software projects. It looks at several traditional cost-estimating methods and proposes a two-step approach. In the first step, the product is estimated from a functional and technical point of view, with resource estimates being derived from that process. Then, a bottom-up real-dollar estimate is done for each workpackage, and after the two are compared and discussed, a final estimate is agreed upon. One of the references used in the first step is a distribution of the effort over the main portions of the development life cycle.

Part 4
PRODUCT REALIZATION

If we go back to the project life cycle presented in Figure 2.5, we see that we have arrived at a very important milestone: the beginning of production. Although many activities have already been performed, the bulk of the resources (50% to 80%) have yet to be consumed. Why, then, are only three chapters of the book devoted to product realization? The answer is twofold.

In the first place, there are several types of projects, and at least an entire book would be required to describe the technical problems involved in each of them. In addition, a large amount of literature and teaching material is already available for system development. This brings us to the second point: our principal focus is project management, rather than how to carry out a project. We have already seen that the project manager's main management function during product realization is control, although technical involvement is still a factor.

System development is not the only type of project, but it remains the largest and most difficult to carry out. We will examine some of the managerial and technical concerns of a project manager supervising the development of a system. The uncertainty surrounding design, programming, and testing makes control the most critical task in system development management, and this task will also be studied. Finally, we will investigate the mechanics of another type of project: computer selection. In this case, the technical aspect of the activities is less well-known and will be examined more closely.

Chapter 12
PROGRAMMING PROJECT: DESIGN, PROGRAMMING, TESTING

INTRODUCTION

Managing a system development team is an exciting experience. The boring tasks like debugging or documenting are carried out by staff members, and only "problems"—in other words, what is of interest to a computer scientist—are brought to the attention of the leader. After one or two experiences, however, the novice team leader discovers that before getting to the niceties of module decomposition or programming style, he has some homework to do: organizing the team, assigning responsibilities, and selecting a strategy.

Once the set has been erected, the play may begin: Act 1, design; Act 2, programming; Act 3, testing. The only problem is that system development is a play that is always in rehearsal. There are many disagreements concerning the way each scene should be played, and sometimes even the director is not certain of his own preference. We will examine the many options available for design, programming and testing and, to carry on the parallel with theatre, we will try to establish the principles on which the performance of any play can be based. The team leader, like the director, may have to demonstrate how a certain scene is to be played; however, he must remember that he is the manager, not the performer, and that the performer might be a better actor than he is—this is as it should be if the leader is a good project manager.

EXAMPLE A: SMT PORTFOLIO MANAGEMENT SYSTEM

In Chapter 4, we met Michael Bernstein, who was put in charge of developing a portfolio management system for SMT. A summary of the specifications was given in Chapter 8 and will be reviewed here.

Inputs include:

clients (enter, modify): any time

stocks: any time

quotations: any time

transactions: any time

Outputs include:

clients list: any time

stocks list: any time

client cash reports: monthly

client portfolio reports: monthly

client portfolio estimates: monthly

We will also reintroduce the project team: Michael Bernstein, project manager, will be the senior analyst. Susan Pratt, senior programmer, will also assist Michael in the design activities. Marvin Phister and John Paintree will both program. No database management system is to be used; a text-editor and report generator are available; and COBOL is the programming language.

Michael Bernstein has never been in charge of more than one programmer. Andrew Crawford, Director of Computing, knows this, and in order to give him some leads about what to do, he asks, "How did you organize your team?" Bernstein does not answer—he goes to his office to do his homework.

MANAGEMENT CONCERNS

The Realization Process

The process of producing a software system appears to be quite straightforward (see Figure 12.1). Design comes first, followed by programming and finally by testing. We already know that this perfectly sequential development cycle might end up with many loops being added to it. We also know that loops mean rework, and that rework often amounts to patching. A patched product is of poor quality—something the project manager does not want. Minimizing the possibility of loops will therefore be a major concern. This will be accomplished through careful design, disciplined programming, and well organized testing. The technical role of the project manager is just that: using his expertise to help his staff achieve a sound design, produce "proper" programs, and test the system instead of merely debugging it.

Looking at Figure 12.1, one might ask why the development cycle contains no documentation activity. It was stated in Chapter 4 that the documentation is embedded in each of the activities, rather than performed afterwards. One might also ask what each of the milestones in Figure 12.1 means. Does milestone 2 mean that the general design is completely finished before the detailed design is begun? Does programming take place only after the detailed design has been completed in its entirety? Is it the same for testing? Chapter 8 contained some clues that such might not always be the case: top-down implementation, for example. The process must therefore be more carefully examined.

Production Strategies

Deciding on a production strategy means determining in which order the many activities will take place. Production strategies may be grouped according to their particular orientation: activity oriented, level oriented, or operation oriented.

Activity Oriented Strategy

This is the strategy presented in Figure 12.1. All design work is completed before programming and all programming work before testing. The primary objective

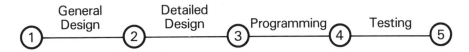

Fig. 12.1. Software product development cycle.

is safety: no design omission or error should be discovered during testing only; no programs will be forgotten, and so forth. Regarding use of personnel, a project is like a bus. People get on, stay a while, and get off—analysts first, then programmers, and finally testers. With the activity oriented strategy, this situation may lead to trouble if problems arise in a later stage of the project. However, the main disadvantage of this approach is the complete lack of visibility of results. The system will be running only in the last stages of the process; until then, progress is largely theoretical. This particular approach may work in highly structured environments with clearcut division of tasks as well as sophisticated documentation and progress report standards.

Level Oriented Strategy: Bottom-up

A system is composed of one or several hierarchies of programs (see Figure 12.2). In bottom-up production, the work begins with the lowest levels of programs, which are designed and written first so that they will be available to the upper levels. Historically speaking, this constituted the first organized approach, and it worked rather well. The method does, however, have two drawbacks. First of all, the lowest levels are close to machine-oriented operations, and this trend tends to be reflected at the higher levels, resulting in a "computer oriented" instead of a problem oriented design. Second, designing the lower levels first may result in integration problems at higher levels, given the absence of overall implementation decisions. The strategy almost inevitably leads to reworks and is now rarely used.

Level Oriented Strategy: Top-down

Here, design starts at the top, with each level being programmed as soon as it is well enough defined (see Figure 12.2). Lower levels to be developed later are

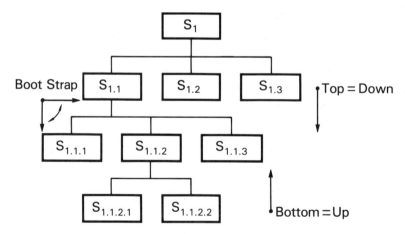

Fig. 12.2. Three strategies for system development.

replaced by "stubs"—dummy programs whose sole purpose is to test the behavior of the upper levels (Boehm, 1977). In this way, once a particular level has been designed, it can be tested, and design work can then proceed to lower levels with less risk of rework.

The process is visible and coherent. There are two drawbacks, however, when it is applied to large systems. First, a given resource (a program or a set of programs) which initially existed in "stub" form may well create many problems once it must actually be designed. Second, a situation in which one resource could be used in two different and possibly quite distant portions of the system could well go unnoticed, resulting in duplication of effort when the resource is produced twice in two different versions. Although top-down implementation seems to be the best strategy, we agree with Tausworthe (1977) that at least some bottom-up iterations must take place.

Operation-Oriented Strategy: Bootstrap

Used successfully by this author, this strategy complements top-down implementation. Let us return to Figure 12.2 and consider the first level: $S_{1.1}$, $S_{1.2}$, $S_{1.3}$. How do we proceed, using the top-down method? Do we begin with $S_{1.1}$, $S_{1.2}$ or $S_{1.3}$? The component selected is the one which can be tested independently of any results from the others; at the lower levels, it is the one which needs no dummy results in order to be tested. In other words, its inputs are produced by modules which are already available.

The strategy is highly visible, since intermediate results are operational parts of the system. It works very well for systems which are composed of independent subsystems, as is often the case in business. It is also attractive in cases where users are pressing for results, since it makes step-by-step implementation possible. Being a variant of top-down implementation, it, too, has the disadvantage of potential problems at the lower levels. However, the risk of the same requirement being programmed twice does not exist, since a product has already been developed at the time the second programming occurs.

In conclusion, it is important to select some development strategy, since any method is better than none at all. Top-down plus bootstrap works very well, but the final choice should take into account the environment, the work traditions of the team, and the skills of the project manager. If the manager is well trained in a given method, that is the one he or she should choose.

Team Organization and Structure

That a team should be organized is an obvious statement. Mantei (1981) noticed that team organization affects both the quality of the work and the productivity of the personnel involved. Four major programming-team structures may be identified:

chief programmer team

egoless programming team

controlled decentralized

cooperative decentralized

Chief Programmer Team

Through the article by Baker (1972), this type of organization has acquired wide recognition. It has sometimes been considered the organizational side of the structured design and programming methodology. Summarily described, it is a team composed of three members (see Figure 12.3a).

The *chief programmer* is a skilled and responsible software engineer who performs all of the technical work. (A project manager takes care of the administrative work.) The back-up programmer, who is also a senior level programmer, assists the chief programmer and acts as a back-up. The librarian is in charge of the program support library.

This structure worked very well in the instance reported by Baker, and has been hailed as "the solution." It is obviously a programmer's dream, designed

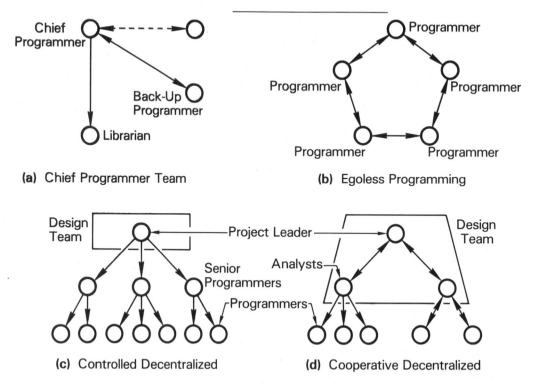

(a) Chief Programmer Team   (b) Egoless Programming

(c) Controlled Decentralized   (d) Cooperative Decentralized

Fig. 12.3. Programming team structures.

by high-level programmers for high-level programmers. The chief programmer is completely in charge of the interesting elements (design and programming) and is surrounded by assistants who do the "dirty work" of management and documentation. The structure works well in difficult projects involving a high degree of pressure, but also requires an exceptional type of professional who may be quite difficult to find. If these two conditions coexist, however, it is undoubtedly one of the best structures to implement.

A major problem with this particular type of organization is that all of the risk is concentrated at one point, on one person. What happens if that person fails to rise to the challenge, or quits? Few managers are likely to be comfortable with such a concentration of risk. Finally, this structure perpetuates the old "one-man show" tradition in computing, where one undertaking equals one person. It fits poorly into the present trend toward true teamwork in which several people having the same skills and experience cooperate with a view to achieving a common goal.

Egoless Programming Team

Proposed by Weinberg (1971), this approach is democracy in action (see Figure 12.3b). Several programmers (up to 10) share all of their decisions and accomplishments. No one is formally in charge. Depending on the particular circumstances, the person whose skills best correspond to the problem at hand assumes an informal leadership role for the period of time required to solve the problem.

It is obvious that working in such an environment is very pleasant. Too, the quality of the final product should be enhanced because the collective study of problems and solutions is usually better than individual work. It is also quite obvious that this structure is more research-oriented than project-oriented; costs and schedules can hardly be met.

Egoless programming is unrealistic in present-day organizational structures. Moreover, even in a democracy, someone eventually has to decide between two opposing positions.

Controlled Decentralized

This term was chosen by Mantei (1981) to designate the classical hierarchical structure found in almost all organizations. A project leader does the design and planning, assisted by senior programmers who manage small programming teams (see Figure 12.3c).

The structure is well suited to large undertakings with strict time requirements. It furthers modular design and reduces communications overhead. The fact that all of the design work is concentrated in one person (the project leader) results in good performance in projects where the level of difficulty is low. But what if the project is large, time-restricted, and difficult? This concentration of high-level work on one person then constitutes a problem. The structure may, nonetheless, have some advantages.

Cooperative Decentralized

This author has always loved design and enjoyed sharing his design proposals with others. The team structure shown in Figure 12.3d was used both in highly technical software projects (compilers, database management systems) and in more classical business applications. The structure is nearly the same as in controlled decentralized, except that senior programmers are replaced by analysts who manage small teams of programmers of all skill levels.

The major difference is in task allocation. The project leader is in charge of the mangerial aspects. But when it comes to general design, he *and* the analysts nearly become an egoless programming team: solutions are drawn up, discussed, and modified by this "peer group," with the project leader acting as leader only to decide between two or more opposing solutions for a given problem, and to keep track of the time and cost requirements of the design activity.

Once the general design has been completed, each analyst becomes the leader of his own team. He then has the option of doing the detailed design himself or involving his team. To turn out a good product (i.e., to have homogeneous detailed design practices), rigorous standards must be implemented and enforced. This works exceptionally well in stable environments such as large data processing centers or close-knit teams where standards have been formally or informally in force for a long time. It usually results in very good designs because, as noted earlier, even if the project manager is a good one, his analysts may well be better designers than he is. Why not put all of these skills to work?

As is always the case, quality must be paid for, and cooperative decentralization is quite expensive. This may be a drawback in some instances as compared with the controlled decentralized approach.

There is no magic solution to the team structure problem. The main guidelines come from the organization itself, where existing structures provide the best framework for solving the problem. In addition, the profiles, skills, and personalities of the team members usually lend themselves to the selection of one particular structure or another.

Personnel Profiles

In a paper on software engineering management, Bruggere (1980) distinguished between a *coder* (someone who knows how to write a program) and a *software engineer*, who is able to write reusable programs. Developing a software product which will be modified or used by others for a long time is a job for professionals, not for computing amateurs. The team must be composed of highly trained, highly skilled individuals. In actuality, a proper mix of skills and experience works best; a good team is not exclusively composed either of aces or of novices.

Let us look first at the technical profiles. In principle, there are three types of professionals: analysts, programmers, and testers.

Analysts are responsible for designing the system. They should all have university degrees in computer science or information systems. If not, they should be programmers who were promoted to this level because they showed an interest in problems beyond the level of simply trying to decide which programming trick to use.

Analysts should obviously have a deep understanding of the computer's operating system, possess database or files management expertise, and be familiar with the problem to be solved. All of this implies experience. In addition, they should know or at least be familiar with some design methods.

Today's *programmers* usually come from colleges where they have learned good programming practices and bits and pieces about detailed design, and where they have gained a good understanding of an operating system's capabilities. In many organizations, programming is the first assignment given to an analyst who has just graduated from university; it provides an excellent training ground.

A good programmer knows several programming languages, but is an expert in one. He also knows the machine very well and how to use the many tools supplied by the operating system. If, in addition, he is familiar with the problem to be solved, he is then both an expert and a future analyst.

Highly technical systems present a special case. In pure software projects such as operating systems and database management systems, or in highly technical applications like defense or real-time health systems, the analyst and the programmer merge to become one single entity: the *software engineer*. He has a university degree in computer science or in a scientific discipline related to the project, as well as a minor in computer science. This merger makes sense when the complexities of the problem at hand are not solved at the design level, but go all the way down to the programming task. It takes longer to explain or write the specifications of a program than to write and test the program itself.

We come now to the profile of the *tester*. Unfortunately, there is nothing resembling a course or degree in testing. Many people, confusing testing with debugging, assume that it is done by programmers. In principle, testing should be done by specialists who have extensive programming experience and are therefore familiar with the most common *and* uncommon programming errors. They should also have a deep understanding of the particular problem at hand; their main source of information is the specifications, not the program. The tester's goal is not so much to find bugs as it is to determine that the program works correctly.

Let us leave the technical aspects of the team profiles and turn our attention to the human qualities involved. The three most important are:

1. Ability to work on a team. Except for the case of the chief programmer team, system development is a collective task, and strong individualists do not adjust well to such a framework.
2. Reliability. If a manager wants to avoid having to monitor his personnel constantly, he will select people who can be left alone once their assignments have been defined.
3. Love of challenge. A project is both a race against time and a fight against costs. Doing a good job and meeting time and cost requirements constitute a challenge which some people would prefer not to accept; they perform better in routine environments or unscheduled time frames.

DESIGN

Overview

According to many people who have developed not just programs, but entire systems, design is the most difficult part of the production process (see Mantei, 1981). Boehm (1976) reported that more errors are introduced during design than during programming. For Rajaraman (1983), it is the best design that produces the best software. If well defined, a poorly written program can always be rewritten properly. A poorly designed system, on the other hand, has to be redone completely—there is no way it can be patched. For years, this author has claimed that good design—not good programming—makes good systems, and that it is the former which should be investigated first. At the time, it was like preaching in a wasteland, with the only response from programming experts being: "What's design?" Fortunately, the situation has changed.

For many people, design is equivalent to programs design. This, too, is wrong; it deals with data as well as processes, and it is our opinion that data design is the more important. In business applications, the programs *process* the organization's information, while the data *are* the information. The data usually outlive the programs, with an error in data design affecting all of the programs. An omission discovered after years of use cannot be repaired; the information is gone.

Design can be summarized by the diagram in Figure 12.4. Before being implemented, both data and processes have to be designed. This is done in two successive steps:

1. General design, which deals with objects and concepts related to the whole system; and

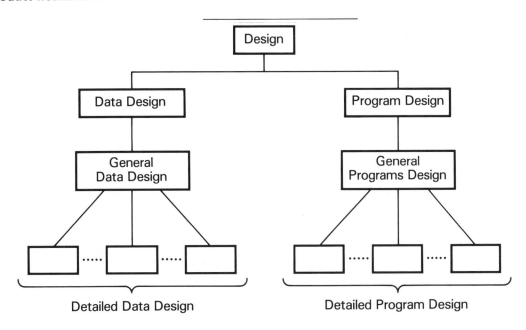

Fig. 12.4. Overview of design.

2. Detailed design, which performs the same work, but on increasingly smaller parts of the whole.

In a well timed progression, each step of data design should take place before the corresponding step related to programs. There will obviously be iterations both vertically (from detailed to general) and horizontally (from programs to data), but the starting framework should be the one shown in Figure 12.4.

General Design

General design is the process of defining (a) the data processing objects which will perform the functions required by the specifications, and (b) the interrelations among these objects.

The way in which the objects will be implemented is not a part of this definition; rather, it belongs to detailed design. To get an idea of what the functions are, one need only look at the entries in the table of contents in the specifications manual (see Figure 7.13): these are the functions referred to in the definition.

EXAMPLE B: SMT.PM SYSTEM

Simply looking at the description given in Example A allows us to draw the scheme shown in Figure 12.5. The lines connecting the data objects mean that

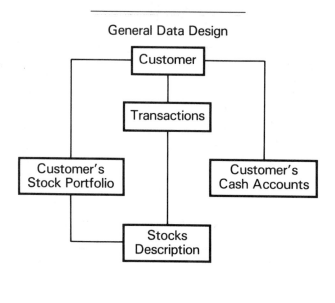

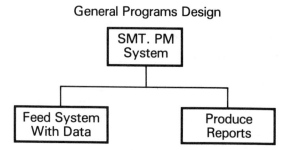

Fig. 12.5. A very simple case of very general design.

there is a relation (something in common) between them. It does not mean that pointers exist from one to another. (For the time being, we do not know what pointers are.)

Data Design

The first step is to define the data objects to be stored by the system, as well as their relationships. General data design is often called *data modeling* because a model is used to represent the problem's information world. To demonstrate the process, we will use Chen's well-known and efficient "entity relationship model" (Chen, 1976).

entity: An entity is an object which can be recognized and distinguished from others (e.g., a customer, a transaction).

attribute: An object has a certain number of properties which are used to describe it (e.g., name of customer, date of transaction).

entity set: All of the entities described by the same attributes are in the same entity set; they are distinguished from each other by the values of their attributes.

relationship: Often, entities from different entity sets are linked by some relation (e.g., a transaction was done for a given customer).

EXAMPLE C: SMT.PM SYSTEM DATA DESIGN

Figure 12.6 contains two entities: customer and transaction. An entity is represented by a rectangle, an attribute by an oval linked to the entity it characterizes. Relations are in lozenges with lines going out to the related entity-boxes.

Figure 12.7 contains a summary of the SMT.PM system data model. Here it can be seen that:

o A transaction is linked to a customer (for whom it was performed) and to a stock (the object of the transaction).

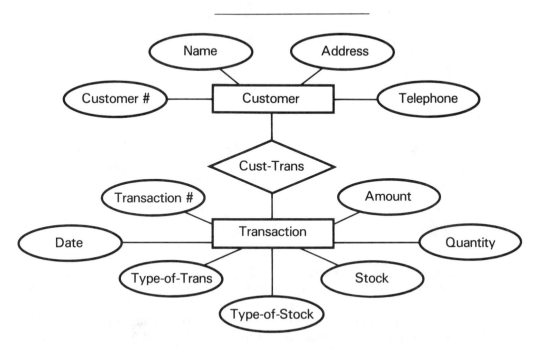

Fig. 12.6. Entity relationship model of CUSTOMER and TRANSACTION entities in SMT.PM system.

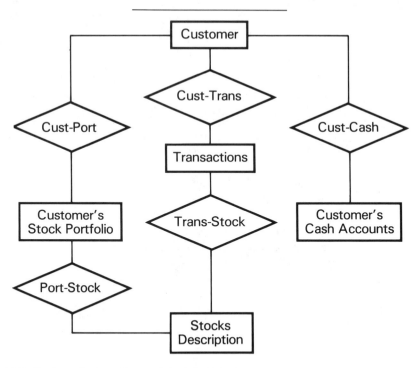

Fig. 12.7. Entity relationship model of SMT.PM data.

○ A portfolio is linked to a customer (possession).
○ A cash account is linked to a customer (possession).

The data structure is not designed based on the programs structure. It is designed independent of available files or database management systems. A common error in data design is to begin by defining files and records—that is detailed design.

Process Design

The word *process* is used instead of *program* because we are not yet at the program level. The result of general design could be a single program or a set of several hundred.

Many good methods have been defined (see Chapter 8). The method presented here and summarized in Figure 12.8 is inspired by Constantine's Structured Design. It will allow us to introduce some principles which are applicable regardless of the method used (see Stevens, Myers, & Constantine, 1974).

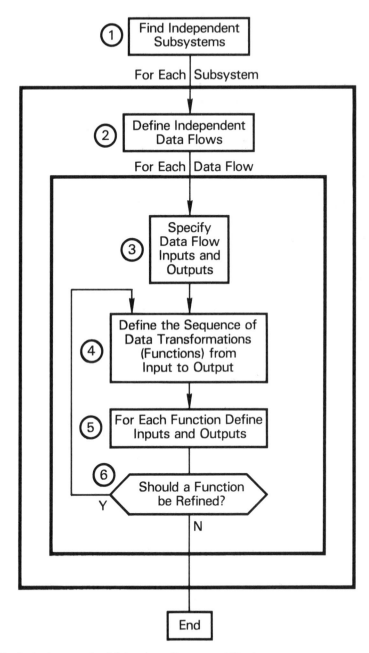

Fig. 12.8. A design method based on Structured Design.

Step 1: Find independent subsystems.

A business system (and many others) is often composed of processes which execute independently, and this should be reflected in the design. If two systems are independent, changes required by one are not required by the other; if, however, they are in the same program or set of programs, implementing changes would be much more complicated and hazardous.

We find the subsystems by going back to the specifications and looking for the triggering events of a function.

EXAMPLE D: SMT.PM SUBSYSTEMS

By examining the specifications summary in Example A, it can be seen that:

○ Inputting and outputting any data are independent operations.
○ One group of outputs can be required at any time.
○ One group of outputs requires special conditions (monthly reports).

The independent subsystems come out very simply and are shown in Figure 12.9.

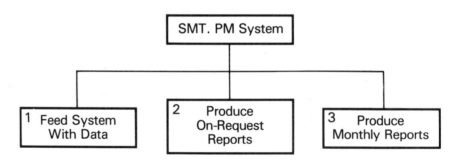

Fig. 12.9. Independent subsystems of SMT.PM.

Step 2: Define independent data flows.

We are now dealing with one particular subsystem. An independent data flow is a sequence of data transformations in which all inputs come from outside the computer and/or data bank and all outputs go directly to the outside world or data bank. In other words, when the data flow is processed, it receives no input from and sends no output to any other process.

EXAMPLE E: SMT.PM INDEPENDENT DATA FLOWS

One independent data flow is the entering of transactions: it starts with an external input (the transaction) and ends in the data bank. Another example is the monthly customer cash report, which starts with data from the data bank (transactions and cash account entities) and ends with a report.

Step 3: Specify data flow inputs and outputs.

This is an easy task since we have all the information we need: (a) system input descriptions from the specifications; (b) system output descriptions from the specifications; and (c) data bank description from the model.

EXAMPLE F: TRANSACTION PROCESSING DATA INPUTS AND OUTPUTS

The inputs are:

○ Transaction provided by the user.
○ Customer entity from the data bank (to check if the customer number on the transaction is valid).
○ Stock entity from the data bank (to check if the name of the stock on the transaction is valid).

The outputs are:

○ A transaction added to the TRANSACTIONS entity in the data bank.
○ The CUSTOMERS-CASH-ACCOUNTS entity (the customer entity is updated).
○ The CUSTOMERS-STOCK-PORTFOLIO entity (the customer entity is updated).

One problem with defining the inputs and outputs is whether to start with the inputs and work forward or to start with the outputs and work backward. In general, if the main data object is a system input like in example F, one starts with the inputs; the opposite is done if the main data object is a system output as, for example, in the customer cash report mentioned in Example E. In some cases, however, the answer is not as clear, and some iterations will be necessary.

Step 4: Define the sequence of data transformations.

The goal is to define the sequence of functions which transform the data along the data flow. In this case, we will define as a function any operation or set of operations which executes one data transformation. In any case, according to Constantine (Stevens et al., 1974), a function should be expressed by a very simple sentence containing one verb and one or two objects.

EXAMPLE G: SEQUENCE OF DATA TRANSFORMATIONS OF A TRANSACTION

This very simple sequence is comprised of three steps:

1. Enter transaction.
2. Process transaction.
3. Update data bank.

Step 5: Define function inputs and outputs.

A function is completely defined once the inputs and outputs, as well as the operation, are defined. Inputs and outputs are interfaces between the different system components. Well-defined interfaces result in a modular system and make separate work assignments possible.

EXAMPLE H: INPUTS AND OUTPUTS OF THE PROCESS TRANSACTION FUNCTION

The inputs are made of the validated data of the transaction:

TRANS #

DATE

CUST #

TYPE-OF-TRANS

TYPE-OF-STOCK

STOCK #

QUANTITY

AMOUNT

We have all of the data we need to update the cash account. Such is not the case, however, for the portfolio. If the transaction involves shares, what we need is the unit cost, not the total amount of the transaction. The outputs are:

TRANS #

DATE

CUST #

TYPE-OF-TRANS

TYPE-OF-STOCK

STOCK #

UNIT-COST

QUANTITY

AMOUNT

Step 6: Determine whether function refinement is needed.

By comparing the inputs and outputs of a function, one is able to determine if the transformation is straightforward or if it needs to be examined more closely. If a closer study is called for, the function is broken down by going back to step 4. We see here the importance of defining the inputs and outputs of a function precisely.

EXAMPLE I: REFINEMENT OF UPDATE DATA BANK FUNCTION

The transaction must first of all be added to the TRANSACTIONS entity. In addition, we have just seen in Example H that updating the cash account and updating the portfolio require slightly different data. To update the cash account, we have only to add the transaction amount to or subtract it from the customer's balance. To update the portfolio, however, we must:

○ Check to see whether the customer has this type of stock (in case of a purchase); if not, a new entity has to be created.
○ Add the quantity of shares to, or subtract it from, the present amount of stock.
○ Update the average cost per share.

It is clear that the process should be refined into three phases: transaction update, cash account update, and portfolio update. The result of the design process as carried out from step 1 through to the end for transactions input is contained in Figure 12.10.

General Principles

Several principles can be drawn from the process which we have just followed. For any method dealing with both data and process design, their application will produce a sound and durable design.

1. *Top-down*: Decomposition is performed by starting at the top and working down.
2. *Data-directed decomposition*: At any time, what prompts a decomposition is the problem's data. Subsystems are decomposed by recognizing independent data

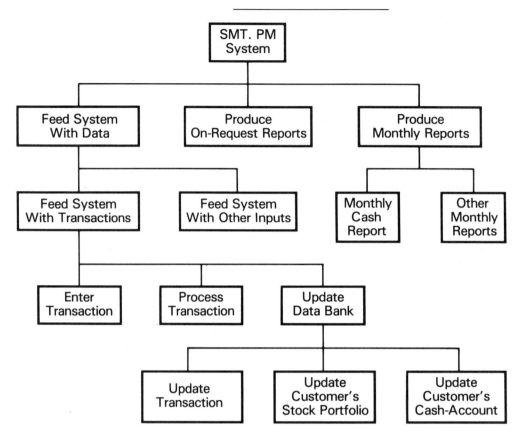

Fig. 12.10. Partial process decomposition of SMT.PM system.

flows, and the functions along a data flow are defined by the successive transformations experienced by the data along that data flow.

3. *Interface definition*: At any level, the inputs and outputs of a process are carefully defined.

4. *Modularity*: Once a function is completely defined (operations, inputs, outputs), it need not know anything about the other functions.

5. *Stepwise refinement*: Each object (subsystem, function) is first defined globally and then broken down, if necessary, into more elementary parts.

A sixth general principle can be summarized as a piece of good advice: *"Design to change."* In a business system, changes in the specifications will invariably be required, either during development or once the system is in operation. A good design must take this into account and make any new requirement easy, or at least not too difficult, to implement. Most changes occur in three areas:

1. New functions are added. This is why it is useful to have an Extension section in the specifications. Decomposing the system into independent subsystems also helps.
2. Modification occurs in the processing of data. The way some calculations are done will often change, and isolating each data transformation within a function will facilitate the implementation of changes.
3. New data are to be entered into the system, either in an existing entity set or a new one. The first case can be handled properly if interfaces are well defined. The second corresponds to a new independent data flow; if these are properly isolated, adding a new one will be easier.

Detailed Design

The dividing line between detailed design and general design or programming is not very clearcut. General design may go as far as specifying programs, and some program design decisions may be made during programming. Making a precise distinction between activities in one or the other stage does not matter as much as knowing exactly what is being done.

Detailed design is the process of deciding how the objects defined during the general design stage will be implemented.

Here we are at last, starting to shape the data processing system. It will be recalled that detailed design deals with processes *and* data, and that data implementation considerations are handled before programs.

Detailed Data Design

This process involves deciding how to implement the data bank on the storage tools available: files and/or DBMS. The first step is to decide how each object will be implemented. If we still use the entity relationship model, we have to assign an implementation for entity sets and relation sets.

If files are available (no DBMS), an entity set is assigned to a file. Usually, a relation set is split among the related files by adding the identifier (key) of the related entities to each entity. In complicated cases, a special file should be set up to handle the relationship.

In cases where DBMS is available, each DBMS has an object equivalent to an entity set (*relation* in the relational model; *record* in CODASYL; *segment* in hierarchical). An entity is therefore assigned to such an object. Relationships are handled according to the specific model. The decision depends on the DBMS model and the complexity of the relationships.

EXAMPLE J: SMT.PM DATA BANK

As noted in Chapter 8, no DBMS is available. Five conventional files will be used:

1. CUSTOMER: one record per customer.
2. TRANSACTIONS: one record per transaction. The CUST # and the STOCK # are already on the transaction and will be part of the record.
3. PORTFOLIO: one record per stock held by a customer. To keep track of the relationships, the record will hold the CUST # and the STOCK #.
4. CASH-ACCOUNTS: one record per customer, containing the CUST #.
5. STOCK-DESCRIPTION: one record per stock.

The file organization must also be determined during this step. It is usually selected according to the way the file will be used (direct access to the record, processing of the whole file, high update rate, etc.). It is not wise to mix too many file organizations in the same system, since a large amount of memory space would then be required to hold the various access methods. In the SMT.PM system, the decision was simple: all files were to be indexed sequential.

Next, each file record format must be defined precisely. The items to provide are:

o Record format (fixed or variable length)
o Record length
o Record key, if required
o The list of data items in the order in which they will appear in the record, including (for each one) name, starting position, length, format, and explanation.

EXAMPLE K: CUSTOMER FILE

Record type: fixed

Record length: 256

Record key: CUST #

Items	Start	Length	Format	Explanation
CUST #	1	6	PIC X(6)	customer number
CUST-NAME	7	20	PIC X(20)	customer name
ADDRESS1	27	30	PIC X(30)	address 1st line
ADDRESS2	57	30	PIC X(30)	address 2nd line
ADDRESS3	87	30	PIC X(30)	address 3rd line
PHONE	107	12	PIC X(12)	phone # with area code

The total length of the data items is 119 characters. The record length has been fixed at 256, however, on the wise assumption that new items will eventually be added. This is the first law of design-to-change when defining a record format.

Program Design

This time, we can talk about programs because detailed design is precisely that: deciding how the functions defined during general design will be translated into programs. Also, if required, we will structure the individual programs. Once more, the key word is modularity, and to be precise we will borrow Zmud's definition (1980, p. 47).

Modularity "is the segmenting of a software product's function into small, well defined independent modules."

The functions have already been determined by general design. They are defined by their interfaces and the problem function they have to carry out. Some guidelines should be applied so that the segmentation will be done properly.

TYPES OF OPERATIONS. There are three basic operations to perform when implementing a function:

1. Problem operations: what the function is about.
2. Data manipulation: converting the data from the input interface format into the data processing format, and the result into the output interface format.
3. Housekeeping: performing such tasks as clearing the buffers, setting or resetting indexes, initializing zones, and so on. Although housekeeping is often spread throughout a program, sometimes it can be localized in one module which can be struck from the memory once it has been used.

These operations should be kept separate as often as possible. In a milestone article, Parnas (1972) offered, among others, two decomposition criteria: The first is *information hiding*: "Every module knows one design decision which it hides from all others." The second is *abstract data types*: "A data structure, its internal procedures and modifying procedures, are part of a single module." The use of abstract data types is also discussed by Meyer (1982).

The following approach integrates these principles: Every function can be put into the form

I–P–O

where I = input, P = process, O = output (see Figure 12.11). The process P requires data to be provided in a specific form I(P) suitable for processing, and releases its results in a form O(P) defined by the process. Input data and output data, defined as interfaces between functions or as part of the data bank, have no reason to be in the format I(P) or O(P). The I and O modules will act as data transformers and present (take) data in P form. In this way:

o The set I(P), P, O(P) may become rigid, i.e., its interfaces are not to change if the outside world does.
o The data transformations and any change in input or output data formats will be handled by the I and/or O modules. We have achieved the criteria of information-hiding and design-to-change.

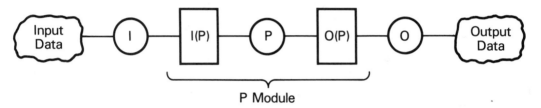

Fig. 12.11. Application of abstract data types to I–P–O decomposition.

The last principle of interest is that of levels of processing. When going from the problem level to that of physical implementation of data, we can distinguish three levels of processing:

1. Problem level (process P in Figure 12.11)
2. Conversion of data into format required by P
3. Access to data as it is implemented (often provided by access methods)

These three levels will be illustrated in the following example.

EXAMPLE L: PRODUCING THE PORTFOLIO ESTIMATE

To produce the estimate of a customer's portfolio, we must take each stock the customer holds, multiply the amount of shares he has by the current stock value, print the result, and add the current values of all stocks. To do this, we need to access the following files:

1. CUSTOMER: to obtain his name and number.
2. PORTFOLIO: to determine the contents of his portfolio.
3. STOCK: to obtain the share names and quotations.

The three levels of processing are shown in Figure 12.12. Let us suppose, for example, that the record format changes in a given file; only the interface

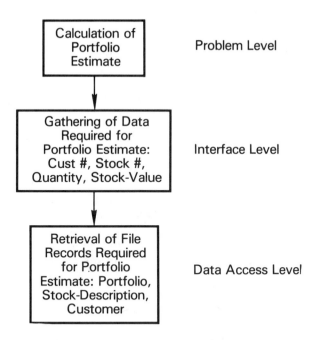

Fig. 12.12. Three levels of processing to access stored data.

level would have to be modified. If the files are replaced by a DBMS, only the data access level will have to be modified. Each level acts as a shock absorber with regard to the others.

Summary

The guidelines for program design may be summarized as:

o One program = one function.
o A function is either a problem function, a data manipulation function, or a housekeeping function.
o Design-to-change at the detailed levels deals with implementation changes, and is handled by applying the principles of information hiding, abstract data types, and levels of functions.

PROGRAMMING

Initial Assumptions

Let us begin by getting rid of a stone-age computer belief: programming is the most extensive activity in system development. First, is programming the most resource-consuming activity? No, it is not. For Bruggere (1980), programming plus individual unit testing account for 25% of the total, while 30% is spent on specifications. Wolverton's (1974) statistics show no more than 20% assigned to programming against 34% allocated to design. Griffin (1980) estimates 23% for programming and unit testing, and 62.5% for testing. Second, is programming really the most crucial activity? No, it is not. Boehm (1976) reports that 60% of all errors are introduced during design, while only 40% are traced to programming.

Assumption 1: the importance of programming in the system development process has been blown out of proportion in computer science literature (Sheil, 1981). This is not to say that careful programming is unnecessary but rather, that everything should be put in the proper perspective.

Assumption 2: A program which is well designed will be well coded, no matter which programming method or language is used.

To support these assumptions, we will try to find out where the qualities of a good program come from, and then discuss the coding activity itself.

What Makes a Good Program?

Like any product, a good program is well-defined, well-designed, and well-manufactured (programmed). Let us explore these three attributes in greater detail.

Detailed design is supposed to provide precise definition of each program. Just because it is precise, however, does not mean that the definition is a good one. According to Gane and Sarson (1979) and Stevens and colleagues (1974), programs may be characterized by three attributes:

1. *Cohesiveness* evaluates the extent to which all parts of a program belong together. A scale has even been established ranging from coincidental (parts are grouped simply for convenience) to functional cohesion (parts are grouped together because they all contribute to the function accomplished by the program). We have seen in detailed design that a program should accomplish one function. Strong cohesiveness is therefore a result of good design.

2. *Connection* defines the way in which two programs communicate. For example, one program could access and modify a variable in another; this is obviously a bad connection. Good connections should be limited to parameters in the program invocation. Connections are related to program interfaces, which are also a result of detailed design.

3. *Coupling* measures the strength of association by a connection. There are two forms of coupling: data and control. Again we are dealing with program interfaces which should have been defined during detailed design.

Well-defined programs are thus the result of good design.

Aspects of a good program design include the following maxims:

o A good program is a "proper program," with one entry point and one exit point.
o A good program is short.
o A good program accomplishes only one well-defined function of the design; if such is the case, the program should by nature be short.
o The structure of a good program follows the same rules as those applied to design. It is separated into distinct sequences of the three basic operations: problem processing, data manipulation, and housekeeping. The hierarchical structure of the program should reflect the hierarchy of operations, *not* their sequence in time.

EXAMPLE M: CUSTOMER CASH ACCOUNTS REPORT

Let us analyze the program which produces such an output. There is one report per customer. Each report contains:

customer name, date, balance forward;

one line per transaction; and

final balance.

To produce the report, three files are needed: CUSTOMER, TRANSACTIONS, and CASH-ACCOUNTS.

We can distinguish three levels of operations (see Figure 12.13).
Level 1 deals with everything related to all customers:

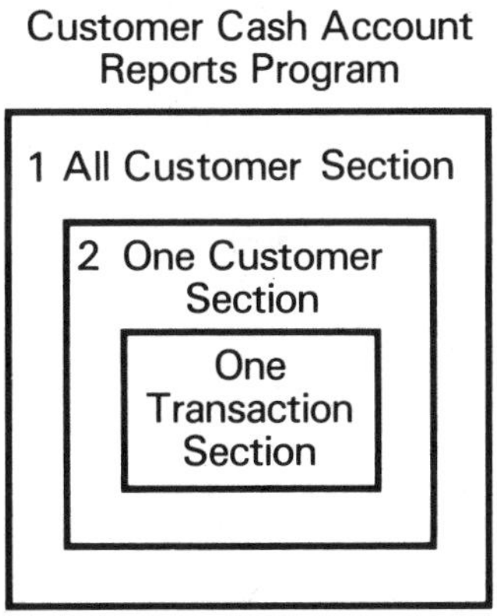

Customer Cash Account
Reports Program

1 All Customer Section

2 One Customer
Section

One
Transaction
Section

Fig. 12.13. The three levels of a report-producing program.

operating the files;

setting the counters.

Level 2 deals with what is specific to one customer:

getting his CUSTOMER record and printing his name, number, address, etc.;

obtaining his balance and printing it;

managing the page numbers if the report has more than one page;

calculating and printing the final balance;

determining if this is the last customer.

Level 3 deals with individual transactions:

getting the transaction from the TRANSACTIONS file;

printing the transaction;

managing the line counter;

determining if it is the last transaction for that customer.

As we have seen, a good program is the result of good detailed design (1 program = 1 function), and also the result of applying the same principles to program design as to system design.

Programming Practices

If programming practices affect neither the quality of the product nor the productivity of the programmers, the project manager need not worry about them. Should the opposite be true, however, he would do well to be concerned. Whether or not good programming practices are the key to a good product and to high production rates—and if so, which ones—is a longstanding topic of debate in computer science.

For this author, the choice of one programming tool versus another has never been a subject of such great concern. The relative importance of programming in projects is steadily decreasing, and there are more important matters to be attended to (specifications, design, planning, control). In addition, the programmer's overall training and discipline is of far more importance than which particular method or language he chooses. Using PASCAL plus structured programming will not enable a poor programmer to produce good programs; they will be badly structured even in PASCAL. Sheil (1981) reviewed some experiments concerning computing practices. The results are very disappointing: there is no evidence that programming notations (including available statements) are a factor in the difficulty of programming. The effects of practice (experience) and of individual variations overwhelm the slight differences which could exist among different practices.

There is thus no experimental proof that one practice is really better than another. It is necessary, however, to make use of a given practice and discipline, and here we must pay tribute to those who created and spread the discipline of structured programming. By designing one method, they defined the principles of good programming practices which can be applied to any good method, in any language (Programs *can* be structured, even in assembly language).We have already seen stepwise refinement applied to project analysis and design; programming is no exception. In addition to stepwise refinement, structured programming supposes the existence of only three control structures:

the sequence,

the iteration (WHILE exp. DO instruction), and

the alternative (IF exp. THEN instruction 1 ELSE instruction 2).

A language is required, making stepwise refinement possible and providing the three basic control structures. However, it need not be the coding language. One may well design the program in PASCAL and then code it in COBOL since it is the only available language. This can be done manually and even automatically. Several preprocessors have been designed to add structured programming capabilities to languages like FORTRAN or COBOL (see Evans, 1982; Tausworthe, 1977).

In conclusion, it may be said that:

o A good program is defined beforehand.
o A good program is carefully designed before being coded; and if a language like PASCAL is used as a design tool, flowcharting becomes a nuisance!
o A good program is coded using one particular discipline (for control flow, variable names, labels, presentation, comments, etc.).

TESTING

What We Know about Testing

"Program testing can be used to show the presence of bugs but never to show thaeir absence" (Dahl, Dijsktra, Hoare, 1972, p. 6). The first step towards achieving program correctness is to *write* the programs correctly. We know that testing is lengthy and expensive. In the 90%-ready program syndrome, the remaining

10%—which sometimes lasts forever—is spent debugging. In no reports on resource consumption have we seen less than 30% set aside for testing, and in Griffin's (1980) results, 62.5% of the resources were spent on tests.

We know what kind of errors are made. At the overall development cycle level, 60% of the errors are introduced during design, and 40% during coding (Boehm, 1976). At the programming level, we find that special cases and erroneous or extreme input data are often overlooked, both during programming and debugging (Myers, 1978). Errors are introduced either during coding (writing one variable's name for another, forgetting a comma or period) or in the program's logic (loop left open or incorrectly closed, array indexes out of range, test incorrectly stated). In summary, errors are made because of sheer optimism on the part of programmers. Errors stem more from design than from coding, and they cost time and resources to eliminate.

But is testing really debugging or, in other words, finding and correcting errors? In fact, it is not.

Testing a system is the process of showing that it performs according to its specifications.

Testing is a much more positive task than simply debugging. This is also why it is much more difficult at the overall system level. For example, a program might be shown correct, in terms of its specifications, but still might be wrong as a result of design errors. Therefore, the process of system testing is, in fact, comprised of two tasks:

1. Assessing the performance of a given task and, if the system does not perform as specified,
2. finding the origin of the discrepancy and eliminating it (debugging).

Both tasks are tedious and time-consuming. Ways to make them as short and efficient as possible will be discussed in the next section. Indeed, the best way to shorten the process is, in fact, to start at the design stage.

The Testing Process

As Dijkstra observed, debugging proves nothing, and writing programs correctly to begin with is the crux of the matter. Accordingly, a large amount of research devoted to formal proofs of programs and formal verifications has emerged (see Tausworthe, 1977). These methods are, however, quite sophisticated, and one wonders if the average programmer without a degree in formal logic could apply them. In addition, they are very impractical for large programs. Until these methods are better adapted to large systems, we will have to make use of the testing process.

As shown in Figure 12.14, there is a hierarchy of tests to be performed. From bottom to top, we find:

o Individual module tests which test the correctness of each program or module. The problem of possible design errors (in module specifications, as well) results in the fact that they are of limited range.

o Subsystem integration tests, which are aimed at eliminating the above-mentioned design problems.

o System integration tests, which are geared toward verifying the correctness of very high-level design decisions. A system is often made up of independent subsystems which communicate only through stored data banks, and this must be tested.

o Acceptance tests, which are a prelude to implementation. Their aim is to assess a "certain level of correctness." This new approach recognizes that although it is impossible to be sure that the system works properly; it is possible to state that for a certain amount of input data, the errors should be no more than X%.

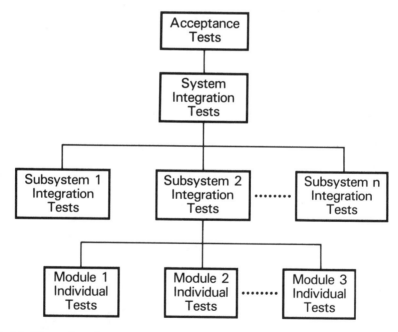

Fig. 12.14. Hierarchy of tests.

Figure 12.15 shows that the testing process is the same at all levels of the hierarchy. The process contains two loops: one concerning what to test, the other how to do it.

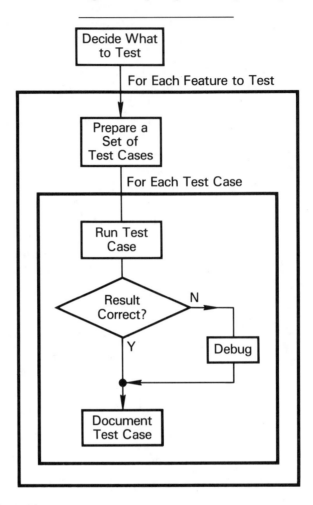

Fig. 12.15. The testing process.

What to Test

Determining what to test can be approached from two perspectives. The first is *from the outside*, meaning, looking at the system through the user's eyes. Here one is interested in the output for a given set of inputs. A good approach is described in Duran's (1981) report on random testing, where the inputs are partitioned in domains, and test cases are prepared to cover each domain extensively. It is the most widely used method in the field, even though in practice the domains are not always covered as they should be. However, if rigorously applied, the method seems to yield results as good as those of the more analytical methods.

The second approach looks at the system *from the inside*. Popular in research circles, the idea is to check every statement, path, and branch of the set of programs. A good analysis of this approach can be found in Ramamoorthy, Siu-Bun, & Chen (1976), who present a test case generator and discuss some problems such as loops or arrays checking (See also Zeil & White, 1981, who concentrate on path analysis.)

An excellent synthesis of both approaches is proposed by Redwine (1983), who identifies five domains to cover: functions, input, output, function interaction, and code execution. Whatever the method chosen, the problem is to be sure that all possibilities are covered.

How to Test

The objective of any case is to test a given topic: input or output domain or subdomain, function, path, etc. In each instance, the following guidelines should be followed:

- No input data should be prepared without the corresponding output data.
- In each case, normal *and* abnormal values should be tested. There is wide agreement that programmers tend to concentrate their efforts almost exclusively on normal behavior (see in particular Duran, 1981, and Myers, 1978).
- A test should not try to check too many things in the same case. The domain covered by the run becomes fuzzy, and if it fails, debugging is very difficult.
- When running a test, the outputs should be carefully analyzed to see if everything is correct. Myers (1978) discovered that several errors were overlooked by experienced programmers because they had neglected to check the output carefully. Duran (1981) made the same point.

If a test fails, debugging must be done, an activity which programmers find unpleasant. Therefore, when left on their own, they try to rush through as quickly as possible, the result being that the search for bugs becomes a panicky situation. Tons of paper are dumped from the printer, the same set of six or seven statements is looked at over and over again, and so on. Bugs in programming are a fact of life, and as with everything in system development, debugging should be done methodically. Following are some debugging suggestions:

- First, locate the module which is responsible for the error.
- Do not repeat the same test twenty times. Surround the faulty section by outputting increasingly close values of "state variables." (We will see an approach to this in the following section.)
- Ask a colleague to help you; there is no shame in having difficulty locating a bug.

○ Take a break! It helps to calm down and clear one's mind.

○ Don't hurry; things will end up taking more time if you do.

Finally, when a test case is successful, it must be documented and filed. Each test case should have the following documentation: description of the test (what is to be tested); test case (description of inputs); date test is performed; results (outputs); and outcome: correct or incorrect.

Testers

We have seen that programmers usually make poor testers (see Myers, 1978). Specialists should therefore be in charge of this activity. Large organizations operate in this manner, and so should sizeable projects. Although on the surface these specialists appear to constitute an additional resource, such is not the case. They will perform the testing better, faster, and more thoroughly than the system authors. In small projects and especially in small organizations, there is often no tester available. The project manager should at least involve himself in designing the process, controlling the choice of test cases and seeing that they extensively cover the specifications.

A Development Approach for Testing

Several methods and tools have been introduced in this chapter, in order to produce a final product of quality. Some of them will be reviewed with a new objective in mind: facilitating the testing process.

COMMENTS.   In principle, they are introduced to help a programmer understand programs written by someone else. However, when some time has elapsed, any programmer has difficulties understanding his own production.

PROGRAMMING DISCIPLINE.   The use of structured programming gives a framework for organizing the code. During the testing process, it also eases program understanding.

PROGRAM SHIELDING.   It has already been mentioned that programmers are optimists who believe that only user objects can be wrong while their own creations (array indexes, constants, counters, and so on) are always correct. The introduction of statements which, at the beginning of critical sequences, check the supposed values of these items, speeds up the debugging activity. These shielding statements should not be removed once the program runs correctly but left in the code during the whole life cycle of the system.

Design to Test

Almost all design methods decompose a system into data flows. Such a flow is illustrated in Figure 12.16a. If an error exists in the program, $O(I_t)$ is wrong. In order to debug, the first step to take is to locate the error in a sequence of transformations. It is therefore more efficient to break the process down into a succession of transformations $T1$, $T2$, ...Tn so that for each T_i the output O_i may be defined in terms of its inputs (see Figure 12.16b).

The testing process is similar to that of bootstrap implementation: test T_i only when all T_j ($j < i$) have been checked for correctness. It is not sufficient, however, because interface errors do exist. The program shielding strategy is therefore implemented. At the start of each T_i, data are checked for correctness even if they are supposed to be correct. Performing what is termed subsystem integration tests in Figure 12.14 then becomes an easy task. The advantages of this approach compared to that shown in Figure 12.16a are as follows:

1. The complexity of locating a faulty module (or interface) is greatly decreased. (It is in the order of the sum of the complexities of each module, while otherwise it would be in the order of their product.)
2. There is no need to prepare test data for each module in the chain.
3. The visibility of the testing process is greatly enhanced.

Condition

In order for this approach to work, it must be possible to define the O_i's. Parnas (1972) demonstrated convincingly that in the first approach to the KWIC program (used as an example), it is almost impossible to find the faulty program if

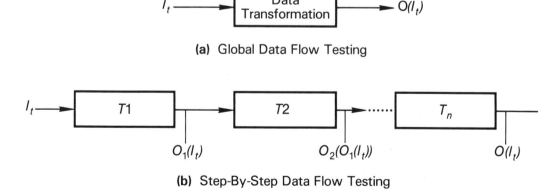

(a) Global Data Flow Testing

(b) Step-By-Step Data Flow Testing

Fig. 12.16. The two ways of testing a data flow.

the data turns out to be wrong, since all modules access and process the same data structure.

Therefore, the design principles and method described in the section on general design not only lead to clean systems and clear, well-defined programs, but they also facilitate and speed up the testing process.

Test Plan and File

Everybody is familiar with the following situation: "I am sure I tested this case; let me just try to remember." Unfortunately, the human mind is sometimes a poor file for details. When users keep coming back with systems supposedly tested and still not working properly, the test results file becomes an asset for clearing up the case. Test planning then becomes a natural thing to do when one realizes, with the help of the test file, that the same item is checked several times.

In this section, we have seen that one way of looking at the development process is to orient it toward the testing activity (see, for example, Bruggere, 1980, for an early error detection strategy). In conclusion, we may pose the following question: Which objectives should the development strategies and methods try to achieve? There are few:

good product quality,

adaptability to change,

stepwise development (each step should facilitate the accomplishment of the next one), and

high productivity.

SELECTED REFERENCES

Baker, F. T. 1972. Chief programmer team management of production programming. *IBM Systems Journal*, 11, 1, 66-73.

> This paper, a hallmark, presented the first application of the chief programmer team (CPT) structure. It also introduced the concept of the program support library, which has proven to be a powerful program management tool. The CPT concept has long been considered the managerial side of structured programming because of its ability to overcome the problems introduced by different levels and styles of programming skills.

Boehm, B. W. 1976. Software engineering. *IEEE Trans. on Comp.*, C-25, 12 (December), 1226-1241.

> This is a complete state-of-the-art survey of all problems related to software development. In particular, the author insists on the importance of design, the high cost of maintenance, and the management causes of project failures. He

rightfully concludes that scientists should pay more attention to the fields of requirements analysis, testing, maintenance, and so forth in economic-driven contexts. (The author has shown the way in many other publications.)

Bruggere, T. H. 1980. Software engineering: Management, personnel and methodology. *Proc. 4th Int. Conf. on Soft. Eng.*, Sept. 17-19, Munich, Germany, 361-368.

The author states that project failures are not solely the manager's responsibility. He cites three causes: management, personnel, methodology. A manager should have one foot on the management side and one on the technical side; he should be able to select the right people and methodology. After differentiating between a coder and a software engineer, the article describes a development methodology whose objective is to detect errors as early as possible.

Duran, J. W. 1981. A report on random testing. *Proc. 5th Int. Conf. on Soft. Eng.*, March 9-12, San Diego, 179-183.

This is a successful attempt to rehabilitate random testing, which had been cast as "the worst testing method." The author, after citing some results that showed it worked quite well, presents an approach in which a partition of the input domains is built. Following some simulations, the approach is tested on published programs. The results show that almost all errors are found after a reasonable number of tests.

Evans, M. 1982. Software engineering for the COBOL environment. *Com. of the ACM*, 25, 12 (December), 874-882.

The paper presents a "macro-COBOL" with structured statements, program skeletons, an interactive debugging facility, and so on. It is a good example of how to achieve structured programming with an unstructured language.

Mantei, M. 1981. The effect of programming team structures on programming tasks. *Com. of the ACM*, 24, 3 (March), 106-113.

This article is important reading for anyone interested in the organization of programming teams. It describes the three classic team structures (chief programmer team, egoless programming, and controlled decentralized). After discussing the advantages of each, the author studies a number of factors involved in system development and assesses each structure with regard to these factors.

Meyer, B. 1982. Principles of package design. *Com. of the ACM*, 25, 7 (July), 419-428.

Here, "package" means utilities for application programmers; it is, in fact, the software warehouse. This article shows that the same principles which apply to application systems design (i.e., information hiding, hierarchical design, and abstract data types) apply to utility packages as well.

Myers, G. 1978. A controlled experiment in program testing and code walkthrough/inspections. *Com. of the ACM*, 21, 9 (September), 760-768.

This is a wonderful and not-so-often performed experiment in comparing several test methods. Very carefully designed, the experiment yielded some surprising results, such as a poor error detection rate and a large variation among individuals and the types of errors detected. In addition, there was no significant difference between the methods for the number of errors detected. The article also concluded that programmers pay too much attention to normal cases and not enough to special ones.

Parnas, D. L. 1972. On the criteria to be used in decomposing systems into modules. *Com. of the ACM*, 15, 12 (December), 1053-1058.

> This milestone article begins by presenting two designs for a small KWIC documentation system. Obviously, there is a good one and a poor one. By showing the problems introduced by the latter and overcome by the former, the author introduces his well-known decomposition criteria: 1 module per processing step; information hiding; each data structure and access in one module; etc. He argues that the order in time in which operations are performed (which is what results from flowcharting) should not be a decomposition criterion.

Rajaraman, M. K. 1983. Structured techniques for software development. *Journal of Systems Management*, March, 36-39.

> The article starts as a general presentation of structured methods. It then turns to the organizational problems which could result from the introduction of some of them, such as chief programmer team or structured walkthrough. In the last part, the author deals with the problem of choices. For him, it is the best design which produces the best software, and if forced to choose between good design–bad coding and bad design–good coding, he would select the first; software reliability and maintenance depend closely on design.

Ramamoorthy, C. W., Ho, S. F., & Chen, W. T. 1976. On the automated generation of program test data. *IEEE Trans. on Soft. Eng.*, SE-2, 4 (December), 293-300.

> The generator described in this article should produce tests in order to be sure that each statement has been executed at least once, each path followed at least once. There are three major components in the generator: path selector, constraints generator, and test data generator. The authors define symbolic execution and present solutions for especially difficult topics like loops of an unknown number of iterations, arrays, and subroutine calls. Finally, the generator is used to test a 10,000-statement program. It is a very good example of the "from-the-inside" approach to testing.

Redwine, S. T., Jr. 1983. An engineering approach to software test data generation. *IEEE Trans. on Soft. Eng.*, SE-9, 2 (March), 191-200.

> This is a very systematic approach to testing and test data generation. The idea is to define five domains which the tests must cover: functions, input, output, function interaction, execution coverage. For each domain, a metric is defined in order to assess whether the tests have been complete. The problems related to the coverage of each domain are then discussed and solutions presented. It is an excellent example of a dual approach to testing, encompassing "from-the-inside" and "from-the-outside" methods.

Sheil, B. A. 1981. The psychological study of programming. *ACM Computing Surveys*, 13, 1 (March), 101-120.

> This article is a shock to programming methodology worshippers. It is a survey of published experiments regarding programming topics and practices. The results are disappointing. Here are some excerpts: performance differences between people using languages with IF-THEN-ELSE and languages without were from 4% to 15% in favor of the former; but differences between session performances showing the effect of experience were in the range of 13% to 27%. There is no positive result for other programming features such as control

flow, data types, and use of comments. The only positive findings are that practice and individual variations are the most important factors. The author wonders why so much importance is attached to studies of a topic which seems to be overrated in significance and performance.

Tausworthe, R. C. 1977. *Standardized development of computer software*. Englewood Cliffs, N.J.: Prentice-Hall.

The book presents an approach to system realization based on top-down hierarchical design, structured programming, and modularity. After reviewing the definition of a "proper program," the author analyzes in detail the realization of structured non-real-time and real-time programs. The CRISP (Control-Restricted Instructions for Structured Programming) is introduced in the form of instructions to be added to a nonstructured language. Part nine is an excellent presentation of formal program correctness assessment techniques.

Zmud, R. D. 1980. Management of large scale software development efforts. *Management Information Systems Quarterly*, June, 45-55.

The author insists on the necessity of a change-receptive development, with modularization being one of the ways to achieve it. A further benefit of good modularization is that tasks can be defined so as to minimize participant interaction.

Zeil, S. J., & White, L. J. 1981. Sufficient test sets for path analysis testing strategies. *Proc. 5th Int. Conf. on Soft. Eng.*, March 9-12, San Diego, 184-191.

This is another example of the "from-the-inside" approach, the objective being to find a minimal set of cases making it possible to test a specific path.

Chapter 13
CONTROL OF A PROGRAMMING PROJECT

INTRODUCTION

As far back as Chapter 1, the problems surrounding system development have been mentioned: cost overruns, unrespected schedules, unexpected and disappointing results, and so on. In order to cope with some of these, the structure and tools described thus far have been set up and put to work: the life cycle, the opportunity study, specifications, planning, and sound design and programming methods. However, for two reasons, this is insufficient. Simply setting a course of action does not guarantee that it will be followed: it must be monitored. In addition, whatever plans have been made, the unexpected will inevitably occur to disrupt them, thus requiring urgent action. Controlling is just that: keeping the project on the tracks, looking for obstacles and coping with them.

The classic definition of control as a management function is taking steps to ensure that the plans are carried out. This somewhat limited definition implies that all plans are perfect and that deviations should be avoided. In the case of programming projects, we already know that such an assumption is unrealistic. A less rigid concept is required in order to cope with the real world.

The control function of project management consists in "taking the steps to ensure that these plans are carried out, or, if conditions warrant, that the plans are modified" (Merchant, 1982, p. 43). This broader definition gives the project manager more room to maneuver, but also implies more risks. If conditions arise which make the plan unworkable, the manager must set new objectives, derive new plans, get them approved, and set them into motion.

EXAMPLE A: THE ADT SYSTEM

In Chapter 7, we met Donald White, the man in charge of the Admission-Discharge-Transfer system at Good Samaritan Hospital. He went through system analysis, set up and negotiated the specifications, planned the development, and submitted a budget (see Table 11.6) which was approved. He now has to produce the system according to the schedule proposed in Example A, Chapter 11.

The hospital is anxious to see the new system in operation because the old one is much too clumsy. White is therefore in charge of a fixed-deadline project. His staff is composed of two analysts and four programmers. The department has a good tradition of standards and documentation, and uses a design method similar to the one presented in Chapter 12. Some structured programming principles are used, although COBOL is the programming language. This is not the first project White has managed, and having been with the hospital for many years, he is well aware of what may happen.

THE CONTROL FUNCTION IN PROJECT MANAGEMENT

Scope and Process

The control process can be summarized in four steps (see Figure 13.1):

1. Assess situation. In system development, this may not be easy; some requirements for product and progress assessment will be discussed later in this chapter.
2. Compare with plan. Estimates, plan, schedule, and budget will all be used again, this time as reference documents.
3. Decide on a course of action. Depending on the degree of difference between the actual situation and the plan, the decisions will be left up to the project manager or will require upper management involvement.

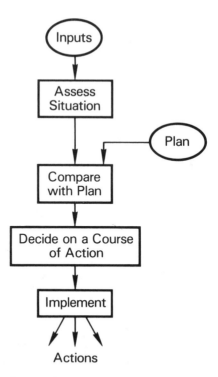

Fig. 13.1. The process of control.

4. Implement. This will involve modifying the plan and often reallocating or finding other resources.

Let us now look at the inputs which represent the controls put on the project structure. What should be monitored? From a very broad point of view, Merchant (1982) proposes the following classification:

o *Specifications control* involves procedures, reviews, and so forth. In system development, it can be accomplished to a certain extent by adopting design and programming methods and reviewing the results by using structured walkthroughs and design and code inspections. Although useful, these kinds of controls have limited value; in system development they need to be complemented by additional measures.

o *Results control* implies clearly defining the results to be achieved and the ability to evaluate performance. This time we are on familiar ground. If the plan has been developed with well-defined milestones and if the modules are clearly defined, it becomes easy to recognize that a given result has been achieved. Results control is the best way of assessing the progress of a project.

○ *Personnel control* essentially involves careful selection of the team members, and can be enhanced by training programs. Although very valuable in a project environment, it has limited use, and is seen more as a planning tool than as a control device.

Which results should be monitored in order to assess progress? Is it the number of lines of code produced, the amount of dollars spent, or the number of modules already tested? The variables to monitor will depend on the constraints of the project. In Chapter 9, we examined three types of projects:

○ *Fixed resources project*. Results will have to be achieved at the forecasted cost, and resource consumption will become the second variable to monitor in addition to results.
○ *Fixed schedule project*. The schedule will be the yardstick by which performance required to achieve a given result is measured.
○ *Fixed team project*. The main problem here will be staff availability and productivity; deadlines and costs go hand in hand.

It is a well-known fact that a project without controls will veer off its path and fail. Does this mean that increasing the number of controls will increase the chances of success? Again, excess destroys the purpose. Too much control may have side effects both on productivity and on quality of work (Johnson, 1977; Merchant, 1982). Obsessive adherence to schedules, for example, will incite people to program "quick and dirty." Too much emphasis on productivity in lines-of-code-per-day turns programmers into statement factories. A proper balance must be achieved between the needs of project control and what people can endure.

Major Problems in System Development

In a project, Murphy's Law is a truism: what can the manager expect to befall him . . . at the worst time? Let us assume that the project has been well planned, that specifications do indeed exist, and that the schedule is realistic provided the estimates are accurate. In this author's experience, the three problems encountered most often are the following, in decreasing order of importance:

1. *Delays*. They are not a cause but rather a symptom of an underlying problem: technical difficulty, estimation error, poor productivity, and so on. Wooldridge (1976) identified up to twelve reasons for project delays. One does not cope with delay problems without determining their origin.
2. *User changes*. Why do users exist? And why do they keep asking for changes once the specifications have been agreed upon? These questions have lengthy

answers which are outside the scope of this book. But the problem does exist. The solution lies in configuration management, which will be described later in this chapter.

3. *Personnel availability.* Among the many reasons why personnel may not be available, thereby putting the most carefully designed plan in jeopardy, are illness, leave of absence, resignation, other urgent assignments, and maintenance. There is no sure method of dealing with personnel availability problems, but they will inevitably be encountered.

Other problems, far less influential on the outcome of the project, include lack of availability of machine, technical difficulty, and estimation errors. Regardless of the problems encountered, good project management implies an awareness of the fact that problems may arise, setting up communication channels so as to be quickly informed if anything does happen, and, when possible, planning and implementing ways of dealing with problems as soon as they occur.

PRODUCT CONTROL

In manufacturing, product control consists in checking to see whether the product satisfies some predefined quality requirements. The only problem with programs is defining what their quality is. In system development, there is an even more difficult problem: the final product may well not perform the way it is supposed to. Product control will therefore consist of two tasks:

1. Obtaining a final product which conforms to a known set of specifications.
2. Obtaining a final product of good quality (provided that the definition of good quality has been established).

Configuration Management

System developers must face two problems regarding requirements. First, the product may not conform to the specifications. Figure 13.2 illustrates three ways in which a system does not meet the specifications:

1. The final result delivers less than expected (which is often the case with late schedules or cost overruns).
2. The final result delivers more than expected (unrealistic, but possible).
3. The final product performs differently than expected.

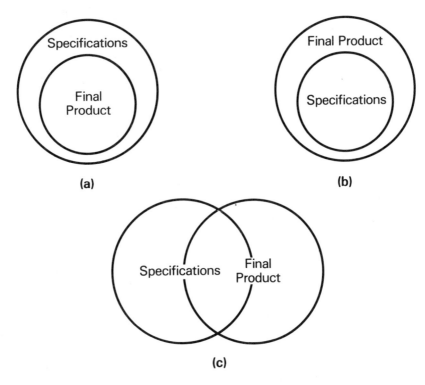

Fig. 13.2. How the final product can miss the specifications.

Second, it is impossible to know what the exact specifications are because of the runaway demands for changes coming from the user. These two problems can be solved by using two procedures: baseline configuration management and change control.

Baseline Configuration Management

The objectives of baseline configuration management are (a) to know exactly what the system's requirements are, and (b) to ensure that the final product meets the stated specifications. If the project's life cycle has gone through the steps described in Chapter 7, the first objective has already been met: the specifications have been established *and* negotiated with the user. It is because they are a contract that they can be considered a baseline document, i.e., the description of what is to be delivered. If not agreed upon, the specifications will remain the analyst's view of the final product, open to all challenges from the user.

To ensure the second objective, the baseline document (the specifications) will be used as a testing ground through all steps of development.

GENERAL DESIGN.   We saw in Chapter 12 that the inputs for general design are the specifications, *nothing else*. (This is supposed to eliminate cases b and c depicted in Figure 13.2.) Once general design has been completed, the results are checked against the specifications. Each feature of the specifications should have a counterpart in the general design. One way to facilitate this process is to associate each object in the design documents with the corresponding element(s) in the specifications. Fagan (1976) pointed out that not only do design and code inspections contribute to a final product that is in compliance with requirements, but they also greatly decrease the amount of testing and rework in the final stages of the development. When the general design documents have passed these tests, they are considered "agreed upon."

DETAILED DESIGN.   At this stage, the process is exactly the same, except that this time the general design documents act as the baseline and reference for the inspection.

PROGRAMMING AND TESTING.   The baseline is made up of the detailed design documents. Code inspections may be used for checking the program's compliance with requirements, but the real check is done during system testing. It has been noted that programmers are notoriously poor testers. This is even more true when the tester is the author of the program because he is testing his own understanding of the program. The baseline document for testing is neither the general design nor the detailed design, but the specifications manual. It is in fact the only document in which the description of what the system is supposed to do was agreed upon by the user.

The process is summarized in Table 13.1. Although it does not guarantee that the system will perform as expected, this process eliminates most of the risks of straying from the user's expectations.

Change Control

One way to be sure of what to develop would be to stick to the "contract" and reject all user requests for changes. Such a solution would make system developers happy; it would also make them jobless. One cannot expect the user to

TABLE 13.1
BASELINE CONFIGURATION MANAGEMENT

Development Step	Baseline Document	Checking Operation	Reference Document
General Design	Specifications	Inspection	Specifications
Detailed Design	Approved General Design Documents	Inspection	Approved General Design Documents
Programming	Approved Detailed Design Documents	Testing	Specifications

foresee everything he will need in a system which will come into being months or years later. In addition, a business system is supposed to support the operation of the business, and there are changes coming from the outside which must be complied with, such as new regulations, new procedures, and new products. Dismissing any change after specifications approval is therefore highly unrealistic. The problem is to assess them and to ensure that those accepted are included in the successive steps shown in Table 13.1.

Change control has three objectives:

1. Screening user requests.
2. Keeping track of the accepted changes.
3. Updating the development process as a result of the changes.

SCREENING USER REQUESTS. Harrison (1981) takes a strong stand regarding user requests for changes. "It is the project manager's responsibility to resist changes unless they are absolutely essential to the objectives of the projects and in the company's interest" (p. 242). Unfortunately, in business data processing, the objectives of the project and the company's interests are not always easy to assess with regard to a change request.

In any case, a procedure to help ensure that only vital changes are accepted consists of the following steps:

1. Changes are asked for on a "request-for-change form" which is always directed to the project manager. A basic rule of change control is that nobody in the project team, except the project manager, is allowed to accept user changes.
2. The consequences of the change are assessed.
3. If the request introduces no change in the project's objectives, final deadline, or resources required for completion, it can be accepted by the project manager. If not, the request and the consequences involved in accepting the change should be brought to the attention of the authority to whom the project manager reports.

KEEPING TRACK OF ACCEPTED CHANGES. When a change is accepted, the specifications must be updated. In addition, all authorized changes must themselves be kept track of. The best way to do this is to have a file containing the updated specifications and the associated requests.

UPDATING THE DEVELOPMENT PROCESS. All the documents referred to in Table 13.1 must be updated and the corresponding updates forwarded to the developers. Once again, this implies quick and effective channels of communication among all members of the team.

EXAMPLE B: A NEW ADMISSION FORM

While general design is in progress, it is announced that a new admission form will have to be used when the system goes into operation. The only change introduced is that, in addition to the Medicare card number, the social security number (SSN) must also be entered (In Canada, the two are different.) Donald White assesses the consequences of this request. (He cannot refuse it, since it is government regulation.) Simply adding one new attribute to the patient entity is no problem at the general design stage.

Before routinely filing the change as accepted, he discusses the matter with Jean Coolidge, his senior designer. "What," she asks, "will they use that for? Everybody in Canada has a social security number, but Medicare numbers are issued by provincial authorities and are not the same from one province to the next—so the patient identification system should accept the SSN as a patient retrieval key." White is less confident now that the change is without consequences; the design group in charge of the patient identification system must be consulted.

Yes, it does introduce a change into the design. A new relationship will have to be created, linking the SSN to the patient entity whose key is the hospital number. Moreover, the identification system should accept the SSN as an input and retrieve the patient's entity.

White and his assistants assess what this means: four more weeks of programming effort. He authorizes the change but sends a memo to his boss, Michael Greenwood, informing him that the final deadline will be pushed back two weeks and that the cost might increase by $2,500.

Quality Control

What are the qualities of a software system? They cannot be measured in terms of life span (a program works better and better as time passes), nor can they be expressed by MTBF (mean time between failures) as with a hardware device. Trying to describe a system qualitatively as "well designed" and "correctly programmed" is unacceptably vague.

The discipline of software quality assurance has taken a much more modest but more useful approach. Buckley (1979) cites the following definition: "Quality assurance: A planned and systematic pattern of all actions necessary to provide adequate confidence that the item or product conforms to established technical requirements" (p. 46).

Quality assurance requires, therefore, that all steps, procedures, and actions mentioned in previous chapters of this book be implemented, enforced, monitored, and evaluated. The emphasis is on watching for:

establishment of written specifications,

checking of design against specifications,

establishment and enforcement of standards,

definition of documentation format and content,

inspections, reviews, and audits during the different steps of the development,

and so forth.

In large projects, a software quality assurance group takes charge of this function. Under the authority of the project manager, it defines the plan and then intervenes on a regular basis to verify that all products (documents, programs, etc.) comply with the predefined terms of reference. It formalizes the process shown in Table 13.1 but broadens its scope to cover all aspects of the project involving the product.

Let us now return to the concept of quality as discussed at the beginning of this section and try, nonetheless, to find some indications concerning the quality of a system. If we consider a consumer product, we will find it to be of quality if it is easy to use, lasts a long time, and looks attractive. It seems that we overlooked some indications of quality in the manufactured product example.

In an article devoted to the management of the information system function, Ahituv and Neumann (1982) defined the qualities of a system as flexibility, ease of maintenance, interface with other systems, compatibility, expansibility, and efficiency. These characteristics will give the system a long life and make it easy to use. In addition, if not quantified, they can at least be specified. *Flexibility* is the ability of the system to cope with changes. It can be achieved through knowledge of forecasted changes (this is where the usefulness of the Extensions section in the specifications becomes visible), and through modular design and application of the principles of bounded context, abstract data types, one function per module. *Ease of maintenance* depends on three factors: modular design, disciplined programming (structured, if possible), and good, up-to-date documentation. *Interface with other systems*, although it is an attribute defining quality, is more properly a requirement which should be part of the specifications. *Expansibility* is the ability of the system to handle an increase in volume of processed data. Once again, it is not a quality of a system, but a requirement. *Compatibility* is important because software systems outlive machines and operating systems. If the development of a system makes too much use of a particular computer's unique features (or of its software), any change in the hardware will become a problem (see Chapter 8). Finally, *efficiency* is a measure of whether the developed system performs its functions in an efficient way with respect to hardware utilization. This is obviously a respectable goal, but too great an emphasis on efficiency may be detrimental to the achievement of the other qualities.

Suggestions for achieving these five attributes include the following:

1. Develop for adaptability to future changes.
2. Design using a good method and good tools.
3. Use disciplined programming.
4. Document with the principle of risk management in mind.

PRODUCTION CONTROL

Progress Control

Results control has been described as the best way to monitor the progress of a project. It has also been repeatedly noted that, in a system development undertaking, the percentage of a given activity that has been completed does not constitute a result. The only way progress can be truly asserted is by the attainment of well-defined milestones. Johnson (1977) defined a meaningful milestone as "a point in time when a task or a number of tasks can be completed at 100%, not 95% or 98%" (p. 27).

In Chapter 3, we determined that to be defined as a milestone, an event should have a "deliverable." This is the key to progress control. If a milestone does not deliver a "product" defined in advance, we will fall back into the 95% swamp. Two kinds of achievements can be distinguished:

A *macromilestone* is a significant achievement in the set of activities. At the project level, the macromilestones are those of the development cycle: general design completed, all individual tests accomplished, etc. At lower levels, it is the same for subsystems.

EXAMPLE C: ADT SYSTEMS MILESTONES

For Donald White, the macromilestones are those mentioned in Table 11.3 and which will be restated here:

General design finished: July 15, 1978

Waiting list subsystem ready: October 10, 1978

Identification subsystem ready: January 10, 1979

Admission-discharge-transfer subsystem ready: June 10, 1979

Patient movements subsystem ready: August 31, 1979

Reports subsystem ready: August 31, 1979

Any task, group of tasks, activity, or group of activities can end with a *micromilestone* if it delivers something. The finished detailed design of a given module (the document is delivered) is a micromilestone. A program free of compiler errors is another, as is the description of a file or the end of the individual tests of a module (in this case, the test documentation must be provided with the program listing).

Acknowledgement of Milestones

The key to real progress monitoring through milestones is in making the producer of the deliverable and the controller two different people. Milestone recognition is usually performed by two groups of people: (a) the project hierarchy, where the producer always delivers to his immediate superior, although there may be "certification groups" as well; and (b) specialized groups. If a project has a quality assurance group, it will have to accept a deliverable before the milestone is considered reached. Even without quality assurance groups, items have to be delivered through particular channels: programs are received by the librarians, documents by the person in charge of documentation, and so forth.

Progress Reporting

Once a milestone has been attained, it must be recorded in such a way that it can be used to draw a broader perspective. In Chapter 10, we saw that the two basic tools for recording milestones are the milestone chart and the Gantt chart (also called the bar chart). Once more, control is designed in advance, during the planning stage.

The simplest milestone chart is presented in Figure 10.9. It can be used not only for an individual but also for a team by adding a column for the person in charge of each activity. Figure 13.3 gives an example of such a chart, which can be used at all project levels.

The problem with milestone charts is that they are not very "pictorial." They do not place achievements (or lack thereof) in the context and perspective of the overall workload. Already described as a planning tool, the Gantt chart needs just a few additions to become the simplest but most visual progress report to date.

EXAMPLE D: DESIGN PORTION OF ADT SYSTEM DEVELOPMENT

Figure 13.4 shows a bar chart which is related to the milestone chart presented in Figure 13.3. It shows that there is already some trouble in the design activity. Each activity is represented by a bar. At update time, the portions of the bars that correspond to activities in progress or completed are darkened up to the point in time of the update. A hollow triangle at the end of the bar shows the expected completion date. If achievement meets objective, then the triangle is darkened, as is the case for three of the activities in Figure 13.4. If not (as with the identification subsystem), then the bar is extended to the actual completion

Milestone Chart			
Project: ADT System			
Work Package: General Design			
Assigned to: Jean Coolidge			
Task or Activity	Assigned to	Completion Date	
		Planned	Actual
Data Design	C. Blain	3/15/78	3/15/78
Identification	C. Blain	5/30/78	6/7/78
Waiting List	R. Norton	4/8/78	4/8/78
Ad.-Dis.	R. Norton	6/8/78	6/8/78
Transfer	C. Blain	6/22/78	

Fig. 13.3. Team milestone chart.

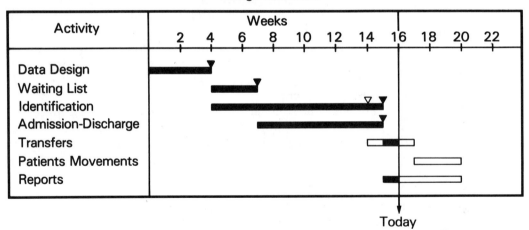

**ADT System Development:
Design Activities**

Fig. 13.4. Gantt chart as a progress report tool.

date. We can see that the identification subsystem design was one week late. We can also see that transfers design started one week late. It is likely that the same person was in charge of both subsystems.

Progress control enables a manager to know how the project is progressing, but it does not tell him at what cost. If schedule is his only concern, he needs no more information. If, however, he must also control costs, then resource consumption must be monitored as well.

Resource Consumption Control

Costs, along with schedules, are the most important problems in project management. In system development, 95% of the costs are represented by the purchase of goods (hardware, software), human resources, and computer time. Although hardware or software acquisitions may lead to budget overruns, they are not an ongoing activity. We will focus on the two other cost factors: people and computer time.

Human Resources Costs

People are usually paid at a fixed hourly or daily rate, even though their salary is determined on an annual basis. Therefore, the cost is proportional to the time spent working, and monitoring time is equal to monitoring expenses.

Time sheets are practically the only way to monitor time spent on the various project activities. An example is given in Figure 13.5. In some organizations, people work on several projects at the same time, so a project number is used to extract the relevant data. The workpackage number is of interest in large projects split into subsystems, for example; the activity code is obvious. Usually, time sheets are fed into a computer system which processes them and produces integrated reports. Often, they are already being routinely used in the organization, and there is no reason for a project manager not to use the best of the existing control structures.

Time sheets do, however, have some drawbacks. They are often used as charging tools, and items like the workpackage number or activity are present only if they have an effect on billing. Without this information, the project manager cannot link resource consumption to a given activity, and the time sheet becomes nothing more than an accounting tool which is insufficient for project control. The second problem is that employees often regard time sheets as performance evaluation tools and have a tendency to "adapt" the way they spend their work time. A project manager should make it clear to his team at the very beginning that they will not be evaluated on number of hours spent working, but primarily on the ability to deliver results on time and within requirements.

Some authors argue that time sheets represent the least useful progress control method (Wooldridge, 1976). It is true that no indication of progress can come out of a time sheet. It does not measure progress; rather, it provides information on resource consumption. Progress can only be measured through results control by using milestone and bar charts. Time sheets are needed to relate progress to costs—nothing more, but also nothing less.

Employee Number: Period Ending:

Employee Name:

Project Number	WP Number	Activity Code	Description	1	2	3	4	5	6	7	8	9	10
Totals													

Activity Codes: D = Design   H = Holiday
                   P = Programming   I = Illness
                   T = Testing   A = Absence
                   W = Documentation   T = Training
                   M = Management

Fig. 13.5. Example of a time sheet.

Computer Costs

If a project manager has to worry about computer costs, it implies that computer usage is measured in some way, usually by the computer system's accounting program. Reports are therefore available and the task of monitoring costs becomes simply one of reading these reports.

A manager who takes the time to analyze these bills over a long period of time (at least six months) will find that CPU time is not the largest entry. The real cost centers are disc space, connection time (which is the time a terminal is hooked into the system), and operator's time, if discs or tapes are often mounted or removed. For users of remote computers, the long-distance telephone calls used to access the computer may also become a significant expense. An analysis of the computer and telecommunications bills can tell the project manager (or team leader) a great deal about the way his staff works.

Crisis Management

Problems encountered can be classified according to their extent and magnitude as microcrises or as macrocrises.

Microcrises

A *microcrisis* is a small problem that usually occurs at the task or small activity level. For example, a micromilestone is missed, computer availability is insufficient, or an employee is sick or has been called away because of an emergency.

Microcrises are often not reported on the control tools previously described, and the project manager might not even be aware of them if he limits his controls to those tools. Indeed, why should he care about such small problems which are, moreover, limited in time? Because, answers Brooks: "How does a project get to be a year late? . . . one day at a time" (see Brooks (1975) in Chapter 9).

Meeting with the project team members is a good way to keep abreast of daily problems. A good project manager in a small project holds one team meeting per week. If unplanned, team meetings are a waste of time. However, if planned, they provide the project manager with more information than any other means. To be successful, team meetings must have all of the following attributes:

1. They are held every week at the same time.
2. The timing is such that the meeting does not encroach on the staff's most productive hours, and it does not last too long. (After 90 minutes, a meeting is like a record that skips, the same points are made again and again.)
3. The meeting has only one focus: to review progress and problems. Technical discussions should take place in other surroundings.
4. The project manager chairs the meeting, and should by all means organize his regular schedule so that he is available. Even in exceptional cases where he really cannot attend, the meeting still takes place, and is chaired by his assistant.
5. The meeting has an established order and an agenda (e.g., news (announcement by the chairman), follow-up of previous week's decisions, individual progress and problem reports, and decisions for the coming week).

To keep the meetings as informal as possible, the project manager should take notes himself and, if he wants, have them typed up afterwards. All notes should be kept in a file.

In large projects where it is impossible to gather all staff together on a weekly basis, the project manager should promote team meetings among his assistants. They will solve the problems at their own levels and come to the project manager with the more important ones. It is not possible to provide general solutions to all of the small problems arising in a project; they must be dealt with according to their nature, intensity, and the environment in which they occur. But most important, they must be detected early enough and then solved, so that they do not become macrocrises.

Macrocrises

A *macrocrisis* is a situation which puts the success of the project in jeopardy. The most common cases are delays, cost overruns, loss of a key team member, and outside events (see Table 13.2). Obviously, a macrocrisis happens late in the schedule, thus making it impossible to react within project boundaries.

DELAYS.   Whatever the reason, it is too late at this point to rectify the errors. The manager cannot maintain the original deadlines, expecting that by some miracle everything will fall into place in the end. Adding more people will only result in further delays (Brooks, 1975).

The manager must face the facts and define a new deadline, which must then be negotiated. In this situation, step-by-step delivery is one way to avoid harming the user too greatly. All subsystems are not usually of the same critical importance, and there is always a nucleus which is the one most badly needed. The other subsystems can be put into operation one after another according to their nature.

EXAMPLE E: STEP-BY-STEP DELIVERY

If Donald White were faced with a delay crisis, he could suggest the following order of subsystem delivery, with others to follow later.

1. *Identification subsystem.* Identification as such is an acute problem in hospitals.
2. *Admission-discharge.* Although the waiting list is needed to select patients to admit, it is less urgent than admission.
3. *Patient movements.* Compiling the daily admissions and discharges every month is the next heaviest burden on the admission staff.

COST OVERRUN.   There is only one way to deal with a forecasted cost overrun: curtail the system. This has come to be known as design-to-cost, which means

TABLE 13.2
MOST FREQUENT MACROCRISES IN A PROJECT

Nature of Crisis	Possible Reasons
Delay	Estimation errors Technical problems Poor productivity
Cost overrun	Same as above Unexpected wage increase
Loss of a key team member	Any reason
Outside events	Strike Fire, flood . . .

producing only what can be paid for in the initial estimation (see Harrison, 1981). There are two ways of tailoring the system to the estimated cost:

1. Classifying the subsystems in terms of priority and deleting as many secondary subsystems as are required to meet the initial cost estimate.
2. Taking advantage of the fact that in a system, 20% of the costs account for processing and 80% for housekeeping and user friendly interfaces. In case of need, cut from the 80% fat (see Mills, 1980).

In our opinion, the first solution is preferable. The second is analogous to the way cars are sold: The "basic model" barely includes an engine, four seats and a top; whatever makes them livable is an option added to the basic price. Users do not like "basic systems;" for them, it is important that they be user friendly.

LOSS OF A KEY TEAM MEMBER. Although a project should not be built around a single "key team member" (see recipe no. 9 in Chapter 10), if such a member is lost, he should be replaced by someone who knows his work. Added personnel from the outside should take care of less important duties. Unavoidably, there will be delays, and all of the consequences will have to be evaluated from the standpoint of their effect on deadlines, including the final deadline.

OUTSIDE EVENTS. These involve the whole organization, not simply the project, and solutions have to be examined in this larger context. Strikes are more likely than other types of risks (see Table 13.2). Contingency plans should be made during the planning stage, in accordance with the policies of the organization.

AN INFORMATION SYSTEM FOR PROJECT CONTROL

Outline of the System

The expression *information system* should be taken here in its broad meaning "a set of people, tools, procedures, etc., processing information to achieve the objective of project control." The outline of such a system is depicted in Figure 13.6. What is important in this drawing is the box composed of two parts: the project manager and the project management system.

Project management systems exist either in manual or computerized forms. They are used for planning, scheduling, and controlling the undertaking. The control function provides a variety of reports that help to answer such questions as the following:

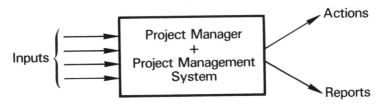

Fig. 13.6. The project control system.

Are we on schedule?

Are we within budget?

What will be the consequences of the present situation on costs and schedules?

How has the time (money) been spent? (In other words, what has each activity cost?)

For more about these systems, see Gray (1981) and Harrison (1981).

Note that project management systems do not manage projects; they enable the project managers to do so. In data processing projects, the uncertainty of estimates might require so many revisions to the input data that all of the time would be spent feeding the system and analyzing the outputs. It seems that as long as planning can be handled manually, so can control. The dividing line therefore lies in the size of the project and the complexity of the relationships. But regardless of whether a manual or computerized system delivers information, the project manager has to process the information in order to make decisions and take appropriate action. As Johnson (1977) observed, success does not depend on reporting technique. Rather, it depends on making the right decisions and having them implemented.

Inputs

The inputs to the control system are all of the information the project manager needs to assess the present state of the project and to compare it with the plan. If we suppose that the project has been planned according to the guidelines given in Chapters 7, 9, 10, and 11, then the manager already has the references for comparison. We will therefore concentrate on what is needed to assess the situation.

The first characteristic of a progress report system is that it should encumber the team members as little as possible. If it is too much of a burden, two things may happen:

○ In an environment where loose controls are the tradition, the progress reports will either be late (and thereby useless) or will not be done at all.

○ In a tightly controlled working environment, adding controls to the already existing structures will have a detrimental effect on productivity and morale.

This leads us to the second point: the project manager should make use of the existing control structures and add to them only what he feels is lacking in control requirements. For example, the minimum control inputs in a small to medium-sized project could be identified as (a) weekly meetings, (b) milestone charts and/or bar charts, and (c) change control requests. If the expenditures are also to be controlled, the manager needs time sheets and computer and telecommunications usage reports.

In most organizations, time sheets and computer usage reports already exist, and therefore do not add to the team's paperwork. The first three control inputs are the true additions required by the project structure. If one considers that bar charts are maintained by the project manager himself (and by his assistants in large undertakings), team members only have milestone charts to update and weekly meetings to attend.

Process

Let us suppose that both results and resource consumption have to be controlled. The first part of the process is to obtain the inputs, and this involves the problem of frequency.

Frequency of Inputs

MILESTONE CHARTS. One way of updating the milestone chart is to ask for results only when the need arises, i.e., when a milestone is to be reached. However, this requires that the project manager keep abreast of all milestones. It is much easier to make the updating of milestone charts a regular item on the agenda of the weekly meetings. Follow-up of missed targets thus becomes part of the same routine.

TIME SHEETS. If these are already being used in the organization, it is necessary to comply with the existing frequency. If introduced for the project, they should be on a one- or two-week basis. If a longer time interval is used, people will lose track of the way they spent their time.

BAR CHARTS. To update bar charts, milestone results and time sheets are required. The charts should be updated according to the frequency of these two inputs.

COMPUTER AND TELECOMMUNICATIONS REPORTS. When available, these reports are provided on a monthly basis. Moreover, most computer accounting systems provide both monthly and cumulative consumption data.

Comparing Present State with Plan

Results are easily compared with the plan by examining the milestone and Gantt charts. Resource consumption is compared with the detailed budget described in Chapter 11 (p. 000). For human resources consumption, the work sheet presented in Table 11.7 can be used: forecasts are expressed in man-months, thereby allowing easy comparison with time sheet results. If a project management system is used, it will provide both actual consumption and results. If not, at least a time sheet processing system should be used.

Decision

Once the results have been compared with the plan, the manager must make a decision. We exclude, of course, cases where everything is on schedule and within cost; project managers in this happy situation need no advice. If something is not consistent with the plan, action taken depends on

the extent of the difference,

the moment in the development cycle when it happens, and

the type of project.

If the difference can be made up within the available slack time, there is no need to revise the plan. The problem should be investigated and closely followed. If the difference does not involve just one or two milestones but is recurring, it might be a productivity or estimate problem. Estimates should be revised according to the actual results, and if the revision pushes the final deadline back, the project manager has a major problem.

In fixed-deadline projects, where costs are more flexible than schedules, a deadline problem can in some cases be solved by asking personnel to work overtime to make up for the delays and for the estimate differences. This implies that the deadline can be met, given the additional amount of work. If the delay involves early milestones, putting additional personnel on the project may also provide a solution.

We already know that for fixed-cost projects it will be impossible to keep both schedule and costs in line. Some concessions will have to be made, either in the product (design-to-cost), schedule (late delivery), or costs.

Unfortunately, nothing like overtime exists for money resources. An 8-hour workday may be expanded to 10 or 12, and people may agree to work on weekends, but there is no way to make up for overruns. In this case one can design-to-cost or negotiate an increase in the budget.

In summary, if the results make the final specifications impossible to meet, there is not much a project manager can do except change the plans—add resources, add time, or decrease the scope of the product to be delivered.

Outputs

There are two main outputs from the process: actions and progress reports.

Actions

When final deadlines or costs are not at stake, internal measures are sufficient. The manager should try to remedy any existing problem by adding people assigned to less urgent tasks, obtaining help for technical problems, and so forth. The manager must also update the plan; a problem may not change the final forecast, but it surely takes away some degrees of freedom which were available. Further assessments should be made in the new context, not the previous one.

If the final objectives are to be changed, the project manager must do so in a formal manner. There are three steps to follow:

1. Justify the reasons for change. It is never easy to admit either an error (estimates) or a predicted failure, but doing so is much better than hiding it and ending up without the desired results. Moreover, the reasons for change are often well accepted, especially when they are out of the project manager's control. (Examples of such reasons would include user changes and staff assigned to other duties.)
2. Propose new solutions. This means both new objectives (time, costs) and new means of achieving those objectives.
3. Obtain approval of one of the proposed solutions from upper management and from the user.

Progress Reports

Up to now, we have been concerned with how the project manager keeps informed of the progress made. Upper management also needs to be informed of what is happening. If this is done on a regular basis, problem events such as those described in this chapter are likely to have a much better outcome than if they came as a total surprise.

Progress reports should be made on a monthly basis and forwarded to upper management. If well designed, they even become the project manager's control file, since they condense all the information related to the progress of the undertaking. There are many variations of progress reports (e.g., Harrison, 1981; Spinner, 1981). The basic framework is made up of two parts: qualitative data and quantitative data.

QUALITATIVE DATA. The first part of the report should be in narrative form. It may often be the only part read by executives, and should contain: (a) an assessment of the overall situation (whether or not the project is proceeding according to plan, etc.); (b) problems encountered since the last report, and how they were settled; (c) objectives for the coming period. This portion of the report should be no longer than one to two pages, and should be written in the same spirit as the executive summary in Chapter 5.

QUANTITATIVE DATA.   This section of the report should be short. It should contain: (a) a bar chart of the overall project showing the major activities and milestones (reached and expected); (b) resource consumption to date on an overall project basis as compared with expectations. Differences between actual and forecasted results should be explained in short notes.

The monthly progress report in fact achieves two objectives. First, it keeps upper management informed of the project's progress. Second, by its existence and content, it shows that the project manager does indeed care about controlling the undertaking.

SELECTED REFERENCES

Ahituv, N., & Neumann, S. 1982. Controlling the information system function. *Journal of Systems Management*, 33,9 (September), 10–16.
> The article deals with the information systems function at the organization level and at the project level. Regarding the latter, the emphasis is on the control function of the project manager. Mentioned are progress reports, project management documentation, and the qualities of a system.

Buckley, F. 1979. A standard for software quality insurance plans. *Computer*, August, 43–49.
> The paper presents the IEEE standard for quality assurance plans. It details in particular the documents which should exist in software development and the reviews the quality assurance group should conduct.

Fagan, M. E. 1976. Design and code inspections to reduce errors in program development. *IBM Systems Journal*, 15,3, 219–248.
> This well-known article presents design and code inspections in great detail. These inspections differ from walkthroughs in that their focus is not on quality but on error finding. The inspection teams and process are described, as are some results: it significantly decreases the number of errors remaining at the test stage, and it teaches designers and programmers which errors they are more prone to commit. In addition, by compelling the team members to study the product in depth early in the development process, it gives them extensive knowledge of the system under development.

Harrison, F. L. 1981. *Advanced project management*. Aldershot, England: Gower Pub. Co.
> Controls, especially regarding costs, are a major focus of this book. The author insists on the necessity of having a project management information system and a change control system. A definition of design-to-cost is also provided.

Johnson, J. R. 1977. Advanced project control. *Journal of Systems Management,* 28,5, May, 24–27.
This article covers all aspects of project management in a 10-step planning procedure. The key to control, according to the author, is the definition of meaningful milestones. He also maintains that control procedures should not be a burden, and that success in a project does not depend on reporting techniques.

Merchant, K. A. 1982. The control function of management. *Sloan Management Review,* 23,4 (Summer), 43–55.
After analyzing the functions and methods of control, the author presents the three types of controls and defines the environment in which every type works best. He points out the possible side effects of having too many controls.

Spinner, M. 1981. *Elements of project management: Plan, schedule and control.* Englewood Cliffs, N.J.: Prentice-Hall.
The book presents the basis of network-oriented project management. For control, however, the author prefers the bar chart and explains how to prepare and update one. He also proposes a model for project status reports.

Wooldridge, S. 1976. *Project management in data processing.* New York: Petrocelli/Charter.
This is one of the few books which discusses the problems associated with the management of data processing projects. The different progress reporting tools are presented in detail and their specific usefulness discussed. Once more, the percent-complete syndrome is described, as are time sheets as progress reporting tools.

Chapter 14

A NONPROGRAMMING PROJECT: COMPUTER SELECTION

INTRODUCTION

Selecting a computer system is one of the most exciting projects in data processing. All aspects of the computing field are covered; it puts one in contact with a wide variety of people and problems; and it has an impact on everything involving data processing for the next five to seven years. In addition, it has all the fascination of a shopping spree, which is where the problems begin.

We have seen in preceding chapters that the main problems of system development lie more in the management of the process than in the process itself. Unfortunately, shopping is an activity with a poorly defined pattern for most individuals, except maybe for advertisers. If we want the outcome here to be more successful, we first need to define the process by which the system will be selected (see Figure 14.1).

Next, we need to specify guidelines on how to perform the different activities making up the process. Here, requirements play the same role as in system

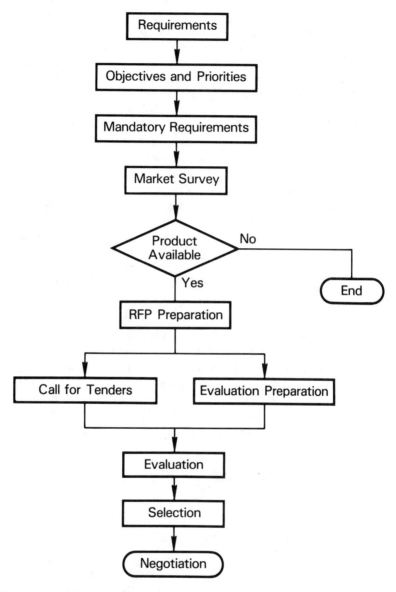

Fig. 14.1. The process of computer system selection.

development. Setting objectives and priorities is necessary in order to avoid losing track of what is essential while looking at all the wonderful state-of-the-art systems presented by vendors. We will examine the set of mandatory requirements which represents their translation into system terms. The RFP (Request For Proposal) process, which is now considered standard for system selection, will also be discussed, along with evaluation methodologies. Finally, a selection step very similar to the decision step in an opportunity study will be presented. The main objectives are: (a) to produce a deliverable (the final choice) of high quality; and (b) to reduce the cost of the process itself. These objectives will be met by: using functional instead of technical requirements; not trying to mix objective and subjective factors into a single assessment; putting the maximum amount of responsibility on the vendor's shoulders; and standardizing the procedures and documents of the process.

Once more, the project manager will have to possess a balanced mix of technical and managerial capabilities. A strong background in hardware and software is required to validate vendor claims and evaluate the products—or to control the members of the team who are performing these tasks. The manager will have to ignore his technical background, however, in order to produce functional requirements and to avoid evaluating the proposals exclusively according to technical criteria. This pattern should now be familiar to us: it is that of the data processing manager of the 1980s, not the 1960s.

EXAMPLE A: THE GREAT RIVER TRANSIT COMMISSION (GRTC)

When we met the Commission in Chapter 5, it already had a computing department. Let us go back in time two years, when no machine and no data processing department existed. Payroll is done by an outside service bureau and everything else is performed manually. Realizing that data processing will help keep costs in line and enable the Commission to handle the administrative workload better, the Board of Directors decides to create a data processing department and hires Bill Mason to head it. His first duty is to select a computer system to handle the processing requirements of the Commission.

SYSTEM SPECIFICATIONS

Functional Requirements

Requirements should specify what the system is to do, not how it will do it (see Timmereck, 1973). Historically, three approaches to requirements can be distinguished.

In the *technical approach*, requirements were expressed in terms of hardware performance: CPU cycle, memory size and speed, and so forth. Little mention was made of the accompanying software except perhaps the programming languages available. This approach was discarded long ago because it was grossly inadequate.

In the *handling-of-the-workload approach*, the first objective of the computer is to handle the existing or forecasted workload and the efforts concentrated on defining its parameters. Volume, throughput, and response time are the main variables. Evaluation concentrates on benchmarks performance, simulation, and so on. A closer look reveals that this approach still deals with the second generation of computers (or the beginning of the third) where applications are mainly batch-oriented, CPU-bound, or use tapes; the CPU is both the main part of the machine and its potential bottleneck.

Since the beginning of the 1970s these computers (and this way of using them) have slowly been fading away. They are being replaced by more balanced hardware in which the CPU is only one component among others of equal importance, with the applications being more and more geared toward remote access and information storage and retrieval. In addition, the systems themselves have decreased in size and price, while increasing in available power and storage space. Today's systems limitations can be encountered in:

disc channels (it is very often *the* bottleneck),

core, be it in a real or virtual memory,

number of active users,

disc space,

speed of the printers (especially at the end of the month),

operating system (design, performance, and services provided), and

telecommunications possibilities (hardware and software).

This evolution in the systems and the way we use them has led to the third and present-day approach. In the *global approach*, the workload concept is enlarged to take into account not only the CPU function but all aspects of the applications: data storage and retrieval, interactive use, teleprocessing. It considers the software (operating system, languages, tools, and utilities) to be an integral part of the system. In addition, life cycle considerations lead to a focus on such related factors as reliability of the vendor, quality of service, and compatibility.

Functional Specifications of System Components

How does one express the requirements of a given piece of hardware or software? One need only keep in mind the definition given for specifications in Chapter 7: the detailed description of the tasks that the product will have to perform for the user. Table 14.1 gives some examples of technical and functional specifications of hardware.

Preferring functional to technical specifications does not mean that one should be unconcerned with the technical aspects of the system. It means that

TABLE 14.1
EXAMPLES OF TECHNICAL VERSUS FUNCTIONAL SPECIFICATIONS OF HARDWARE

Item	Technical Specifications	Functional Specifications
Disc	Size (number of bytes)	Number of characters of information to be stored
Memory	Real or virtual	Ability to process simultaneously n programs of sizes S1, S2, . . . Sn
	Direct or relative addressing	
	Size in kilo- or megabytes	
Ports	Synchronous or asynchronous	Ability to support n terminals for specific functions
	Number of ports	
Printer	Speed, fonts, width of page	Ability to print a given number of outputs in a given time.

the requirements should be expressed in functional terms—nothing more. Respecting those requirements will be the vendor's responsibility, but validating his claims will be the responsibility of the project team.

Requirements Analysis

In Chapter 7, it was mentioned that the system analysis method as such could not be applied to computer selection, but that the same principles could be used. Let us restate them:

1: top-down

2: modularization

3: abstraction

4: bounded context

5: data and functions

6: visibility of results

7: automated if possible

Principle 7 has already been mentioned as being difficult to achieve, while principle 5 is specific to development. But the others can still be applied. Figure 14.2 shows a decomposition of requirements. Principles 1, 2, and 4 lead to the decomposition shown in the figure; principle 3 (abstraction) is obtained by specifying for each box the functional requirements (what to achieve in user terms) instead of the technical requirements (how to achieve it).

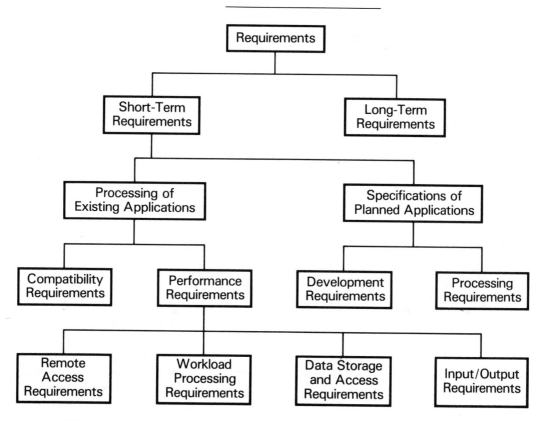

Fig. 14.2. Requirement analysis.

EXAMPLE B: REQUIREMENTS OF THE GRTC

Short-term requirements. As there is currently no computer, there is no processing of existing applications. (The payroll service is not to be converted but replaced.) The *planned applications* are:

Phase 1: payroll, general accounting

Phase 2: inventory control

Phase 3: budget control.

Phase 1 applications should be realized by acquiring packages; phase 2 could be purchased or developed; and phase 3 will depend on the products available for phase 1. Note that short-term requirements are expressed in successive phases. This approach allows a staged development of the hardware and software sought.

Long-term requirements. The Commission plans to use data processing for:

purchasing management,

bus maintenance management,

fixed assets,

database on the transit network, and

driver work assignments.

Long-term requirements are those planned for the one to two coming years. They usually have no precise timing, nor are they as firmly decided upon as short-term requirements. However, if they are likely to be put into operation during the system's life cycle, they should be mentioned.

Mandatory Requirements

Shopping for a computer system is much like shopping for a car. There are so many new and attractive features touted by vendors that a person can easily forget what his real needs and means are. It is true that new features can help him better fulfill his needs, but he should never lose sight of his basic requirements.

Mandatory requirements are those without which the system will not meet the objectives and constraints (see Joslin, 1977; Lustman et al., 1978). A system will be a good candidate for acquisition only if it meets the mandatory requirements; all others will be considered optional, useful, or suitable—but not essential.

Defining mandatory requirements is a problem. Very often the tendency is to settle for mandatory requirements that are simply within the parameters of the present way of doing things or the knowledge of the team regarding technology. Another danger is stating them too rigidly, as, for example, with price limits. Joslin (1977, p. 135) stated that price should never be a mandatory requirement: "What if the system costing only one dollar more offers 50% more capability?" It leaves room to maneuver during the selection step, when it will always be possible to reject overly costly proposals.

Examples of Mandatory Requirements

HARDWARE REQUIREMENTS.   Examples include: direct access storage (again in terms of user data, not in disc capacity); number of terminals which can be connected to the system; compatibility with existing equipment. In fact, so many solutions exist for any given problem that few hardware requirements are mandatory.

PROCESSING REQUIREMENTS. Workload characteristics are mandatory only if no conversion is to take place. If applications are to be converted, the processing requirements have to be converted into applications specifications.

SOFTWARE REQUIREMENTS. Examples include language processors, database management systems, telecommunications, and multiprogramming. Software requirements are more often mandatory than hardware requirements, since applications and programming practices outlive machines.

SERVICES. The existence of a local branch of the supplier with repair facilities (technicians, parts, etc.) is often considered a mandatory requirement.

FINANCING REQUIREMENTS. It may well happen that the organization wants to rent the system. Because not all suppliers offer this formula, it could be considered mandatory.

EXAMPLE C: MANDATORY REQUIREMENTS FOR THE GRTC

To define the mandatory requirements, Bill Mason has consulted the Commission's lawyer, the head of the purchasing department, and the head of finance. The result is shown in Table 14.2. The system requirements cannot be contested; they correspond to the use the GRTC wants to make of the system.

When looking at the application packages requirements, one is somewhat surprised to see that the Commission wants to have access to the code. Although the disappearance of a company is common in data processing, such a clause could in fact discourage the largest suppliers, who have rigid contract formulas from which such a condition is surely excluded.

The back-up center requirement in the proposal part of Table 14.2 is very wise, except that few suppliers would guarantee it themselves or negotiate it with some other user. If the system must already be in use in Great River (according to another clause), it is up to Bill Mason to negotiate a back-up agreement.

The last clause, obviously introduced by the lawyer, is a wise one: if the solicitation document is part of the contract, the vendor is responsible for his product's performing according to what he claims in the proposal. However, it is obvious that the lawyer is not very familiar with data processing contracts; if considered mandatory, this requirement will create problems, as we will see later on.

Replacement of an Existing System

When the future system is to replace an existing one, its primary objective is to process the existing workload. The first part of the requirements is therefore

TABLE 14.2
MANDATORY REQUIREMENTS FOR THE GRTC

Part of the RFP	#	Requirement	Reason
Computer system	1	Multiprogramming (up to 5 tasks)	Long-term requirement
	2	Interactive (up to 16 terminals)	Maximum expected number of terminals to be installed
	3	RPG or COBOL	Local programming
	4	Scientific language	Statistics on network use
Application packages	5	Compatibles	Integration planned
	6	Well tested	Wants no trouble with bugs
	7	Can be shown in operations	Replaces benchmark and proves that they work
	8	Source code provided or in escrow	If the supplier goes out of business
Supplier	9	Large, well-equipped branch in city	To decrease downtime
	10	References for the same equipment in city	Not to be alone
Proposal	11	Single bidder for all products	In case of trouble, one phone number
	12	Back-up center	Payroll cannot wait
	13	Solicitation document part of the contract	Makes the vendor responsible for his statements in proposal

made up of the description of this workload. It is not a very difficult task, since precise quantitative data are available.

Let us follow the decomposition shown in Figure 14.2.

○ *Hardware compatibility requirements.* All of the equipment with which the system will have to interact is described.

○ *Software compatibility requirements.* If the existing applications are not to be converted, the programming languages, file organizations, utilities used, etc., are enumerated. If they are to be converted by the user, all tools required for the conversion are listed.

○ *Workload processing requirements.* These are first provided on a global basis by specifying parameters such as: number of systems, of programs; number of jobs processed at the same time (the classical batch workload); throughput time; number of transactions (per hour or per minute); average response time for a transaction; number of terminals connected to the system; volume of stored data per storage device type (disc, tape); volume of printing (average, peak); and so on.

Forecasted Increase in Volume of Present Applications

If an increase is forecasted, it has to be specified. This should be done for all the parameters mentioned in the workload. Once the existing workload is described completely, the planned applications have to be specified. There is at this point no difference between the replacement of an existing system and the case of a first computer in the organization.

EXAMPLE D: EXISTING WORKLOAD AT THE INSTITUTE OF CARDIOLOGY

The GRTC cannot be used as an example, since it has no existing applications. Let us therefore go back to the Institute of Cardiology system described in Chapters 9 and 10. It did not have its own computer, and so developed and processed its applications on the university's machine. Therefore, a workload does exist and has to be described.

COMPATIBILITY REQUIREMENTS.

1. The vendor must supply or find a supplier for a version of the SPSS package (Statistical Package for the Social Sciences), running on the proposed system.
2. The following software tools are needed to enable the Institute's staff to convert the programs: FORTRAN compiler, and indexed sequential and direct access files organizations.
3. The system must have a card reader.
4. For the next two years, a telecommunications link with the university's computer will have to be provided. It will have to emulate the U200 terminals accepted by the mainframe and run as a task concurrently with others in the Institute's computer.

WORKLOAD PROCESSING REQUIREMENTS.

Total number of programs: 220

Workload profile:
  4 daily batch jobs (average)
  2 jobs twice a week
  6 jobs monthly

Average daily processing requirements (on a CDC 6600):
  CPU time: 1 minute
  I/O time: 30 minutes

Average end of month processing requirements:
  CPU time: 30 minutes
  I/O time: 2 hours

Average size of a program: 25000 60-bit words*

Maximum size of a program: 40000 60-bit words*

DATA STORAGE REQUIREMENTS.

Disc space: Around 10 million bytes of data.

Tapes: Around 100 tapes (half full on the average) are in use.

INPUT/OUTPUT REQUIREMENTS.

Average daily input: 500 cards

Average daily output: 650 pages

Specifications for a First System

When a system is required, it is obviously for some specific purpose which must be expressed. As shown in Figure 14.2, forecasted applications (or system use) are usually divided into two categories: those that are planned (i.e., well defined) and those that are long-term (less precisely defined in terms of time, scope, and detail). Both have to be presented, but at different levels of detail.

Planned Applications

If specifications exist, one could simply include them as part of the requirements. This is, however, a poor method of defining requirements. The document is too big for the purpose and must be condensed. The requirements should focus on everything that has an influence on the system's configuration (hardware and software) and size. Each application will therefore be described according to the following guidelines:

1. Overall description;
2. Functions performed, frequency, mode of processing (batch, remote batch, interactive); and
3. Volumes of input and output data for each instance.

If packages are to be used for an application, required input and output data should be described carefully.

---

* Many programs are in overlays; the size given is for the largest segment.

EXAMPLE E: PLANNED APPLICATIONS AT THE GRTC

Payroll and general accounting are the first two systems to be put into operation. Moreover, they will not be developed by the Commission; packages are to be provided by the vendor. In Table 14.3, we can see the requirements for the accounting package.

Note that this application requires two terminals. It will be up to the vendor to assess the speed of the printer required to output the reports for this application as well as for all others presented in the requirements. Bill Mason should, however, be able to validate the vendor's claims. He has to know what volume of printout will be produced by the various applications.

Why, therefore, does he not specify these figures directly as requirements? Once more the answer is functional requirements: specifying a volume of input (in number of lines, for example) is being very specific. Since the supplier has to provide the package, let him do the calculations according to his package specifications.

Development Requirements

For those applications which will be developed inhouse, the requirements should specify all development tools considered necessary, such as programming languages, text-editors, file organizations, DBMS, and so on. One can trust a computer professional: he will never overlook any of them.

TABLE 14.3
REQUIREMENTS FOR THE GENERAL ACCOUNTING APPLICATION

Function	Characteristics	Inputs	Reports
Accounts payable	500 suppliers	Daily, interactive (1 terminal) 25 invoices/day	Journal of purchases (weekly, monthly) Accounts payable (monthly) Age of accounts (monthly) Checks (monthly) Disbursement cash (monthly) List of suppliers (on request)
General ledger	Accounting chart has 800 entries Account number has 8 digits	Monthly, interactive (1 terminal) 100 entries monthly	General ledger (monthly) Bank conciliation (monthly) Trial balance (monthly) Financial statements

Long-term Requirements

These are usually described in less precise terms because no real investigation or system analysis has been performed. They are similar to the Extension section in a specifications manual (see Chapter 7). Regardless of this lack of precision, long-term requirements should be indicated, since they have an influence on the expansion possibilities of a proposed system. The system should be able to handle them with or without additions, but should not need to be replaced.

THE RFP PROCESS

Definitions and Objectives

Request For Proposals (RFP) is a formal procedure by which the buyer solicits proposals from vendors for a specified set of products and/or services. The various steps are depicted in Figure 14.3. The process is mandatory in public administrations and was designed to give all bidders equal opportunities and to

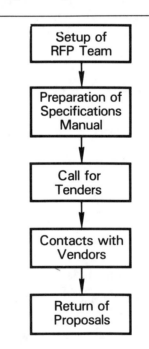

Fig. 14.3. The RFP process.

eliminate or at least decrease favoritism. However, it goes further than that and can be used advantageously in private enterprise, as well.

Its main objectives are:

1. Fairness toward the vendors: (a) all have the same information; (b) all start at the same time; and (c) all follow the same path.
2. Decrease in the workload for both the vendors and the team members: (a) the vendors have all the information at the outset; (b) they know exactly what information they have to provide; (c) the team is less disrupted by requests for information concerning the solicitation; and (d) the proposals are much easier to analyze.

Public and Selective RFPs

There are two formulas for RFPs. In the case of the *public tender*, the request is made through public media (usually newspapers); anybody can bid, provided he or she fulfills the conditions for submission. This procedure is often used by public administrations because it is the law or the official rule. The disadvantage lies in being flooded with proposals of no interest.

The second formula is the *tender on invitation* or *selective tender*. In this case, the buyer screens the market and asks selected vendors (usually in writing) to come pick up a specifications manual if they are interested. The screening process mentioned in connection with Figure 14.1 is also geared toward determining if the product or service sought is available on the market.

The RFP Team

Typically, the RFP team is interdisciplinary in its composition. The project leader is always a data processing professional, often the head of data processing. The other members include:

o Other data processing specialists (operations, systems, development, market).
o The head of the purchasing department or one of his assistants. He will be in charge of the RFP procedure and of the part of the manual dealing with the conditions of the deal.
o The company's lawyer for the contractual aspects. Sometimes it is even necessary to consult a lawyer specializing in data processing contracts.
o The head of finance or one of his representatives for the procurement aspects.

Joslin (1977) suggests that a single person should be the contact for all vendors and that this person should not participate in the preparation of the specifications. In principle, the specifications manual is prepared before the bidders are called in. The contact person should obviously be the head of purchasing (or his representative). Dealing with vendors is his usual job, and if any questions are of a technical nature, he will forward them to the right specialist.

The Specifications Manual

Everything a would-be supplier needs to know should be in the specifications manual. Its scope is therefore much broader than merely stating the system's requirements. An example of a table of contents is as follows:

1 General Conditions

1.1 Procedure

1.2 The Tenderer

1.3 Conditions of the Deal

1.4 Responsibilities

1.5 Miscellaneous

2 The Requirements

2.1 The Company

2.2 Short-term Requirements

2.3 Long-term Requirements

2.4 Services

3 Proposal Forms

General Conditions

This section covers the details of the procedure and all of the conditions of the projected deal. In particular, it will specify the responsibilities of the vendor and buyer should an agreement be reached. According to a panelist in a discussion between vendors and buyers, there are a potential 5,000 lawsuits in this area for the 1980s in the United States alone (Martin, 1981).

Examples of clauses found in this section are as follows:

○ Procedures for picking up the RFP and for returning proposals.
○ Format and content of the proposals. Two good documents to ask for are the annual report of the vendor's company and a copy of each contract form the vendor intends to submit for signature should he obtain the deal.
○ Right of the buyer to reject any proposal.
○ Impossibility for a bidder to change his proposal after the closing date.

o Single bidder; whenever possible, a single vendor should be required.
o Conditions of the deal should be outlined: how, when, where the product should be delivered and installed; any case in which the deal could be off, and under what conditions, and so forth. A very good clause is to make the returned RFP document itself an integral part of the contract. This is recommended by Schaeffer (1981) and has been used successfully by this author.
o The respective responsibilities of the buyer and vendor should be outlined.
o Miscellaneous clauses like some of those mentioned in Table 14.2 can be added: packages (or system) well tested, source in escrow, etc.

The Requirements Section

It is useful for a vendor to have information about the company asking him to bid. The information provided should be of a very general nature, such as that given in Example F.

The requirements themselves, both short-term and long-term, will be stated as described earlier in this chapter. It is the data processing professionals' section: they produce it; they are responsible for its content and evaluation.

The services section describes the requirements or asks for information on topics such as maintenance, documentation, training, access to a similar system before delivery (remember the Institute of Cardiology case in Chapter 9), and analyst and programmer time.

EXAMPLE F: COMPANY DESCRIPTION OF THE GRTC

The Great River Transit Commission is a public company providing transportation in the city of Great River and its suburbs. The network is composed of 15 lines and is serviced by 300 buses. The maintenance of the buses is handled in two garages, one on Harbour Road, the other on Rosedale Street. The staff is composed of:

drivers	387
repair staff	104
office staff	43
management	41

Bus maintenance requires the use of more than 5,000 items including parts, tires, fuel, motor oil, etc.

Up to now we have been paying particular attention to the vendor. We provided him with all the information he needed, and told him the rules by which he should abide. But what about the project team? It is time to think of its well-being, and this is the subject of the last section of the RFP document: the proposal forms.

A Format for Proposals

In such selection projects the team is burdened by returned proposals in the form of huge stacks of paper, as well as the immense and boring task of going through all the manuals, reference books, pamphlets, etc. to find the right information. In addition, no two vendors adopt the same format, so the search begins over again for each proposal.

Joslin (1977) suggested using a "solicitation document," and Schaeffer (1981) supports that idea; it is a turn-around document on which the vendor has to fill in the blanks with the requested answers. After one bitter experience of rummaging through nine proposals (Lustman et al., 1978), this author switched definitively to questionnaires as proposal-recording documents. After some adjustments, he never regretted the move. Best of all, the vendors were happy too: they knew exactly what the selection team wanted to know and how it wanted the information to be presented.

The objective of forms to record proposals is twofold: obtaining standard answers to requests, both in format and content, and obtaining all the information needed. It allows team members to find easily the information they are looking for and it decreases the amount of interaction between them and the vendors, thereby decreasing the cost and duration of the process.

The proposal forms constitute the third chapter of the specifications manual as shown in the table of contents (p. 328). It usually starts with a section explaining how to fill out the different forms and how to interpret the different questions.

EXAMPLE G: INSTRUCTIONS REGARDING FORM 20 (PAYROLL PACKAGE COSTS)

"When applicable, the amounts entered for the first year will be considered definite; the amounts for the following years will be considered to be ceilings. If royalties are to be paid, their amount should be entered on that formula. As long as the Commission does not process volumes beyond those mentioned in the present document, it should incur no additional expenses."

General and Specific Forms

General forms correspond to very general requirements and can be used in any selection. Figure 14.4 shows a form requiring the description of the local branch of the vendor. Another general form of particular interest is shown in Figure 14.5. It requires the vendor to list all points on which his proposal does *not* conform to the specifications manual! Vendors usually do not like this form, but they

FORM 3
LOCAL BRANCH

Name: _____

Address: _____

_____

_____

General manager: _____

Sales manager: _____

Service manager: _____

Staff: Sales: _____

Service (hardware): _____

Service (software): _____

Others: _____

Total: _____

Fig. 14.4. Form for local branch description.

know that they have a greater chance of being rejected if they do not fill it out correctly. A very useful form!

Specific forms are intended to record all of the information specific to the given selection. There will be forms to describe hardware (e.g., Figure 14.6), forms to describe software packages (e.g., Figure 14.7), forms to describe maintenance formulas and costs, documentation, training, and so on. These forms are not difficult to design. The little extra effort necessary to set them up results in great savings of time and work when it comes to analyzing the proposals. If, however, something has been missed when designing the formulas, there is still the possibility of going through the vendor's literature which accompanies the forms; after all, his claims have to be validated.

Application to Small Equipment

When the project concerns small equipment (up to $20,000), the procedure is obviously too clumsy and has to be reduced. This is even more true in a private

FORM 4

DIFFERENCES BETWEEN THE PROPOSAL AND THE SPECIFICATIONS MANUAL

Section	Clause #	Page #	Topic	Explanation

Fig. 14.5. Form for recording differences from the specifications manual.

FORM 7
COMPUTER SYSTEM DESCRIPTION

Piece of equipment	number or quantity in the proposal	maximum possible
CPU model: _____	_____	_____
Storage (kilobytes)	_____	_____
Virtual memory: yes ___ no _____		
Disc drives (number)	_____	_____
Disc capacity (unit)	_____	_____
Disc capacity (total)	_____	_____
Tape drives (number)	_____	_____
Printer model: _____	_____	_____
terminals model: _____	_____	_____

Fig. 14.6. Example of form for hardware description.

FORM 17
PAYROLL PACKAGE DESCRIPTION

Manufacturer (if different from vendor): _____

Programming language: _____

Functional specifications:	YES	NO
hourly rate:	___	___
daily rate:	___	___
weekly rate:	___	___
yearly rate:	___	___
tax tables updated by programming:	___	___
tax rates updated by data:	___	___
deduction tables updated by programming:	___	___
deduction tables updated by data:	___	___
payroll register:	___	___
checks with cumulative vouchers:	___	___

Limits:
    number of employees: _____
    number of digits in employee number: _____
    number of deductions: _____
    number of unions: _____

Fig. 14.7. Form for payroll package description.

business. It can be done provided the basic principles are enforced and the best tools are retained. The basic principles include functional specifications and mandatory requirements. Tools are the RFP and the proposal forms. Following is an example of microcomputer selection in a private business.

EXAMPLE H: SELECTION OF A MICROCOMPUTER IN A SMALL PRIVATE BUSINESS

Requirements:

1. Word processing: average of 5 reports per week
2. Mailing lists: 6 per week
3. Personalized letters: 25 per week
4. Spread sheet: 4 persons involved
5. Access to inhouse computer
6. Text transmission outside the office
7. Payroll (28 employees)

Request for proposals:

The following document was sent to four microcomputer retailers: the letter shown in Figure 14.8, the information form in Figure 14.9, and a pricing form not shown.

Mandatory requirements:

1. Display screen with 24×80 characters (for user convenience)
2. Storage of at least 128k–bytes (size required for payroll and telecommunications software)
3. Diskettes: at least two drives and 300k–byte capacity
4. Printer: 132 positions (budget) and daisy wheel
5. Software: CPM or MSDOS, well-known word processing and spread sheet systems and a payroll system available on the computer
6. Telecommunications: at least one serial port (in addition to the one needed for the printer); TTY and 2780 or 3780 protocols.

The forms seemed simple enough to prompt four retailers to answer the request, and nine systems were submitted. The evaluation and selection process will be described in subsequent sections.

THE WORLDWIDE TRADE COMPANY

4378 Main Street
Montreal

Dear Sir:

Our company is considering the purchase of one or several microcomputers. In order to facilitate our selection process, could you answer the questions on the attached forms? Please use one form per system.

We thank you for your cooperation and hope that we will be able to do business with you.

Yours truly,

Richard Hackett
Head, Data Processing

Fig. 14.8. Solicitation letter for small equipment.

EVALUATION

Overview

The evaluation step has three objectives:

1. To validate vendor claims in several ways (documentation reading, site visits, references, personal experience, etc.).

THE WORLDWIDE TRADE COMPANY
Information sheet regarding microcomputers

Vendor: _____

Make and model of the system: _____

ITEM

_____

display screen 24 × 80 characters: Yes: __   No: __

storage: minimum size (kilobytes): _____

          maximum size (kilobytes): _____

diskettes: number of drives: _____

            diskette size (in inches): _____

            diskette capacity (in kilobytes): _____

printer: 132 positions:

          daisy wheel:

Software: —operating system: _____

           —programming languages available: _____

           _____

           —word processing system: _____

           —spread sheet system: _____

           —payroll system: _____

Telecommunications: number of ports: _____

                     protocols available: _____

           _____

Fig. 14.9. Example of form for microcomputer selection.

2. To eliminate those proposals which do not meet the mandatory requirements.
3. To assess the value of the remaining proposals with regard to the objectives of the selection project.

One may be surprised to find that the selection itself is not an objective of this step. Evaluation is intended as a technical assessment of proposals, regardless of all the other considerations which may intervene during the decision stage, some of which may be purely subjective or out of the field of jurisdiction of the project team.

The evaluation does not focus on the system itself. In fact, three evaluations are carried out simultaneously:

○ The product is assessed from a technical and life cycle point of view.

○ The vendor is evaluated both as supplier and candidate for a long-term partnership.

○ The proposal itself (that is, all the aspects of the proposed deal) is looked at from a business point of view.

As in other projects, the evaluation team changes with the particular stage of the project. The user who was involved in the requirements definition step, but did not participate in the RFP process itself, comes back to evaluate the products he is being offered. If no specific application products were sought, the users are the operation and development staff of the data processing department. But if, as was the case for the GRTC, products for the end-user were specifically part of the requirements, those end-users will be part of the evaluation team. They will have to assess whether or not the product fits their functional requirements.

In addition to users, we will find the core of the team—those hardware, software, and market specialists who set up the requirements and who will evaluate the products from a technical point of view. A lawyer, the director of finance or a member of his staff, and the head of purchasing will complete the make-up of the evaluation team.

The Screening Step

The mandatory requirements were defined as those without which the system could not fulfill its needs. To be of any interest, a system must meet those needs. The screening step is aimed at *eliminating* those systems which do not. In principle it should be an easy task, although its conclusions may be harsh and even painful to some of the team members.

The process should be easy because, for each mandatory requirement, the question "Does this system meet it?" should have a clear, unequivocal, and definite answer. If it does not, the requirement should not have been considered mandatory. This brings us to the controversial question of performance requirements.

It is very difficult to assess the performance of a system without seeing how it handles the real workload. Because this cannot realistically be done, we are left with approximations: hand calculations, benchmarks, or simulations.

Although valuable, these tools cannot provide a completely convincing answer to a question such as "Will the response time be less than 4 seconds?" (And what if the response time is 4.1 seconds?)

Performance requirements are very difficult to assess. The assessments can always be challenged, and drawing an arbitrary line to eliminate what may be close approximations is itself debatable. For Joslin (1977), whose book is the reference in computer selection, performance requirements should be desirable, rather than mandatory requirements which can only be used to evaluate the systems, not eliminate them.

Mandatory requirements should be such that the information necessary to screen a system can be easily obtained:

in the proposal itself,

in the accompanying documentation, or

by established facts.

EXAMPLE I: MANDATORY REQUIREMENTS SCREENING IN THE GRTC PROJECT

Let us suppose that Bill Mason followed our advice and removed requirement 8 (source code in escrow) and requirement 12 (back-up center) from the list of mandatory requirements. The RFP process yielded six proposals, which we will name P1 to P6. Figure 14.10 shows the results of the screening process, and the following explanations are keyed to the corresponding footnote number in the figure.

[1]The system is intended exclusively for business applications and has no scientific programming language.

[?]It was impossible to obtain a clear answer on this point from the vendor; the next remarks will help understand why.

[2]Payroll was licensed by the vendor from one software supplier, and accounting from another.

[3]The supplier of P1 was making the final tests on the accounting package. The supplier of P5 was in the process of converting payroll to his proposed machine.

[4]The supplier of P1 was a very small company reselling software; the complete staff numbered 12 people, two of whom were currently being trained to become maintenance technicians. The supplier of system P5 had his office in a nearby city and no branch in Great River.

[5]The proposed system had not been installed in the city. One was installed in the vendor's city three months ago.

GREAT RIVER TRANSIT COMMISSION
COMPUTER SYSTEM SELECTION
Situation of proposals in relation to mandatory requirements

Requirement	System					
	P1	P2	P3	P4	P5	P6
1:multiprogramming (up to five tasks)	yes	yes	yes	yes	yes	yes
2:interactive (up to 16 terminals)	yes	yes	yes	yes	yes	yes
3:RPG or COBOL	yes	yes	yes	yes	yes	yes
4:scientific language	no[1]	yes	yes	yes	yes	yes
5:application packages compatible	?	yes	yes	yes	no[2]	yes
6:packages well tested	no[3]	yes	yes	yes	no[3]	yes
7:packages can be shown in operation	no[3]	yes	yes	yes	no[3]	yes
9:large, well-equipped branch	no[4]	yes	yes	yes	no[4]	yes
10:same equipment already installed in city	yes	yes	yes	yes	no[5]	yes
11:single vendor	no[6]	yes	yes	yes	yes	
13:solicitation document part of the contract	yes	no[7]	no[7]	no[7]	yes	no[7]

Fig. 14.10. Screening proposals for the mandatory requirements.

[6]The supplier of P1 intended to contract for the software and the system maintenance; the hardware had to be bought from another company which was selling machines but no programs.

[7]Vendors submitting P2, P3, P4, and P6 were very large companies using contract forms explicitly rejecting such a clause.

Outcomes

Three outcomes of the screening process and discussion are possible:

1. Some proposals have been retained, and nobody in the team argues about the outcome. (Yes, it can happen, although not very often.)
2. Some proposals have been retained, but team members feel unhappy that one or several proposals they considered good have been eliminated. Joslin recommends that if the mandatory requirements were well defined, there should be no revision, especially not for the purpose of retaining those systems in the competition which the team especially likes.
3. No proposals have been retained. (This is exactly what happens in the GRTC case.) Usually, this occurs when the set of mandatory requirements was too rigid. A close examination of the requirements and the reasons behind the eliminations should be performed, and could reveal the problem clause(s).

EXAMPLE J: REVISION OF THE MANDATORY REQUIREMENTS AT THE GRTC

The numbered explanations discussed in this example correspond to the numbered items in Example I. Explanation 1 (lack of a scientific programming language) is sound: the Commission needs to perform scientific calculations on its data. Explanations 2 to 6 correspond to a need for smooth operation and quick and efficient service. Explanation 7, however, is debatable, as was requirement 8 in Table 14.2 (code source in escrow); its aim is to put the maximum number of legal safeguards on the side of the Commission should a problem arise between supplier and buyer. It is surprising to see that those vendors who agreed to this clause had products which would almost certainly create problems for the Commission, while those rejecting it were large, well-known companies. In this case, the clause in question should not have been mandatory but desirable: vendors which agree to it should receive some points for doing so.

Evaluation Methodologies

Evaluation methodologies try to quantify all aspects of a system in order to come out with a single number representing its "value." Methods dealing with only one aspect of the system, such as cost or performance, are not considered to be methodologies. With this definition, there are only two groups of methodologies, depending on the quantification unit used: the *weighted-scores* group, which uses marks to evaluate system characteristics, and the *cost-related* group, which uses dollars (Joslin, 1977). Both have one thing in common: they are applied to systems which meet the mandatory requirements.

Weighted-scores Methodologies

PRINCIPLE: The items considered factors in the evaluation are assigned a relative weight; each is then evaluated according to a point system and assigned a mark. A general score is obtained by adding the weighted marks. The formula is:

$$S = \Sigma \, w_i \times m_i$$

where

$$w_i = \text{weight of item } i$$

and

$$m_i = \text{mark of item } i$$

EXAMPLE K: GRTC COMPUTER SYSTEMS EVALUATION

After the selection step, modified by the removal of clause 13 from the mandatory requirements (see Figure 14.10), there are four systems left: P2, P3, P4, and P6. After long discussion, the team arrives at the following items and weights:

computer system: 20%
application packages: 30%
vendor: 30%
proposal: 20%

After evaluating all items, they arrive at the results shown in Figure 14.11. The following questions might be posed concerning these results:

1. What marking scheme did they use?

Obviously there has to be one; the meaning of a mark of 60% (or 6) for an item must be explained to some extent. Part of the methodology consists in defining a marking scheme. If this is not done, and everybody is left free to use his own, it will in fact modify the weighting scheme (not the marking scheme, because the same item is evaluated by the same person or group of people).

2. Just one evaluation for the whole computer system (or all the packages)?

In actuality, Figure 14.11 shows the *final* result. Each item can itself be divided into more elementary components, grouped together by another weighting scheme, and so forth. We now have a hierarchical approach to evaluation in which each level can be evaluated independently of the others; the method becomes more cumbersome but more flexible.

3. What about costs?

This is one of the main criticisms of weighted-scores techniques: they do not take costs into consideration. This topic will be discussed later in this section.

ADVANTAGES.   When performed correctly, this is an objective methodology. It is easy to understand and easy to implement. It makes it possible to assign a value related to the objectives of the acquisition of the system to each of its aspects. For example, Ghandforoush (1982) designed a weighted-scores method with a program enabling one to modify the weights on demand; the program automatically recalculates the results, and with several trials, it is possible to see the effects of different weighting schemes.

GREAT RIVER TRANSIT COMMISSION
COMPUTER SYSTEM SELECTION
Results of Evaluation

ITEM		SYSTEM			
		P2	P3	P4	P6
Computer system	(20%)	81	84	74	78
Application packages	(30%)	85	84	63	78
Vendor	(30%)	91	81	55	84
Proposal	(20%)	92	85	79	62
Final score	(100%)	87.4	83.3	66	76.6

Fig. 14.11. Example of use of the weighted scores methodology.

DISADVANTAGES.   It does not take costs into account. It is cumbersome and requires a large number of calculations. To a certain extent, it mixes elements which have nothing in common: for example, vendor and hardware.

Cost-related Methodologies

Under this name are two evaluation methodologies designed by Joslin (1977), and which many consider the best to date. They are differential methods in that they *do not* evaluate the mandatory requirements parts of a system; only the desirable ones are looked at. The principle is to assign a basic dollar value to each desirable item and then to evaluate the dollar value of the item as present (or absent) in each proposal.

COST-VALUE TECHNIQUE.   The starting point is the total cost of a proposal. If an item is offered in a proposal and if its proposal cost is lower than the basic value established by the team for that item, the difference is *deducted* from the total cost of the proposal. The idea is that this difference is an earned value. The proposal with the lowest cost wins.

EXAMPLE L: COST-VALUE TECHNIQUE APPLIED TO THE GRTC SELECTION

Let us suppose that the desired items offered in the different proposals are:

○ System performance: time to issue a payroll if less than one hour ($100 per hour).
○ Additional disc space in the basic configuration; valued at $300 per megabyte.
○ Site preparation costs; a complete preparation including raised floor, special power supply, and air conditioning is evaluated at $15,000.

In Figure 14.12, we see the results of the process on the four remaining proposals. The figures have been obtained as follows:

THE GREAT RIVER TRANSIT COMMISSION
PROPOSALS EVALUATION BY THE COST VALUE METHOD

ITEM	SYSTEM			
	P2	P3	P4	P6
Cost of proposal	180200	211500	224750	172000
System performance	0	−2166	−4333	0
Additional disc space	−6000	−3000	−15000	−600
Site preparation costs	−10000	0	0	−15000
Final results	164200	206334	205617	156400

Fig. 14.12. Use of the cost value technique for evaluating proposals.

For system performance, the difference between one hour spent processing the payroll and the system's performance was taken into account during the life cycle: 5 years with 26 payrolls per year. P2 took one hour to perform payroll (no value deducted); P3 took 50 minutes (10 minutes benefit); P4 took 40 minutes; and P6 took 1 hour and 5 minutes.

For additional disc space, P2 offered 20 additional megabytes in its proposed configuration; P3, 10 megabytes; P4, 50 megabytes; and P6, 2 megabytes.

For site preparation, P2 needed special power supply ($5,000); P3 and P4 needed everything; P6 needed nothing.

Questions

1. How is the list of desirable items arrived at? This has to be done before the proposals come in because a basic value has to be established. It usually comes out of the specifications from which mandatory requirements have been removed.
2. How does one calculate the basic value of an item? It is, in fact, possible to attach a dollar value to almost any item. Sources will be market prices, inhouse costs (for example, cost to develop a program offered by some vendors and not by others), and so forth.

Advantages. The cost-value technique provides a unique and objective yardstick for evaluating all aspects of a proposal. In addition, this evaluation unit—money— is clearly understandable by management. It takes into account all aspects of the proposals.

Disadvantages. The technique is cumbersome, and requires a very sophisticated team to produce basic dollar values for the items. When those dollar values cannot be obtained from the market or any data, their estimation becomes merely a guesstimate.

REQUIREMENT COSTING. This is a refinement of the cost-value technique. In this case, if an item is *not offered* (or is offered at a price higher than the basic value), its basic value (or the difference with that listed in the proposal) is *added* to the cost of the system. Here too, the least costly proposal wins. The advantages over the cost-value technique are that it gives the true, complete cost of the proposal and it forces the evaluator to find a dollar value for everything he considers. According to Joslin, if he cannot find one, he should not have considered that item to be a selection criterion. In addition, it takes into account the life cycle cost and not just that of the proposal.

Discussion

Joslin (1977) is quite harsh toward the weighted-scores technique. His main criticisms are that it does not enable the establishment of meaningful and understandable relative values between the desired items, and that it does not incorporate life-cycle costing. Regarding the second argument (life-cycle costing), we will see later how to use it in conjunction with the weighted-scores techniques. It should be mentioned however that not everybody agrees with the idea of incorporating costs in the evaluation step: for some, costs should be handled in a separate step (see Foss, 1976; Lustman, 1978). On the other hand, using life-cycle costing instead of proposals costs is sound business practice. If the project team is not aware of this practice, the financial expert should remind the team to use it and, if necessary, teach the team members how to proceed.

With regard to Joslin's first criticism (namely, the relative values of the various items), the basic cost value of some items is extremely difficult to establish. (Vendor support is one example.) Remember, a contract contains provisions that enable the supplier to avoid fulfilling many of his obligations without incurring any penalties. In these instances, the evaluator has to assign dollar values which are as meaningful as weighted scores.

This brings us to another point of discussion. Does everything have to be expressed in dollar figures? If they are used simply as a yardstick, their cost meaning is lost. In addition, not every consideration in computer selection is related to money; trying to pretend that it is, even in the name of so-called "sound business management," is just an effort to hide subjective matters behind a pretence of cost efficiency. We saw in Chapter 5 that some benefits of a system are nonfinancial or impossible to evaluate financially. This is true of computer systems as well, and should be clearly acknowledged.

An interesting observation is that in both methodologies (weighted-scores and cost-related) the differences between the results for the different systems are very small. A possible explanation lies in the fact that mandatory require-ments are given consideration before evaluation. Therefore, what really differ-entiates the systems are not basic features—they all have them—but "secondary" ones.

In conclusion, carefully designed weighted-scores techniques and Joslin's methods both have merit. The distinction lies not so much in their value as in their field of application. Joslin's much more sophisticated approaches should be used if (a) the system to be acquired is a large one (over half a million dollars), because the cost of finding basic values is important and not proportional to the size of the system; or (b) if the team is already trained or at least familiar with the method. (Several basic cost evaluation techniques are not trivial.)

Weighted-scores techniques should be used (a) if the system in question is medium to small in size; (b) if the team is not familiar with Joslin's methods or does not have sufficient data to apply them (as would be the case, for example, in a first system selection); or (c) when money is of lesser concern than technical considerations, as in research-and-development-oriented machines.

Evaluation Methods

Three evaluations must be performed: product, vendor, and proposal.

Product Evaluation

Two aspects have to be looked at: configuration (hardware and software) and performance.

CONFIGURATION EVALUATION. If a system meets the mandatory requirements, evaluating the configuration (both hardware and software), consists in assessing how the system meets them and what it offers in addition to meeting them: extra power, additional space, additional terminal accesses, more sophisticated operating system, and so forth.

An important aspect of the configuration evaluation is the age of the system itself. The obsession with obsolescence is misplaced. Vendors and the media have created a paranoia about the fast evolution of hardware and software and have led people to believe that if they do not acquire the latest state-of-the-art system, they will be left with an outdated product before the end of its expected lifetime. Here are some facts: the IBM 360 systems were on the market for over 10 years; the popular DEC PDP 11's for over 12 years. As for software, COBOL was born in the late 1950s, as was FORTRAN. This does not mean, however, that one should accept old systems. It is wise to ask that the year the system was introduced be given in the RFP; a system over five years old could become obsolete. On the other hand, even a system which came out less than two years ago could have problems, especially in the area of software.

PERFORMANCE EVALUATION. This is probably the most difficult part of the evaluation. When acquiring a first system, it is largely guesswork. Four techniques are used (see Joslin, 1977, for an investigative analysis of the first three).

o *Hand timing.* By using the system's time data (CPU cycle, memory access time, etc.) and the known characteristics of the workload, an estimation of the time required to process the workload is obtained. The method is very difficult to use and is applicable only to workloads of a simple uniform pattern.

o *Benchmarking.* A benchmark is a meaningful representation of the workload, composed of several programs and run on each vendor's system. Preparing representative benchmarks is a difficult task, especially when the workload is not strongly batch-oriented but is heavily interactive. It is difficult to obtain a workload sample, and interactive applications are heavily dependent on the way the operating system handles them. If the vendors are ready to adapt the programs to their system, benchmarking is an excellent evaluation tool.

o *Simulation.* Programs exist which can simulate a computer system in operation. They are fed with a description of the computer system and of the workload, and provide as results the behavior of the simulated system under the simulated workload. One of the advantages of the simulation technique is that it provides a large amount of information about the various elements of the system's behavior while processing the workload. Another is that it can simulate an interactive environment. However, the quality of a simulator depends on the quality of the model used.

o *Use of references.* This method is to be used when no other is available, such as in the case of a new system. It consists simply in visiting sites which already have the proposed system and the same kind of applications. It is then possible to obtain a fair appraisal of a system's capabilities by asking users about system performance. Joslin argues that one should never visit the sites suggested by the vendor, for he will select only happy users and the evaluation will be biased. This author, on the other hand, has found that such users were very candid in answering questions and provided useful and valuable information.

EXAMPLE M: PERFORMANCE EVALUATION OF THE GRTC PROPOSALS

Because there was no workload, but only specifications, Bill Mason was left with user references—some given by the vendors, some obtained through personal contacts. Results were as follows:

1. Bill Mason could see P2 performing a payroll within the required time (in fact, a little less). In one installation they had the inventory package, and it performed well. Nine terminals were connected to the system, which maintained a good response time.

2. There was one P3 system to be seen in the vicinity, handling a workload twice as large as the one expected at the GRTC.

3. One P4 system could be observed. It was obviously very powerful—so powerful, in fact, that it required two full-time operators in the site visited. Mason was a little worried about that; the machine was put on the market eight years ago and worked much like the old batch-oriented systems. Interactive capabilities were visibly patched on a batch-oriented system.

4. Four P6 systems could be seen in Great River. Users were very happy with the system. However, by asking some questions, Mason concluded that if more than five terminals were interacting with the system, response time increased dramatically. One of the users told him that he was planning to upgrade to a larger compatible model. Once back at his office, Mason discovered that this larger system also cost $40,000 more. The proposed system could handle the short-term workload, but surely could not absorb long-term requirements.

Vendor Evaluation

Three elements should be considered in relation to vendor evaluation: the vendor's company, the vendor's local branch, and the vendor's salesman. The company can be evaluated through public knowledge, professional journals, and financial specialists. The objective is to assess the company's reputation, reliability, and chances of survival. There are only two ways of evaluating the local branch—by visiting it and by asking users. Here the objective is to ensure that the branch will provide good service. The salesman is the channel through which a customer deals with his supplier. Regardless of the company and the local branch, his qualities (or lack thereof) determine the quality of the service.

SELECTION

Rationale

Many procedures do not have a separate selection step. Instead, the result of the evaluation determines the winner: lowest cost-value in Joslin's methods, highest score in the weighted-scores methods. There are, however, several reasons to support the separation of evaluation and selection as two operations. First, it is desirable that costs be handled separately from product. Second, arriving at one single value (score or dollar) for elements that are very different in nature may be considered a little arbitrary. At the very least, the evaluations of these different aspects of the proposals should be made known to the decision makers (who often are not the team members).

Finally, those with experience in performing evaluations know that the results have a definite pattern: systems end up in clusters (the very good ones, for example, having marks or dollar values differing sometimes by less than 1%). Looking at the evaluation methodologies carefully, one discovers that the margin of error (or imprecision) in the individual evaluations is larger than the difference between the final results. The order in which the best systems come out should therefore not be accepted blindly as their relative order of quality when the differences are slight.

For all these reasons, a selection step is desirable. This step will allow latitude for discussion and for the introduction of other relevant considerations. Despite many efforts, computer system evaluation is not a purely quantitative discipline.

The Life Cycle Cost

One of the reasons for considering costs in a distinct step is that the cost of the proposal accounts for only a fraction of the expenses related to using a computer system. First of all, some expenses will be recurring. Examples include maintenance, insurance if the system is purchased, hardware supplies like disc packs, and so on. Second, the system will not remain in its proposed configuration but will grow. Storage, terminals, disc drives, and printers may have to be added to absorb the increasing workload. Third, in addition to the cost of the system, one has to take into consideration installation costs such as site preparation, training, and special furniture. Finally, the problem of the cost of money itself must be considered. The dollar of today is not the dollar of three years from now, and the same is true for prices. In the assessment of the true cost of a system, all of these factors have to be taken into consideration.

One-time Costs

SITE PREPARATION. With small to medium-size computers, site preparation requirements have been steadily decreasing. But some remain, and for large systems they still have to be incurred. A *raised floor* is convenient for hiding the cables and wires, but if the system needs air conditioning, a raised floor is almost a necessity for providing good air circulation. With regard to *power supply*, systems often require a regulated power line or at least a line without anything else connected on it.

Air conditioning, when required, may represent the major site preparation expense. If new terminals will be connected to the system in the same building, *cables and wires* will have to be put in the walls and ceilings. If new terminals are to access the system via telecommunications means, *modems* will have to be added. All of these costs must be added to the cost of the proposal as one-time expenses.

TRAINING. Usually, a new system comes with some basic training included in the contract, but these courses are never enough. It is therefore a wise precaution to ask for the prices and schedule of the supplier's training program in the RFP.

UPGRADE COSTS. The forecasted increases have to be added to the basic configuration asked for. A well designed RFP usually includes the request to submit the successive configurations of the system with time associated costs.

CONVERSION COSTS. If a conversion has to be performed, its costs should be evaluated. This is a project estimation in itself, as was seen in Chapters 9 and 10. The cost can be low when only cosmetic changes such as small differences in a programming language or in control commands are required. It can be quite high when the new and the old systems are very different. In some cases, emulators are offered which make it possible to avoid conversion problems. However, this only postpones the problem or makes poor use of the new machine; the applications not converted will perform very poorly on the new system and reduce its true performance capabilities.

Ongoing Costs

The first is the cost of the system itself. This is obvious if the system is rented or leased. But even if the system is purchased, its cost must be considered ongoing. Either the company will borrow the money and make monthly payments, or it will pay for it all at once and will enter the amount as amortization in its books. Therefore, the cost of the system is always considered over its lifetime, and the formula to select is usually determined by finances or upper management. It requires sophisticated financial calculations which require an accounting and finance background.

MAINTENANCE.   The nice thing about the rental formula is that it includes everything. A purchase, on the other hand, leaves maintenance and insurance in the hands of the buyer. Maintenance contracts are revisable more and more on a yearly basis and do not decrease as do hardware costs.

STAFF.   New systems operations usually require less staff than their predecessors. However, when a first system is to be installed, provision for operators and even a complete data processing department have to be made.

SUPPLIES.   Although never representing a large part of the cost, supplies do have to be taken into account. Paper, printer ribbons, magnetic tapes, and discs are the main items. In particular, disc packs of large capacity are expensive, and if used for back-ups, their cost could well make a tape drive attractive.

EXAMPLE N: LIFE-CYCLE COSTS IN THE GRTC COMPUTER SELECTION

The system was to be purchased; staff costs were already accounted for, except for system P5 in which an additional half-time operator had to be added. Moreover, after his visits to other sites, Bill Mason decided, in agreement with the other members of the team, to exclude system P6 for not meeting long-term mandatory requirements.

The costs to be taken into consideration were:

equipment proposed,

site preparation,

training,

upgrade (storage, disc drive, terminals),

maintenance, and

supplies.

The result of the life-cycle costing exercise is shown in Figure 14.13. As can be seen, the bill has increased significantly—almost double the "basic" price.

THE GREAT RIVER TRANSIT COMMISSION
COMPUTER SYSTEM SELECTION
Life cycle costs

ITEM	SYSTEM		
	P2	P3	P4
Equipment and packages, phase 1:	180200	211500	224750
Site preparation:	5000	15000	15000
Maintenance of equipment, phase 1:	90100	84600	101138
Training:	1500	2000	500
Additional staff:	—	—	35,000
Additional equipment, phase 2:	48600	42500	37200
Maintenance of equipment, phase 2:	14500	10200	10040
Supplies:	8000	12000	12000
Total costs:	347900	377800	435628

Fig. 14.13. Example of life cycle costs.

Selection Alternatives

One of the reasons for having a distinct selection step is to enable the decision makers to evaluate the factors which are the most important to them. Money will often be the prime factor, but this is not always the case; reliability of the system or of the service can be deciding factors, as can be pure technical performance or even subjective motivations like ego, marketing, or friendship. It is all very well to say that a system should not be selected on subjective criteria, but they do exist and it is unwise to dismiss them. That is why evaluation and selection are two separate operations.

The selection step has excluded any system not meeting the mandatory requirements. Any system still remaining is able to fulfill the stated needs, and even if the winner is not the best of the group (e.g., if subjective considerations prevail), it will still be a good choice. In addition, the evaluation—especially when it leads to more than one result—provides the decision makers with valuable information to explore different selection alternatives.

Selection on Cost Criteria

In public administrations, the rule is often to award the contract to the lowest bidder. This could be interpreted as either the total life cycle cost (which would make system P2 the winner in Figure 14.13) or as the face value of the proposal. If no regulations apply, it is the total life cycle cost which determines the winner.

Selection on Purely Technical Grounds

It may happen, especially when systems are intended for research and development work (as in universities and research laboratories), that a certain amount of money is available for the system. In this case, people are interested in the best system from a technical point of view. Compatibility considerations and even quality of service may become secondary; these institutions often have better technicians than the vendors themselves. A system's state-of-the-art and performance then become almost the only selection factors, and to have a purely technical evaluation is useful.

Selection Based on Other Criteria

Any criteria or combination thereof can be used. The evaluation step has provided all the information on—and all the limitations of—the different systems still in the race. A system may be selected because the vendor is a large company which is well-known for quality and service; or it may be selected because the vendor's branch is a few steps away from the future system's location. It may even be selected because the salesman or branch manager is well known to the company. (As long as the system is among the best being evaluated, the fact of knowing somebody in the branch *is* a presumption of good service.) Another reason for selecting a given product is compatibility; here the objective is to have access to a wide variety of products and services, as shown in the following example.

EXAMPLE O: MICROCOMPUTER SELECTION

Let us go back to the RFP seen in Example E. Of the nine systems proposed, three were eliminated for not meeting the mandatory requirements. As these represented almost all of the requirements, the selection process immediately followed the elimination step. Price considerations were limited to the proposal costs, the results of which are as follows:

S1:	$9124
S2:	$7985
S3:	$8680
S4:	$11530
S5:	$14890
S6:	$15030

The team recommendations were:

We recommend buying either system S1 or system S2. Both are well tested products from large and reliable manufacturers. Although system S3 is attractive because of its price, we do not recommend it: it was put on the market three months ago and is the first microcomputer produced by this manufacturer of mainframes and minis. System S4 is expensive, and it offers nothing more than S1 and S2. Finally, systems S5 and S6 are too expensive because they are much more powerful than the others and we forecast no use of these extra capabilities.

The management of the company decided on system S1 and was happy with its choice.

SELECTED REFERENCES

Foss, W. B. 1976. Guidelines for computer selection. *Journal of Systems Management*, 27,3 (March), 36–39.
This article gives an excellent overview of the process. It insists on mandatory requirements, gives selection criteria, and suggests that functional specifications will give the vendor more opportunities to provide efficient solutions to needs. The author suggests that vendors should not be aware of the evaluation and selection criteria used.

Joslin, E. O. 1977. *Computer selection* (augmented edition). Fairfax Station, Va.: The Technology Press.
This is *the* book on computer selection. Not only did the author design the cost-value and cost-requirement methodologies, he also covers all aspects of the process almost completely. Several chapters are devoted to evaluation tools, financing, negotiating the contract, etc. Anyone interested in computer selection should study this book carefully.

Lustman, F., Lanthier, P., Charbonneau, D., DeLadurantaye, P., & Gagnon, M. 1978. A systematic approach to choosing a computer. *Canadian Data Systems*, April, 24–32.
This is an example of the weighted-scores method. The overall process involves three distinct evaluations: product, vendor, and proposal, as well as a separate selection step.

Martin, J. 1981. Coping with vendor failings. *Computer Decisions*, 13,5 (May), 131–144.
This article reports a panel discussion between frustrated customers and vendors. The emphasis is on small businessmen who do not speak "computerese" and are often confused and misled by salesmen. The basic problems seem to involve a lack of understanding and excessive expectations.

Schaeffer, H. 1981. *Data center operations.* Englewood Cliffs, N.J.: Prentice-Hall.
All aspects of data center management are covered in this book. Chapter 6 is devoted to computer system acquisition and is filled with valuable advice. The author suggests, for example, preselecting the vendors before the RFP, making the solicitation document a part of the contract, and so on. A complete section is devoted to contract negotiation.

Part 5

PRODUCT DELIVERY

At last, the product is ready. If it is a computer system, the selection has been made, the contract negotiated and signed. If an application was to be developed, all of the programs have been tested on an individual basis and as a whole. Unfortunately, a data processing system cannot simply be delivered in a box with a user manual composed of a sheet of paper. Some pre-operation tasks have to be performed:

○ *Environment preparation.* If hardware is part of the product, the site has to be prepared to enable the equipment to work properly. If the product contains application programs, files, among other things, have to be set up.

○ *Setup of the system.* Delivering a "kit" with instructions on how to assemble the system is not acceptable in the world of information systems.

○ *Training.* The delivered product is usually unfamiliar to its users and much more complicated to operate than a pocket calculator; even microcomputer-based systems should not be installed without user training.

When the project involves installing a computer system, the first-line users are data processing professionals. Although the system is new, its principles are familiar to them, and problems are of a technical nature. As noted elsewhere, technical elements usually create no real problems in a project.

If the result of the project is an application program, the users are not computer specialists and the integration of the system into their daily work may create serious problems for them and for the project team. For this reason, Chapter 15 will deal with the implementation of an application program. Although hardware may be involved, it is not the source of the major trouble spots. These stem from the interfacing of the system with the final client of the project team: the end user.

Chapter 15
PRODUCT
IMPLEMENTATION

At the end of Chapter 13, we left Donald White controlling the development of the ADT system. In July 1978, he took a short vacation and is now back at work. After inquiring about the state of the project, he updates his plans and arrives at the schedule shown in Figure 15.1. Up to now, there has been no discussion about the way the system would be implemented, and White realizes that nothing was really planned regarding this last stage of the project. Since development is proceeding without any real problems, he decides to start implementation planning immediately.

IMPLEMENTATION IS MORE THAN DELIVERY

The Stage That Nobody Likes

Nobody feels at ease with the implementation stage of a project. For developers, the interesting part is finished once the system is ready, and implementation

THE GOOD SAMARITAN HOSPITAL
COMPUTER DEPARTMENT
ADT System Development Schedule (August 1, 1978)

Subsystem	Date Ready
Waiting list	Nov. 1, 1978
Patient Identification	Feb. 1, 1979
Adm.-disch.-transfer	July 1, 1979
Pat. mvts.	Sept. 15, 1979
Statistics	Oct. 1, 1979

Fig. 15.1. ADT system development schedule as of August 1, 1978.

only brings trouble from ever-complaining users. On the other hand, it is not without mistrust and even some fear that users brace themselves for all of the perturbations that the new system will certainly cause.

As is often the case with tedious problems, people try to forget them. The implementation is forgotten (as was the case with Donald White and the ADT system), its planning is forgotten, and no resources are committed to it. Indeed, projects which were flawless from a technical point of view often failed because of a lack of care regarding the implementation stage. This stage involves no technical or managerial difficulties; it needs only be dealt with.

The Process

There are six groups of activities in system implementation:

acceptance tests

site preparation

system setup

user training

system introduction

cut-over

The order in which they occur is shown in Figure 15.2.

Acceptance tests allow the user to determine if the system performs properly. The testing team is part of the project team, but the user must have the last word. *Site preparation* is required if new equipment is involved. It has to be taken care of, but does not really present any serious problems. *System setup* is exactly

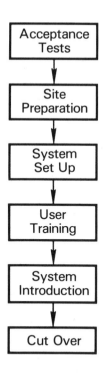

Fig. 15.2. The implementation process.

the same as assembling the parts of a kit: files have to be created, programs put together in working order, etc. It is data processing work.

One of the two most critical activities is *user training*. Handing a system over without providing any training is almost a guarantee of failure. How the user will start operating the new system *(system introduction)* is the other critical aspect of implementation.

Cut-over is the action of discarding the old system and working only with the new one. The only problem is one of timing because once the cut-over has been done, there is no way to go back. It marks the end of the project and the first assessment of the team's work.

Preparation Activities

The top four activities shown in Figure 15.2 make it possible for the system to be operational and the user to work with it.

Acceptance Tests

At the end of the development phase, the system works properly as far as the project team is concerned. It is only fair, however, that the last word belong to the user. Acceptance tests represent the formal trial by which the user acknowledges that the system conforms to what was agreed upon at the specifications stage. In order that these tests do not continue indefinitely, *acceptance tests specifications* are determined: in other words, which tests will make up the trial, under what conditions, for how many runs. In principle, this should be determined at the end of the development stage by the users and the project team.

Acceptance criteria are the conditions the system must meet in order for the user to accept it. Obviously, these conditions include bug-free programs and results that are in agreement with specifications. They also contain performance criteria such as response time, throughput time, borderline cases, etc. Acceptance criteria are usually defined by the user and presented to the project team for approval or discussion. In principle, this happens long before implementation, and in some cases is even part of the specifications.

Depending on the acceptance tests specifications, the tests themselves will take place either at the development site or at the operations site. They are usually run by the user's staff or under user-representative supervision. If the acceptance criteria are not met, the system goes back to the team's testing group. If they are, implementation can proceed; the system is fit for the user.

Site Preparation

Site preparation is necessary if hardware is involved as part of the system or if the entire project is concerned only with installing equipment. In the case of a computer (larger than a micro or small mini), site preparation consists of:

1. Computer room preparation (doors, windows, lighting, furniture, etc.)
2. Air conditioning (if required)
3. Raised floor (if required)
4. Electric power for the computer and its peripherals
5. Cables and wires for remote access
6. Telecommunications hardware (modems, network accesses, etc.)

It appears that the project manager should become a construction contractor or coordinator at this stage! He can, however, expect some help from two sources. The organization usually has a department or at least a team dealing with these problems. In addition, the supplier has site preparation specialists whose responsibility it is to help the customer with site preparation.

Even if only small equipment like terminals, word processors, or microcomputers is involved, some site preparation is required. One of the most common oversights is ignoring seemingly minor considerations. "They fit on a desk corner, don't they?" No, they do not! In fact, a terminal may require a complete desk-top and a microcomputer a large table for the screen, the keyboard, the printer, the diskette holders, the manuals, etc. A system could well end up not being used just because the location and work setting of the equipment are inadequate.

System Preparation

This activity is more than just putting all programs together in working order. System preparation involves:

FILES SETUP. Some files have to be created for the system to be operational: tax tables in a payroll system; customers in accounts receivable; patient records in an identification system. Files setup can be very time consuming. A hospital's patient file, for example, may contain several hundred thousand entries. In addition, many errors may be introduced during the file setup process; the data entered will have to be checked and double-checked. Time and resources will therefore have to be forecast in large amounts for this activity.

PROCEDURES. Working with a new system implies doing things in new and different ways which must be specified for users and for data processing people. Users need to know how to function with the new system. But is this information not contained in the user manual? Not exactly. In principle, the user manual describes how to use the system—nothing more. Procedures describe how one should perform his or her job in the new context.

Data processing procedures include how to start the system or system components, how and when to run batch jobs with what data, and recovery and back-up procedures. Data processing professionals know what this involves.

EXAMPLE B: PATIENT IDENTIFICATION PROCEDURE

In the Admission Department, the old procedure for patient identification was:

1. Ask the incoming patient if he already has a hospital card; if yes, call the Medical Records Department to check if the number is still valid.
2. If the patient has no such card, ask for name (last, then first), date of birth, and address, then call the Medical Records Department to see if the patient has a hospital number; if not, ask the Department to issue a number and fill out a Patient Identification Form.

With the new system, the procedure will be as follows:

1. Ask the patient for the hospital card; if he or she has one, enter the number into the system (see User Manual, Section 4.1.1).

2. If the patient has no hospital card, ask for name and date of birth, and enter with patient's sex into system (see User Manual, Section 4.1.2).

User Preparation

The development team has worked on the system for months or years, and for its members the system has no secrets. Such is not the case, however, for the users. Most of them have never seen it live; some have no idea what it looks like. If they were to be given user manuals and turned loose, the system would not be used at all. Users have to be informed and trained according to the kind of interaction they will have with the system.

There are two kinds of users: operators and end-line users. *Operators* will interact with the system, either by filling out forms to feed into it or by operating a hardware device such as a terminal. Not only do they need to understand what the system does, but they also have to be trained in the operation of the hardware or the filling out of the forms. *End-line users* are generally at the supervisory or managerial level. They receive the system's reports. These outputs are very often new to them, both in format and content. The meaning of the various reports and their details have to be explained.

There are three basic forms of preparation: A *general introduction to the system* is more an information tool than a training course, and is usually provided through information sessions. In *end-line user training*, formal lectures are provided for the users of the various reports, one or several sessions for each group of users. *Work training sessions* are directed to those users who interact directly with the system. These sessions have to be specialized according to the different functions performed by the various users.

User preparation is a long and costly activity for both the project team and the users. Unfortunately, it is often poorly handled or even overlooked. Many implementation problems are the result of a lack of serious user training.

EXAMPLE C: USER PREPARATION FOR THE ADT SYSTEM

The ADT system is quite complex, and involves many hospital departments. White knows that if one group does not use the system, the entire undertaking will be in jeopardy. He therefore carefully plans his training program, presented in Figure 15.3. The overall training program consists of five lectures with audiences ranging from three to fifteen people, and two different training courses for terminal users, one to be given to six people, the other to ten. Preparing the users of an Admission-Discharge-Transfer system is decidedly not a small task, especially since all involved users have busy schedules.

ADMISSION-DISCHARGE-TRANSFER SYSTEM
User Training Requirements

Type of preparation	Type of training	Departments involved	Number of users
General presentation	Conference	Med. Rec.	4
		Mgt.	3
		Adm. Office	6
		Emergency	2
Patient identification subsystem:			
—general presentation	Conference	Med. Rec.	4
		Adm. Office	6
		Emergency	2
—training	Work session	Med. Rec.	4
		Adm. Office	4
		Emergency	2
Admission-discharge-transfer subsystem:			
—presentation	Conference	Adm. Office	4
		Emergency	2
—training	Work session	Adm. Office	4
		Emergency	2
Reports:			
—Patient movements	Seminar	Hospital Mgt.	3
		Adm. Office Mgr.	1
—General statistics	Seminar	Hospital Mgt.	3

Fig. 15.3. Training requirements for the ADT system.

STRATEGIES FOR SYSTEM INTRODUCTION

Replacement Strategies

When planning the introduction of a new system, the question of how to do it arises. Should the old system be thrown away and immediately and completely replaced, or should both run in parallel in case the new one runs into trouble? This question can be answered in three different ways depending on the system, the costs, the reliability requirements, and the users.

Immediate Replacement

This case is outlined in Figure 15.4a. The old system is shut down altogether and the new one takes over in every aspect. Choosing this strategy requires very careful training of the users, and presumes great confidence in the new system's reliability or no choice to do otherwise.

The advantages of immediate replacement are as follows:

1. It is the least costly alternative, since it does not involve the double expenses incurred from the running of both systems.
2. It is the fastest way of introducing the system.
3. It decreases the period of instability created by the change.

Unfortunately, regardless of how carefully users are trained, it creates chaos, the pace of change and the impossibility of going back often results in simple rejection of the system, thereby negating in the end the goal of the strategy.

The immediate replacement strategy is often used for going from one computer system to another because of cost or simply because of a lack of space. The replacement usually takes place during the weekend, and the computing department staff (the users, in this case) work almost 48 hours nonstop. But except for such extreme cases, immediate replacement is strongly advised against. Although upper management likes it because of its low cost, the project manager should argue against it whenever there is another alternative.

Parallel Running

In this case, shown in Figure 15.4b, the new system is introduced in its entirety while the old one is kept running. This parallel activity lasts long enough for everybody to become familiar with the new system and to eliminate the old one.

Parallel running is used when the requirement for correct system results outweighs all others. Good examples are banking and patient monitoring systems. A sense of security is a distinct advantage of this choice. If something is wrong with the new system, the old one is still there providing its results and working methods. Reliability is another advantage. Parallel operations will be maintained as long as every detail of the new system has not been proven correct. Cost and overload are the two disadvantages. It requires keeping two systems running to perform the same functions, and it also requires doing everything twice.

Phased Replacement

When the system's structure allows it, phased replacement consists in introducing one subsystem after another (see Figure 15.4c). Each new subsystem is usually

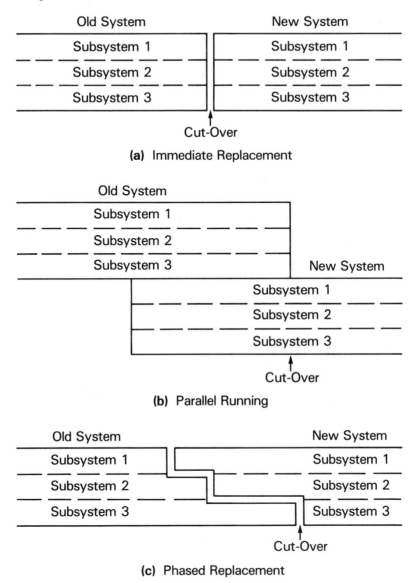

Fig. 15.4. Replacement strategies.

introduced once the preceding replacement has been assimilated. Its advantages are that the system is more easily integrated and accepted, there is less disturbance in the overall working environment, and costs are kept to an acceptable level. However, if chaos reigns when the new system is introduced, this strategy will only perpetuate it. Depending on the strategy used for introducing each subsystem (parallel or immediate), the disadvantages of each of those will also be experienced.

This author's experience leads him to favor phased replacement, with each subsystem being introduced by immediate replacement. If users are well informed and well trained, minor problems can be solved on a local level without disturbing everything, and the users themselves usually ask for the next stage of replacement. Moreover, phased replacement is the natural strategy when the system is to be delivered in successive steps, as advocated in Chapter 10 (step-by-step delivery).

EXAMPLE D: REPLACEMENT STRATEGY FOR THE ADT SYSTEM

An examination of Figure 15.1 reveals that phased replacement is the thing to do, because the different subsystems will be completed one after another. Looking at this chart, Donald White plans the following sequence of introduction of each subsystem:

1. *Waiting list.* This subsystem will be ready before the others. Moreover, the waiting list is handled by a group of two people only, and does not interfere with other functions.

2. *Patient identification.* This subsystem will be introduced first in the Medical Records Department where, unlike the Admissions Office, staff are not disturbed by incoming or outgoing patients. Therefore, if something goes wrong (a program bug or anything else), the disruption will have minimal effects. Once the identification system has been operationally tested by the Medical Records staff, it will be introduced in the Admissions Office and Emergency Department. There, the staff will use the new system to identify patients, while keeping the old admission procedure long enough to become acquainted with the equipment and processing procedures.

3. *Admission-discharge-transfer and patient movements.* The next step will be to introduce simultaneously all of the functions related to patient movements. Phased or department-by-department introduction is impossible because, in order to work properly, the system requires that it be provided all data regarding all patients.

4. *General statistics.* To provide statistics, the system must have at least one month of data, so statistics production will start after admission has been in operation for a while.

Implementation Approaches

Once the overall strategy has been defined, the details must be taken care of. This requires determining *when* and *how* to introduce a system or subsystem.

Timing

We have seen that the introduction of a new system requires time and effort on the part of the users. Careful timing will increase the chances of easy acceptance. Donaldson (1979) points out that workload peaks, holiday dates, and Mondays are to be avoided. Introducing an accounting system at budget preparation time, for example, is surely a poor decision. In the ADT system, Mondays and Fridays should be discarded because elective patients are usually admitted on Mondays and many discharges occur on Fridays; Sundays should be avoided as well, if the Emergency Department is involved, since there is usually a rush of car accident casualties being admitted. For systems where transactions are entered on an ongoing basis with monthly processing, a good time is just after the end of a given period.

Implementation Method

Although the system has been tested, some bugs will be discovered only during operation by the user. And, despite the training they have received, the users will run into problems because they have forgotten some of the lessons learned or because they are faced with an unexpected situation. In order for these problems to create only a minimal amount of disturbance, several approaches can be used.

DRY RUN. Under the supervision and with the help of team members, selected users operate the system using old but real data. The method requires extra work from the users involved, but it enables them to check the system's outputs and become used to its operation.

MINI-IMPLEMENTATION. A small group composed of selected users and project team members is created, and starts using the system on live data. Once the users master the system, they progressively introduce it to their colleagues, or another group of users comes to work with the project team. This method is particularly useful when a system has to be introduced in different locations such as the branches of a large organization. Some people have even recommended that a special facility be set up for system introduction (see Harrison, 1982).

EXAMPLE E: PATIENT IDENTIFICATION SYSTEM

A dry run would create too many problems. Because the patient file is already set up and complete, entering old patients would always yield the same results: those patients are already in the file. White therefore opts for the mini-implementation approach.

Under the guidance of a project team member, one clerk in the Medical Records Department will start working with the new system while the other clerks continue to use the old Rolodex card system for retrieving patient names. Once trained, the clerk will be able to help his or her colleagues. The team member will then move to the Admissions Office, where the same pattern of events will be followed.

IMPLEMENTATION PROBLEMS

The history of data processing is full of stories about projects which failed at the implementation stage. This sad outcome can be attributed to three causes:

the system itself,

user management, and

user staff.

If the system is poorly designed or full of bugs at delivery time, users will reject it or repairs will be expensive and time consuming. The project team has done a bad job and bears the responsibility for the failure. Let us discard this eventuality by stating that the preceding chapters should help preclude such an outcome.

Even if the system is well designed and bugless, two problems can arise: lack of commitment from upper or middle management regarding the implementation requirements; and resistance to change coming from first-line users. Systems have been rejected for these reasons more than once, and project managers should be aware of the risks involved in overlooking them.

Commitment

The usual attitude of management regarding the project's outcome is to keep asking the project manager when the system will be ready. When he finally announces it, management thinks that the system will be operational overnight—as, for example, with a newly ordered photocopier. We have seen that this is not the case, and that the user has a long way to go before that happens. Unfortunately, management is not conscious of this fact and is therefore reluctant to get involved in the implementation stage. A good analysis of this lack of awareness and commitment can be found in Koogler, Collins, & Clancy (1981).

The root of the problem is that management at all levels does not (or does not want to) realize that implementation is a normal stage of the project, that management involvement is required, and that user resistance to change is a natural attitude. The following ingredients are required in order to make the implementation stage possible.

Organization Commitment

Site preparation and system setup are necessary for the system to operate. In addition, user preparation requires some or all of the resources listed in Table 15.1 The list implies that users will be given the time to attend the training sessions on the new system. If parallel operation is adopted, users should receive extra help in order to handle the work overload. If a dry run is the introduction approach selected, the involved users should be freed from their present tasks in order to devote themselves seriously to the new system. Too often management does not recognize that the implementation represents a great deal of additional work for the user and neither forecasts nor allocates resources for this extra effort.

An even worse situation arises when, for financial reasons or out of a desire to save time, management is not ready to commit the resources required to set up the training programs, especially when outside-provided courses have to be paid for. A classic example from the time of key-punch cards was to put a clerk or secretary in front of the new key-punch machine with the manual, instead of paying for a three-day training course. The same approach applied to the introduction of a microcomputer for word processing is a more up-to-date example. It may take the beleaguered operator weeks to be able to produce anything substantial.

Middle Management Commitment

Another, more subtle problem involves middle managers who will be directly affected by the new system. Although they will be in contact with it, they seem reluctant to participate in the preparation program. They always have some

TABLE 15.1
RESOURCES REQUIRED FOR USER PREPARATION

Nature of training activity	Resources involved
Courses provided from outside	User time Extra personnel to handle the workload Money to pay for the courses
Course provided by the project team	User time Extra personnel to handle the workload Project teamwork to prepare the training program Project teamwork to train the users Training material

urgent task to finish when the time comes to go live; they think that learning the new system is their staff's concern, not their own (see Koogler et al., 1981).

The reasons for such an attitude are difficult to define, but it seems that ego is deeply involved. First, they do not feel at ease being on the same training benches as their employees. Second, they firmly believe that as managers, they do not have to be involved in operations details. Finally, although they, too, feel uneasy with the changes the new system will bring into their working environment, they do not feel comfortable expressing these views openly, so they try to avoid the new system as long as possible. Employees have extrasensory perception with respect to this kind of behavior. If they see that their manager is not actively participating in the introduction of the new system, and if they themselves are already worried about its potential effects, they will not push for its introduction.

Resistance to Change

Resistance to change may often pose the most serious problem when introducing a new system. Most human beings like the security of familiar surroundings, and see any change as a threat to their way of life. Koogler (1981) describes the stereotype of an elderly clerk who will not even let the deliverymen bring in the new computer. A thorough analysis of the attitudes of people toward innovation can also be found in Lee and Steinberg (1980). Before exploring the reasons for these attitudes, let us review the consequences of resistance to change on the introduction of a new system. In increasing order of seriousness, we find:

○ *Poor use of the new system.* This consequence contradicts the initial objective which was, in many cases, increased productivity.
○ *Chaos.* People are unable or unwilling to use the new system correctly, and a formerly harmonious working environment gives way to permanent disorder, resulting in tension, frustration, and even the resignations of good employees.
○ *Rejection of the new system.* If frustrations are too high, people can simply refuse to use the new system, or else use it badly (to demonstrate its inadequacy) while continuing to perform their work in the old way. After a while, management recognizes that the new system is useless or unworkable and decides to eliminate it.

It is possible that a profile of persons who will never be willing or able to accept innovations does in fact exist. More generally, however, resistance to change is fostered by errors committed at some point in the project life cycle. The main reasons for induced resistance to change are the following.

Lack of Line-user Participation

In Chapter 7, it was stressed that line users should be involved in system analysis and specifications approval. Although many middle managers feel uneasy about this, project managers should insist on involving the line users in the process. Management often suggests that involving them at so early a stage would create useless worries and that, in any case, they will be informed at the proper time. This attitude usually has the opposite result. In addition, middle managers often do not know or tend to forget the operational details of a function, while line users live with them. If these details are not taken care of at the specifications level, the system will not achieve its primary goal of making the user's task easier.

A poorly designed system can also result in a very inefficient way of performing certain tasks. A classic example is a log of money transactions with a single final balance and no debit and credit totals. If the clerk verifying it finds a discrepancy between the computer log total and his own, he has no other alternative but to check all transactions.

Finally, well-specified and well-designed systems can also be a source of frustration if the user interface is poor. A well-known example of poor user interface is the Wordstar® word processing system available on almost all microcomputers.* It is a very well-specified system: almost all needed functions are included. The system is well designed (at least from the user's point of view) because all functions are easy to perform. But there is almost no command with a code having the slightest mnemonic connotation relating it to the function it performs; all commands have to be known by heart or found on the screen, thereby slowing down the working pace.

For the user, drawbacks such as these make a system unpleasant to use.

Lack of User Consideration

The importance of allocating resources for good user preparation has already been stressed. If this is not done, the new system will become a burden for the user. If, in addition, he is left to handle the overload created by the system's introduction, his work will become a nightmare. In such a situation, the user will consider the system hard to learn and hard to work with, and he will conclude that it is a poor system.

Lack of Consideration for Resistance to Change

There is another, deeper reason why users feel uneasy about a new system: *fear*; fear of anything new, fear of losing one's job, fear of becoming a robot. In the

---

*Wordstar® is a registered trademark of MicroPro International Corporation.

early days of data processing, the way of dealing with these feelings was to brush them aside as belonging to old-fashioned people who should be "educated" or avoided altogether.

In reality, feelings of fear are legitimate. First of all, in the past, data processing has indeed resulted in job losses. Second, one could wonder why being "old-fashioned" should be a serious enough sin to prevent someone from earning a living. User fears regarding a new system should be respected and taken into consideration.

Conditions for Success

○ Users, especially those destined to operate the system, should be deeply involved in all steps of system development which are of concern to them. The result should be a system adapted to their needs and not just to those of the far-removed manager who receives the final reports.

○ The project team should provide a well-designed, user-friendly system which "works," not a patchwork full of bugs.

○ Resources and time should be allocated for user preparation.

○ When possible, a phased introduction strategy should be adopted even if it increases the duration of the transition period. Donaldson (1979) suggests that in a phased approach, the module which will be the simplest for the user should be the one first introduced.

END OF THE PROJECT

Cut-over

Cut-over involves the complete and definitive elimination of the old system if such a system exists (see Figure 15.4). It then becomes impossible to go back if the new system runs into trouble.

Many computer professionals have experienced the weekend or holiday phone call: "Come back quick, the new system is down" (or working incorrectly). In principle, cut-over should occur once every function of the system has been shown to be working properly on live data. If a system has monthly reports, for example, the cut-over should take place after, not before, the monthly updates.

In principle, the user (or, more precisely, user management) should decide that there is enough confidence in the new system to abandon the old one. The project manager should realize, however, that as long as the old system is in existence, the project is not over and the team is not available for other tasks.

If development and acceptance tests have been performed seriously, he can try to reason with managers who are sometimes overconcerned with safety.

Conclusion

Cut-over signifies the end of the project. If a system was developed, the responsibility of dealing with remaining bugs is handed over to a maintenance team or department. How can success or failure be assessed?

A successful project is, first of all, one in which users are happy with the system. Second, it is one in which project constraints (i.e., time and resource expenditures) have been respected, or overruns or delays kept within acceptable limits (10% to 20% overruns). If one had to choose which is more important—user satisfaction or adherence to strict constraints—the former would be given priority. If users like the system, it means that it will be useful for a long time. Once more, long-term considerations take precedence over short-term ones.

If, after a short while, users request additions to the planned and delivered system, the project team and manager will know that they have done a really good job: satisfied customers always come back.

SELECTED REFERENCES

Donaldson, H. 1979. *A guide to the successful management of computer projects.* New York: John Wiley & Sons.

> The author stresses the importance of the implementation stage. He insists on the right timing of system introduction and favors a phased implementation.

Harrison, R. 1982. User acceptance testing facility. *Journal of Systems Management*, 33, 8 (August), 13-15.

> The author suggests setting up a "user acceptance facility," a special environment set up for the purpose of testing the new system as operated by users. The facility looks much like a branch in a multi-branch organization, is completely staffed, and has a testing and operating program.

Koogler, P., Collins, F., Clancy, D. K. 1981. The new system arrives. *Journal of Systems Management*, 32, 11 (November), 32-37.

> After presenting an extreme case of resistance to change, the authors analyze the consequences of the stress induced by the change. The major reasons are cited, such as lack of commitment by management. The article then presents strategies for reducing the stress created by the introduction of a new system.

Lee, W. B., & Steinberg, E. 1980. Making implementation a success or failure. *Journal of Systems Management*, 31, 4 (April), 19-25.

> Although the article is about manufacturing systems, all of its findings are applicable to other systems. In the first part, innovation is analyzed, as is the attitude of people with respect to it. The authors then present results concerning reasons for success or failure of system implementation. The attitude of management, the characteristics of the users, and the cooperation between users and the project team are all discussed.

BIBLIOGRAPHY

Abdel-Hamid, T. K., & Madnick, S. E. 1983. The dynamics of software project scheduling. *Com. of the ACM*, 26,5 (May), 340–346.

Abe, J., Sakamura, K., & Aiso, H. 1980. An analysis of project failure. *Proc. 4th Int. Conf. on Soft. Eng.*, Sept. 17–19, Munich, Germany, 378–385.

Ackoff, R. L. 1967. Management misinformation systems. *Management Science*, 14,4 (December), B140–B156.

Ahituv, N., & Neumann, S. 1982. Controlling the information system function. *Journal of Systems Management*, 33,9 (September), 10–16.

Alter, S., & Ginzberg M., 1978. Managing uncertainty in MIS implementation. *Sloan Management Review*, 20,1 (Fall), 23–31.

Alter, S. 1980. *Decision support systems: Current practice and continuing challenges*. Reading, Mass.: Addison-Wesley.

Ansoff, H. I. 1977. The state of practice in planning systems. *Sloan Management Review*, 18,2 (Winter), 1–24.

Aron, J. D. 1974. *The program development process*. Reading, Mass.: Addison-Wesley.

Aron, J. D. 1976. Estimating resources for large programming systems. In *Software engineering: Concepts and techniques*, edited by J. M. Buxton, P. Naur, B. Randell. New York, N.Y.: Litton Educational Pub.

Bachman, C. W. 1969. Data structure diagrams. *Data Base*, 1,2 (Summer).

Bailey, J. W., Basili, V. R. 1981. A meta model for software development resource expenditures. *Proc. 5th Int. Conf. on Soft. Eng.*, San Diego, Ca., March 9–12, 107–116.

Baird, L. L., Jr. May 1974. An analytical approach to identifying computer vulnerability. *Security Management*, American Society of Industrial Security.

Baker, F. T. 1972. Chief programmer team management of production programming. *IBM Systems Journal*, 11,1, 66–73.

Belford, P. C., Bond, A. F., Henderson, D. G., & Sellers, L. S. 1976. Specifications: a key to effective software development. *Proc. 2nd Int. Conf. on Soft. Eng.*, Oct. 13–15, San Francisco, 71–79.

Bell, T. E., Thayer, T. A. 1976. Software requirements: are they really a problem? *Proc. 2nd Int. Conf. on Soft. Eng.*, San Francisco, Ca., Oct. 13–15, 61–68.

Bell, T. E., Bixler, D. C., & Dyer, M. E. 1977. An extendable approach to computer-aided software requirements engineering. *IEEE Trans. on Soft. Eng.*, SE-3,1, 49–60.

Benbasat, I., & Vessey, I. 1980. Programmer and analyst cost/time estimation. *Management Information Systems Quarterly*, 4,2 (June), 31–44.

Benjamin, R. I. 1971. *Control of the information system development life cycle*. New York: John Wiley and Sons.

Berry, D. M. 1975. Structured documentation. *Sigplan Notices*, 10,11 (November), 7–12.

Berthaud, M. 1977. Towards a formal language for functional specifications. *Proc. IFIP Working Conf. on Constructive Quality Software*, 379–396. New York: North Holland Pub. Co.

Biggs, C. L., Birks, E. G., & Atkins, W. 1980. *Managing the systems development process*. Englewood Cliffs, N.J.: Prentice-Hall, Inc.

Black, W. W. 1976. The role of software engineering in successful computer applications. *Proc. 2nd Int. Conf. on Soft. Eng.*, San Francisco, Ca., Oct. 13–15, 201–205.

Block, E. B. 1971. Accomplishment/cost: Better project control. *Harvard Business Review*, May–June, 110–124.

Boehm, B. W. 1973. Software and its impact—a quantitative assessment. *Datamation*, 19,5 (May), 48–59.

Boehm, B. W. 1974. Some steps toward formal and automated aids to software requirements analysis and design. *Proc. IFIP 74*, 192–197.

Boehm, B. W. 1976. Software engineering. *IEEE Trans. on Computers*, C-25, 12 (December), 1226–1241.

Boehm, B. W. 1977. Seven principles of software engineering. *Infotech state of the art report on software engineering*. Infotech International Ltd., Nicholson House, Maidenhead, Berkshire, England, 77–113.

Boehm, B. W. 1981. *Software engineering economics*. Englewood Cliffs, N.J.: Prentice-Hall, Inc.

Bohm, C., & Jacopini, G. 1966. Flow diagrams, Turing machines and languages with only two formation rules. *Com. of the ACM*, May.

Boland, R. J., Jr. 1979. The process and product of system design. *Management Science* 24,9 (May), 887–895.

Boyer, R. S., Elspas, B., & Levitt, K. 1975. SELECT—a formal system for testing and debugging. *Proc. Int. Conf. on Reliable Software*, 234–245.

Brandon, D. H., & Gray, M. 1970. *Project control standards*. Brandon/Systems Press.

Brandon, D. H. 1972. Computer acquisition methods analysis. *Datamation*, 18,9 (September), 76–79.

Bratman, H., Court, T. 1975. The software factory. *Computer*, 8,5 (May), 28–37.

Brooks, F. T. 1975. *The mythical man-month: Essays on software engineering*. Reading, Mass.: Addison-Wesley.

Brown, P. L. 1972. Redesigning an information system. *Journal of Systems Management*, January, 26–31.

Brown, P. J. 1974. Programming and documenting software projects. *ACM Computing Surveys*, 6,4 (December), 214–220.

Bruggere, T. H. 1980. Software engineering: Management, personnel and methodology. *Proc. 4th Int. Conf. on Soft. Eng.*, Sept. 17–19, Munich, Germany, 361–368.

Bryce, T. 1978. Evaluating a systems design methodology—part 1. *Infosystems*, November.

Buckley, F. 1979. A standard for software quality assurance plans. *Computer* (August), 43–49.

Burch, J. G., & Strater, F. R. 1974. *Information systems: Theory and practice.* Hamilton Pub. Co.

Burton, B. J. 1975. Manpower estimating for systems projects. *Journal of Systems Management,* January, 29–33.

Caine, S., & Gordon, E. 1975. PDL—a tool for software design. *Proc. AFIPS NCC,* 44, 271–276.

Canning, R. G., ed. 1972. The data administrator function. *EDP Analyzer,* 10,11 (November).

Canning, R. G., ed. 1977. Getting the requirements right. *EDP Analyzer,* 15,7 (July), 1–14.

Canning, R. G., ed. 1979. The analysis of user needs. *EDP Analyzer,* 17,1 (January), 1–13.

Carlson, W. M., & Kerner, D. V. 1979. The new horizon in business information analysis. *Data Base,* 10,4 (Spring), 3–9.

Caroll, J. M. 1977. Computer security. *Security World,* Los Angeles.

Cave, W. C., Salisbury, A. B. 1978. Controlling the software life cycle—the project management task. *IEEE Trans. on Soft. Eng.,* SE-4,4, July, 326–333.

Chand, D. R., & Yadav, S. B. 1980. Logical construction of software. *Com. of the ACM,* 23,10 546–555.

Chapin, N. 1979. Some structured analysis techniques. *Data Base,* 10,3 (Winter), 16–23.

Chen, P. P. 1976. The entity-relationship model—Towards a unified view of data. *ACM Trans. on Database Systems,* 1,1 (March), 9–35.

Chen, P. P. 1980. *Entity relationship approach to system analysis and design.* Amsterdam: North Holland Pub. Co.

Chu, Y. 1976. Introducing a software design language. *Proc. 2nd Int. Conf. on Soft. Eng.,* Oct. 13–15, San Francisco, 297–304.

Churchman, C. 1969. *The systems approach.* New York: Dell.

Cleland, D. I., & King, W. R. 1975. *Systems analysis and project management.* New York: McGraw-Hill.

Condon, R. J. 1982. *Data processing system analysis and design.* Reston, Va.: Reston Pub. Co.

Cooper, R. B., & Swanson, E. B. 1979. Management information requirements assessment: The state of the art. *Data Base,* Fall, 5–15.

Corbato, F. J., & Clingen, C. J. 1980. A managerial view of the Multics system development. In *Research Directions in Software Technology,* edited by P. Wegner. The MIT Press, 138–158.

Couger, J. D. 1973. Evaluation of business systems analysis techniques. *ACM Computing Surveys,* 5,3 (September), 167–198.

Couger, J. D., & Knapp, R. W. 1979. *Systems analysis techniques.* New York: John Wiley & Sons.

Couger, J. D., Colter, M. A., & Knapp, R. W. 1982. *Advanced systems development and feasibility techniques.* New York: John Wiley & Sons.

Crowston, W. B. 1971. Models of project management. *Sloan Management Review,* 12,3 (Spring), 25–42.

Dahl, O. J., Dijkstra, E. W., & Hoare, C.A.R. 1972. *Structured programming*. London: Academic Press.

Daly, E. B. 1977. Management of software development. *IEEE Trans. on Soft. Eng.*, SE-3,3, 230–242.

Date, C. J., 1977. *An introduction to database systems*. Reading, Mass.: Addison-Wesley.

Davis, G. B. 1974. *Management information systems*. New York: McGraw-Hill.

Davis, G. B. 1982. Strategies for information requirements determination. *IBM Systems Journal*, 21,1, 4–30.

Davis, W. S. 1983. *System analysis and design: A structured approach*. Reading, Mass.: Addison-Wesley.

Davis, C. G., & Vick, C. R. 1977. The software development system. *IEEE Trans. on Soft. Eng.*, SE-3, 169–184.

Davis, A. M., & Rauscher, T. G. 1979. Formal techniques and automatic processing to ensure correctness in requirements specifications. *Proc. Specifications of Reliable Software Conference*, Cambridge, Mass., 15–25.

Dearden, J. 1972. MIS is a mirage. *Harvard Business Review*, January-February, 90–99.

DeBrander, B., & Anders, E. 1977. Successful information system development. *Management Science*, 24,2, October, 191–199.

Delaney, W. A. 1966. Predicting the costs of computer programs. *Data Processing Magazine*, October, 32–35.

Dijkstra, E. W. 1976. *A discipline in programming*. Englewood Cliffs, N.J.: Prentice-Hall.

Donaldson, H. 1979. *A guide to the successful management of computer projects*. New York: John Wiley & Sons.

Donelson, W. S. 1976. Project planning and control. *Datamation*, 22,6, 73–80.

DPMA 1981. *DPMA model curriculum for undergraduate computer information systems education. DPMA*, Park Ridge, Il.

Dreyfus, J. M., & Karacsony, P. J. 1976. The preliminary design as a key to successful software development. *Proc. 2nd Int. Conf. on Soft. Eng.*, Oct. 13–15, San Francisco, 206–213.

DeMaagd, G. R. 1970. Matrix management. *Datamation*, 16,13, October 15, 46–49.

DeMarco, T. 1978. *Structured analysis and system specification*. New York: Yourdon, Inc.

Duran, J. W. 1981. A report on random testing. *Proc. 5th Int. Conf. on Soft. Eng.*, March 9–12, San Diego, 179–183.

Eppen, G., & Gould, F. 1979. *Quantitative concepts for management*. Englewood Cliffs, N.J.: Prentice-Hall.

Evans, M. 1982. Software engineering for the COBOL environment. *Com. of the ACM*, 25,12 (December), 874–882.

Ewers, J., & Vessey, I. 1981. The system development dilemma—A programming perspective. *Management Information Systems Quarterly*, 5,2, 33–46.

Fagan, M. E. 1976. Design and code inspection to reduce errors in program development. *IBM Systems Journal*, 15,3, 219–248.

Fireworker, R. B., & Bogner, L. J., Jr. 1980. Improved software development through project management. *Data Management*, 18,2 (December), 27–31.

Foss, W. B. 1976. Guidelines for computer selection. *Journal of Systems Management*, 27,3 (March), 36–39.

Frankwicz, M. S. 1973. A study of project management techniques. *Journal of Systems Management*, 24, October, 18–22.

Freeman, P. 1980. A perspective on requirements analysis techniques. *Tutorial on Software Design Techniques*, 3rd edition, P. Freeman, A. I. Wasserman, editors, IEEE Computer Society.

Gane, C., & Sarson, T. 1979. *Structured system analysis and design.* Englewood Cliffs, N.J.: Prentice-Hall.

Gass, S. I. 1981. Documentation for a model: A hierarchical approach. *Com. of the ACM*, 24,1, 728–733.

Gaydash, A. 1982. *Principles of EDP management.* Reston, Va.: Reston Publishing Co.

Gehring, P. F. 1976. Improving software development estimates of time and cost. *Proc. 2nd Int. Conf. on Soft. Eng.*, Oct. 13–15, San Francisco.

Geller, D. P. 1976. How many directions is top-down? *Datamation*, 22,6 (June), 109–112.

Gerrity, T. P., Jr. 1971. Design of man-machine decision systems: An application to portfolio management. *Sloan Management Review*, 14 (Winter), 59–75.

Gewirtzman, R. 1983. Controls in automated information systems. *Journal of Systems Management*, 34,1 (January), 34–41.

Ghandforoush, P. 1982. Model for mini computer selection. *Journal of Systems Management*, 33,6 (June), 11–13.

Gildersleeve, T. R. 1970. *Decision tables and their practical application in data processing.* Englewood Cliffs, N.J.: Prentice-Hall.

Gildersleeve, T. R. 1973. The time-estimating myth. *Datamation*, 19,1 (January), 47–48.

Gildersleeve, T. R. 1974. *Data processing project management.* New York: Van Nostrand Reinhold.

Glass, R. 1979. *Software reliability guidebook.* Englewood Cliffs, N.J.: Prentice-Hall.

Golden, J. R., Mueller, J. R., & Anselm, B. 1981. Software cost estimating: Craft or witchcraft. *Data Base*, 12,3 (Spring), 12–14.

Goodenough, J., & Gerhart, S. 1975. Toward a theory of test data selection. *IEEE Trans. on Soft. Eng.*, SE-1,2 (June), 156–173.

Gore, M., & Stubbe, J. 1979. *Elements of systems analysis for business data processing*, 2nd ed. Dubuque, Ia.: W.C. Brown.

Gorry, G. A., & Scott-Morton, S. A. 1971. A framework for management information systems. *Sloan Management Review*, 12, Fall, 55–70.

Gray, C. F. 1981. *Essentials of project management.* New York: Petrocelli Books.

Griffin, E. L. 1980. Real time estimating. *Datamation,* June, 188–197.

Gunderman, J. R., & McMurry, F. W. 1975. Making project management effective. *Journal of Systems Management,* February, 7–11.

Gustafson, G. G., & Kerr, R. J. 1982. Some practical experience with a software quality assurance program. *Com. of the ACM,* 25,1, 4–12.

Hall, T. P. 1980. Systems life cycle model. *Journal of Systems Management,* 31,4, April, 29–31.

Hallam, J. A., Hallam, S. F., Hallam, T. A. 1983. Control of MIS: A comprehensive model. *Journal of Systems Management,* 34,1 (January), 20–22.

Halstead, M. H. 1977. *Elements of software science.* New York, N.Y.: North Holland Pub. Co.

Hamilton, M., & Zeldin, S. 1976. High order software—A methodology for defining software. *IEEE Trans. on Soft. Eng.,* SE-2,1, 9–32.

Hammer, M. M., Howe, W. G., & Wladawsky, I. 1974. An interactive business definition system. *Sigplan Notices,* 9,4 (April), 25–33.

Hammer, M., Howe, W. G., Kruskal, V. J., & Wladawsky, I. 1977. A very high level programming language for data processing applications. *Com. of the ACM,* 20,11, 832–840.

Hammer, M., & Ruth, G. 1979. Automating the software development process. In *Research Directions in Software Technology,* edited by P. Wegner. Cambridge, Mass.: The MIT Press, 767–790.

Hammond, J. S., III. 1974. Do's and don'ts of computer models for planning. *Harvard Business Review,* March-April, 110–122.

Hancock, S. 1978. An approach to hospital data processing development. *Management Accounting,* March, 51–55.

Harrison, F. L. 1981. *Advanced project management.* Aldershot, England: Gower Pub. Co.

Harrison, R. 1982. User acceptance testing facility. *Journal of Systems Management,* 33,8 (August), 13–15.

Harvey, A. 1970. Factors making for implementation success or failure. *Management Science,* 16,6 (February), B312–B321.

Hauesein, W. D., & Camp, J. L. 1982. *Business systems for microcomputers: Concepts, design and implementation.* Englewood Cliffs, N.J.: Prentice-Hall.

Head, R. V. 1971. Automated system analysis. *Datamation,* August, 22–24.

Hershauer, J. C. 1978. What's wrong with our system design methods? It's our assumptions. *Journal of Systems Management,* April, 25–28.

Herzog, J. P. 1975. System evaluation techniques, selected references for users. *Journal of Systems Management,* 26,5 (May), 30–35.

Hetzel, W., ed. 1973. *Program testing methods.* Englewood Cliffs, N.J.: Prentice-Hall.

Hice, G. F., Turner, W. S., & Cashwell, L. F. 1979. *System development methodology*, 2nd ed. North Holland/American Elsevier Pub.

Highsmith, J. 1981. Structured systems planning. *Management Information Systems Quarterly*, 5,3, 25–54.

Higley, R. S., Eason, T. S., & Fitzgerald, J. M. 1977. *Data processing control practices report*. Prepared for the Institute of Internal Auditors. IBM.

Horowitz, E. 1975. *Practical strategies for developing large software systems*. Reading, Mass.: Addison-Wesley.

Howard, P. C. 1973. Measuring system performance with benchmarks. *EDP Performance Review*, I,9, September, 1–7.

Hsia, P., & Petry, F. E. 1980. A framework for discipline in programming. *IEEE Trans. on Soft. Eng.*, SE-6,2, 226–232.

Ingrassia, F. S. 1975. Combating the 90% complete syndrome. *Datamation*, January, 171–176.

Ingrassia, F. S. 1976. The unit development folder (UDF): An effective management tool for software development. *TRW Software Series*, TRW-SS 76–11, October.

Inmon, B. 1976. An example of structured design. *Datamation*, 22,3 (March), 82–86.

Irvine, C. A., & Brackett, L. W. 1977. Automated software engineering through structured management. *IEEE Trans. on Soft. Eng.*, SE-3,1, 34–40.

Jackson, M. A. 1975. *Principles of program design*. London: Academic Press.

Jackson, M. 1983. *System development*. Englewood Cliffs, N.J.: Prentice-Hall.

Janusz, E. J. 1982. Performance measurement in times of turbulence. *Data Base*, 13,4 (Summer), 3–6.

Jeffrey, D. R., & Lawrence, N. J. 1980. An inter-organizational comparison of programming productivity. *Proc. 4th Int. Conf. on Soft. Eng.*, Sept. 17–19, Munich, Germany, 369–377.

Jinks, D. W. 1977. Systems documentation. *Journal of Systems Management*, June, 24–33.

Johnson, J. R. 1977. A working measure of productivity. *Datamation*, February, 106–108.

Johnson, J. R. 1977. Advanced project control. *Journal of Systems Management*, May, 24–27.

Jones, M. M., & McLean, E. R. 1970. Management problems in large scale software development projects. *Sloan Management Review*, 11,3 (Spring), 1–15.

Jones, T. C. 1978. Measuring program quality and programmer productivity. *IBM Systems Journal*, 17,1, 39–63.

Jones, G. H. 1978. Project management: An overview. *Proc. SMIS Conf.*, Washington, DC., 161–168.

Joslin, E. O. 1977. *Computer selection* (augmented ed.). Fairfax Station, Va.: The Technology Press, Inc.

Kahn, J. 1975. How to tackle the systems maintenance dilemma. *Canadian Data Systems*, 7,3 (March), 30–32.

Katzan, H. 1976. *Systems design and documentation: An introduction to the HIPO method*. New York: Van Nostrand Reinhold.

Kay, R. H. 1969. The management and organization of large scale software development projects. *Proceedings, AFIPS 69*, SJCC, 34, 425–433.

Keane Associates, 1979. Aiming for project control. *Data Management*, 17,1 (January), 51–53.

Kearney, J. M., & Mitunovich, J. S. 1976. *A guide to successful computer selection*. Park-Ridge, Ill.: DPMA.

Keen, P. G., & Scott-Morton, M. S. 1978. *Decision support systems: An organizational perspective*. Reading, Mass.: Addison-Wesley.

Keen, J. S. 1981. *Managing systems development*. New York: John Wiley & Sons.

Keider, S. P. 1974. Why projects fail. *Datamation*, December, 53–55.

Kelly, J. F. 1970. *Computerized management information systems*. New York, N.Y.: MacMillan.

Kernighan, B. W., & Plauger, P. J. 1974. *The elements of programming style*. New York: McGraw-Hill.

Kerzner, H. 1981. Project management. *Journal of Systems Management*, October, 26–31.

King, J. 1975. A new approach to program testing. *Proc. Int. Conf. on Reliable Software*, 228–233.

King, W. R., & Cleland, D. I. 1975. The design of management information systems: An information analysis approach. *Management Science*, 22,3 (November), 286–297.

King, J. L., & Schrems, E. L. 1978. Cost benefit analysis of information systems development and operation. *ACM Computing Surveys*, 10,1 (March), 19–34.

Knuth, D. 1974. Computer programming as an art. *Com. of the ACM*, 17,12 (December), 667–673.

Knutsen, K. E., & Nolan, R. L. 1974. Assessing computer costs and benefits. *Journal of Systems Management*, February, 28–34.

Koenig, M. H. 1978. Management guide to resource scheduling. *Journal of Systems Management*, January, 24–29.

Koogler, P., Collins, F., & Clancy, D. K. 1981. The new system arrives. *Journal of Systems Management*, 32,11 (November), 32–37.

Krauss, L. I. 1979. *Administering and controlling the company data processing function*. Englewood Cliffs, N.J.: Prentice-Hall.

Kustanowicz, A. L. 1977. System Life Cycle Estimation (SLICE): A new approach to estimating resources for application program development. *Proc. IEEE Comp. Soft. and Appl. Conference*, Chicago, 226–232.

Land, F. F. 1976. Evaluation of systems goals in determining a design strategy for a computer based information system. *The Computer Journal*, 19,4, 290–294.

Langefors, B. 1973. *Theoretical analysis of information systems*. Philadelphia, Pa.: Auerbach Publishers.

Langefors, B., & Sundgren, B. 1975. *Information systems architecture*. Princeton, N.J.: Petrocelli/Charter.

Lecht, C. P. 1967. *The management of computer programming projects*. American Management Association.

LeDuc, A. L., Jr. 1980. Motivation of programmers. *Data Base*, 11,4 (Summer), 4–12.

Lee, W. B., & Steinberg, E. 1980. Making implementation a success or failure. *Journal of Systems Management*, 31,4 (April), 19–25.

Levy, F. K., Thompson, G. L., & Wiest, J. D. 1963. The ABC's of critical path methods. *Harvard Business Review*, September-October, 98–116.

Lienz, B. P., Swanson, E. B., & Tompkins, G. E. 1978. Characteristics of application software maintenance. *Com. of the ACM*, 21,6 (June), 466–471.

Liskov, B. H. 1972. A design methodology for reliable software systems. *Proc. AFIPS*, FJCC, 41, 191–199.

Liston, D. M., Jr., & Schoene, M. L. 1973. A systems approach to the design of information systems. *Journal of the American Society for Information Science*, March-April, 115–122.

Lucas, H. C., Jr. 1973. *Computer-based information systems in organizations*. Palo Alto, Cal.: Science Research Associates.

Lucas, H. C., Jr., Clowes, K. W., & Kaplan, R. B. 1974. Framework for information systems. *Infor*, 12,3 (October), 245–260.

Lucas, H. C., Jr., & Moore, J. 1976. A multiple-criterion scoring approach to information project selection. *Infor*, February, 1–12.

Lucas, H. C., Jr. 1981. *The analysis, design and implementation of information systems*. New York: McGraw-Hill.

Lucas, H. C., Jr. 1982. *Information systems concepts for management*. New York: McGraw-Hill.

Lucas, P. 1980. On the structure of application programs. *Lecture notes in Computer Science 86: Abstract specifications*, New York: Springer-Verlag.

Lundeberg, M. 1979. An approach for involving the users in the specification of information systems. In *Formal models and practical tools for information systems design*, edited by M. J. Schneider. New York, N.Y.: North Holland Pub. Co.

Lundeberg, M., Goldkuhl, G., & Nilsson, A. 1979. A systematic approach to information systems development, (2 parts). *Information Systems*, 4,1, 1–12.

Lundeberg, M., Goldkuhl, G., & Nilsson, A. 1981. *Information system development: A systematic approach*. Englewood Cliffs, N.J.: Prentice-Hall.

Lustman, F., Lanthier, P. Charbonneau, D., DeLadurantaye, P., & Gagnon, M. 1978. A systematic approach to choosing a computer. *Canadian Data Systems*, April, 24–32.

Lustman, F. 1983. Project management in a small organization. *Journal of Systems Management*, 34,12 (December), 15–21.

Lynch, H. J. 1969. ADS: A technique in systems documentation. *Data Base*, 1,1 (Spring), 6–18.

Maciariello, J. A. 1974. Making project management work, part 1. *Journal of Systems Management*, June, 8–15.

Maciariello, J. A. 1974. Making project management work, part 2. *Journal of Systems Management*, July, 20–27.

Mahmood, M. A. 1982. Choosing computer services for small businesses. *Journal of Systems Management*, 33,7 (July), 22–24.

Mantei, M. 1981. The effect of programming team structures on programming tasks. *Com. of the ACM*, 24,3, 106–113.

Martin, J. 1977. *Computer data base organization*, 2nd ed. Englewood Cliffs, N.J.: Prentice-Hall.

Martin, J. 1981. Coping with vendor failings. *Computer Decisions*, 13,5 (May), 131–144.

Menard, J. B. 1980. Exxon's experience with the Michael Jackson method. *Data Base*, 11,3 (Winter-Spring), 88–92.

Mendes, K. M. 1980. Structured system analysis: A technique to define business requirements. *Sloan Management Review*, 21,4, 51–63.

Menkus, B. 1970. Defining adequate systems documentation. *Journal of Systems Management*, December, 16–21.

Merchant, K. A. 1982. The control function of management. *Sloan Management Review*, 23,4, 43–55.

Merton, A. G., & Severance, D. G. 1981. Data processing control: A state-of-the-art survey of attitudes and concerns of DP executives. *Management Information Systems Quarterly*, 5,2, 11–32.

Metzger, P. 1973. *Managing a programming project*. Englewood Cliffs, N.J.: Prentice-Hall.

Meyer, B. 1982. Principles of package design. *Com. of the ACM*, 25,7, 419–428.

Miller, R. W. 1962. How to plan and control with PERT. *Harvard Business Review*, March-April, 93–109.

Miller, W. B. 1978. Fundamentals of project management. *Journal of Systems Management*, November, 22–29.

Mills, H. D. 1975. The new math of computer programming. *Com. of the ACM*, 18,1 (January), 43–48.

Mills, H. D. 1976. Software development. *IEEE Trans. on Soft. Eng.*, SE-2-4, December, 265–273.

Mills, H. D. 1980. Software development. In *Research Directions in Software Technology*, P. Wegner editor, The MIT Press, Cambridge, Mass., 87–105.

Mohanty, S. N. 1979. Models and measurements for quality assessment of software. *ACM Computing Surveys*, 11,3, 252–275.

Moore, J. H. 1979. A framework for MIS software development projects. *Management Information Systems Quarterly*, 3,1, 29–30.

Morgan, J. H., & Lightman, M. S. 1976. System for developing systems. *Datamation*, 22,4 (April), 62–65.

Munro, M. C., & Davis, G. B. 1977. Determining management information needs: A comparison of methods. *Management Informations Systems Quarterly*, June, 55–67.

Murdick, R. G., & Ross, J. E. 1975. *Information systems for modern management*, 2nd ed. Englewood Cliffs, N.J.: Prentice-Hall.

Murdick, R. G. et al. 1978. *Accounting information systems*. Englewood Cliffs, N.J.: Prentice-Hall.

Murdick, R. G. 1980. *MIS concepts and design*, Englewood Cliffs, N.J.: Prentice-Hall.

Myers, G. 1976. Forms management, part 1: Why forms management? *Journal of Systems Management*, 27,9, September, 6–9.

Myers, G. 1976. Forms management, part 2: How to design forms. *Journal of Systems Management*, 27,10, October, 15–19.

Myers, G. J. 1978. A controlled experiment in program testing and code walkthrough/inspections. *Com. of the ACM*, 21,9 (September), 760–768.

Myers, G. J. 1979. *The art of software testing*. New York: John Wiley & Sons.

McFarlan, F. W., & Nolan, R. L. 1975. *The information systems handbook*. Homewood, Il.: Dow Jones-Irwin Inc.

McFarlan, F. W. 1981. Portfolio approach to information systems. *Harvard Business Review*, September-October, 142–150.

McGowan, C. L., & Kelly, J. R. 1975. *Top-down structured programming techniques*. Princeton, N.J.: Petrocelli/Charter.

McGowan, C. L. 1980. Software management. In *Research Directions in Software Technology*, edited by P. Wegner. Cambridge, Mass. and London, England: The MIT Press, 207–253.

Naumann, J. D., Davis, G. B., & McKeen, J. D. 1980. Determining information requirements: A contingency method for selection of requirements assurance strategy. *The Journal of Systems and Software*, 1, 273–281.

Nelson, E. A. 1975. *Management handbook for the estimation of computer programming costs*. Springfield, Va.: U.S. Dept. of Commerce–Clearing House for Federal Scientific and Technical Information. Publication #AD648750.

Newmann, P. S. 1982. Towards an integrated development environment. *IBM Systems Journal*, 21,1, 81–107.

Nolan, R. L. 1973. Plight of the EDP manager. *Harvard Business Review*, 51,3 (May-June), 143–152.

Nolan, R. L. 1973. Managing the computer resource: A stage hypothesis. *Com. of the ACM*, July, 399–440.

Norden, P. V. 1970. Useful tools for project management. In *Management of Production*, edited by Starr. Baltimore: Penguin Books.

Norden, P. V. 1977. Project life cycle modeling: Background and application of the life cycle curves. Airlie, Va.: *Software Life Cycle Management Workshop*.

Nunamaker, J. F., Jr. 1971. A methodology for the design and optimization of information processing systems. *Proceedings AFIPS, SJCC Conf.*, May 18–20, Atlantic City, N.J. AFIPS Press, Montvale, N.J., 283–294.

Nunamaker, J. F., Jr., Ho, T., Konsinsky, B., & Singer, C. 1976. Computer aided analysis and design of information systems. *Com. of the ACM*, 19,2, 647–687.

Orilia, L. S. 1982. *Introduction to business data processing*, 2nd edition. New York: McGraw-Hill.

Orr, K. T. 1977. *Structured system development*. New York, N.Y.: Yourdon Press.

Osborne, A. 1980. *An introduction to micro computers*, 2nd ed. New York: McGraw-Hill.

Parnas, D. L. 1971. Information distribution aspects of design methodologies. *Report AFOSR-TR-0547, Dept. of Computer Science*, Carnegie Mellon University, Pittsburgh, Pa. 26pp.

Parnas, D. L. 1972. A technique for the specification of software modules with examples. *Com. of the ACM*, 15,5, 330–336.

Parnas, D. L. 1972. On the criteria to be used in decomposing systems into modules. *Com. of the ACM*, 15,12, 1053–1058.

Parnas, D. L. 1974. On a buzzword: hierarchical structure. *Proc. IFIP74*, 336–339.

Parr, F. N. 1980. An alternative to the Raleigh curve model for software development effort. *IEEE Trans. on Soft. Eng.*, SE-6,3, 291–296.

Paster, D. L. 1981. Experience with application of modern software management tools. *Proc. 5th Int. Conf. on Soft. Eng.*, March, 18–26.

Peters, L. J., & Tripp, L. L. 1976. Is software design wicked? *Datamation*, 22,5 (May), 127–136.

Putnam, L. 1976. A macro estimating methodology for software development. *Proceedings, COMPCON76*, Washington, D.C., September, 138–143.

Putnam, L. H. 1978. A general empirical solution to the macro software sizing and estimation problem. *IEEE Trans. on Soft. Eng.*, SE-4,4 (July), 345–361.

Putnam, L., and Fitzsimmons, A. 1979. Estimating software costs. *Datamation*, September, 189–198; October, 171–178, November, 137–140.

Rajaraman, M. K. 1983. Structured techniques for software development. *Journal of Systems Management*, March, 36–39.

Ramamoorthy, C. W., Ho, S. F., & Chen, W. T. 1976. On the automated generation of program test data. *IEEE Trans. on Soft. Eng.*, SE-2,4 (December), 293–300.

Redwine, S. T., Jr. 1983. An engineering approach to software test data generation. *IEEE Trans. on Soft. Eng.*, SE-9,2, March, 191–200.

Reuter, V. G. 1979. Using graphic management tools. *Journal of Systems Management*, April, 6–17.

Rolefson, J. F. 1978. Project management—Six critical steps. *Journal of Systems Management*, 29,4 (April), 10–17.

Ross, D. T., Goodenough, J. B., & Irvine, C. A. 1975. Software engineering: Process, principles and goals. *Computer*, May, 17–27.

Ross, D. T., & Schoman, K. E. 1977. Structured analysis for requirements definition. *IEEE Trans. on Soft. Eng.*, SE3–1, January, 6–15.

Ross, D. T. 1977. Structured analysis: A language for communicating ideas. *IEEE Trans. on Soft. Eng.*, SE-3,1, January, 16–34.

Ross, D. T. 1977. Reflections on requirements. *IEEE Trans. on Soft. Eng.*, SE-3,1, 2–5.

Rubin, M. L. 1970. *Introduction to the system life cycle.* Princeton, N.J.: Brandon Systems Press.

Ryge, S. 1981. Evaluating structured COBOL as a software engineering discipline. *Data Base*, 12,3 (Spring), 3–6.

Salter, K. G. 1976. A methodology for decomposing system requirements into data processing requirements. *Proc. 2nd Int. Conf. on Soft. Eng.*, Oct. 13–15, San Francisco, 91–101.

Sanders, L. L. 1980. Barriers to estimating DP projects effectively. *Infosystems*, December, 64–70.

Schaeffer, H. 1981. *Data center operations.* Englewood Cliffs, N.J.: Prentice-Hall.

Schoderbek, P. 1971. *Management systems*, 2nd ed. New York: John Wiley & Sons.

Scott, L. R. 1978. An engineering methodology for presenting software functional architecture. *Proc. 3rd Int. Conf. on Soft. Eng.*, May 10–12, Atlanta, 222–229.

Semprevivo, P. C. 1976. *Systems analysis: definition, process and design.* Palo Alto, Cal.: Science Research Associates.

Sharp, W. F. 1970. *The economics of computers.* New York: Columbia University Press.

Shaw, J. C., & Atkins, W. 1979. *Managing computer systems projects.* New York: McGraw-Hill.

Sheil, B. A. 1981. The psychological study of programming. *ACM Computing Surveys*, 13,1 (March), 101–120.

Spinner, M. 1981. *Elements of project management: Plan, schedule and control.* Englewood Cliffs, N.J.: Prentice-Hall.

Stephens, S. A., & Tripp, L. L. 1978. Requirements expression and verification aid. *Proc. 3rd Int. Conf. on Soft. Eng.*, May 10–12, Atlanta, 101–108.

Stevens, W. P., Myers, G. J., & Constantine, L. L. 1974. Structured design. *IBM Systems Journal*, 13,2, 115–139.

Stuckenbruck, L. C. 1981. *The implementation of project management.* Reading, Mass.: Addison-Wesley.

Swanson, B., & Cooper, R. 1979. Management information requirements: The state of the art. *Data Base*, 11,2 (Fall), 5–16.

Swartout, W., & Balzer, R. 1982. On the inevitable intertwining of specification and implementation. *Com. of the ACM*, 25,7, 438–440.

Taggart, W. M., Jr., & Tharp, M. O. 1977. A survey of information requirement analysis techniques. *ACM Computing Surveys*, 9,4 (December), 273–290.

Tausworthe, R. C. 1977. *Standardized development of computer software.* Englewood Cliffs, N.J.: Prentice-Hall.

Tausworthe, R. C. 1980. The work breakdown structure in software project management. *The Journal of Systems and Software*, 1,3, 181–186.

Teichroew, D. 1969. A methodology for the design of information processing systems. *Proc. Fourth Australian Comp. Conf.*, Adelaide, Australia.

Teichroew, D., & Hershey, E. 1977. PSL/PSA: A computer-aided technique for documentation and analysis. *IEEE Trans. on Soft. Eng.*, SE-3,1 (January), 41–48.

Thayer, R., & Hinton, E. 1975. Software reliability—a method that works. *Proceedings, AFIPS, National Computer Conf.*, May 19–22, Anaheim, Ca., AFIPS Press, Montvale, N.J., 877–882.

Thayer, R. A., Lipow, M., & Nelson, E. C. 1978. *Software reliability*, Amsterdam, The Netherlands and New York, N.Y.: North Holland.

Thayer, R. H., Pyster, A. B., Wood, R. C. 1981. Major issues in software engineering project management. *IEEE Trans. on Soft. Eng.*, SE-7,4, July, 333–342.

Timmereck, E. M. 1973. Computer selection methodology. *ACM Computing Surveys*, 5,4 (December), 199–222.

Tripp, L. L., Wah, P. N. 1980. How much planning in systems development? *Journal of Systems Management*, October, 6–15.

Tsichritzis, D. 1982. Form management. *Com. of the ACM*, 25,12, 453–478.

Ullman, J. D. 1980. *Principles of database systems*. Rockville, Md.: Computer Science Press.

Van Leer, P. 1976. Top down development using a program design language. *IBM Systems Journal*, 15,2, 155–170.

Walston, C. E., & Felix, C. P. 1977. A method of programming measurement and estimation. *IBM Systems Journal*, 16,1, 54–73.

Warnier, J. D. 1981. *Logical construction of programs*. New York: Van Nostrand Reinhold.

Wasserman, A. I. 1980. Information system design methodology. *Journal of the American Society for Information Science*, 31,1, January, 5–24.

Weinberg, G. M. 1971. *The psychology of computer programming*. New York: Van Nostrand Reinhold.

Weinworm, G. F. 1970. *On the management of computer programming*. Philadelphia, Pa.: Auerbach Publisher.

Williams, R. D. 1975. Managing the development of reliable software. *Proc. 1975 Int. Conf. on Reliable Software*, 3–8.

Willoughby, T. C. 1975. Origins of systems projects. *Journal of Systems Management*, October, 19–26.

Wolverton, R. W. 1974. The cost of developing large-scale software. *IEEE Trans. on Comp.*, June, 615–636.

Wooldridge, S. 1976. *Project management in data processing*. New York: Petrocelli/Charter.

Wynant, L. 1980. Essential elements of project financing. *Harvard Business Review*, May-June, 165–180.

Yadav, S. B. 1983. Determining an organization's information requirements: A state of the art survey. *Data Base*, 14,3 (Spring), 3–20.

Yourdon, E., ed. 1977. *Structured walkthroughs*. New York, N.Y.: Yourdon Inc.

Yourdon, E., & Constantine, L. L. 1979. *Structured design*. Englewood Cliffs, N.J.: Prentice-Hall.

Zalud, W. 1983. Take high risk out of high tech through negotiation. *Data Management*, 21,4 (April), 26–28.

Zave, P. 1982. An operational approach to requirements specification for embedded systems. *IEEE Trans. on Soft. Eng.*, SE-8,3 (May), 250–269.

Zeil, S. J., & White, L. J. 1981. Sufficient test sets for path analysis testing strategies. *Proc. 5th Int. Conf. on Soft. Eng.*, March 9–12, San Diego, 184–191.

Zelkowitz, M. V. 1978. Perspectives on software engineering. *ACM Computing Surveys*, 10,2, 197–216.

Zilles, S. N., & Hebalkar, P. G. 1980. Graphical representation and analysis of information system design. *Data Base*, 11,3, 93–98.

Zloof, M. N. 1977. Query by example: A data base language. *IBM Systems Journal*, 16,4, 324–343.

Zmud, R. W. 1980. Management of large scale software development efforts. *Management Informations Systems Quarterly*, 4, 45–55.

INDEX

APL, 55
Abdel-Hamid T. K., 192, 196, 201
Abstract data type, 273, 275, 279
Acceptance tests, 356, 358, 371
Activation condition, 146
  see also Triggering event
Activity, 21–23, 213
  dummy, 21
  duration of, 40–41
  ending date of, 67
  starting date of, 67
Ahituv N., 299
Analysis
  tools for, 98
  top down, 44, 53, 96, 101, 132–133
Analyst, 16, 259
Ansoff H. I., 209

BASIC, 156
Bailey J. W., 193, 198
Baker F. T., 256
Bar chart, 227, 301, 303, 309, 312
Basili V. R., 193, 198
Belford P. C., 132
Bell T. E., 129, 133
Benbasat I., 193
Benchmark, 317, 336, 344
Benefits
  direct financial, 107
  indirect, 107
Benjamin R. I., 20, 30, 64
Bixler D. C., 133
Black W. W., 129
Black box concept, 17, 41, 77, 167, 184
Block E. B., 235
Boehm B. W., 20, 29, 123, 260, 276, 280
Bond A. F., 132
Brandon D. H., 228
Bratman H., 167
Breakdown, 42, 47, 51–53, 55, 138
  hierarchical, 49
Brooks F. P., 56, 193, 198, 215, 305–306
Brown, B. W., 255
Brown P. J., 117
Bruggere T. H., 258, 276, 286
Buckley F., 298
Budget, 88–89, 232–233, 246, 291, 308
  activities summary, 245
  detailed, 238, 240, 244, 247, 310
  functions of, 234
  of a project, 237
  summary, 238
  time summary, 245–246
Budgeting phase, 120
Burch J. G. Jr., 28
Burton A. Jr., 55

COBOL, 67, 154, 156–157, 191, 194, 252, 279, 291, 344

CPM, 5
  see also Critical Path Method
Canning R. G., 93–94, 102, 129
Cave W. C., 27–28
Change control, 296, 309
Chen P. P., 160, 262
Chen, W. T., 283
Chief Programmer Team, 165
  see also Programming team structure
Chief programmer, 256
Churchmann C. W., 15–16
Clancy D. K., 366
Cleland D. I., 16, 133
Clingen C. J., 154–155, 163
Collins F., 366
Compatibility, 174
Computer accounts, 246–247
Computer selection, 32, 156, 249, 314, 337
  see also Hardware selection
Computer system requirements
  technical approach, 316
  workload handling approach, 317
  global approach, 317
Configuration management, 149, 294–295
Constantine L. L., 159, 264, 267
Control, 290
  loss of, 60
  of costs, 61, 245
  of personnel, 293
  of quality, 298
  of resource consumption, 234, 303
  of resources, 20, 247
  of results, 292, 300, 303
  problems of, 237
  structures, 309
Control tool, 229
Control process, 291
Controlled decentralized team, 257
  see also Programming team structure, 307
Conversion of programs, 22
Cooperative decentralized team, 257
  see also Programming team structure
Corbato F. J., 154–155, 163
Cost accounts, 246–247
Cost/benefits analysis, 106–107, 139, 246
Cost-value technique, 341–342
Costs
  fixed, 107
  hidden, 246
  of human resources, 303
  of installation, 243
  of maintenance, 244
  of site preparation, 243
  of the project, 57
  operational, 107

  overruns, 306
  proportions in system development, 241
Couger J. D., 64
Court T., 167
Crisis management, 304
Critical Path Method, 5, 10, 218
  see also CPM
Critical path, 22, 49, 52–53, 213–214, 218, 220, 225
Cutover, 29, 356–357, 370–371

DBMS, 158–160, 172, 188, 271–272, 275, 325
  see also Data Base Management System
DFD, 134, 136, 138
  see also Data flow diagram
Dahl O. J., 279
Daly E. B., 117
Data Base Management System, 158, 252, 264, 321
  see also DBMS
Data dictionary, 134, 136
Data flow, 132–134, 138, 267, 269, 285
Data flow diagram, 134
  see also DFD
Data modeling, 160, 262
  see also Data modelization
Data modelization, 160, 172
  see also Data modeling
Data store, 134, 136
Date C. J., 158
Davis G. B., 64, 99
De Marco T., 132
Deadlines, 7, 60, 220
Debugging, 253, 280, 283
  tools, 158–159
Decision tables, 136, 146
Decision trees, 136, 146
Design
  as a contract, 64
  detailed, 65, 159, 192, 223, 253, 258, 261, 271, 273, 276, 278, 296, 300
  general, 65, 159, 163, 192, 253, 258, 260–261, 273, 286, 300
  methods, 159, 259
  structured, 159, 162, 172, 256, 264
  to cost, 306, 310
  top down, 159
Design and code inspections, 292, 296
Design to change, 270, 273–275
Development phase, 19–20
  see also Development stage
Development stage, 65
Diagrams, 132
  detailed, 69
  overview, 69
Difficulty, 56–57
Dijkstra E. W., 162, 279, 280

Document
as a contract, 75–76, 124
as a decision tool, 75
as production tool, 74
baseline, 71, 75–76, 124,
142, 149, 234, 295
different roles of, 71
of system design, 74
primary function of, 66
reference, 73, 76
target of a, 67
Documentation, 61–64
of a program, 172
of operation, 61
of programs, 61
of tests, 87, 172
user, 61, 67
Documents
key product, 89
key project, 87
of detailed design, 172
product control, 89
project control, 89
Donaldson H., 365, 370
Dry run, 365, 367
Duran J. W., 282–283
Dyer M. E., 133

Egoless programming team,
257–258
End user, 354
Entity, 269, 271
Entity relationship model,
160, 172, 262, 271
Estimates, 213, 245–246,
291, 293, 311
adjustments to, 206
factors affecting, 185
global, 41
inaccurate, 121
incorrect, 55, 129
integration of, 204, 206
of productivity, 187
raw, 187
revision of, 186–187
Estimating, 155
errors, 196–197, 294
of required resources, 192
of resources, 20
process of, 184
Estimation, 182–183
data, 38
methods of, 205
of resources, 187
problems, 38
Evaluation methodologies,
346
cost related, 339–340
weighted scores, 339
Evaluation methods, 343
Evans M., 279
Event, 21–23, 40, 213
Executive summary, 108–
109
Expenses
hardware related, 243
salary related, 243

FORTRAN, 55, 156, 170,
182, 188, 190–191, 195,
279, 322, 344
Factors of influence, 196
Fagan M. E., 296

Feasibility study, 18, 25, 92
Felix C. P., 193, 198
Foss W. B., 343
Frankwicz M. S., 6, 31
Freeman P., 123, 130
Functional requirements,
316, 318, 336

Gane C., 134, 136, 276
Gantt H. L., 227
Gantt chart, 64, 227–229,
301, 310
see also Bar chart
Gaydash A., 56, 92
General design stage, 172
Ghandforoush P., 340
Gildersleeve T. R., 196
Gray C. F., 4, 210, 213, 216,
228, 308
Griffin E. L., 276, 280

HIPO method, 64, 68, 190
Hall T. P., 25, 28
Hardware selection, 7, 28–
29, 173–174, 176, 178
see also Computer
selection
life cycle, 176
objective approach, 175,
178
pragmatic approach, 175
subjective approach, 174
Harrison F. L., 209, 213,
235, 247, 297, 307–308,
311
Harrison R., 365
Henderson D. G., 132
Hershauer J. C., 141
Hershey E. A., 133
Hoare C. A. R., 279

I-P-O (Input-Process-
Output), 159
ISAC method, 127, 134,
138–139, 141, 143
Implementation, 29
approach, 364
bootstrap, 163
method, 365
problems, 366
top down, 162–164
Implementation stage, 355–
356, 366
Implementation strategy,
224
bootstrap, 216, 285
top down, 216, 223, 253,
255
Ingrassia F. S., 64
Integration
problems of, 254
Integration process, 49–50,
52, 56
Interviews, 98, 100
Invitation to tender, 28, 176,
178

Jackson M. A., 159
Johnson, J. R., 198, 293,
300, 308
Joslin E. O., 176–178, 320,
327, 330, 337–339,
341–343, 346

Katzan H. Jr., 64
Kay R. J., 38
Keen J., 61–62
King W. R., 16, 133
Knutson K. E., 106
Koenig M. H., 220
Koogler P., 366, 368

Land F. F., 106
Lee W. B., 368
Librarian, 165–166, 256
Life cycle, 15, 17, 25, 27, 42,
290
Norden/Putnam curve, 19
of a project, 19, 23, 118,
249
of a system, 15, 19–20
Life cycle costing, 342–343,
347
Lines of code (LOC), 192
Lucas H. C. Jr., 4–5, 25,
60–62, 92
Lundeberg M., 93, 100, 138
Lustman F., 176, 178, 194,
320, 330, 343

MIS
see also Management
Information System
Maciariello J. A., 235, 244
Macrocrisis, 304–306
Macroestimates, 43, 51, 53,
56, 184, 206
factors influencing the,
200
scope of, 44
Macromilestone, 300
Madnick S. E., 192, 196, 201
Man–months, 192, 310
Management
middle, 95
Management Information
System, 9
see also MIS
Management Information
Systems, 133
see also MIS
Manager
middle, 8, 367, 369
senior, 8–9
Manatory requirements, 176,
320–321
see also Requirements,
mandatory
Mantei M., 255, 257, 260
Martin J., 158
McGowan C. L., 162
Merchant K. A., 291–293
Mendes K. M., 132
Menkus B., 60, 62
Metzger P. W., 20, 190, 198
Meyer B., 273
Microcrisis, 305
Microestimates, 43, 49, 51,
53, 55–56, 184, 194,
200
Micromilestone, 305
Milestone, 23–25, 26, 223,
249, 253, 301, 310, 312
Milestone chart, 228–229,
301, 303, 309–310
Milestone schedule, 233
Milestones, 214–216, 292, 300

Miller W. B., 117, 216
Mills H. D., 158
Mini implementation, 158
Minimal set of requirements, 176
see also Mandatory requirements
Modularity, 270, 273
Modularization, 130, 132, 138
Modularization principle, 318
Murdick R. G., 16, 44
Myers G. J., 159, 264, 280, 283–284

Nelson E. A., 38, 54
Neumann S., 299
Network, 21–22, 32, 39–40, 212–213, 216, 218, 220–221, 223, 226–228, 230
detailed, 215
general, 214–215
intermediate, 215
levels of detail of, 214
of activities, 37
of the project, 65
user of, 214
Newman P. S., 167
Nolan R. L., 106
Norden P. V., 18
Nunamaker J. F. Jr., 64

On going costs, 347
One time costs, 347
Opportunity study, 24–26, 32–33, 92, 99, 116
overview, 94
results of, 105
stage, 91, 94
team, 96
Opportunity study report (OSR), 65, 70, 75, 89, 108

PASCAL, 156, 169–170, 278–279
PERT, 11, 218
PL/1, 155–156
PSL, 157, 165
see also Program Support Library
PSL/PSA system, 133
Parnass D. L., 273, 285
Performance criteria, 358
Performance evaluation
benchmarking, 344
hand timing, 344
simulation, 344
use of references, 345
Performance requirements, 336–337
Piecemeal delivery, 223
Pietrasanta A. M., 38, 53, 55–57, 121, 197
Planning, 183, 209, 211–212, 230, 232–233, 307
formal, 213
poor, 117
process of, 215
strategic, 210
tactical, 210
techniques, 223

Planning stage, 39, 301
Planning systems, 210
Preliminary analysis, 18
see also Preliminary survey
Preliminary survey, 18, 92
see also Preliminary analysis
Problem Statement Language, 134
Process design, 264, 269, 273
Product control, 29, 89, 246
Product delivery, 353
Product delivery stage, 29–30, 33
planning of, 34
Product design, 28
Product design stage, 32–33
Product realization, 25, 249
Production stage, 187–188
Production strategy
activity oriented, 253
level oriented: bottom up, 254
level oriented: top down, 254
operation oriented: bootstrap, 255
Production tools, 156
Productivity, 206
adjustments to, 200
factors affecting, 185
factors of influence, 196, 198–199
Program design, 273, 275
Program Support Library, 157, 165–167, 256
see also PSL
Programmer, 259
back-up, 256
Programming, 9, 18, 31
errors, 61
practices, 277
structured, 87, 160, 162, 199, 256, 278–279, 284, 291
Programming language, 27, 156–157, 159
Programming team
structure, 255
chief programmer team, 256
controlled decentralized, 256
cooperative decentralized, 256
egoless programming team, 256
Progress control, 23, 29, 300, 302–303
Progress report, 89, 308, 311–312
Progress reporting, 301
Project
concept, 3
goal, 6
team, 8
Project analysis, 37–39, 41, 159, 279
Project design, 24–25, 27, 117
Project design stage, 25, 27, 34, 118, 153, 155

Project management problems, 38, 129
Project management packages, 11
see also Project management systems
Project management systems, 307–308, 310
Project manager
administrative involvement, 34
in the estimating process, 205
involvement of, 32
responsibilities, 38
skills, 33
technical concerns of, 249
technical involvement, 34
technical role of, 253
Projects
with a fixed deadline, 202, 291, 293, 310
with a fixed number of personnel, 202, 293
with fixed total resources, 203, 293, 310
Putnam L. H., 18–19, 54–58
Pyster, A. B., 38

Quality assurance, 64
see also Software quality assurance
Quality assurance group, 301
Questionnaires, 98, 100

RFP, 315, 326, 328, 344, 347
documents, 329–330
procedure, 327
process, 326, 336–337
public, 327
selective, 327
team, 327
Rajaraman M. K., 260
Ramamoorthy C. W., 283
Redwine S. T. Jr., 283
Relational model, 136
Relationship, 263
Replacement strategy
immediate, 30, 364
modular, 30, 362, 370
parallel running, 30, 362, 367
Request for proposals, 315, 334
see also RFP
Requirements, 103, 322–323
hardware, 320–321
long-term, 319–320, 326, 328–329, 345
mandatory, 320–321, 333–339, 341–344, 347, 350
of a system, 101–102
optional, 320
processing, 321
short-term, 319, 328–329
software, 321
Requirements analysis, 318
Requirements Statement Language (RSL), 133
Requirements cost evaluation technique, 178–179, 342

Resistance to change, 368–369
Resource bounded projects, 221, 223
Resource load chart, 229
Resources, 28, 40
  acquisition of, 4
  allocation of, 213, 220
  availability of, 12
  consumption of, 18–19, 26, 29, 241, 245, 247, 280, 293, 310, 312
  estimation of, 119–120
  gathering of, 31, 118
  human, 118–119, 247
  library of, 220
  monetary, 119
  scheduling of, 220
Results (visibility of), 163, 254
Rework, 224
Risk analysis, 171
Risk management, 300
Rolefson J. F., 5, 11
Ross D. T., 102, 132
Rubin M. L., 25, 61

SADT method, 132, 134
SAMM method, 133
SREM method, 133
SSA, 134, 138
  see also Structured System Analysis
Salisbury A. B., 28
Sanders J., 38
Sarson T., 134, 136, 276
Schaeffer H., 329–330
Schedule, 28, 75, 89, 291, 302–303
Schedules, 227
  individual, 229
  of activities, 213, 227
  of resources, 213, 229
Scheduling, 209, 211–213, 246, 290, 307
Scheduling techniques, 223
Scoring method, 178–179
Scotto M., 117
Screening process, 337–338
Sellers L. S., 132
Sheil B. A., 276, 278
Simulation, 317–336
Site preparation, 10, 356, 358, 367
Slack, 22, 213–214, 218, 223, 226, 310
Software engineering, 117, 130, 258
  seven principles, 20
  specialists, 124, 141
Software quality assurance, 29–30, 298–299
Software warehouse, 166–167, 193
Solutions
  evaluation of, 105
  survey of, 103, 105
Specifications, 75, 123–124, 147–149, 292
  approval process, 148
  as a contract, 148
  change in, 166
  document, 126
  errors, 129

functional, 177, 316–317, 333
  of a module, 167
  qualities of, 125
  user involvement in, 199
Specifications manual, 124, 176–177, 179, 261, 296, 327–328, 330
Spinner M., 311
Standards, 62
  absence of, 60
  enforcement of, 299
  of design, 167–168, 170
  of development, 27
  of documentation, 27, 171
  of programming, 27, 62, 168, 170
Start–up, 29–30
Steinberg E., 368
Step–by–step implementation, 255, 306
Stephens S. A., 133
Stepwise refinement, 161, 172, 270, 279
Stevens W. P., 159, 264, 267, 276
Strater F. R. Jr., 28
Structured English, 136, 146
Structured System Analysis, 132, 134
  see also SSA
Structured walkthrough, 62, 291
Stubs, 162, 255
System
  influence of, 17
  life cycle of, 18
  limits of a, 17
System design, 18, 28
System set–up, 356, 367
Systems analysis, 8, 18, 25, 31, 126, 130, 134
  methods of, 126
Systems analysis principles, 138
  abstraction, 131, 138, 318
  bounded context, 132–133, 138–139, 299, 318
  data and functions, 138
  levels of abstraction, 131, 133–134
  principles of, 130, 139
  visibility of results, 132

Task, 23
Tausworthe R. C., 255, 279–280
Team
  meeting, 305
  organization and structure, 255
Teichroew D., 133
Test case, 284
Tester, 259
Testing, 279–280, 284
  operational, 28
  team, 356
Testing tool, 170
Tests
  acceptance, 281
  individual, 191
  of integration, 281

Thayer R. H., 38
Thayer T. A., 129
Throughput time, 358
Time bounded projects, 221, 223
Time sheets, 246, 247, 303, 309–310
Time-cost tradeoff, 58
Time-cost-product tradeoff, 58
Timmereck E. E., 174–175, 316
Training, 30
  costs, 347
  of the users, 29, 356–357, 360
Triggering event, 134, 141
  see also Activation condition
Tripp L. L., 44, 47, 55, 121, 133

UDF, 64
  see also Unit Development Folder
Ullman J. D., 158
Uncertainty, 6, 12, 15, 20, 25, 99–100, 223, 225, 249, 308
Unit Development Folder (UDF), 64
  see also UDF
Upgrade costs, 347
Upgradibility, 174
User manual, 73, 87, 359–360
User needs, 149
User preparation, 360, 367
Users (involvement of), 7, 138

Vessey I., 193

WBS, 44–45, 46, 48–49, 53, 55–56, 65–66, 99, 131, 187–188, 205, 213, 216
  see also Work Breakdown Structure
WP, 47
  see also Workpackage
Wah P. N., 44, 47
Walston C. E., 193, 198
Warnier J. D., 132, 159
Wassermann A. I., 130
Weighted scores, 342, 346
Weinberg G. M., 60, 62, 66, 257
White L. J., 283
Willoughby T. C., 94
Wolverton R. W., 276
Wood R. C., 38
Wooldridge S., 293, 303
Work Breakdown Structure, 44, 96, 124
  see also WBS
  of project design, 118
Workload, 321–323, 344–345
Work unit, 191
Workpackage, 47, 215, 244, 303
  see also WP

Zeil S. J., 283
Zmud R. D., 117